The Architecture of Global Governance

The Architecture of Global Governance

An Introduction to the Study of International Organizations

James P. Muldoon Jr.

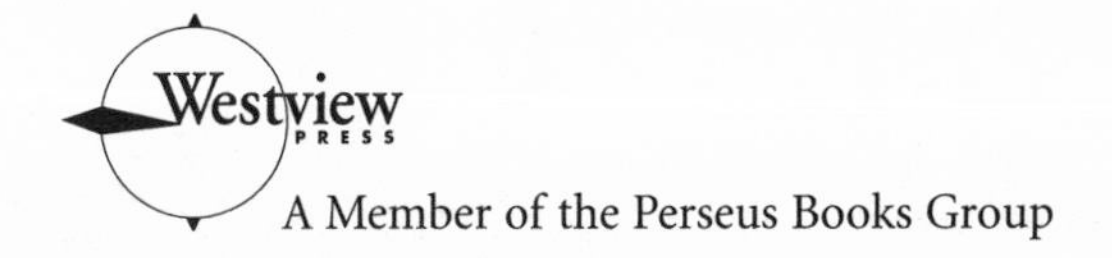

A Member of the Perseus Books Group

Published in the United States of America by Westview Press, A Member of the Perseus Books Group, 5500 Central Avenue, Boulder, Colorado 80301-2877, and in the United Kingdom by Westview Press, 12 Hid's Copse Road, Cumnor Hill, Oxford OX2 9JJ.

Find us on the world wide web at www.westviewpress.com

Westview Press books are available at special discounts for bulk purchases in the United States by corporations, institutions, and other organizations. For more information, please contact the Special Markets Department at the Perseus Books Group, 11 Cambridge Center, Cambridge, MA 02142, or call (617) 252-5298, (800) 255-1514 or email j.mccrary@perseusbooks.com.

Library of Congress Cataloging-in-Publication Data

Muldoon, James P.
The architecture of global governmance : an introduction to the study of international organizations / James P. Muldoon Jr.
p. cm.
Includes bibliographical references and index.
ISBN 0-8133-6844-8 (pbk. : alk. paper)—ISBN 0-8133-4136-1 (hbk. : alk. paper)
1. International organization. 2. International agencies. 3. Globalization. I. Title.
JZ5566.M85 2003
341.2—dc21

2003006403

The paper used in this publication meets the requirements of the American National Standard for Permanence of Paper for Printed Library Materials Z39.48-1984.

10 9 8 7 6 5 4 3 2 1

CONTENTS

List of Figures, Tables, and Maps vii
List of Acronyms ix
Preface xiii

1 Introduction: In Search of Global Governance 1

PART 1

SCHOOLS OF THOUGHT
The Foundations of International Order and Organization

2 The Classical Schools of Thought 15
3 "Peace Plans," "Reformers," and "Realists"—Thinkers of the Seventeenth to the Nineteenth Centuries 37
4 Modern International Theory and the Idealist/Realist Debate 65

PART 2

MANIFESTATIONS OF INTERNATIONAL ORDER

5 From the World of Ideas to the Real World 99
6 Architects of International Order: States, Markets, and Civil Society 151
7 International Organizations and the Management of International Change 211

8 Conclusion: The "New World Order" and the Future of International Organizations 259

Appendix: List of International Organizations by Location and Year of Founding 275
Bibliography 297
Index 311

Figures, Tables, and Maps

Figures

1.1 Three Institutional Pillars of Global Governance 10
3.1 Subdivisions of the Traditions 63
5.1 A Typology of International Organizations 100
7.1 The Dimensions of Legalization 216
8.1 Select List of Global Public Goods and Bads 263
8.2 Intersectoral Processes Between the Three Pillars of Global Governance 273

Tables

5.1A Classification of International Organizations, 1924 121
5.1B Number of International Organizations Founded from 1863 to 1954, in Five-Year Periods 122
5.2 Postwar Planning During the War: Declarations and Doctrines 127
5.3 Distribution by Function of IGOs Comprised Exclusively of Members of Particular Political-Economic Groups Established from 1960 through 1981 (in percentages) 133
5.4 International Governmental Organizations by Year, 1954–2000 142
5.5 International Nongovernmental Organizations by Year, 1954–2000 144
6.1 Multilateral Treaty Subjects by Period, 1648–1995 156
6.2 Multilateral Treaties and International Organizations, 1648–1995 157
6.3 The World's Top Ten TNCs in Terms of Transnationality, 1998 175
6.4 Industry Composition of the Top 100 TNCs, 1990 and 1998 176

7.1 Forms of International Legalization 217
7.2 Decolonization and Growth in U.N. Membership, 1945–2000 232

Maps

5.1 Europe in 1812 105
5.2 Europe in 1914 110
5.3 Europe in 1919 111
5.4 The Cold War World 131

Acronyms

ACM	Andean Common Market
ACCT	Agence de Coopération Culturelle et Technique
APEC	Asia-Pacific Economic Cooperation
APSA	American Political Science Association
ARF	ASEAN Regional Forum
ASEAN	Association of South East Asian Nations
BIS	Bank for International Settlements
CACM	Central American Common Market
CARICOM	Caribbean Community
CEO	Chief Executive Officer
CIS	Commonwealth of Independent States
CMEA	Council of Mutual Economic Assistance
CSBM	Confidence- and Security-Building Measure
CSCE	Conference for Security and Cooperation in Europe
CTBT	Comprehensive Nuclear Test Ban Treaty
DONGO	Donor-Organized Nongovernmental Organization
ECLAC	Economic Commission for Latin America and the Caribbean
ECOSOC	Economic and Social Council
ECOWAS	Economic Community of West African States
EEC	European Economic Community
EFTA	European Free Trade Area
EU	European Union
FAO	Food and Agricultural Organization
FDI	Foreign Direct Investment
FRELIMO	Frente de Libertação de Moçambique

FTAA	Free Trade Area of the Americas
GA	General Assembly
GATT	General Agreement on Tariffs and Trade
GC	Global Compact
GDP	Gross Domestic Product
GNP	Gross National Product
GONGO	Government-Organized Nongovernmental Organization
GRI	Global Reporting Initiative
G-77	Group of 77 Developing Countries
G-7	Group of 7 Industrialized Countries
IAEA	International Atomic Energy Agency
IBEC	International Bank for Economic Cooperation
IBRD	International Bank for Reconstruction and Development
ICANN	Internet Corporation for Assigned Names and Numbers
ICAO	International Civil Aviation Organization
ICBL	International Campaign to Ban Landmines
ICC	International Criminal Court
ICC	International Chamber of Commerce
ICJ	International Court of Justice
ICOMIA	International Council of Marine Industry Associations
ICRC	International Committee of the Red Cross
ICT	Information and Communications Technology
IFI	International Financial Institution
IGO	Intergovernmental Organization
IIB	International Investment Bank
ILO	International Labor Organization
IMF	International Monetary Fund
IMO	International Maritime Organization
INGO	International Nongovernmental Organization
IO	International Organization
ION	Interorganizational Network
IR	International Relations
IRD	Integrated Rural Development
ITU	International Telecommunications Union
LAFTA	Latin American Free Trade Area
LDC	Least Developed Countries
M&A	Merger and Acquisition

MERCOSUR	Common Market of the South
MNC	Multinational Corporation
MNE	Multinational Enterprise
MPLA	Movimento Popular de Libertaçao de Angola
NAFTA	North American Free Trade Agreement
NAM	Non-Aligned Movement
NATO	North Atlantic Treaty Organization
NEPAD	New Partnership for African Development
NGO	Nongovernmental Organization
NIC	Newly Industrialized Country
NIEO	New International Economic Order
OAU	Organization of African Union
OAS	Organization of American States
ODA	Official Development Assistance
OEEC	Organization for European Economic Cooperation
OECD	Organization for Economic Cooperation and Development
OFDA	U.S. Office of Foreign Disaster Assistance
OIC	Organization of the Islamic Conference
OPEC	Organization of Petroleum Exporting Countries
OSCE	Organization for Security and Cooperation in Europe
POW	Prisoner of War
QUANGO	Quasi-Nongovernmental Organization
RENAMO	Resistência Nacional Moçambicana
SAARC	South Asian Association for Regional Cooperation
SAL	Structural Adjustment Loan
SC	Security Council
SEATO	South East Asian Treaty Organization
SG	Secretary-General
SIPRI	Stockholm International Peace Research Institute
SRSG	Special Representative of the Secretary-General
TCP/IP	Transmission Control Protocol
TNC	Transnational Corporation
UDEAC	Union douanière et économique de l'Afrique centrale
UIA	Union of International Associations
UN	United Nations
UNCHE	United Nations Conference on the Human Environment
UNCED	UN Conference on Environment and Development

UNCTAD	UN Conference on Trade and Development
UNDP	UN Development Program
UNEP	UN Environment Program
UNESCO	UN Educational, Scientific, and Cultural Organization
UNHCR	UN High Commissioner for Refugees
UNHCHR	UN High Commissioner for Human Rights
UNICEF	UN Children's Fund
UNIFEM	United Nations Fund for Women
UPU	Universal Postal Union
UNU	United Nations University
USAID	U.S. Agency for International Development
USSR	Union of Soviet Socialist Republics
VER	Voluntary Export Restraint
WILPF	Women's International League for Peace and Freedom
WFP	World Food Program
WHO	World Health Organization
WMO	World Meteorological Organization
WOMP	World Order Models Project
WTO	Warsaw Treaty Organization
WTO	World Trade Organization
WWF	World Wide Fund for Nature

PREFACE

When I initiated this project in the fall of 1998 the world seemed to be a lot less troubled and the future more certain. At least that's how it appeared from my study in Shanghai, China. International organizations as a field of study had been revitalized by the end of the Cold War and the dramatic changes in the world caused by globalization. There was a growing interest in international organizations among scholars, policymakers, and international affairs experts and a certain amount of enthusiasm for expanding the role of international organizations. I thought that under the circumstances, putting together an introductory textbook about international organizations would be relatively straightforward and swift. On both counts, I was definitely overly optimistic. Neither the world nor international organizations are ever static, especially in these times of change and uncertainty.

The research and writing of this book over the past four years have been both challenging and rewarding. As much as I enjoyed getting lost in the world of ideas and exploring the incredible mosaic of today's global reality, the best part of the enterprise has been the time spent in the company of others, my fellow travelers on this journey of discovery. Indeed, there are many people who have assisted me throughout this long drawn-out process. I owe a debt of gratitude to the Shanghai Academy of Social Sciences and the many Chinese scholars there, especially Li Yihai, for giving me an exciting intellectual environment at the very beginning of this project and important insights into the Asian worldview. I am especially thankful to the Carnegie Council on Ethics and International Affairs, which brought me into its family of exceptionally talented intellectuals when I returned to the United States. Joel Rosenthal, CCEIA president, and the Council's first-rate staff not only expanded my appreciation of the ethical challenges of living in today's complex interdependent world, but also of the importance of examining the philosophical roots of contemporary international thought. I am also grateful to the Center for Global Change and Governance at Rutgers University–Newark and the center's director, Richard Langhorne, for including me in their exciting work and deepening my understanding of the many facets of globalization. The United Nations University has been an inspiration both intellectually and practically to my endeavors. UNU's Jean-Marc Coicaud in Tokyo and Jacques Fomerand in New York, in particular, generously gave me much support and encouragement.

Over the course of this undertaking, I also received incredible assistance and guidance from many within the United Nations Secretariat and the UN diplomatic community who have first-hand experience in the art of global governance, including Susan Markham, Kevin S. Kennedy, Henk-Jan Brinkman, Jan Fischer, Georg Kell, J. P. Kavanagh, Don Mills, Syed Azmat Hassan, Chen Luzhi, and Hugh Dugan. And this book has been much improved from the insights and detailed suggestions of several scholars and experts—Jan Kooiman, Dennis Dijkzeul, Shareen Hertel, Lotta Hagman, Abby Stoddard, James Cairns, Jonathan Bach, Newton Bowles, Juergen Dedring, Benjamin Rivlin, Edward C. Luck, Shepard Forman, Jeremy Taylor, Jeffrey Laurenti, Richard Reitano, JoAnn Aviel, and Wilfred Grey—all of whom gave generously of their time to share with me their views and experience on the dynamic features of our times. I also owe a great debt to those who contributed directly to this enterprise and to whom I am eternally grateful—Melissa Semeniuk, who compiled the appendix to Chapter 5 and spent numerous hours in the library poring over yearbooks and other dusty reference works on the earliest international organizations; Gautum Goon, who was able to make out my "scriblings" and put some of the earliest drafts of the manuscript into the computer; and Kathleen Tinkel, who was enlisted at the end to create the maps. And, I am grateful for the patience and constant support of everyone at Westview Press, especially my editor, Steve Catalano.

But my greatest appreciation goes to my wife, Reeta Roy, who has supported me in all ways. Her generous spirit and unflagging enthusiasm made this book possible and it is to her I dedicate this book.

James P. Muldoon Jr.
Lake Forest, Illinois
January 1, 2003

1

Introduction: In Search of Global Governance

On September 11, 2001, the world was turned upside down. The unthinkable unimaginable happened—the greatest power on earth had become the victim of the most spectacular acts of terrorism in world history. The "new" world order, barely a decade old, was being challenged, but not by conventional foes and means as in the Persian Gulf war. A much more insidious, elusive enemy was the perpetrator—a global network of militant Islamists called Al Qaeda. The first "war" of the twenty-first century was declared and the international machinery geared up to vanquish not only Al Qaeda but also the multifaceted, disembodied, complex phenomenon of terrorism as a whole.

September 11 (or 9/11 as it is now commonly called) was a wake-up call for the international community, pointing out the inadequacies of the interstate system to govern a rapidly changing, globalizing world. The underside of globalization had demonstrated its destructive power and ability to exploit the international system's vulnerabilities. Reflecting on the condition of international politics since September 11, Professor Fred Dallmayr of the University of Notre Dame writes:

> In many ways—to use currently fashionable vocabulary—the international arena hovers precariously between "clash" and "dialogue" between civilizations. Stated in different and more customary terminology, the arena is wedged between inter-nationalism and trans-nationalism, that is, between traditional inter-state politics and emerging transnational or global politics (possibly guided by a hegemonic superpower). This situa-

tion is risky and hazardous because of the lack of historical precedents and clear guidelines. There have been frequent assertions in recent times, by experts and non-experts alike, concerning the imminent demise of nation-state politics; but the alternative is far from obvious or readily intelligible.

The hazards of contemporary international politics were clearly brought out into the open by September 11 and its aftermath: the so-called "war on terrorism." From the beginning, this war was ambivalent and amorphous. The initial attacks were launched not by a state but by a private "war-lord" and his followers (although they may have enjoyed the protection of a regime). The American response was swift, but also ambivalent. In the press and the media, the response was firmly proclaimed as a "war"—evident in the rhetoric of the "war on terrorism" or "America's new war." But a war against whom? Against a public regime or state (say Afghanistan)? In that case, the normal rules of warfare applied (*ius ad bellum, ius in bello*). Or was it a military action against a private band of outlaws or terrorists? In that case, the action hovered in a legal vacuum—since neither international norms nor domestic civil laws (of America or Afghanistan) could be invoked. The hazards of the situation were further illustrated in later phases of the military campaign, when large numbers of Taliban and other enemy fighters were captured. Given the repeated designation of the campaign as a "war," one could with reason expect that fighters captured in that war would become prisoners of war (POW) entitled to the protection of familiar international conventions. When the United States suddenly chose the term "detainees," it seemed to indicate that the campaign had not been a war after all, but rather something like a global police action or global "domestic" conflict (akin to a global civil war). But what are the rules authorizing or regulating such action?

In this respect, September 11 brought into the open a global political "deficit": the lack of norms and institutions mediating, or bridging the gap, between the emerging globalism and the traditional system of nation states. Here a major lesson comes into view: the need to build viable institutions and multilateral conventions able to remedy the dangers implicit in the mentioned legal vacuum or no-man's land. (Dallmayr 2002, 9)

Dallmayr's conclusions echo the analyses of many other scholars and specialists that have emerged since the Berlin Wall came down in 1989–

1990. The major lesson from all the post–Cold War conflicts and humanitarian emergencies (Somalia, Rwanda, Sierra Leone, Liberia, the Balkans, Kosovo, East Timor) is the same: The architecture of the international order—international institutions and organizations—needs to be strengthened and buttressed with additional resources and structures. International organizations, despite their many problems and limitations, are essential building blocks of a global governance architecture. They form the core of an evolving infrastructure of global institutions that will shape the way cooperation is organized and complex interdependence is managed. In other words, multilateralism matters.

Governing the Global Village

The world of 2002 is a sharp contrast to the kind of world many analysts and political leaders had thought would emerge after the Cold War. Initially, there was a naive belief that the demise of the Soviet Union and communism had ushered in a "New World Order" of peace and prosperity based on core Western values—justice and democracy, free and open trade within a global market economy, and international security—and secured by the unprecedented harmony that had emerged among the permanent members of the U.N. Security Council. "As the cold war ended in 1989, revolution in Central and Eastern Europe extended the movement towards democratization and economic transformation, raising the prospect of a strengthened commitment to the pursuit of common objectives through multilateralism. The world community seemed to be uniting around the idea that it should assume greater collective responsibility in a wide range of areas, including security—not only in a military sense but in economic and social terms as well—sustainable development, the promotion of democracy, equity and human rights, and humanitarian action." (Commission on Global Governance 1995, 1) But, over the course of the 1990s, the commitment and "unity" fractured under the pressure of a string of events—the increase in intra-state conflicts in places like the Balkans (Bosnia-Herzegovina and Kosovo) and throughout Africa (Somalia, Rwanda, Democratic Republic of Congo, Liberia, Sierra Leone, Ethiopia/Eritrea); crises in the global economy such as the Asian financial crisis of 1997–1998, the crash of the Russian ruble in 1999, and the debt crisis of developing countries (particularly the Least Developed Countries in Africa); and humanitarian calamities like the HIV/AIDS epidemic, burgeoning flows of refugees and the rise in the numbers of people internally displaced, and a range of natural disasters (drought, famine, and earthquakes). Today, we know how misplaced the optimism was at the time and that it was dangerously premature to believe the end of the ideological conflict between the Soviet Union and the West was sufficient for world peace and prosperity to reign.

Various forces of globalization have changed the political, economic, and social landscape, eroding sovereignty—the core principle of the international order—and redistributing power within the international system away from the nation-state to new international non-state actors. "The end of the Cold War has brought no mere adjustment among states but a novel redistribution of power among states, markets, and civil society. National governments are not simply losing autonomy in a globalizing economy. They are sharing powers—including political, social, and security roles at the core of sovereignty—with businesses, with international organizations, and with a multitude of citizens groups, known as non-governmental organizations (NGOs). The steady concentration of power in the hands of states that began in 1648 with the Peace of Westphalia is over, at least for a while." (Mathews 1997, 50). Immense changes on a global scale—some of it integrative, and some disintegrative—continue to unfold; new patterns of interaction are being developed; a global system is emerging. But the most important and difficult challenge to meet has been and continues to be establishing a new world order, a global order. Today, the challenges of globalization are just as pronounced and complex as they were in 1989, as are the challenges of governing the seemingly unending turbulence in the world that globalization creates.

Governance and Order

For thousands of years, humanity has searched for the best form and method of organizing itself. It is an endless journey, a perpetual quest for answers to fundamental questions—How should or could the world be organized? What are the rules and laws that people should follow and obey? And, who shall govern? As we enter a new millennium, this quest begins anew. However, the dimensions of the search have dramatically changed, even if the questions have not. Today, we are exploring the global dimension for the first time, a dimension no longer constrained by physical or temporal realities of previous eras. Embarking on this latest adventure, humanity once again is asking itself these perennial questions and in so doing is taking a fresh look at the architecture of global governance that has been built.

The idea of global governance is not necessarily new. It stems from a long history of thought on and experience with various ways of ordering and organizing political, economic, and social relations. The concept of global governance has been bundled up in the expansion of the system of sovereign nation-states and discussed as part of the notion of an international society or world polity. Seyom Brown argues:

> For three centuries the world polity has been premised on a particular pattern of governance/society congruence: the expectation that the most intensive patterns of human interaction would take place within territorially defined jurisdictions, each having its own regime of governance (or "state") whose supreme authority over what happened in its jurisdiction would be recognized and respected by the other states. Attempts to intervene in another's jurisdiction would be considered illegitimate, and grounds for war.
>
> Each of the presumably sovereign states would control interpersonal and intergroup behavior within its jurisdiction so as to provide at least the minimum personal and institutional security necessary for the performance of basic societal functions: the protection of persons and property from physical attack; the enforcement of laws and contracts; the orderly exchange of goods and services; the husbanding of resources essential to the healthy survival of the population; and the maintenance of the society's cultural, moral, and legal norms, including the rights and obligations of individuals and standards of distributive justice.
>
> Because these basic functions of society and governance in the traditional world polity were to be provided *within* each of the sovereign "nation-states," international or transnational interactions could be relatively sparse and could be managed for the most part by negotiation or periodically (in cases of conflict unresolvable through peaceful bargaining) by war. Looking at the world from this perspective, there was no crucial incongruence between the configuration of global society and the anarchic structure of global governance, for global society itself was compartmentalized into national enclaves of human interaction. Most

> countries would be willing to take their chances in the anarchic world polity when it came to handling international relations, in preference to subordinating the sovereignty of their territorial unit to "supranational" governing bodies purporting to act on behalf of some larger inchoate international community, let alone a nonexistent worldwide community of humankind. (Brown 1996, 108–109)

The anarchic structure of global governance is inherent to international society, according to Hedley Bull, and "the fact that states form a society without government reflects features of their situation that are unique." (Bull 1995, 49) International order is possible without world government because states have come to recognize that they do have certain interests and some values in common, regard themselves bound by a common set of rules in their relations with one another, and share in the working of common institutions (for example, diplomacy, war, international law, balance of power) (Bull 1995, 13). The point is that governance is present when there is order in a system; government is not a necessary condition of social order. In this regard, James Rosenau argues that "governance and order are clearly interactive phenomena. As intentional activities designed to regularize the arrangements which sustain world affairs, governance obviously shapes the nature of the prevailing global order. It could not do so, however, if the patterns constituting the order did not facilitate governance. Thus order is both a precondition and a consequence of governance. Neither comes first and each helps explain the other. There can be no governance without order and there can be no order without governance (unless periods of disorder are regarded as forms of order)." (Rosenau 1992, 8)

The end of the Cold War and radical shifts in power away from states to non-state actors were the impetus behind the initial surge of interest in the concept of global governance, but in a new way. The state-centric international order was coming undone as the mechanisms of cooperation and coordination among states no longer seemed capable of managing the rapidly expanding global agenda. The architecture of the international order had become too rigid and seemed unable to adapt to the fast pace of change or to accommodate the crowds of non-state actors that were coming onto the world stage. In this confused and conflicted international environment, governments, businesses, and nongovernmental organizations have been struggling to manage and restructure their relationships. For some, the disarray of traditional relationships in international affairs indicates a dangerous deterioration of the international order and portends collapse of the system into chaos or anarchy. Others consider the turbulence of the 1990s as a part of the process of evolution, an inevitable consequence of the transformation of the international system into a global system. In some respects, both are right. The international order has indeed deteriorated into "disorder" in large measure, but there is growing evidence that a global system is emerging out of this "chaos." Hence, the concept of global governance shifted its focus onto the dynamics of globalization so as to identify the new patterns of interaction between actors, institutions, and organizations on the global level.

Core Characteristics of Global Governance

This shift in focus is reflected in the "rapidly proliferating number of publications, countless conferences throughout the world, blueprints for the future prepared by academic think tanks and international organizations, as well as numerous ceremonial addresses dealing with the far-reaching structural changes that are affecting all spheres of life and have been reduced to the overused, not to say hackneyed, common denominator of 'globalization.'" (Nuscheler 2002, 156) The "global governance project" has become a vibrant exercise of global thinking and the most ambitious effort to chart a new course for humanity as a whole. It is still a fragile project and its conceptualization is still evolving. At this stage, we can merely speculate as to what physical attributes the still emerging global system may have and the principles upon which such a system is likely to operate. At the same time, there are a few fundamental characteristics of global governance that have emerged:

- Multipolarity of power and decentralization of authority: The traditional hierarchy of power and authority in the world has become more and more flat or horizontal over time. The allocation of power is gradually spreading to new centers and places on the planet. This inexorable trend of decentralization and widening connectivity is not as revolutionary as some might think because it seems to fit a general pattern in human history. As technology and knowledge advance and spread, the form and structure of governance becomes more "universal" and inclusive. Yet, the gradual convergence of governance values (namely, transparency/accountability, participation, fairness in the rule of law, equity and equality, and so on) does not necessarily mean that governance will be "homogenized" into one form/structure or another. Rather, this convergence only reflects an increasing consistency in approach to governance among the diverse collection of organizations and networks.

The emergence of "new forms of governance without government" (see Rosenau and Czempiel 1992) is a critical aspect of the transformation of the international system to the global. The globalization process of the past decade has increased both the value and significance of non-governmental mechanisms in governance. While nongovernmental mechanisms are perceived by many as an assault on the exalted position of the state in world affairs, the idea of governance without government does not preclude the existence of governments. Rather, it simply points out that non-governmental governing structures will develop and that governments are sharing governance responsibilities increasingly with two other societal actors—namely, markets and civil society.

- Institutions, regimes, and organizations: Historically, societies have created structures to order and regulate human relations. These structures have been established to define and differentiate authority, power, the allocation of resources, and the rules and procedures for intercourse within and among social systems. Such structures are essential elements of governance. Institutions reflect an organized pattern of group behavior that is generally accepted as a fundamental part of a social system or order. Regimes, in much the same way as institutions, are arrangements—a style or tenure of rule or management—for managing and regulating group behavior, but in a specific area. Organizations are the most formal expression of structure that define in explicit terms the relationship of the power and authority of its constituent elements.

Global governance cannot be actualized without institutions, regimes, and organizations. Such structures are essential intermediaries that tie together the different components of social systems. They are also historical realities in that their composition, raison d'être, and manifest purposes are derived through social experience and evolve out of earlier structures and forms. Therefore, the trans-

formation of international institutions, regimes, and organizations will likely retain many of the features that currently define them and add new features as needed or desired to address the particular, unique, or distinct demands of the global system in the future.
- Stability, responsiveness, and order: People establish institutions, regimes, and organizations to meet several categories of needs. Among these categories three are essential to the emerging global system—stability, responsiveness, and order. J. Martin Rochester argues that these three categories are key factors of system transformation and the political development of the international system. Global governance is closely tied to the international system's "capacity to cultivate a political order which combines stability with responsiveness to new demands and, hence, avenues for peaceful change" (Rochester 1993, 35). Governance structures only survive if they promote stability in the system, if they can effectively and sufficiently respond to the demands made of the system, and if order is achieved within the system.

The concept of global governance involves three primary actors—governments, markets, and civil society—who operate within three basic governance domains—the political domain, the economic domain, and the socio-cultural domain (UNDP 1997, 14–18). Thus they form three institutional pillars of global governance as portrayed in Figure 1.

Each pillar has distinct institutions and organizations on three different levels that support the system as a whole. The interaction among the levels and their contents produce both integration and differentiation within and between institutions and organizations. But as we go forward in the twenty-first century, the analytical lines that have traditionally divided these domains, as well as the institutions and organizations in each, will blur and perhaps even disappear.

This model recognizes four important aspects of global governance. First, global governance recognizes non-governmental mechanisms as having as much influence on how the global system is governed as do governmental mechanisms. Second, the actors involved in creating or forming instruments of global governance include "individuals, voluntary groups, localities, regions, ethnic groups, nation-states and all kinds of transnational actors" (Axford 1995, 7). Third, global governance infers

Political Pillar	**Economic Pillar**	**Socio-cultural Pillar**
International	*International*	*International*
Diplomacy International Law Intergovernmental bodies — e.g., UN, WTO, NATO, ASEAN, etc.	MNCs/TNCs ICC Industry Associations	NGOs Labor Unions Professional Associations
National	*National*	*National*
Government Military/defense Court system Regulatory bodies— commerce healthcare education	Banking system Retail system Industries— manufacturing technology construction	Education system Healthcare system Performing Arts Religious Organizations
Community	*Community*	*Community*
Local government Police and judges Public services: roads, bridges, water, sewage, public assistance, etc.	Banks Stores Manufacturers Restaurants	Schools/teachers Hospitals/doctors Theater/performers Churches/pastors Families

FIGURE 1.1 Three Institutional Pillars of Global Governance

the gradual integration of the three domains of governance—political, economic, and socio-cultural—and the fragmentation of world order due to transitory and contested spheres of authority which are disaggregative or anti-systemic (Rosenau 1997, chapter 8). And fourth, global governance architecture is projected to be predominantly non-hierarchical in structure and to operate at multiple levels.

International Organizations and the Development of Global Governance

Clearly, international organizations play an important role in the governance of international society. They constrain the predilection of individual and organized interests to diverge from a common or shared perspective of the "good." They help states and non-state actors manage the competition among identities and values and create conditions whereby conflicting ends can be accommodated and reconciled. They function as bridge-builders, coordinators, information centers, transmitters, and adjudicators of social processes and interactions that go on within and beyond the frontiers and borders of national life. They structure the "dynamic" of human relations, and thus facilitate order in the world.

International organizations make up the core of the infrastructure of a global system, providing the institutional framework for an orderly transition from the "international" to the "global." International organizations have been at the forefront in current thinking on global governance in terms of envisioning the future as well as translating this vision into action. According to Martin Hewson and Timothy Sinclair:

> Although there have been several programmatic statements of how the world organizations should have global governance as their aim, by far the most influential is that of the Commission for Global Governance. In this process, the idea of global governance has gained some prominence beyond academia and into some sectors of public debate.
>
> In response to the new prominence of the UN during the Gulf conflict (1990–1991), an initiative of the Swedish prime minister Ingvar Carlsson brought together a Commission on Global Governance to suggest ways of building upon and consolidating the apparent revival of the UN. What resulted was a manifesto in the social democratic tradition of Willy Brandt's North-South report of 1980 and Gro Harlem Brundtland's sustainable development report of 1987. However, there is one striking difference in tone between the earlier global reform reports and the global governance report. The earlier reports had focused on solving a particular problem facing the world. The global governance report is more concerned with conveying the argument that pervasive global changes have altered the terrain on which global problem solving was to take place.
>
> On the one hand, the commission's report envisages that the ending of the Cold War enables a considerable strengthening of the world organizations. For instance, the report recommends establishment of a standing military force, a facility for automatic taxation, and a tribunal to oversee

> global competition. On the other hand, the commission also envisages a situation in which the agencies of global civil society increasingly become involved in the functions of global governance. For example, it proposes a widening of the institutional forums in which Non-Governmental Organizations (NGOs) can gain an effective presence on the world stage. (Hewson and Sinclair 1999, 13–14)

The report of the Commission on Global Governance—*Our Global Neighbourhood*—gave a much-needed focus to the different strands of thinking on global governance that have flourished since its publication in 1995. Its effort to imagine the future and to set out practical steps to realize that future has generated renewed interest in the study of international organizations and has challenged scholars and policymakers to see international organizations in a global perspective. In nearly every study of global governance, international organizations loom large in the analysis and are often characterized as the building blocks for establishing a new global system. At the same time, there remains considerable skepticism about the ability of international organizations to meet the ongoing challenges of globalization and to manage the growing complexity of the nascent global system. Policymakers and scholars have expressed serious concerns about the capacity of international organizations for reform and innovation, which in turn deepens doubts of international organizations' relevance and legitimacy in today's world. Although this skepticism may be warranted, it does not detract from the historical significance of the role international organizations play in the governance of world order.

This book is divided into two parts. The first part traces the various intellectual roots of international organizations and the architecture of governance. The section highlights the contributions of major thinkers to international thought from ancient times to the present. The second part examines the different forms, structures, and functions of international institutions and highlights how international organizations have evolved as agents of structural change. This survey of international organizations represents an effort to contextualize international organizations in an evolutionary perspective and to bring out the significance of international organizations—their past, present, and future forms—in the architecture of global governance.

PART ONE

Schools of Thought

The Foundations of International Order and Organization

2

The Classical Schools of Thought

To make sense of the intellectual dilemma of global governance today, we must turn our attention to those thinkers of ancient times whose thoughts have shaped and forged our understanding of the world. Much of what we understand and think about international relations and international organizations is rooted in the "academic scribblings" of the earliest political philosophers—men such as Plato, Confucius, Aristotle, and Augustine. The schools of thought of today emanate from the rich and profound insights of these great thinkers of an earlier and "simple" time.

Although the earliest thinkers did not think of the "international" as we know it, they inform most of the fundamental principles of contemporary political theory and international thought. It is they who first contemplated the essence of political life; examined key relationships among man, the state, and society; and sought out enduring truths within the messy and confused reality of human existence. The matter of their inquiry remains of considerable significance today. In addition, the foundation of a global society is the final reckoning of competing worldviews (civilizations) that once existed in isolation to each other but now intermix.

The Ancient Traditions

Classical political thought comes out of traditions developed over centuries by the world's most ancient civilizations—the Egyptians, the Mesopotamians, the peoples of the Indus Valley, the Chinese, and the Mesoamerican peoples. These traditions reflected the ways in which the ancient kingdoms and empires organized themselves, politically and socially, and distinguished themselves from each other. They define values and sanction practices, thus shaping people's worldview and notion of community.

But these traditions were also born out of great adversity and conflict. "Most of the ancient kingdoms and empires arose out of the turmoil of warring families, villages, or tribes. For almost all of them, the establishment of political and social order became the most important task. Often, order was imposed by force alone. When threatened by immediate and painful death, most people, then as now, would remain quiet and obedient—as long as the force remained. The problem became, then, how to keep order when force was not present, as it could not be at all places and times." (Van Doren 1991, 23–24) The solution to this problem was an order based on a hierarchy. The gods stood at the top, humanity at the bottom, and the ruler(s) occupied a special place as the interlocutor between the gods and humanity. The rulers were joined with priests whose purpose was to interpret the will of the gods, thus keeping the people in submission. The Egyptians created and maintained a rigid social hierarchy that went unchanged for 3,000 years; the Indians stratified their society through a caste system that fixed one's place in the hierarchy by birth; the Mesopotamian civilizations made literacy a distinguishing aspect of their social system, giving a powerful minority control over most of the business of the state; and the Chinese developed a test by which the distinction between people is determined on a superior knowledge of Confucian texts. "These empires gave their people law, which is to say, a measure of peace and security against the violence of other people like themselves. But they provided no security against the rulers themselves, who ruled by violence and guile, and whose will was absolute." (Van Doren 1991, 3)

The Sages of the East—Buddha and Confucius

The great teachers of antiquity all shared a concern about the inequities and injustices that were rampant in the social order of their place and time. Although their worldview was limited to the boundaries of the society in which they lived and did not challenge the labeling of outsiders as enemies and inferior, their doctrines came to shape millions of people's view of how society should be organized and governed. An interesting coincidence is that perhaps the three greatest minds of all times emerged around the same time—Siddhartha Gautama (the Buddha), Confucius, and Socrates—and although they never crossed paths, their teachings and thought had a profound effect, albeit in different ways, on the political culture of society, particularly through their respective students and followers.

The Buddha's search for truth in the fifth century B.C. was to become one of the great systems of ethical thought in the world. The Buddha's thought reflects the understanding he had achieved of the reasons for human suffering and goodness. The "Truth" that he had found was actually four truths—life is full of conflict, sorrow, and suffering; the cause of life's pain and suffering is our selfish desire; it is possible to liberate oneself of this condition and achieve freedom, or Nirvana; and the way to Nirvana is the "eightfold middle path" (right view, right thought, right speech, right action, right mode of living, right endeavor, right mindfulness, and right concentration). He taught that all living beings, not just priests or ascetics, could aspire to enlightenment and that all people are equal in their common destiny. Buddhism's simple optimistic message stood in stark contrast to the social inequalities of Hinduism and the caste system, which by the fifth century B.C. had become deeply rooted in the political systems of India.

Buddhism took a great leap forward when in the third century B.C. the most powerful emperor of the Mauryan dynasty, Ashoka, reached his own "enlightenment" somewhere around thirty years of age, embraced Buddhism and renounced warfare forever. Ashoka's rule inaugurated India's Golden Age with its emphasis on making peace with his people and neighbors. During this period Buddhism spread throughout Ashoka's extensive empire—an area of nearly a million square miles and a population of over fifty million persons—and ultimately throughout Asia, playing a vital role to this day in the politics of many Asian countries. However, Buddhism did not overcome subsequent challenges of other belief systems such as Islam, Hinduism, and Confucianism in those places where it had spread, though "its emphasis on social equality, and its doctrine that many human ills are caused by poverty, have inspired liberal reform movements in numerous places" (Van Doren 1991, 22–23) and it remains powerfully influential in the world (most notably in the recent Asian values debate).

The other great sage of the East is Confucius. The teachings of Confucius were in response to the grave injustices of ancient China's feudalism and the failure of the ruling class to meet their duty to set an ethical example. Confucius viewed the chaos and disorder that had descended on Chinese society in the fifth century B.C. as symptoms of moral decay. In an effort to reverse this destructive course, he called for a return to the classics and the enduring wisdom of the rulers of the Shang and early Zhou dynasties.

Whereas the Buddha espoused social equality, Confucius taught that all should recognize their place in society and act accordingly. Social order was best maintained if correct relationships were strictly observed on a hierarchical basis or subordination. These relationships were defined in a group of texts: the Five Classics (*Book of Songs*, *Book of Documents*, *Book of Changes*, *Spring and Autumn Annals*, and the *Record of Ritual*); and the Four Books (the *Analects*, the *Mencius*, and two chapters, "Great Learning" and the "Doctrine of the Mean," from the *Record of Ritual*). (Wood 1993, 47–53) Confucius "propounded an ethical philosophy based on respect for traditions, and the careful observation of religious obligatory rituals. He projected an ideal moral man whose primary virtues were self-restraint, good-heartedness and the setting up of good examples to others. He taught that the key to good government was the education of the princely class, and the perpetuation of good values in each ruler that are desirable in his subjects." (Aero 1980, 192). Confucius's teachings were further refined by one of his most eminent disciples, Mencius (371 B.C.–289 B.C.). "Mencius held onto and solidified the Confucian belief in the inherent goodness of man. . . . He elevated the virtues of humanity and righteousness above all else, and proposed a system by which 'humane government' could replace 'the way of the despot'. Mencius maintained the traditional Confucian values of reverence for tradition and respect of ancestors. His concept of humanity began with the performance of duties to the family. Morality was located in every individual, making the people the most important elements of government, and therefore giving them the right to revolt against injustice." (Aero 1980, 194)

Confucianism came to dominate Chinese philosophy and ultimately the political order. According to Sun Rongrong:

> The veneration of the Sages is a cultural pattern of thought of pre-modern China. In the period before the Qin dynasty (Qin lasted from 221 B.C.–207 B.C.), the various philosophical schools, especially the Confucians, all held a deep respect for the Sages. After the unification of China during the Qin and Han (206 B.C.–220 A.D.) dynasties, the emperors of the feudal period respected and worshipped Confucius, regarding him as the highest Sage and the first great Teacher, firmly establishing Confucius's

> position as a sage. Moreover, when Emperor Han Wudi (157 B.C.–87 B.C.) "eradicated the hundred schools of thought, in order to honor only the Confucians," Confucianism became the dominant thought of the ruling class. Thus the Confucian classics and the words of the sages became the single standard and only model for speaking and acting. Throughout China's long-lasting feudal society, the dominant and collective way of thinking remained the Confucian persuasion. Further developments of the neo-Confucian school of the Song dynasty (960–1279) only helped to strengthen the dominant position of Confucianism by the Ming (1368–1644) and Qing (1644–1911) dynasties. (Sun 1999, 1)

Confucianism didn't spread much beyond China, but its values—social order and harmony, "good government" based on merit, love of learning, duty to the family, and respect for authority—have spread with the waves of Chinese migrations throughout Asia and the rest of the world. Indeed, the intermingling of Confucianism and Buddhism in popular beliefs throughout the Far East was to prove a potent and enduring "partnership" in Asian ethics and social philosophy.

The Sages of the West—Socrates and the Ancient Greeks

Emerging in the West in the fifth century B.C. was the Greek philosopher Socrates. He shared with Buddha and Confucius an interest in (or even passion for) ethics and politics, challenged the orthodoxies of the times in Athens, and considered "man" the most important subject to study and understand. During his day, Greece was a hotbed of science and philosophy that dared to believe the human mind could comprehend the workings of the world. The incredible explosion of knowledge emanating in the city-states of ancient Greece is unique in world history and had a profound effect on societies and peoples of antiquity. The creativity of such men as Thales, Pythagoras, Euclid, and Democritus revolutionized human thought in mathematics, the physical sciences, ethics, and politics. Socrates's contribution was solely in the fields of ethics and politics. Although Socrates wrote nothing, his ideas and his quest for the truth were recounted and advanced in the writings of his most famous student, Plato.

> The Platonic dialogues take up Socrates' quest for truth and, in the words of some commentators, improve on it. Plato speaks of Socrates as being

> "rejuvenated and beautified" through political discourse. Nothing is settled in the dialogues, yet everything is somehow clarified and illuminated. Philosophy for Plato and Socrates is love of the quest for wisdom rather than the pronouncement of truth. Plato's world is a world of ideals and values, but, in John Dewey's phrase, it is also "a realm of things with all their imperfections removed." In a feigned spirit of ignorance Socrates questions, not as the sophists did, leading their students toward some desired end, but in an effort to gain a fuller understanding of the essence or the essential form and character of an idea or a virtue. Socrates' method is dialectical, the tracing of an idea to its underlying postulate. For example, he asks on what premise or assumption the idea of security rests, or equality, or justice. He searches for examples that will explain and illuminate the principle. (Thompson 1994, 27–28)

The ancient Greek city-states were different from other societies in that they had "attained rough-and-ready democratic constitutions, founded on the premise of equality or isonomia—the condition said to pertain between and among citizens in whom final political authority was lodged and who determined the course of their city's fate by majority vote. . . . This equality meant equality in the *agora*, the open place where citizens assembled and debated, where rhetoric took primacy. Government was not by *all* the people, given the restrictions of citizenship, but it must be *for* all the people. For her defenders, like Pericles, democracy was the name given to the model city in which the power of the people and of law, political liberty and freedom of speech, political equality and rotation of offices, and, above all, justice between and among citizens defined political life." (Elshtain 1995, 93 and 96–97).

Although this form of government was not to last on the world stage for more than a few centuries, the idea was planted and became a focal point in the perpetual discourse of Western political thought.

Plato, through Socrates, was to challenge the superficial rhetoric and the corruption of virtue that had taken hold in Athenian democracy. Plato's politics are enumerated in two works—*The Republic* and *The Laws.* He creates or imagines a perfect city in *The Republic* whereby each individual fulfills his intended role and each class realizes its intended purpose in an architectonic and hierarchical social order. At the top of this order are philosophers and rulers whose role is to govern the state, then there is the guardian class in which warriors and loyal administrators rest, and at the bottom is the worker class. "Each has his own peculiar virtue—for example, philosophers wisdom and guardians courage. Each does for the state what certain virtues do for the individual. Warriors are to the state what courage, loyalty, and enlightened passion are to the individual. The worker class, which participates in the physical and industrial activities of the state, aspires to temperance and discipline. If all the classes perform in accordance with their intended virtues, justice will prevail in the state." (Thompson 1994, 29) *The Laws*, on the other hand, is Plato's assessment of how to determine the best regime. In theory, Plato argues that the regime is the order that gives society its character. Plato further argues that it is difficult to realize the best regime since what will be best depends on chance or contingencies no one can foresee.

Another important figure in the Greek tradition was Plato's student, Aristotle. Although Plato and Aristotle did not agree on all things, "Aristotle shared with Plato, as Plato shared with Socrates, an overweening concern and fascination with politics and morality. None of them ever questioned the idea that the most important being in the world is man. Mankind in the abstract, for only men, they agreed, have rational souls. Real men, also, because with them we must live, our happiness or misery depending on how well or badly we do so." (Van Doren 1991, 44) Aristotle is credited with inventing the science of logic and with being one of the first fathers of natural sciences. His interest in the empirical world sets Aristotle apart from his teacher Plato in that Aristotle did not dispense with the reality of man's condition as an irrelevant factor of political thought. In his exploration of virtue and justice, he sought to understand how politics and the "good life" come together. He was a practical man and emphasized limits, moderation, and restraint in his teachings, particularly when he tutored Alexander of Macedon, who was to conquer and rule most of the known world. Aristotle's politics focused on the practical expression of his ethics, which he argues is "happiness."

In his greatest work, *Politics*, Aristotle presents his analysis of different states and constitutions and "introduces the concept of *telos*, or the innate purpose that exists for every living thing. . . . In every living being, in men and beasts, a teleological principle exists in which the *telos* is fulfilled." (Thompson 1994, 40) For Aristotle, the *telos* of man is through the state or the political community, which is man's highest community and embraces all others. "In *Politics* and his discussion of different states and constitutions, Aristotle argues that 'statesmen must consider not only the absolute best conditions.' The best government may be a mixture of the actual and ideal. This is the essence of success in forming a government and writing a constitution. The way to think about constitutions is to reflect on the conditions of a people and the constitutions they require." (Thompson 1994, 38)

> Aristotle distinguishes between good and bad constitutions: Each good constitution can degenerate into a bad form. Democracy, Aristotle claims, is the corrupt form of popular government. It is corrupt because within it the mass of people, the poor, take over and do so in a way likely to lead to violence and anarchy as laws are abandoned and unchecked self-interest triumphs. A good constitution, for Aristotle, is directed to the common interest—whether it is a monarchy or a *politeia*, a constitution of and for the people. But a bad or perverted constitution is captured by selfish interests, whether of a few or the majority. For Aristotle, this is baneful because the end of the state is not "mere life" but a "good life," and a good life is one of felicity and fairness. (Elshtain 1995, 105)

Aristotle's core concern in his philosophical discourse about political systems and institutions was justice. A just political order "is based on the principle of equality, but it is in the nature of politics to divide men on the basis of inequality. Rulers 'lord it over others.' The best practical and attainable goal, therefore, is an accommodation, or *modus vivendi*, or some kind of compromise between these antinomies. The essence of politics requires some form of organized relation between political power, political freedom, and political equality." (Thompson 1994, 40) Aristotle's political theory did not deal with those societies outside of the Greek city-states or Alexander's empire, as he is known to have held foreigners in contempt, yet his influence, as well as that of Socrates and Plato, on the development of political thought in the West is perhaps the most profound.

The Roman Experience

The Greek influence was to reach the farthest points of the Western world and the "Near East" through the Roman empire. The Roman form of governance was a compromise formula of the Greek city-state—a republic that forged partnerships between the senate (an advisory group of patrician families) and the people. What sustained the Roman republic for three hundred years was the Romans' respect and love of law. "They considered their ancient laws and customs to be the lifeblood of the state. They were also avid students of law, and they constantly sought to improve their legal system. This was especially true during the two centuries of rapid Roman expansion after the defeat of Carthage in 146 B.C. Everywhere that Rome conquered they took their law with them and gave it to the peoples they ruled. As a consequence, during the greatest days of the empire one law ruled all men from Britain to Egypt, from Spain to the Black Sea. . . . Roman law was complex and ingenious, but Romans never forgot that its purpose was to regulate the lives of ordinary mortals. Thus there were laws of succession and inheritance, laws of obligations (including contracts), laws of property and possessions, and laws of persons (which included family, slaves, and citizenship)." (Van Doren 1991, 67) The practicality of the Romans may not have furthered Western philosophy or political thought, but it did preserve and spread the wisdom of the great thinkers of antiquity.

There is one Roman thinker of some importance who should be noted here, Marcus Tullius Cicero. A leading lawyer of his day, Cicero brought Greek thought to the masses while seeking to apply the principles of Greek ethical thought to the lives of Roman businessmen and politicians. Charles Van Doren notes:

> Cicero's last book, *On Duties*, dealt with a wide range of homely problems. How honest did a businessman have to be? Did shortcuts exist that could honestly be taken? How should a good man respond to the unjust demands of a tyrant? Was it all right to be silent, or should a person always speak up, even if to do so would prove dangerous? How should a man treat his inferiors, even his slaves? Did inferiors have rights that ought to be respected?
>
> Cicero's solution of all such problems seems simple: Always do the right thing, he insisted, because a wrong action, although perhaps apparently advantageous, can never be *really* advantageous because it is wrong.
>
> What *is* the right thing? How do you know? Cicero does not dodge the question. First, the right thing is what is legal, what is required by the law. But beyond that, for the law itself is not always just, the right thing is what is honest, open, and fair. Keeping your word, no matter the conse-

> quences. Telling the truth, even if you have not taken an oath. And treating everyone—foreigners, slaves, and women—alike, because they are all human beings. All are equal in their humaneness, although in no other way. Their humaneness gives them the right to be treated with respect. (Van Doren 1991, 74)

Cicero's simple rule for living epitomizes Roman practicality and insight as to what works in a mass, multiethnic society. Furthermore, he offered a solution to the great political problem of choosing either freedom or security and peace. He believed that a government of laws and not of men would give people both freedom and peace in a state. For Cicero the Roman republic represented such a state, but as we know the republic was not to last, being replaced in relatively short order by a system of institutionalized tyranny of Octavian's (a.k.a. Augustus's) Roman empire.

Religion and Politics

An important element in the evolution of political philosophy is religion. In ancient times, all societies invented belief systems that involved supernatural beings or entities who provided both sustenance and meaning to life. In many places, the gods were the progenitors of law that regulated human behavior and maintained social order. Tradition and custom are clearly steeped in religion's rectification of what we know and of the inexplicable through faith. The Egyptians, the Mesopotamians, the Indians, the Greeks, and the Romans (as well as the Aztecs, Incas, and the Chinese) all followed polytheistic religions and developed elaborate rituals and rites. Religious practices were infused in the governance of communities and were instrumental to those who ruled. This admixture of religion and politics remains a potent (and often explosive) force in society.

The Judaeo-Christian Tradition

The contribution of religion to classical political thought is manifold. It often defined or gave a unique identity to a community or people, while legitimizing a ruler or form of government for the community. As the "law-giving" authority, religion gave society rules to live by and moral standards by which social harmony was achieved. Among the many ancient religions one stands out—Judaism. It was probably the first monotheistic religion. The descendants of Abraham considered themselves the chosen people of God and have a special and permanent relationship with him. This relationship was defined by three things—the law (the Ten Commandments and the rules of diet, behavior, and social intercourse found in the Torah); the Convenant, a promise from God that he would never desert them; and a requirement by God to be a witness to all humanity of his being, goodness, and justice. The Jews have survived as a community for almost four thousand years despite efforts of other communities, faiths, and peoples to destroy them. Its staying power, despite the many adversities the Jewish community has had to endure and the Diaspora, has contributed to its influence and power as a faith and ethical system in the world. However, Judaism's impact on politics and political thought has never been as great as that of two of its "offspring"—Christianity and Islam.

Building on the doctrine of the Jewish community, Christianity was to overcome the severe persecution of the Roman empire to eventually win over the fourth century Roman emperor, Constantine, who made Christianity an official religion of the empire. The steady encroachment of Christianity on the political affairs of the Roman empire eventually led to the creation of a theocracy whereby the Christian church came to exercise "spiritual supremacy over all matters of faith and worship and temporal dominion over Rome and the entire Western empire" (Van Doren 1991, 104). The early part of the "Christian Era" saw two important church thinkers emerge—St. Augustine in the fifth century and St. Thomas Aquinas in the thirteenth century.

Augustine lived during the final decades of the Roman Empire and witnessed the sack of Rome in 410 A.D. It was a treacherous and uncertain time, but, like Aristotle and Plato before and Machiavelli, Hobbes, and Rousseau after, under such difficult circumstances Augustine was to write one of the most influential works of political thought. His most famous work, *The City of God,* was, in part, a defense of the church against those who claimed that Christianity was the cause of the sack of Rome. The significance of *The City of God* goes beyond a mere defense of the church, however, laying out a "plan of world history, showing how two cities had vied with each other for dominance. . . . One city was human—material, fleshly, downward-turning. The other city was divine—spiritual, turning upward toward the Creator of all things." (Van Doren 1991, 93–94)

According to Kenneth Thompson:

> Heir to classical thought, Augustine was the father of Christian philosophy and theology. He sought to maintain traditional ideas while responding to a changing situation . . .
>
> Augustine was a "God-intoxicated man." He maintained that the world was created by God. However, the City of Man was not eternal. It had a beginning and would have an end, which would coincide with the Last Judgment. Man was created good but had lost his goodness and innocence with the Fall. He became a victim of self-pride. He had been created good in God's image but not incorruptibly good. . . . According to Augustine, the root cause of sin is man's prideful self-centeredness. . . . Man's life is a restless and never-ending quest for power and for unremitting self-gratification with one conquest following another . . .
>
> Yet God has not abandoned suffering humanity and never will. By means of unmerited grace, man is enabled to preserve some residual virtue. Through the Incarnation, God has given assurance that an elect group will receive salvation. . . . A small minority will be chosen along with the good angels for eternal salvation. They will constitute the City of God, and will live forever in perfect peace and happiness. But that city is not of this world. No earthly city or state can be said to be representative of or even part of the City of God, not even the Commonwealth of the Hebrews or the universal Catholic church, although each may prefigure and announce the City of God. (Thompson 1994, 45–46)

Augustine laid the foundation for a nascent Christian political order that he thought should emerge out of the ashes of the Roman Empire. Reflecting the decline of the *pax Romana*, Augustine considered war and conflict inevitable because of man's fallibility and thought perpetual peace was impossible in the earthly city. He acknowledged that the state was the highest social community but recognized it was "a coercive order sustained by force and ruling on the basis of fear of pain and punishment. It seeks not to make men good or virtuous but to restrain citizens from evil." (Thompson 1994, 49) His views on virtue—temperance, fortitude, justice, and prudence—were only attainable in the Heavenly City, which is the noblest expression of the state. In essence, the state is a necessary evil since the City of God is not of this world and humanity is incapable of overcoming original sin or prideful self-centeredness. It is evident that Augustine's Christian political order—a system of small states preserved by the balance of power—was prescient of what was to emerge in Western Europe after the total collapse of the Roman Empire. Furthermore, Augustine was probably the first political realist who helped to bridge the thought of classical civilizations of Greece and Rome and the medieval Christian civilization of Western Europe.

St. Augustine's influence in political thought was to dominate the development of Western European philosophy and theology for almost 800 years. During this period, the Roman Empire dissolved and in its stead arose two great Christian empires—the Eastern Empire, with its capital at Byzantium and later at St. Petersburg in Russia, and the Holy Roman Empire in the west. In both cases, church and state were indistinguishable and marked the height of the theocratic state. As a form of governance, the Christian empires were fraught with problems and contradictions that made for an unstable system and engendered conflict.

Another great churchman, St. Thomas Aquinas, emerged 700 years after Augustine and was to synthesize Christian thought with Aristotle's outlook on human nature. Thomas Aquinas's most significant work is the eight-volume *Summa Theologica*, which was published in 1270. According to Kenneth Thompson:

> The twin purposes of *Summa Theologica* are the systematic survey of Christian theology and the elaboration of philosophical and social judgments based largely on Aristotle. . . . In his discussion of politics and the political community, Aquinas follows the thinking of Aristotle. He departs from the pessimism of Augustine, as had other medieval writers. With Aristotle, he finds that man's goal in the state is the good life and that the common good is above the good of the individual. In opposition to Augustine, he argues that the political community is a natural institution based on reason that would have existed whether or not man had sinned. . . .
>
> The aspect of politics that concerned him most was law. For Augustine, the law above all laws is the eternal law, which is beyond the reach of man. Divine law is the expression of the eternal law and is accessible to men. Natural law contains the precepts essential for the attainment of virtue and the good life. Human law is positive law, or what we describe

> as legislation for the ordering of society. Men are not bound to obey an unjust human law if it is contrary to divine and natural law. (Thompson 1994, 58–59)

Aquinas had hoped to bring together the City of God and the City of Man "under one immortal polity" and to rectify the doctrine of the "two truths"—"Faith and reason have nothing whatever in common. Each has its own truth, but the one is vastly more important than the other, with one determining salvation, the other the mere comfort of the body during this life." (Van Doren 1991, 123) The fact that Aquinas failed to win over the Realists before his death simply reflects a trend during the Middle Ages of a growing schism in the political order of the Christian church. Although Aquinas agreed with most aspects of Augustine's plan for a decentralized international system, he goes a bit further and professes that a world order of peace, "a common order of reason" is found in natural law. This departs from Augustine's view that a balance of evils (or power) is the best man can do during this life and places Aquinas in the position of being one of the earliest political "Idealists."

Augustine and Aquinas span the Middle Ages and mark two important schools of Christian thought for the period. While these two men drew upon the wisdom of Plato and Aristotle when developing their views and thinking about the world and society, they also brought to bear new elements of the Christian faith and its morality on Classical thought. Furthermore, these two men defined the principles of the successor system of governance to the Roman Empire, namely *pax Christiana*, which ruled over Europe (both east and west) for nearly a millennium.

Islam

Another monotheistic religion that emerged in the wake of the Roman Empire's collapse is Islam. It was founded by Muhammed, the Prophet, in the seventh century. Muhammed was a preacher who claimed to have been called by the angel Gabriel to be the "Messenger of God" and received revelations from God. Since he was not a scholar or a member of the elite in the society of medieval Arabia, the deck was stacked against him when he started off on his career as a prophet in his native city of Mecca. Due to growing opposition to his message, Muhammed and his followers were forced to leave Mecca for Medina. And yet, "Muhammed had managed, by the time he died in Medina in 632, not only to found a new religion and to unite all the Arabs of Arabia into one nation, but also to inspire a fervor that would, within twenty years of his death, lead his followers to conquer most of the Byzantium and Persian empires and, within a hundred years, to create a land empire rivaling in size and organization the Roman empire at its greatest." (Van Doren 1991, 19)

The revelations received by Muhammed were eventually written down and became the Koran, the sacred scriptures of Islam. The Koran set down the rules of behavior—when and how to pray; the relationships between men and women, father and son, man and God; dietary rules; and so on—which "established a clear, clean line between the rest of the world and themselves, and the sense of close, fraternal community this engendered led to rapid and astounding victories over societies and cultures not so bound together." (Van Doren 1991, 20) Whereas Judaism and Christianity recognized a distinction between the religious and secular realms (even if it was sometimes confused and blurred), Islam from the beginning "acquired its characteristic ethos as a religion that united both the spiritual and the temporal in one community and sought to control not only the individual's relationship to God but also his social and political relationships with his fellow men. Thus there grew up not only an Islamic religious institution but also an Islamic law [the Sharia] and Islamic state." (Van Doren 1991, 20)

One of the most important contributions of the spread of Islam in its early years was its embrace of Greek scientific thought after the second caliph, Omar, conquered Alexandria, where the greatest library of Hellenistic works in the world was situated. Instead of destroying the library, the new rulers of this capital of scholarship assumed the responsibility of codifying and interpreting the immense knowledge of science of the Greeks. Muslims became noted mathematicians, astronomers, physicians, and physicists, bringing Greek thought with them as the Islamic empire spread as far west as Spain and east to the South China Sea. Whereas the Western world under the theocratic rule of the Catholic church was generally bereft of Greek thought during the Middle Ages, the Islamic world (which was no less "God-obsessed" than the West) kept the Greek tradition alive through such men as Avicenna and Averroës, whose works on medicine, science, and philosophy were instrumental to reintroducing Aristotle's work on the natural world and ethics to the West. (Van Doren 1991, 114–115 and 117–119)

Beyond being a repository of classical Greek thought, Islam is not known for any significant contribution to either political thought or international theory, except perhaps as a challenge to the universalist imperial claims of Christendom. However, the ability of Islam as a governance system to survive (or rather adapt to) changes in the world suggests that it is a potent political force of enduring credibility and salience. In short, Islam worked as a theocracy and continues to function within the context of today's international community.

The Middle Ages was perhaps the high point of religion's political ambitions to realize Alexander the Great's ideas for world empire based on the ideal of *Homonoia* (union of hearts) or *Concordia* (being of one mind together). Both Christianity and Islam in their respective political manifestations made claims of their universal jurisdiction over all of humanity and were more than willing to seek "by all means necessary" to bring about their version of heaven on earth. The result of such a "noble experiment" was not the world-state but a bitter enmity between Christians, Jews, and Muslims that has endured into the twenty-first century.

The Renaissance

The end of the Middle Ages and the intellectual dominance of theology was an unassuming transition over three or four hundred years in Western Europe. Historians call this important period the Renaissance, during which time the decline of feudalism, of the universal Church, and of an empire of universal claims was in full swing. It was a period of "rediscovery of the wisdom of antiquity." (Wight 1992, 2) After nearly a millennium of God-centered thought, the Renaissance brought man back to the center of things, reviving both Aristotle and Plato as well as a nostalgia for the Roman Republic and Empire. "For a thousand years since the fall of Rome, men and women had turned over responsibility for their moral lives to surrogates of God on earth: the pope at Rome, his bishops, their parish priests or ministers. . . . Perhaps to their surprise, they discovered that the ancient Greeks and Romans, whom they admired for so many things, had by and large made no such bargain. . . . Classical man had been responsible for himself, and had accepted the consequences of his errors if he made them." (Van Doren 1991, 167)

It is at this critical juncture in history—a revival of the classics and the breakdown of the supranational authority of the Catholic Church that was to result in the Reformation—when the first signs of international theory can be seen. According to Martin Wight:

> International theory can be discerned existing dimly, obscured and moreover partitioned, partly on the fringe or margin of ordinary political philosophy and partly in the province of international law. This is owing to a historical accident, due ultimately to the cultural cleavage in Western society that occurred in the sixteenth century.
>
> One cannot talk properly about international relations before the advent of the sovereign state. This, the state which acknowledged no other political superior, largely came about in Western Europe in the time of Machiavelli, at the beginning of the sixteenth century, the threshold of "modern history." . . . In the sixteenth century, from Machiavelli on, the important and exciting social need was seen as the development of the sovereign state itself, the need to build up strong central authority which would give internal order in place of feudal license. . . . The crystallization of the state was what excited the best minds at that time, and they gave political philosophy that concentration on the state which it has never since lost. Hence the discussion of the nature of sovereignty, of the limits of sovereign power, of popular sovereignty and contract theory, which constitute the familiar highroad of political theory. . . .
>
> The divisive effects upon European thought of the Renaissance and Reformation also produced a partitionment of international theory between international law (as Tocqueville said, "the public law of Europe") and the work of philosophers. International law had its origin in the vague field where theology, ethics and law all meet and seem indistinguishable, and in its second chapter of development it had to borrow its tools and concepts largely from political philosophy. Jean Bodin in his *De Republica* (1576), is usually credited with the invention of the theory of sovereignty, the theory that every state must have a central authority which was the source of laws but not bound by them. But this doctrine of the equality of states became part of the stock-in-trade of international law only much later. Even in Grotius, there is more about sovereignty as a principle of internal organization than as the mark of membership of international society, and more about the extinction of sovereignty by

> dynasties dying out or through dynastic marriage than by cession or conquest. (Wight 1992, 1–3)

The Sixteenth Century and the Birth of the International

The sixteenth century was a significant turning point in the development of political theory and the fundamental principles of the nation-state. It marked the beginning of an important transition (in the West) in world order from the tradition of empire and supranational authority to the international and the sovereign state system. Machiavelli introduced a radical perspective on political philosophy looking for "order and unity within politics, not in some external or transcendent principles as in Plato or Augustine. He offers a set of do's and don'ts for political success." (Thompson 1994, 64) His importance to the evolution of political thought rests in his focus on describing what *is* rather than what *ought to be*. His conclusions that conflict "is a universal and permanent condition in society" driven by man's inherent lust for power and domination, that "the state is the most important instrument for containing and channeling man's selfish nature toward socially desireable goals," and that "the supreme end of politics is the security and well-being of the community rather than the higher moral ends portrayed in the classics" were to become the cornerstone of the "realist" school of thought. (Thompson 1994, 64–67)

In contrast to Machiavelli and the realist school was the work of Desiderius Erasmus. Erasmus challenged the prevailing views of realist and just-war schools of thought in his quest to bring about a lasting peace for war-torn Europe. As Sissela Bok points out:

> Few have spoken out more forcefully than Erasmus about the folly and cruelty of war. Already in his *Adages*, published in 1500 and reportedly more widely circulated at the time than any other book save the Bible, he inveighed against war in an essay entitled "*Dulce Bellum Inexpertis*" ("War Is Sweet to Those Who Have Not Experienced It"). Between 1514 and 1517, when a brief interval in the near-constant wars between European powers made a more lasting peace seem at least possible, Erasmus devoted himself wholeheartedly to helping to bring it about. He suggested summoning a "congress of kings"—a "summit meeting" among

> kings of Europe—for the purpose of signing an indissoluble peace agreement. He revised and expanded his essay on the sweetness of war to the inexperienced for the latest edition of the *Adages*. And he wrote a manual for princes—*The Education of the Christian Prince*—to guide the young Prince Charles of Spain, who was shortly to become Charles V.
>
> This book presents a striking contrast to Machiavelli's *Prince* (written a few years earlier but still unpublished). Where Machiavelli had broken from the stress on virtues so common in previous books of advice for princes and urged the prince to resort to violence, deceit, and betrayal whenever necessary to gain or retain power, Erasmus emphasized moral virtues as prerequisites to a good reign. And whereas Machiavelli had urged the prince to study war above all else, Erasmus gave precedence to learning "the arts of peace": how to establish and preserve a rule of just laws, improve the public's health, ensure an adequate food supply, beautify cities and their surroundings, and master the diplomatic alternatives to war. (Bok 1999, 129)

Erasmus's *The Complaint of Peace* (1517) was "a carefully reasoned attack on the underlying assumption widely shared in his day, as in our own: that violent conflict and organized war are somehow inherent in the human condition." He argues that peace "has to be undertaken at every level of society. Kings must work together for the good of their citizens and consult them before embarking on any war. . . . Erasmus, who never ceased criticizing kings for their exploitative and brutal scheming at the expense of their peoples, here hints at the alternative of government limited by democratic consent—hard to envisage in his time and dangerous for anyone to promote. If nations submitted, further, to an international court of arbitration, they could avert many wars; if need be, peace should be purchased to prevent still others." (Bok 1999, 131 and 133) Unfortunately, Erasmus and his ideas for lasting peace were not to bear fruit in sixteenth century Europe. However, he and others who would follow his lead gave voice to an important tradition within Western thinking about war and peace.

The breakdown of social order that followed in the wake of the Reformation and the civil wars that wracked the European continent were the circumstances that compelled Jean Bodin to take up political writing. He found the theological approach to political rule and the "science of politics" approach taken by Erasmus, Machiavelli, and others both wanting for the times. Martin van Creveld points out that "Bodin turned his back on both traditions. Starting at the beginning, he focused neither on the way God had constructed the universe nor on the education of princes but on the nature of the *république* as such—a problem which both Machiavelli and Erasmus (let alone Charles V who, though he was an astute and conscientious ruler, was anything but a theorist) had entirely ignored. Naturally Bodin's model was Aristotle's *Politics*, which he followed very closely even as he criticized some of the detailed arrangements which it proposed. Seeking a new, nonreligious basis for government, Bodin in *Les six livres de la république* became the first writer in modern history to discuss the difference between government *within* the household, as exercised by the husband over his dependents and by the master over his slaves, and political power which prevailed between people who were, if not yet equal, at any rate born free and possessed of a legal persona of their own." (van Creveld 1999, 176) Bodin endorsed and argued for the rule of law in political affairs, adopting Cicero's definition of a *res publica* (a community of people governed by law). In essence, Bodin replaces God with the sovereign as the entity through which a consensual basis for political life could be provided. He focused his thinking on "the sovereign's ability to create order out of chaos by instituting good laws and governing through them." (van Creveld 1999, 177)

Another contrast to Machiavelli and Jean Bodin were the neo-scholastics of the Catholic Church, namely Francesco de Vitoria O.P. (1480–1546) and Francesco de Suarez S.J. (1548–1617). Building on the pioneering work of Thomas Aquinas, these men were responsible for making the bridge between the medieval tradition of natural law and modern international thought. (Wight 1992, 14) They and the Italian Protestant refugee, Alberica Gentili (1552–1608), are credited with laying the foundation of a new school of thought—the School of Natural Law—one of "three patterns of thought purporting to describe the new international politics, and to prescribe conduct within it." (Bull 1995, 26)

> The mediaeval idea of world-monarchy was an idea foreign to the thinkers of the School of Natural Law. They left to the publicists of the Holy Roman Empire the task of continually reinvoking, on reams of paper, the unsubstantiated ghost of the old *imperium mundi*, but they made the indestructible germ of that dying system of thought yield the

> new and fruitful idea of *international society*. . . . On the one hand, a tendency continually reappeared to harden international society into a world-State, and to arm it with the authority of a Super-State organized on Republican lines: on the other, the stricter advocates of the theory of sovereignty rejected *in toto* any idea of a natural community uniting all States together. But the doctrine which held the field, and determined the future of international law, was a doctrine which steadily clung to the view that there was a natural law connection between all nations, and that this connection, while it did not issue any authority exercised by the Whole over its parts, at any rate involved a system of mutual social rights and duties. (Otto Gierke, quoted in Bull 1995, 26–27)

The Spread of Western Political Thinking

Another important development during the fifteenth and sixteenth centuries was the daring-do of European explorers of the seas—Prince Henry the Navigator, Bartholomeu Dias, Vasco da Gama, Christopher Columbus, and Ferdinand Magellan—who proved that all the oceans were connected and discovered that new places and peoples existed. According to Charles Van Doren, the race among Europeans to discover alternative trade routes to the Far East created a new kind of trade "that ultimately would bring the whole world together into one economic unit, no matter how many separate political units it might hold. Within a century this trade no longer dealt primarily in luxury goods. Large profits were to be made in the bulk shipment of mundane things like cloth, sugar, and rum. It was a far cry from the old overland trade in small amounts of valuable spices and drugs that could be carried on a camel's back. No one complained about the change, for the riches to be gained were incomparably greater. Besides, the trade routes—sea routes—could be controlled by Europeans from one end to the other. No middlemen were needed, Arab or otherwise." (Van Doren 1991, 178) Obviously, there was much more happening when Europe ventured out on the high seas. Besides the trade in goods there was a trade in knowledge and ideas. As Van Doren puts it:

> The ships that plied the oceans of the world during the three centuries after 1492 carried invisible cargoes in addition to the bulk cargoes that were visible to all. These were knowledge and ideas, together with reli-

> gious beliefs, and they flowed in both directions from West to East and from East to West. And in the interchange, ideas were transformed.
>
> Gunpowder, invented in China around 1000 A.D., is a good example of the change. The Chinese used gunpowder primarily to make fireworks and for other peaceful purposes. Arab mercenaries, obtaining gunpowder from the Chinese, made the first guns. The Europeans perfected them. More, they studied the art of using guns and cannon with a unique intensity. By 1500, European military strategy, both on sea and land, was based on the concept of acquiring and maintaining superior firepower. And to this day, in the West, the superiority of firepower over manpower and tactics has persisted as the central idea of military thinking. (Van Doren 1991, 179)

Unfortunately, the exchange of ideas of a political nature was not so straightforward or accommodating. For centuries the economic interaction between Europe and the East was punctuated by conflict and warfare as the great empires clashed with each other. Religion and politics were the great divide between civilizations, and it was rare for soldiers or merchants to take the time to grasp the complexity and distinct characteristics of the political systems with which they were fighting or doing business or to transfer political knowledge of these places back home. By the time Europeans ventured out into the world in the fifteenth and sixteenth centuries, Western civilization was at the start of an extraordinary revolution in science, economics, and politics, while the East cleaved to ancient traditions and political thought.

The influence of non-Western civilizations on international political thought at that time was minimal. The political traditions and systems of the East remained distinct and foreign to the development of Western political thought and vice versa. Only much later and after transportation and communication technologies enabled greater and sustained interaction between East and West would the significance of so-called "Asian values" and non-Western socio-cultural perspectives to international thought and world order be examined or even recognized.

3

"Peace Plans," "Reformers," and "Realists"— Thinkers of the Seventeenth to the Nineteenth Centuries

The seventeenth to nineteenth centuries were a period of dramatic change and progress in the world. Ancient and traditional notions of governance and social order were under siege and the evolution of political thought was to take a tremendous leap towards the "international." The intellectual foundation shifted from the predominance of "faith over reason" to science and humanism. With religious authority on all fronts in retreat, an opening appeared for science to come forward. Galileo Galilei (1564–1646), Rene Descartes (1596–1650), and Isaac Newton (1642–1727) revolutionized understanding of the world and how it works. These men gave us the "scientific method" and the fundamental rules of scientific reasoning. The incredible impact of their discoveries in mathematics, geometry, laws of motion and the principles of mechanics was not only in the natural sciences. Indeed, their influence extended to all human endeavors and paved the way for the important political and industrial revolutions that followed.

The three centuries of this period saw the ultimate demise of the unitary state and the ascendancy of the nation-state. The International Age was born. The bloodshed and chaos that accompanied the collapse of the Holy Roman Empire had an immense influence on the political thinkers of this dynamic period. The consolidation of independent sovereign states in Western Europe during the sixteenth and seventeenth centuries gave cause to some of the most illustrious political writers of this millenium, namely Hugo de Groot (Grotius), Thomas Hobbes, Samuel Pufendorf, John Locke, Émeric Crucé, Maximilieu de Béthune, duc de Sully, Benedict de Spinoza, and William Penn during the seventeenth century; Adam Smith, David Hume, Charles-Louis de Secondat, baron de Montesquieu, Jean-Jacques Rousseau, Edmund Burke, Charles Irénée Castel de Saint-Pierre, Jeremy Bentham, Thomas Jefferson, and Immanuel Kant in the eighteenth century; and George Wilhelm Friedrich Hegel, Karl Marx, Alexis de Tocqueville, David Ricardo, James Mill and his son John Stuart, and Henry George in the nineteenth century.

The expansiveness of thought during this period can hardly be given justice in this brief review, and we cannot indulge in an exhaustive treatment of each of these scholar's writings in one or even a dozen chapters. Therefore, this chapter will only give the relevant highlights and key contributions of these men to international theory. Martin Wight conveniently provides a tripartite framework to review this rich era of international theory:

> If one surveys the most illustrious writers who have treated of international theory since Machiavelli, and the principal ideas in this field which have been in circulation, it is strikingly plain that they fall into three groups, and the ideas into three traditions. Let them be called Rationalists, Realists, and Revolutionists . . . .
>
> These three traditions of political thought can be in some sense related to the three interrelated political conditions which comprise the subject-matter of what is called international relations.
>
> (a) *International anarchy:* a multiplicity of independent sovereign states acknowledging no political superior, whose relationships are ultimately regulated by warfare.
>
> (b) *Diplomacy and commerce:* continuous and organized intercourse between these sovereign states in the pacific intervals: international and internationalized intercourse.
>
> (c) *The concept of a society of states, or family of nations:* although there is no political superior, nevertheless recognition that the multiplicity of sovereign states forms a moral and cultural whole, which imposes certain moral and psychological and possibly even legal (according to some theories of law) obligations—even if not political ones. As Burke observed: "The writers on public law have often called this *aggregate* of nations a commonwealth."

> The three traditions of international theory can be roughly distinguished by reference to these three interdependent conditions of international relations. The Realists are those who emphasize and concentrate upon the element of international anarchy, the Rationalists [are] those who emphasize and concentrate on the element of international intercourse, and the Revolutionists are those who emphasize and concentrate upon the element of the society of states, or international society. (Wight 1992, 7–8).

Wight points out that these groupings are "not clear-cut pigeon-holes, but can overlap" and their utility is found in the rough distinctions between the many thinkers we are considering for this 300-year period. Perhaps more importantly, Wight's categories lead to a grasp of the continuities of thought that reach to the present time. The implication here is that the three traditions have their origin in seventeenth century Western Europe.

The Seventeenth Century—Realists and Rationalists Defined

The writings of Grotius, Hobbes, Pufendorf, and Locke during the seventeenth century helped define the rationalist and realist positions in political thought. Hobbes's most famous work, *Leviathan*, posited that the state of nature is an environment fraught with dangers, perpetual conflict, and constant struggle for survival—the famous line that life in a state of nature is "poor, nasty, brutish and short." He argues that men exchange unbridled liberty in the state of nature for a political order made possible by the Leviathan (or Commonwealth) that is created by an act of compact or social contract. This act is the real source of authority of government or the sovereign, not the divine right theory that dominated the day. Furthermore, it is a declarative rejection of the church's role in the state or the division of authority between church and state (the "two swords" doctrine). The Hobbesian view of politics and "of the doctrine that it is from politics, the conflict for power, that both morality and law derive their authority" (Wight 1992, 17) was a reflection of the terrible civil wars and strife that wracked both England and the European continent, often with religion at the heart of the conflict. (Thompson 1994, 77)

After Machiavelli, Hobbes is considered "the profoundest of Realists" basing his "Realism on a psychological theory which furnishes the first eight chapters of *Leviathan* . . . He was interested in the psychology of the individual mind less for its own sake than as a logical foundation for his secularist, 'naturalist', doctrine of ethics and politics" (Wight 1992, 20). In his effort to describe things as they are and the motivations that created this reality, Hobbes's core idea of the state of nature and the centrality of power in his thinking were to be echoed by other realists of the day—namely Samuel Pufendorf and Spinoza. The international theory that these men have given to us was not some scheme of international governance, but the rationale for the balance of power among states and sovereigns as the way to overcome, or at least manage, the insecurity of the state of nature. They argued that conflicts of interests are regulated through war and that the idea of "right is might" is a major or primary element of natural law. Machiavelli and Hobbes launched the final and decisive assault on the remnants of the church's supranational authority, introducing a new doctrine—"politics as the practical art of obtaining and preserving state power as an end in itself; political power in itself was the natural and sufficient end of government. . . . The state is an organization for survival in an international anarchy, and its policy is determined by the pressure of conflict in the international anarchy. It is an organization for which guns mean more than butter, security more than liberty, and foreign policy more than domestic." (Wight 1992, 103–104)

Obviously, the early thinkers in the realist tradition contributed to the development of the notion of the sovereign state and had influence on the princes, kings, and queens who ruled at the time. But there also emerged a countervailing school of thought in the seventeenth century—the "rationalist" or Grotian school. "This school of thought posits that in the state of nature men are still bound by the law of nature, by which is meant the pre-Hobbesian moral law of nature. . . . Sovereignty had indeed passed to different states, by social contracts, but the original unity of the human race survived; there was a law of nations acknowledged by sovereigns, even if violated, and this was the original natural law, which was legally binding and not just a moral imperative." (Wight 1992, 38) Grotius (Hugo de Groot) is broadly credited with establishing Wight's "rationalist" tradition and is called "the father of international law." A contemporary of Hobbes, "he was an optimist and a rationalist in a time of profound pessimism, the early seventeenth century. His theological outlook led to conflict with Protestants and misunderstandings with Catholics and Deists. He sought peace while at the same time propounding a doctrine of just war, describing war as a lawsuit carried on by armed forces. He pointed to ways of obtaining justice through war, including defending property, regaining possessions, and punishing criminal offenders." (Thompson 1994, 70)

According to Kenneth Thompson:

> Grotius found the basis of international law in natural law. For him, judgment proceeded from the fact that natural law is the source of certain fundamental concepts that underpin international law. Law is seen as universal and justice is determined by right reason. Natural and international law fill the void left by the ecclesiastical law. Because it is universal, natural law binds all human beings, individuals as well as states. It affects the rights of the citizen to bear or not bear arms. Whether states agree or not, natural law, and therefore international law, determines whether war is just or unjust, humanitarian intervention is justified, and war and violence are crimes or police actions . . . .
>
> Looking back as he set out to write *The Law of War and Peace*, which was published in 1625, Grotius observed a world dominated by religious wars. The conduct in war was cruel and barbaric. Grotius employed the Prolegomena to elucidate the philosophic principles of his work. They constitute the search for a fundamental or natural law on which the civil law of a nation rested. The fundamental or natural law was binding on every nation because of its intrinsic justice. There had been such a law in Christian political thought, but Christian unity was breaking up and the authority of the Church had declined. Neither the authority of the Church nor the authority of the Scriptures could provide an effective law binding alike on Protestants and Catholics. (Thompson 1994, 72–73, 74)

Grotius's thinking on natural law was an important bridge between medieval political thought and modern political thought. He saw a "society of mankind, bound by a general law of mankind. But it proved impossible to persist in this generous view; Christendom or Europe was the cultural unit and historical reality which defined the effective international society. . . . Christendom was an inner circle of kingdoms and republics with the duty (and tradition) of confederating against Moslem attacks and making contributions of men or money according to their strengths." (Wight 1992, 72–73) Wight points out that "a picture began to emerge of three concentric circles; the inner circle was the state, with its municipal law or '*jus civile*'; the second circle was international society, subject to a volitional, positive law of nations; and the third, outer circle, surrounding the other two, was mankind, subject to natural law." (Wight 1992, 73)

The consolidation of the nation-states during the sixteenth and seventeenth centuries, which gave rise to international relations, was still a work in progress and therefore in need of rules and explanation appropriate to the new situation. The idea of the social contract provided an explanation for the origins of society and was instrumental in the development of rules that governed society. However, the idea of a contract existing between the societies themselves, thus forming an "international society," didn't happen. The problem with a social contract between societies lies in the weaknesses of international law at the time. Martin Wight contends:

> Machiavelli was a pre-contractual thinker; but the founders of international law who established an anti-Machiavellian position, the Spanish neo-Scholastics who preceded Grotius, spoke of a society of nations or of mankind, and by so doing posed the question whether it was a society needing a contract. Vitoria (1480–1546) speaks of a *societas naturalis* of nations and in a dim way prefigures contract theory: the original state of nature saw common ownership; then the nations formed themselves and appropriated territories but as it were simultaneously and by mutual agreement, each nation reserving its natural rights to persist in international relations hence-forward, such as the right of commerce. Suarez (1548–1617) speaks of mankind, however much divided into states, having a kind of political and moral unity. Even though each state is a perfect community, an organic whole, which is coherent and has everything it needs within itself, and no external superior, nevertheless it is a limb of the human race needing mutual aid, society and communication. Even if economic self-sufficiency were possible, free trade would be better for mankind as a whole.
>
> Here there are already three notions: that an aggregate of nations is an international society; that a dim kind of social contract may bind them; but that states, however, are perfect communities. Grotius (1583–1645)

> like Suarez postulates an international society: the "common society of the human race"; "the great community" or "great university." *In De Iure Praedae* (The Law of Prize and Booty), he speaks of "the city of the world, the society of the earth" "*illa mundi civitas, societas orbis*". But he expressly says he does not believe in a super-state. He is the first writer after Dante to consider practically the possibility of a world-state (earlier writers had dismissed the claims of the Roman Empire as obsolete), but he warns against Dante's arguments that a world state would be advantageous for the human race: "The advantages are in fact offset by the disadvantages. For as a ship may attain to such a size that it cannot be steered, so also the number of inhabitants and the distance between places may be so great as not to tolerate a single government." (Wight 1992, 137–138)

Another important rationalist to appear in the seventeenth century was John Locke. A master theoretician of government, Locke produced two treatises on government—*Of Civil Government*—which were published in 1690 and written to defend the Glorious Revolution of 1688 in England, which established a system of government of the monarchy controlled by Parliament. Kenneth Thompsons points out:

> Locke's thought had its roots in Thomas Hooker's *Ecclesiastical Polity*, which was a summary of English political thought at the close of the Reformation. Hooker's political theory in turn was inspired by Aquinas.
>
> The medieval tradition as it had been developed by Hooker was the basis for the constitutional ideals of the Revolution of 1688. In *Leviathon* Hobbes had found political absolutism to be a necessity to assure peace and order. Locke's *Of Civil Government* was meant to refute Hobbes. Locke asserted that king and parliament were responsible to the people or the community governed. Power in such a political order had to be limited by the moral law and constitutional tradition as well as the history of the realm. For Locke community determines government, but for Hobbes a preexisting community was a fiction. Hence for Hobbes ideas like representation and responsibility required the force and sanction of a sovereign power.
>
> Locke attacked Hobbes's state of nature. Locke saw the state of nature as one of "peace, good will, mutual assistance, and preservation." The

> only defect of Locke's state of nature is its lack of organization, courts and magistrate, and written law. Right and wrong in Locke's state of nature are determined eternally. Positive law merely provides an apparatus for the enforcement of existing rights. Locke asserts that man's right to his own property and his duty to respect another's property *exist*. They are not dependent for their creation on the dictates of the Leviathan. However, rights such as life and liberty are not provable but are merely self-evident axioms. In opposing Hobbe's concept of morality instituted and enforced by the Commonwealth, Locke asserts that morality gives law, not law morality. Why, then, is morality binding? Here Locke draws an analogy with property and natural law. Society exists to protect private property, but property is a right society does not create. By nature property results when man mixes his labor with land. In this Locke is as egoistic as Hobbes. Individual self-interests for both are compelling. As for methodology, Locke joined a psychology that was empirical with a theory of science that was rationalist. (Thompson 1994, 81–82)

Locke, like Grotius before him, propounded an alternative view to Hobbes's state of nature, the doctrine of sociability. They did not believe that there was an absolute distinction between the state of nature and the social condition as purported by Hobbes. Indeed, the social contract inaugurates the condition of society, but the state of nature is a condition of sociability—the capacity for becoming social. Locke argues that "the state of nature is not a state of war; all that the two conditions have in common is the absence of a political superior. The state of war is a state of enmity, malice, and mutual destruction; the state of nature is one of good will, mutual assistance and preservation. The view of the state of nature clearly offers a different answer to the question about international society. Given this view, international society is a true society, but institutionally deficient; lacking a common superior or judiciary." (Wight 1992, 38–39)

Locke's political thought was ahead of its time, articulating principles of governance that were to be central to the development of the state system in the eighteenth and nineteenth centuries. His influence not only changed English politics but also informed the thinking and principles of Thomas Jefferson and the American Revolution that helped to establish what Charles van Doren calls the English-Lockean political doctrine. Van Doren argues that the American victory in 1776 "confirmed the rightness of the English-Lockean political doctrine, and ever since it has been dominant on the world stage. No one in the last two centuries has been able to make a *reasoned* argument against the thesis that it is the people who shall judge whether their government is legitimate or not, and not the government itself, and that a government that becomes illegitimate because it has lost the assent of the governed may be legitimately overthrown. The only denial of this thesis that has worked (and sadly, it has often done so) has been through the barrels of the guns of tyrants, turned against their own people." (Van Doren 1991, 226)

The seventeenth century was a time to experiment with new ideas and the thinkers discussed were instrumental in shaping the debate of a new period in human history. The focus on the state was not surprising, since the reality of several nation-states emerging at the same time had never happened before, and the visible chaos that accompanied this development needed better explanation than political thought at the time was able to provide. As the new nation-state emerged and evolved it was essential for the rulers to establish their legitimacy and the power over the "nation" or people, to defend their claims against rivals internally and externally.

Plans for Peace

Another important watershed reached during this period was the Peace of Westphalia (1648), which brought to a close the Thirty Years War, or wars of religion in Europe. As a result the European nation-state system came into existence and the first serious "peace plans" were formulated or taken more seriously. According to Warren Kuehl:

> The appearance of nations had a greater impact upon concepts of an international organization than did unitary states. As large, purely centralized territorial entities appeared, organized in accordance with the new idea of sovereignty, wars engulfed Europe. Men thus had reason to desire peace and to suggest that countries might obtain a degree of stability by uniting. They faced a difficult task, however, for the very existence of the new nation-state, jealous of its powers and suspicious of others, stood as an obstacle to their dream. Most of the early planners, therefore, realized that governments could never be compelled to join an association and that all action would have to be on a voluntary basis.

> Not until 1623, therefore, did anyone present a plan of merit which considered the changed realities of international life. Émeric Crucé, a French scholar, in the "New Cyneas", suggested a permanent congress of ambassadors, not princes, who would represent nations. He thought in terms of a world-wide league, since he included Ethiopia, Persia, the Indies, and China. A tribunal would hear disputes between states, enforce the assembly's laws, and "pursue with arms those who would wish to oppose it." . . .
>
> A contemporary of Crucé, Maximilien de Béthune, duc de Sully, also presented a plan that influenced later thinkers. This friend and admirer of Henry IV of France suggested that Europe be divided equally among fifteen nations so that none of them would envy or fear the other. A "General Council" with commissioners from each state would then sit continuously as a senate with power to legislate and resolve disputes. Sully also provided for lesser bodies to act as courts with the council serving as an appeals body. Decrees would be binding and would be upheld by the military arm of the commonwealth. Members would contribute to the force on a quota basis, and since the contingent would be larger than those of any country, they could keep the peace. . . .
>
> Near the end of the seventeenth century, William Penn presented his views in an *Essay Towards the Present and Future Peace of Europe* . . . Penn suggested a new European order built around a congress to which all kings should send deputies. It would meet yearly or at least once every two years or on occasion. All disputes which nations could not solve should be referred to this body. Any country refusing to abide by the provisions or ignoring decisions or embarking upon war would face "all the other sovereignties, united as one strength." These powers would "compel the submission and performance of the sentence, with damages" assessed for the part harmed and for the cost of enforcement. (Kuehl 1969, 4–8)

For all their novelty and incredible foresight on the emerging international order, these early thinkers of international organization were marginal to the philosophical center, which was preoccupied with the state and its organization. However, they recognized before most that independent sovereign states could not survive as "islands" unto themselves, self-sufficient and absolutely autonomous. International relations were a fact of life and the need to order and organize this new reality was, for them, a palpable concern.

The Eighteenth Century—Revolution, Liberalism, and Conservatism

The two main schools of thought that emerged in the seventeenth century—realists and rationalists—were to encounter a third in the eighteenth century, namely revolutionists. According to Martin Wight:

> The Revolutionists can be defined more precisely as those who believe so passionately in the moral unity of the society of states or international society, that they identify themselves with it, and therefore they both claim to speak in the name of this unity, and experience an overriding obligation to give effect to it, as the first aim of their international policies. For them, the whole of international society transcends its parts; they are cosmopolitan rather than "internationalist", and their international theory and policy has "a missionary character."
>
> There are three outstanding examples of these international revolutionists: the religious Revolutionists of the sixteenth and seventeenth centuries [Calvinists and the Jesuits]; the French Revolutionists, especially the Jacobins; and the totalitarian Revolutionists of the twentieth century. (Wight 1992, 8)

The philosophical battlefield shifted when the American and later the French Revolutions broke out in the second half of the eighteenth century. They challenged the ancien regime that had put legitimacy into the hands of despots and tyrants. Each in its own way gave expression to some of the important ideas proffered by Montesquieu, Rousseau, and Jefferson. While Thomas Jefferson and the leaders of the American Revolution found their source of inspiration and political thought in John Locke, the Jacobins and the French Revolution, ten years later, were the offspring of Jean-Jacque Rousseau.

Rousseau's political thought reflects the strong influence of Calvinist doctrine, which spelled out the duty of resistance to tyrants and the right of deposing kings. He argued that there exists a general will—*volanté genérale*—undergirding society. "The community has a will of its own, the general will. Government is merely an agent or a committee of the community" (Thompson 1994, 97). Many of Rousseau's precepts have influenced subsequent thinkers and continue to be debated even today. Not only did Rousseau inspire the Jacobins and the populist democracy that replaced Louis XIV, his ideas about the common man and the belief that republican government (an elective aristocracy with the best men chosen for specified terms of office) is the best regime and is capable of transforming human nature put him at odds with the mainstream of the French Enlightenment. His emphasis on the moral rather than the science of society and community made him a gadfly of his time.

Another French thinker, Charles-Louis de Secondat, baron de Montesquieu, shared Rousseau's abhorrence of despots and tyrants but found a different path to "explain the conditions upon which freedom depends." In Montesquieu's most influential work, *The Spirit of the Laws* (1748), he argues that "a sense of civic morality" and "the correct organization of the state is essential" to a free society. The correct organization that Montesquieu envisioned was the classical formulation of "checks and balances" and separation of powers. This treatise was a sociological theory of government and law, derived largely from Locke and the Roman law theorists. In fact, Montesquieu held up Britain's political institutions as a model for strengthening political liberty. (Thompson 1994, 94–95) Obviously, Montesquieu was not a "revolutionist" as Rousseau was, but he was part of the broader movement for popular sovereignty and democratic government, which was revolutionary at the time. The connection between Montesquieu and the American revolutionaries, particularly Thomas Jefferson, is not difficult to see. Montesquieu's praise of the British model in his political theory and the American Revolution's creation of a republican form of government are clearly derived from the Lockean tradition. Furthermore the significance should not be lost of the enduring influence the founding fathers of the United States and Montesquieu have on contemporary theories of government and democracy.

The upheaval in the American colonies and in France reflected the "eighteenth century's preference for new modes of international relations." (Thompson 1994, 93) But the realist school was not to be easily pushed aside. During the eighteenth century, David Hume (1711–1776) is recognized as the most influential of the realists and credited with many writings that expressed the classical realist position for the balance of power. According to Kenneth Thompson, "Hume wrote a series of essays including 'Of Money,' 'Of Interest,' 'Of the Balance of Trade,' 'Of Taxes,' and 'Of the Balance of Power.' In each the gravamen of his argument is the need for the balance and limitation of power—balance in opinion, balance between interest and right, balance of labor and capitalists, and balance of commerce. He maintained that the principle of balance has been demonstrated by experience and is a precept by which all governments should be governed. In international relations, he was always conscious of the need for a balance of power for the sake of the independence of each nation and state." (Thompson 1994, 90–91)

Of course the concept of maintaining a balance of power was not exclusive to the realist tradition, since it had its adherents within the other traditions as well. But Hume's historical approach to both political theory and international relations, which provides the basis for his general observations on human nature and society and principle of "balance," is a core tenet of the realist school of thought and one of the more important contributions to realist thought of the time.

The liberal heritage that took root during the eighteenth century through the experiences of Britain and the newborn United States was a blend of rationalist with the more progressive elements of realist thought. Classical liberalism, as it is called today, embodies the Lockean-Jeffersonian conception of rights and the sovereignty of the people, which spawned another important tradition—"individualism." The Enlightenment's universalist moral claims (for example, property, rule of law, constitutionalism, and citizenship) for governance of societies was to become the foundation of liberalism in political thought and "liberal internationalism" in international thought.

The thinker of greatest consequence for the liberal tradition is Adam Smith (1723–1790), whose famous work *Inquiry into the Nature and Causes of the Wealth of Nations* (1776) introduced economics into the lexicon of political theory. As Kenneth Thompson explains:

> Smith was the great prophet of economic liberalism. He defended man's natural right to private property and favored individual enterprise. He saw the individual being guided as if by a hidden hand. In pursuing selfish interests, man served the common good. Significantly, with all his emphasis on the individual, Smith understood the importance of collectivities. Quite simply, he believed that the interests of the group were best served through providing first the interests of the individual. National wealth depended, however, not only on the economic power of a nation

> but on free trade. Every nation would benefit from free trade. Based on his conclusions about free trade, Smith stipulated that comparative nations ought not produce at home that which can be produced more economically abroad. He was an early proponent of the law of comparative advantage . . .
>
> [Smith] was the foremost defender of a free enterprise economy . . . He stands out as the champion of free trade. He saw economic development as closely linked with nations producing what they are able to produce best. . . . He was untiring in defending the primacy of the individual not only in the economy but in society at large. Smith offered a view of economics that was broader than the traditional approach of economists. His approach was that of political economy . . . For Smith, politics was as important as economics, especially in providing the framework for the working out of economic policies. He clearly acknowledged the necessary functions of government even while making a general argument against the intrusion of government into the economy. . . . Throughout his writings he displayed continuing concern with moral and political ends: freedom, sympathy, and individualism. Not only did he make reference to such values but he placed them at the center of his thinking. (Thompson 1994, 87–89)

Adam Smith provided much of the "liberal" canon of contemporary international thought. Indeed, the liberal school, which combines Smith's political economy with Locke's theory of government and Rousseau's contractarian political theory, largely rests on individual rights and an international order of reason and science. However, the optimism of the Age of Enlightenment was not embraced by another tradition that is found in the eighteenth century—conservatism. This tradition is exemplified by one of the most profound thinkers and politicians of eighteenth century Britain—Edmund Burke (1729–1797). Burke's conservative nationalism was both an expression of political reason (an understanding that derives from experience and tradition) and careful observation of political practice. The hallmark of Burke's thinking was his pragmatism, gradualism, and flexibility when considering change and continuity in society (national and international). Conservatism's main tenets are clearly rooted in the work of Burke and his disciples. According to Russell Kirk:

> there are six canons of conservative thought–

1. Belief that a divine intent rules society as well as conscience, forging an eternal chain of right and duty which links great and obscure, living and dead. Political problems, at bottom, are religious and moral problems. A narrow rationality, what Coleridge calls the Understanding, cannot of itself satisfy human needs . . . .
2. Affection for the proliferating variety and mystery of traditional life, as distinguished from the narrowing uniformity and equalitarianism and utilitarian aims of most radical systems . . . .
3. Conviction that civilized society requires orders and classes. The only true equality is moral equality; all other attempts at levelling lead to despair, if enforced by positive legislation. Society longs for leadership, and if a people destroy natural distinctions among men, presently Buonaparte fills the vacuum.
4. Persuasion that property and freedom are inseparably connected, and that economic levelling is not economic progress. Separate property from private possession, and liberty is erased.
5. Faith in prescription and distrust of "sophisters and calculators." Man must put a control upon his will and his appetite, for conservatives know man to be governed more by emotion than by reason. Tradition and sound prejudice provide checks upon man's anarchic impulse.
6. Recognition that change and reform are not identical, and that innovation is a devouring conflagration more often than it is a torch of progress. Society must alter, for slow change is the means of its conservation, like the human body's perpetual renewal; but Providence is the proper instrument for change, and the test of a statesman is his cognizance of the real tendency of Providential social forces.

Various deviations from this system of ideas have occurred, and there are numerous appendages to it; but in general conservatives have adhered to these articles of belief with a consistency rare in political history. (Kirk 1953, 7–8)

Of course, Burke was particularly concerned about the French Revolution and its impact on the international system. Since the Jacobins' revolutionary zeal repudiated and attacked with arms the "civilized society of states" and "the Commonwealth of Europe," Burke saw the seizure of power by the masses in France just as dangerous to the society of states as seizures of power by kings. If the rise of the masses to power was progress, then Burke would rather do without. But if progress were to reflect and embrace the traditions, customs, and historical reality of a society and political order, Burke would be in the vanguard. (The former depicts Burke's reaction to the French Revolution, and the latter his outlook on the American Revolution.)

While the rationalist tradition was conflicted by liberal and conservative crosscurrents, the revolutionist tradition continued to rise through the end of the eighteenth century. The French Revolution is recognized as the "fountain-head of modern revolutionism. In political theory this means Rousseau; in international theory, Kant. Kant was the funnel through which the intoxicating alcohol of Rousseau was poured into the veins of international society. Kant saw this as his own function: for him Rousseau was 'the Newton of the moral world.'"(Wight 1992, 263)

The revolutionary fervor that was exhibited at the beginning of the French Revolution did indeed overturn the political order of the nation-state and gave impetus to the ideas of democratic rule and the democratic peace. According to Charles Van Doren:

> [The French Revolution] was a true change of society, not just in government. Here at last the people had grasped the rule in their own hands, and would judge the good and evil of laws and legislators—as was their indubitable right—for all ages to come. Here at last was a government whose legitimacy could not be denied by political philosophers save those who had been hired by kings and conquerors to justify their unjust rule. And here at last was a new world filled with men and women all equal and all consumed with hope and energy for a future that could not help but be brighter than the past.
>
> For the most part, Americans applauded what was happening in France. They understood that the Jacobins agreed with them in holding that property in rights is even more crucial than the right to property. In fact, in August 1789 the Jacobins promulgated a Declaration of the Rights of Man and of the Citizen that went beyond the American Bill of Rights in affirming, "Nothing that is not forbidden by Law may be hindered, and no one may be compelled to do what the Law does not ordain," for "Liberty consists in being able to do anything that does not harm others." This doctrine placed an enormous burden on positive law, for it ruled out

> entirely the notion that common or customary law should have any effect on people's actions. (Van Doren 1991, 230–231)

More Plans for Peace

The French Revolution affirmed the notion of "cosmopolitanism" based on the rights of man, bringing the fundamental principles of the American Revolution onto the European continent. International thought began to shift from concepts of monarchy to those of democracy. This profound movement inspired several important thinkers in the final decades of the eighteenth century to put forth new peace plans for Europe and world organization. Rousseau argued in 1782 that a federation of republics (a cooperative union of governments rather than the league of monarchs that Charles Irénée Castel de Saint-Pierre had proposed between 1712 and 1714) should be formed on a permanent basis. It would be empowered to settle all disputes through judicial or arbitral processes and to impose its will upon violators of any treaty provisions and act as a legislative body and the guarantor of the governments and territories of all members. "Jeremy Bentham recorded his views [for a society of nations] between 1786 and 1789 by referring extensively to the American, Swiss, and Germanic federations. In his comments on justice and in a section decrying secrecy, he revealed how far his age had shifted from concepts of monarchy to those of democracy. . . . One of Bentham's fellow-philosophers, Immanuel Kant . . . published the essay *Perpetual Peace* in 1795. . . . Kant's proposal called for a federation which nations could enter and withdraw from at will. It would be a constitutional republic, not a pure democracy." (Kuehl 1969, 9–10)

The creation of the United States, particularly its evolution from the Articles of Confederation to the U.S. Constitution of 1789, had a profound impact on those who put together plans for perpetual peace. Again, Warren Kuehl argues:

> Internationalists had long argued that earlier experiments in confederation, notably the Hanseatic League from the thirteenth to the seventeenth century and the Swiss and Dutch arrangements dating from the thirteenth and fourteenth centuries, provided men with a clue to the organization of nations. . . . But the ideal remained a dream, tried as it had been on so small a scale and without formal constitutions.

> The establishment of the United States seemed to prove that the political theory could be successfully applied on a large geographical basis. Moreover, the American experiment contributed in other ways to emerging concepts. Men like Saint-Pierre had envisaged a federation but only in terms of a semicompulsory arrangement. The achievement of a *voluntary* association in an age of rampant nationalism revealed how far mankind had moved from the concept of a world unitary state. Even more, it showed the transition toward the democratic-republican ideal for which Kant had pleaded shortly after the creation of the United States. It was no league of princes; it was a republic of self-governing states.
>
> Finally, the Constitution of 1789 in provision after provision met structural problems which stood as a challenge to internationalists. Matters of representation, voting, equality of states, financing, allocation of powers, defense, and operation all seemed to be solved. It is not surprising, therefore, to find that men saw in the events of 1776 and 1789 the "great rehearsals" for experiments in world co-operation of the twentieth century. (Kuehl 1969, 11–12)

An often overlooked figure in the evolution of international thought is Thomas Paine. But he was one of the more celebrated political thinkers of the latter part of the eighteenth century and "was the first to offer an integrated, modern, cosmopolitan vision of international relations. . . . Of all the cosmopolitan writers of the Enlightenment, Paine's international thought is one of the most coherent. And basking in the glow of the Enlightenment are Paine's visions of peaceful, democratic, and egalitarian societies interacting within a cosmopolitan international order based on reason and justice. Paine's worldview included the most enduring strands of cosmopolitan thought in international relations: democratic governance, free trade, high degrees of interdependence, nonprovocative defense policies, and a universal respect for human rights." (Walker 2000, 52)

A veteran of the American Revolutionary Army and secretary to the Committee on Foreign Affairs of the Continental Congress from 1777 to 1779, Thomas Paine was a committed and outspoken advocate of democracy for the world and "a pioneering radical progressive in international relations." (Walker 2000, 54) His two most famous works—*Common Sense* (1776) and *Rights of Man* (1791 and 1792)—were the first serious treatments of the idea of "democratic peace" and cosmopolitanism. *Rights of*

Man was to make Tom Paine a household name in Europe and North America within a year of its publication. In fact, "hundreds of thousands of copies in several languages were circulating throughout Europe . . . So by the time a relatively obscure Immanuel Kant penned his ideas on the democratic peace in 1795, *Rights of Man* was already an international best-seller that was often read aloud to the illiterate." (Walker 2000, 55) However, Paine's fame was relatively short-lived and by the time he died in 1809, he was a man "nearly forgotten and surely abandoned by those who played important roles in the American and French revolutions." (Walker 2000, 51)

The significance of Thomas Paine and Immanuel Kant for the development of international thought is in their challenge of realism and conservatism of the time. Paine's worldview reflected the optimism and missionary zeal of Americans that continues to be a characteristic of American self-perception. Kant, on the other hand, was skeptical of human nature's goodness and reflects the European pessimism that endures through modern times. Yet, both men shaped the course of Western political and international thought at the end of the eighteenth century and into the nineteenth century. But the cosmopolitan ideals of the late eighteenth century were to be abandoned in the nineteenth century when the state and nationalism were wed and the "great transformation" of the state from an instrument into an end took hold. (van Creveld 1999, 190–191)

The Nineteenth Century—Modernity and Nationalism

The nineteenth century witnessed the maturity of the nation-state and its reach globally. The political revolutions in the Americas and in France failed to retire the conservative European political system, which was reconstituted after the Napoleonic conflicts of the first decades of the new century. Yet, it was an amazing period, as Charles Van Doren describes:

> During the tumultuous hundred years of the nineteenth century, Europe impressed its brand upon the rest of the world, so that it was possible to boast that the sun never set on the British or the Spanish or the Portugese or the French or the Dutch empire. The burgeoning United States, "the great nation of futurity," discovered that it was not necessary to establish an empire. The promulgation of the Monroe Doctrine in 1823 insured that American influence in the Western hemisphere would remain un-

> questioned while the country was spared the burden of having to administer the affairs of a dozen small nations. Japan, quicker than most to see how the winds of the future were blowing, opened itself up to the West in 1868, thereby obtaining the benefits of Western technology instead of being forced, like China, to remain a mere supplier of raw materials and manual labor. And a century of comparative peace, interrupted only by small wars of position among the colonial powers, allowed the world from 1815 to 1914 to devote its abundant energies to the development of a global market in subsistence goods instead of luxury items. . . .
>
> The nineteenth century saw the discovery of new sources of energy, like oil and electricity. It gloried in new devices for communications on both a world and local scale, such as the telegraph and the telephone. And it welcomed new means of comforting life, from electric light to cheap cast-iron stoves. Manufactured objects, iron deer for the lawn and mass-produced furniture suites for the parlor and bedroom, replaced handmade decorations, which would only regain their cachet in the late twentieth century. Popular literature and journalism demanded universal literacy in a few developed countries, whose missionaries tried to carry the light of learning around the globe. Railroads snaked through forests and across prairies and rivers, joining communities that had been separated for centuries and creating new social ideas while destroying old ones. And at the end of the century, seers in Germany and the United States prophesized that the newly invented automobile would prove to be the most revolutionary, as well as profitable, vehicle that the world had ever seen.
>
> Generally, the nineteenth century was an age that liked to think of itself, and to call itself, "new." The word was apt. (Van Doren 1991, 243–244)

The profound changes that were ushered in during the nineteenth century were practical applications of the advances in mechanical and scientific thinking since the days of Descartes and Newton 200 years earlier. The 1800s was a period of consolidation in Western political thought into three basic ideologies—conservatism, liberalism, and socialism. The territorial nation-state, the focus of political thought for over 200 years, was no longer a novel concept. It had rooted itself in Europe and was fast spreading to the rest of the world as the colonial powers of the period—France, Great Britain, Germany, Spain, the Netherlands, Portugal, and Belgium—competed with each other for control over far-flung places and peoples. Despite the American and French revolutions that had altered the political landscape in the eighteenth century, the 1800s appears to have been less concerned with political revolutions, especially since the defeat of Napoleon and the actions of "Count Metternich, the apostle of reaction at the Congress of Vienna [September 1814–June 1815], had already recreated the old political order of Europe." (Van Doren 1992, 232) Instead the nineteenth century became engrossed in a different kind of revolution, the industrial revolution and the rise of money to the center of peoples' day-to-day lives. As Charles Van Doren points out:

> Once, the ownership of land substituted for having a money income. Today, if we should be so unlucky as to own land without having money to support it, we might end up poorer than the poorest peasant used to be. If we were a king, living off the labor and charity of his people, we might feel dishonored, at least uncomfortable. If we were an honest priest, helping his parishioners, we would be aware that most of our parishioners pitied us because we were so poor even if we thought ourselves as rich because we were doing the Lord's work.
>
> The change from 1800 to today is extraordinary. In 1800, in most places in the world, money was almost invisible. Today, it is omnipresent. Work existed then as now, but the notion that work is life, and life is work, has practically disappeared. We work in order to earn a living, and we may even dream of a day when we will no longer need to work, so that we will have time to 'really live' . . .
>
> For the majority of human beings on earth, that change has occurred during the present century [twentieth century]. That is only because the industrial development of the entire world took two centuries to accomplish, rather than one. Starting during the last half of the 1700s, it was completed during the last half of the 1900s. But the change, essentially, was the work of the nineteenth century alone, the period between 1815, which saw the close of the old regime in Europe, and the onset of World War I in 1914. (Van Doren 1992, 252)

The nineteenth century launched a new "science"—economics. Economic theories proliferated, much of it building on Adam Smith's principles of market economics in his book *Wealth of Nations*. The interdependence of politics and economics was never questioned when the science of economics was born. Therefore, it was common to see stark political agendas interwoven in economic theories that were promulgated during the nineteenth century. Furthermore, many of the classical economists of this period were quite concerned about social and political conditions created by industrialization. In this regard, many sought to find remedies for the most difficult problems of the day through reform of government and politics.

Thomas Malthus (1766–1834), for example, was a political economist who was concerned about the decline of living conditions in the early years of nineteenth century England. In his most famous work, "Essay on the Principle of Population" (1798), Malthus argues that the decline is due to three factors: overproduction of young; inability of resources to keep up with the rising human population; and, the irresponsibility of the lower classes (Simison 1995). Malthusian principles conclude that humans tend not to limit population size voluntarily so famine, disease, poverty, and war are natural and "positive " checks on overpopulation. Malthus's pessimism was provoked by the French Revolution's notion of human perfectibility, a matter he profoundly disagreed with. He influenced Charles Darwin, the father of evolution theory, and continues to be a controversial figure today. Malthus's concerns were shared by other classical economists, namely David Ricardo (1772–1823). Ricardo and his contemporaries contributed to several core principles of economics. Ricardo developed two key economic theories: distribution theory (economic rent and diminishing returns) and international trade theory (comparative advantage). His most significant works were on market economics and included "Essay on the influence of the low price of corn on the profits of stock" (1815) and *The Principles of Political Economy and Taxation* (1817). Ricardo remains a major figure in the field of economics and political economy. As did Adam Smith, David Ricardo easily blended politics and economics in his work. It was, in fact, the norm during the nineteenth century to see it in this way.

Ricardo was also a member of the "Philosophical Radicals" who had rallied around Jeremy Bentham's ideas on utilitarianism. James Mill and his son John Stuart Mill, were also part of this group. The fundamental idea of utilitarianism was the "the proper objective of all conduct and legislation is 'the greatest happiness of the greatest number'. According to Bentham, 'pain and pleasure are the sovereign masters governing man's conduct'. As the motive of an act is always based on self-interest, it is the business of law and education to make the sanctions sufficiently painful in order to persuade the individual to subordinate his own happiness to that of the community." (www.spartacus.schoolnet.co.uk/PRbentham.html)

The most celebrated amongst this group was John Stuart Mill, who wrote extensively on philosophy and political economy. A rigorous thinker and ardent liberal, John Stuart Mill worked tirelessly to overcome the injustices of the class divisions and the grinding poverty of the masses at the time. His greatest work, *Principles of Political Economy* (1848), laid out his thinking of social reform for England (as well as the continent of Europe), and his concern about the direction of society in the middle of the nineteenth century. He wrote in his *Autobiography* (1873):

> In this third period (as it may be termed) of my mental progress, which now went hand in hand with hers [Harriett Taylor, who J. S. Mill married in 1851], my opinions gained equally in breadth and depth, I understood more things, and those which I understood before, I now understand more thoroughly. . . . I was much more inclined, than I can now approve, to put in abeyance the more decidedly heretical part of my opinions, which I now look upon as almost the only ones, the assertion of which tend in any way to regenerate society. But in addition to this, our opinions were far more heretical than mine had been in the days of my most extreme Benthamism. In those days I had seen little further than the old school of political economists into the possibilities of fundamental improvement in social arrangements. Private property, as now understood, and inheritance, appeared to me, as to them, the *dernier mot* of legislation: and I looked no further than to mitigating the inequalities consequent on these institutions, by getting rid of primogeniture and entails. The notion that it was possible to go further than this in removing the injustice—for injustice it is, whether admitting of a complete remedy or not—involved in the fact that some are born to riches and the vast majority to poverty, I then reckoned chimerical, and only hoped that by universal education, leading to voluntary restraint on population, the portion of the poor might be made more tolerable. In short, I was a democrat, but not the least of a socialist. We were now much less democrats than I had been, because so long as education continues to be so wretchedly imperfect, we dreaded the ignorance and brutality of the mass . . . While we repudiated with the greatest energy that tyranny of society over the individual which most Socialistic systems are supposed to involve, we yet looked forward to a time when society will no longer be di-

> vided into the idle and industrious; when the rule that they who do not work shall not eat, will be applied not to paupers only, but impartially to all; when the division of the produce of labour, instead of depending, as in so great degree it now does, on the accident of birth, will be made by concert on an acknowledged principle of justice; and when it will no longer either be, or thought to be, impossible for human beings to exert themselves strenuously in procuring benefits which are not to be exclusively their own, but to be shared with the society they belong to. The social problem of the future we considered to be, how to unite the greatest individual liberty, with a common ownership in the raw material of the globe, and an equal participation of all in the benefits of combined labor. . . . In the "Principles of Political Economy," these ideas were promulgated. (Mill, 1873 81–82)

The ideas of Ricardo, Bentham, John Stuart Mill, and other "radicals" in England also included championing women's political rights and suffrage, parliamentary reform, and the rights and freedoms of people in the British colonies. While many of these ideals were shared on the continent, particularly amongst intellectuals in France, the circumstances for continental Europe during much of the 1800s created two extremes in political thought—Georg Wilhelm Friedrich Hegel's nationalism and the emergence of Karl Marx's communism.

Hegel (1770–1831) is best known for the dialectical method through which "history reveals itself in a continuous and orderly unfolding. . . . The historical process proceeds by opposites, which interact along lines of a moving equilibrium," according to Kenneth Thompson. Hegel delineates this process in his most important work, *The Philosophy of History* (1837). Kenneth Thompson points out that "The heart of the dialectical method, then, is a process of affirmation (thesis), negation (antithesis), and synthesis. With the attainment of synthesis, we arrive at a new thesis or affirmation. All concepts are dialectically related. Analysis advances by a rhythm of opposition, and this, according to Hegel, is the only way the human mind can arrive at the truth about anything. Every proposition or doctrine contains elements of truth and error. Each is the product of self-centered and fallible human beings. Where others see the error of a doctrine, they formulate another doctrine that is opposite to the first but also contains elements of truth and falsity. Only a third action, or a synthesis, can reconcile the thesis and the antithesis. The same process continues as the new doctrine is seen to be flawed. Presumably the testing of each new thesis by its antithesis leads to a new synthesis that each time is closer to the Absolute about which Hegel writes. For him that Absolute is the will of God, and the dialectic is a method for distinguishing what is insignificant and transient from what is important for the long run. What exists is only a manifestation of deep-lying forces and reality." (Thompson 1994, 113–114)

Another significant contribution of Hegel was his idealization of the nation-state and nationalism. Hegel's theory of the state appeared at a time when nationalism was on the rise and people's identification with the nation-state was overcoming loyalties to aristocratic rulers and monarchs. His philosophy strengthened the clear trend of this shift during the nineteenth century. According to Kenneth Thompson:

> If the dialectical unfolding of reason in history is the ultimate reality for Hegel, the nation-state is the incarnation of the world spirit in history and the embodiment of rational freedom. It is the march of God in the world. It is the presence of mind on Earth. . . . the collective group or social morality is the embodiment of reason, and the state is the crystallization of the community. Individual consciences can never be the final court of judgement because they never or rarely agree. They can point to what may be right in a given circumstance but not to what is universally right. The individual has spiritual reality only as he participates in the state. Not individuals but universal reason creates the state. The state prescribes rights and duties. The state is absolute power on earth and is a moral organism. Whatever rights an individual has are drawn from his humanity or nature. World history is but the unfolding of reason. Because the state is a manifestation of reason, every state is sovereign and autonomous in relation to its neighbors. (Thompson 1994, 115)

Karl Marx (1818–1883) was profoundly influenced by Hegel's philosophy. As a student in Bonn and Berlin, Marx joined the "Young Hegelians," favoring Ludwig Feuerbach's focus on materialism rather than idealism, the other Hegelian school of thought at the time. He ultimately "appropriated Feuerbach's views and developed the central thesis that the means of production are the foundation on which the institutional and ideological superstructure of a society are built." Marx's philosophy of history—dialectical materialism—"is a story of linear moral progress driven by economic and technological change. History in Marxist science moves irresistibly from one stage of development to the next. In the same manner that feudalism had proven superior to primitive socieities, capitalism was superior to feudalism. The measure of progress for Marxism was the transformation of material structures and values." (Thompson 1994, 121)

Charles Van Doren suggests that "Marxism is both a theory of history and a practical program for revolutionaries. Many of Marx's predecessors either laid out plans for revolution or laid down a rationale of it. Marx did both, and that is the reason why he is the most famous revolutionary who ever lived, and the most influential. . . . Hegel's rather vague notion of a conflict of historical 'forces' was transformed by Marx into a struggle between social and economic classes, which he believed had been going on throughout history and would only cease with the final triumph of communism. He was a painstaking observer of conditions in the burgeoning industrial world surrounding him, and a brilliant writer. . . . This new order [of communism] was not inevitable, as it has not occurred except in isolated instances in the century and half since the Communist Manifesto appeared [in 1848]. And where it has occurred, it has been reversed in recent times. Nevertheless, it is a comforting thought to a revolutionist to believe that he is riding on a historical roller coaster, whose progress through time is controlled by great forces. Marx never stopped repeating that the communist revolution was inevitable, and here again he made people believe him." (Van Doren 1991, 258–259) Marx's sweeping vision of a classless, stateless, and apolitical world society failed to take into account the power of nationalism and the significance of the nation-state. While the Marxist utopia did capture the imagination of many on the political left (liberals and socialists), most deemed it unattainable or even dubious as a practical platform for governance. Of course, Marxism became an important, indeed defining, ideology in the twentieth century.

By the end of the nineteenth century, Martin Wight's three schools of thought or traditions—realists (Machiavellism), rationalists (Grotianism), and revolutionists (Kantianism)—are clearly apparent, but as we cross into the twentieth century the intellectual landscape was becoming much more complicated. As Wight explains,

> There is overlapping and indistinctiveness between the three traditions. Each tradition can be subdivided into two or more [see Figure 3.1], and

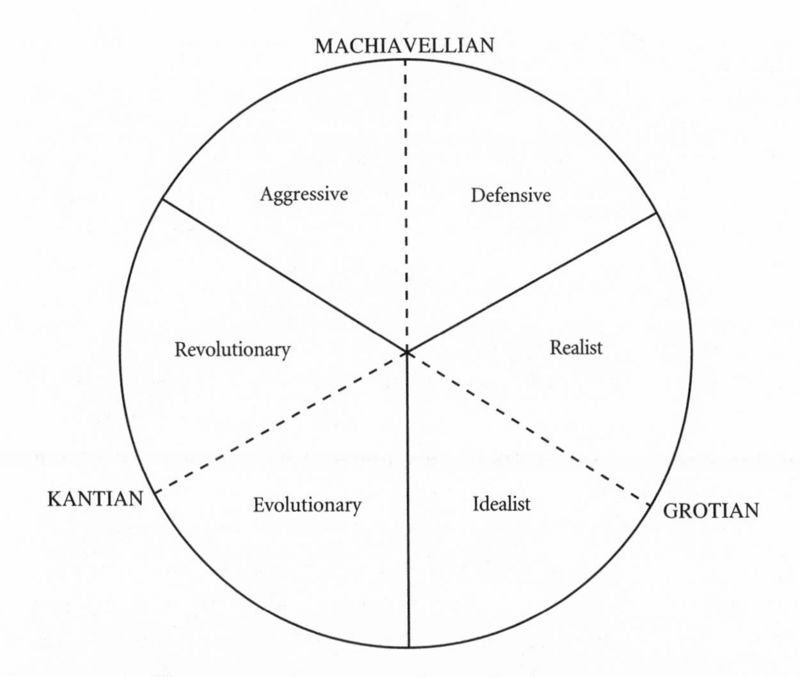

Source: *International Theory: The Three Traditions* by Martin Wight, edited by Gabriele Wight and Brian Porter (New York: Holmes & Meier, 1992). p. 159. Copyright © 1992 by Gabriele Wight. Reproduced with the permission of the publisher.

FIGURE 3.1 Subdivisions of the Traditions

they dove-tail; thus Grotians and Machiavellians agree in being Realist, in accepting facts of the world of politics, although they differ in what they bring under the heading of "fact". Grotians and Kantians agree in being idealist, in pursuing ideals in the world of politics, although they differ in their estimate of the power of ideals and in their method of attaining them. . . .

A conflict between the traditions lies in the emphasis placed on the importance of facts as against ideas, and of men as against ideals. The defensive Machiavellian believes that men, not ideas, guide the world. . . . In contrast, consider the comment of Wilson, an evolutionary Kantian, that 'Men die but ideas live', which he made to Colonel House on his first arrival in Paris in December 1918, when House pessimistically pointed out the obstacles to world security. Similarly the last words of Sturzo, an ideal Grotian, to the Turin congress in 1923 were: 'Victory belongs to the ideal, not to us; defeat falls on us, not on the ideal.'

> Such patterns of dove-tailing and contrasts can be seen in other areas. The Grotian and the Kantian agree that history has a purpose and meaning. The Kantians may regard history as the totality of mankind surging forward and individuals getting trampled underfoot, while Grotians see history as a field in which individuals find their several purposes or meanings and are skeptical about the meaning of the whole; but at least they agree in a sense of history as dynamic, and the individual as having responsibility in it. The Machiavellian however regards history as static or cyclic, and the individual scrapes what corner or burrow in life he can.
>
> Although they disagree in their theory of history, the Machiavellian and Kantian agree that politics have their origin in sin; they believe in the Augustinian doctrine of the state as "poena et remedium pecati"—punishment and remedy against sin—like an age-long Borstal or approved school. . . . The Machiavellian and Kantian agree in seeing politics as dominated by human rapacity and stupidity, but Kantians see it in a special way, as the rapacity of a special set of men, which explains why "man is born free but is everywhere in chains" (Rousseau). In other words, Machiavellians believe that the sinful nature of politics is unchangeable, Kantians believe it *can* be changed. Against them both is the Grotian (Aquinas as against Augustine), who believes that political life is natural to man, and needed for his proper development. As far as international society goes, the Machiavellian and Kantian agree that there is no such thing. The Machiavellian believes that there is not and cannot be one, the Kantian that it must be brought into being. The Grotian however believes the existing diplomatic system is an international society. . . .
>
> Thus the Grotian and Kantian dove-tail in their idealism and their theory of history, whereas the Grotian and the Machiavellian share a certain realism. The Machiavellian and Kantian agree on the origin of politics, on (the absence of) international society, and on the criteria for international morality. Broadly, the Grotian and Kantian approximate over ideals, the Kantian and Machiavellian over methods. (Wight 1992, 158–162)

In the twentieth century, scholars from the United States and the United Kingdom came to dominate the new academic discipline of international relations, and this changed both the direction and focus of international thought.

4

Modern International Theory and the Idealist/Realist Debate

The historian Eric Hobsbawn captured the quintessence of twentieth-century international relations in the title of his 1994 book, *The Age of Extremes*. The 1900s are replete with global conflicts and clashing ideologies as well as magical technological breakthroughs and unprecedented wealth. Modernity, an idea defined by industrialized societies, created new extremes within and between societies—between rich and poor, powerful and powerless, and developed and developing—that all too often clashed in bloody conflicts. The ideas that Hegel and Marx unleashed in the world at the end of the nineteenth century ultimately produced in the twentieth century one of the most excessive periods, in terms of both destruction and creativity, in human history.

At the beginning of the twentieth century, the international system was multipolar, with three contending political ideologies that spanned the political spectrum. To the right was conservatism that advocated state-imposed constraints on free market capitalism and on democratic parties; at the center was liberalism that championed free-market capitalism and liberal democracy; and to the left was socialism that argued for state ownership of major industries and utilities and "social democracy." James Kurth argues that these ideologies were "radicalized" by World War I and the communist revolution in Russia and shifted to more extreme versions—conservatism to nationalism; liberalism to democracy; and socialism to communism. The combination of the Great War (World War I), the Great Fear (the success of the Bolshevik revolution and communism in Russia), and the Great Depression shaped the ultimate emergence of fascism and national socialism in the period between the world wars. Kurth goes on to argue that World War II "served as a great simplifier, . . . leaving the remaining two ideological families—liberalism/democracy and socialism/communism—to confront each other in a long duel, which became the Cold War." Finally, by the end of the twentieth century only one ideology remains—liberalism: "After its victories over fascism and national socialism in World War II, and its victories over Marxism and communism in the Cold War, liberalism now stands alone, triumphant. . . . Advanced by the United States, the sole superpower and the leader of the global economy, liberalism promises to make the new century one of ideological consensus—indeed, the end of ideology—and of international peace." (Kurth 1999, 3–7)

International relations fully blossomed during the 1900s. The nation-state project, which had been the primary focus of political thought for 300 years, had lost its vigor and was eclipsed by a new and more challenging enterprise—the international order project. The population of scholars and thinkers dedicated to the study of international relations grew dramatically, producing an explosion of ideas and approaches that make up modern international theory. International relations became an academic discipline distinct from that of politics, law, and government as the idea that the "international" could be studied scientifically became firmly rooted in the academy.

Idealists Versus Realists

During the twentieth century, the development of modern international thought can be roughly divided into three periods. The first period (1900–1945) coincides with the decline of the international order that was established in the nineteenth century after the Napoleonic wars and that finally dissolved with the two world wars. During this period, the legal approach to international relations was dominant. "This point of view dominated the early stages of thinking on foreign relations in virtually every developed country, and its sources of influence are obvious. As we compared national and international life, the missing elements on the international scene appeared to be law and government. The implicit theory of most international lawyers, who moved self-confidently to fill the void, was that only by substituting law for lawlessness could the unhappy circumstances of international life be rectified. . . . Beginning in the 1930s and 1940s, the study of law merged with the study of organization and, more specifically, the League of Nations. Scholars of extraordinary talents turned to international organization." (Thompson 1992, 38–39)

The second period (1945–1989) reflects efforts to come to grips with the contradictions between the "new world order" that was constructed after World War II and the realities of Cold War international politics. In this period the political approach became dominant in the study of international relations. According to Kenneth Thompson, "The political approach is an attempt to discover a core, or center, for the subjects that make up the totality of international relations. International politics is an effort to order and relate elements of international society to some overarching set of concepts, problems, and questions. . . . The overall interest in the political approach stems in part from the orientation of students after World War II. The postwar generation, schooled in a certain way of looking at international problems, experienced the pathos of World War II and learned that earlier approaches to the world were insufficient. Treatises by Professors Morgenthau, William T. R. Fox, and Frederick S. Schuman had as their objective the regrouping and clarification of those aspects of international studies that they saw as most relevant to contemporary needs and as requiring more rational and systematic treatment. They placed stress on the analysis of the relationships between power and policy, diplomacy and military strength, and statecraft and popular support for policy. A whole clustering of issues not commonly dealt with by those primarily legal concerns prompted attention to political and sociological problems and led to the political approach" (Thompson 1992, 40–41). The shift in approach marked the outcome of the first great debate between the so-called idealists and realists within the discipline of international relations.

The end of the Cold War and globalization mark the third period (1989–present). During this period the institutional approach became dominant in international relations. In fact, this approach blends together, albeit imperfectly, key aspects of both the legal and political approaches, bringing under one umbrella the contending (and often contentious) perspectives within the discipline on international order, law and organization, power, and politics.

The Idealists

During the initial decades of the twentieth century, international thought started to take on a distinct Anglo-American flavor with the likes of Norman Angell, Gladsworthy Lowes Dickinson, Leonard Woolf, Pitman Benjamin Potter, David Jayne Hill, Woodrow Wilson, Westel Woodbury Willoughby, Francis Delaisi, James Bryce, Harold Laski, Ramsay Muir, Mary Parker Follett, Alfred Zimmern, David Mitrany, Quincy Wright, and E. H. Carr dominating the intellectual scene (Osiander 1998; Schmidt 1998).

In the United States, the academic discipline of international relations traces its origins to 1903 when the American Political Science Association (APSA) was formed and included "international law, and politics, which was an amorphous category that dealt with a number of international issues such as imperialism and colonial administration" as two of the Association's seven official sections (Schmidt 1998, 439). But the official history of the discipline begins in 1919 when the University of Wales endowed a dedicated international relations (IR) professorship which was soon followed by IR chairs elsewhere (Osiander 1998, 409 footnote 1). By the time World War I dismantled the remnants of the "old" international order, international relations was defined by the newfound "science" of politics and its concentration on sovereignty and the juristic theory of the state as a sovereign, territorial actor. As Brian Schmidt points out:

> According to juristic theory, the international milieu was one where states led an independent and isolated existence. By dint of their equal possession of absolute sovereignty, states were assumed, in principle, to have complete freedom from all sources of external authority. States were presumed to have no obligations to any other entity but themselves, and compliance with external rules was deemed to be strictly voluntary. Although rejecting the idea of a social contract to explain the origins of the state, adherents to juristic theory nevertheless evoked the pre-contractual image of individuals living in a state of nature to describe the external conditions of states. In depicting states as existing in an international state of nature, proponents of juristic theory conceptualized the anarchic structure of international relations in a manner similar to that of realists. They also pointed to many of the same dilemmas that realists associate with politics in the absence of central authority. . . .

Proponents of juristic theory adhered to the Austinian definition of international law as an authoritative command issued from a political superior to an inferior backed by the sanctions of force. Like John Austin, the absence of a higher source of authority above the collection of states in the international system led many scholars to deny the legal character of international law. [Westel Woodbury] Willoughby maintained that "the term 'law,' when applied to the rules and principles that prevail between independent nations, is misleading because such rules depend for their entire validity upon the forbearance and consent of the parties to whom they apply, and are not and cannot be legally enforced by any common superior." (1896:200) . . .

A second effect of juristic theory was that political scientists were not optimistic about the prospects of world order reform; especially with any plan that infringed on the sovereignty of a state. Regardless of the different manner in which states were being drawn closer together, sovereignty represented a significant obstacle to world order reform. This view was clearly articulated in the series of lectures that David Jayne Hill delivered when he was appointed the Carpenter Foundation Lectureship at Columbia University in 1911, which were later published under the title *World Organization as Affected by the Nature of the Modern State.* Like Willoughby, Hill maintained that the juristic nature of the state was axiomatic. The problem remained, Hill explained, was to extend these same juristic principles to the realm of inter-state relations. This was the task of world organization, which Hill defined as of "so uniting governments in the support of principles of justice as to apply them not only within the limits of the State but also between States" (1911:1). Yet as with other adherents to the juristic theory of the state, Hill insisted that there were severe limitations on the possibility of extending juristic principles to the international realm. Since Hill believed that there could not be a deviation from juristic principles, he embraced arbitration as the most appropriate means to achieving a juristic ordering of international relations and campaigned against the League of Nations on the grounds that it was antithetical to juristic principles.

Third, juristic theory contributed to the view that the structure of inter-state relations was anarchical. In depicting the state as a unitary sovereign actor, the international milieu was conceived as a realm where there was an absence of central authority. This ontology of the interna-

> tional realm was one that directly emanated from the juristic theory of the state and, at the same time, reveals how the principle of sovereignty serves as the constitutive underpinning the claim that the structure of inter-state politics is *ipso facto* anarchical. Recognition of the basic relationship between sovereignty and anarchy provided the framework for much of the interwar discourse of international relations. Yet in many ways, it was less the anarchical structure of international politics than the problem of state sovereignty that was identified as the most pressing theoretical issue. (Schmidt 1998, 442–443)

The so-called idealists are often associated with a specific set of ideas that makes up what many scholars today call liberal international theory. "Kenneth Waltz (1959), in his work *Man, the State and War*, provided what has become the standard interpretation of the liberal tradition of international relations. Liberal theories correspond to what Waltz termed 'second image' explanations for the cause of war; that is, arguments which contend that international conflict is a consequence of flaws in the internal organizations of states. To explicate the second image thesis that the internal arrangements of states determines the character of their external behavior, Waltz turned to the political thought of nineteenth-century liberals. By utilizing the insights of liberal political theorists, such as Jeremy Bentham, John Stuart Mill, and Immanuel Kant, Waltz derived several theoretical assumptions that defined the essence of the liberal view of international relations. These assumptions include: one, that there was an objective harmony of interests in both domestic and international society; two, the war-does-not-pay argument, an idea that Waltz explained was rooted in classic free-trade economic theory; three, a belief in the inherently peaceful proclivities of democratic forms of state; and four, faith in world public opinion as an effective sanction in securing peace." (Schmidt 1998, 435–436) The writings of the early twentieth-century international relations scholars do reflect many, if not all, of the liberal assumptions identified by Waltz and others, but it would be wrong to assume that these thinkers were unrealistic or naive. The idealists were not a monolithic intellectual group and the strands of thought that can be found in their work are diverse. In this regard it is worth quoting at length Andreas Osiander's analysis of the Idealists' work:

Conventional summaries of early twentieth-century IR writing tend to conjure up images of authors naively ignoring the realities of power, which only later, when Realism came to dominate the discipline, at last received due attention. In order to understand the paradigm of world politics underlying much early twentieth-century IR writing it is important to realise that this is a myth, and that many so-called Idealists were conversant with, and took seriously, the way of thinking that would later be labeled Realist. . . .

Curiously, it was a leading figure in the British League of Nations movement, Goldsworthy Lowes Dickinson, who drew attention to the [anarchical character of the international system] and gave it a name that caught on, "the international anarchy." Whether or not he actually coined the term, he contributed greatly to its popularity by making it the central idea of his book *The European Anarchy*. Published in 1916 (a revised version published in 1926 was renamed *The International Anarchy*), this is basically a work of history seeking to explain the outbreak of World War I. . . .

The frequency with which the term or at any rate the concept of "international anarchy" was taken up in interwar IR literature indicates the wide agreement with Dickinson and his Realist analysis. Thus Leonard Woolf (1928:4) declares that during the previous century or so "practical statesmen and political theorists regarded nations as being in a state of perpetual war." Here as elsewhere Woolf takes issue with the notion of the "beneficent inevitability" of this state of affairs. . . . [Norman] Angell had started using the term "international anarchy" after World War I and continued to do so in later writings. But it was merely a convenient shorthand for a conception of international politics of which he himself had provided a striking summary as early as 1914, just prior to the outbreak of war. . . .

A second theme in early twentieth-century IR literature is provided by its assumption that growing interdependence between states rendered popular Realist assumptions on international politics increasingly obsolete and harmful. Early twentieth-century IR authors saw a dangerous discrepancy between the new reality of worldwide economic interdependence and existing political structures, between increasing global integration and traditional foreign-political attitudes and modes of behaviour. Ramsay Muir (1933:vii; quoted in de Wilde, 1991:46) puts it succinctly: "We have entered a new era, the era of interdependence; and this interdependent world is threatened with chaos because it has not learnt how to adjust its institutions and its traditions of government to the new conditions."

In his book *International Government* of 1916 Leonard Woolf contends that the growth of economic links between states meant that conflicts could more easily become global than in the past. . . . To Woolf, it followed from this that the notion (central to Realism) of the state as a self-contained, autonomous entity had become an anachronism, a view that, in *International Government*, he reiterates on numerous occasions. . . . The problem, as Woolf stresses in a later essay, was that people failed to realise the extent and significance of the change. . . . In fact, according to Woolf (1928:28), the Industrial Revolution had altered the nature of international relations in such a way that states now had common rather than competing interests. . . .

Muir, Woolf, [Francis] Delaisi, and Angell are typical representatives of the way the theme of the discordant economic and political evolution of the international system was discussed in the earlier part of the century. . . . The same theme can be identified in the writings of Alfred Zimmern, one of the few IR authors cited (quite frequently even) in *The Twenty Years' Crisis* and still widely regarded as . . . the "consummate" Idealist. . . . Zimmern (1931:14–15) stresses the increasing integration of the world and its component states as a result of technological innovation, more specifically the increasing speed and ease and hence volume of global communications. This process of integration was inescapable: "An inexorable law . . . has made us members of the body politic of the world. Interdependence is the rule of modern life."

However, Zimmern also notes the increasing *fragmentation* of the world as a result of the rise of the idea of national self-determination and the virulence of national feeling. . . . For Zimmern, then, there was a built-in contradiction in the contemporary international system that did not simply result from the persistence of atavistic views on international politics. Rather there was the additional fact that the industrial age confronted governments with a twofold challenge complicating their foreign policy-making. On the one hand, governments had to heed the often strident and aggressive demands of nationalistic domestic opinion on which their legitimacy rested—unlike what Carr implies, Zimmern, like Angell, was very far from seeing public opinion as necessarily a force for peace. On the other hand, governments were forced at the same time to manage their mutual relations against the background of an unprecedented complexity of interconnected interests" (Osiander 1998, 412–418).

Pluralism and Legal Positivism

Much of the work of the early twentieth century IR scholars was an effort to describe and explain the changing conditions of the international system during the first half of the twentieth century. There was a growing skepticism among political scientists on the then-dominant theory of the state, juristic theory, which many believed contributed to the "irresponsibility and unrestraint of the German state both before and during [World War I]." (Schmidt 1998, 444) In response to the traditional doctrine of state sovereignty, a group of scholars found the sociological theory of pluralism to be a more accurate ontological description of world politics. The pluralist writers, which included American political scientists like Harold Laski, Mary Parker Follett, James Garner, and Quincy Wright and legal scholars such as Edwin Borchard and Hugo Krabbe, criticized the monistic doctrine of the state and its claim of absolute internal and external sovereignty. Laski and other pluralists of the period "argued that the state was only one of many forms of human association to which the individual belonged. Moreover, the pluralists asserted that the different associations found in modern society, such as trade unions, civic associations, and religious groups, each, in their own distinct way, possessed sovereignty on a parity with the state. . . . Just as pluralists maintained that the state was not supreme over all the constituent groups present in society, they also argued that, internationally, the state was not completely sovereign with respect to every other state and non-state actor. The interdependent quality of world politics, which pluralists took to be axiomatic, along with the existence of numerous public international unions and international organizations, raised serious doubts about the validity of the claim that each nation-state was entirely sovereign in relation to all other actors in the international realm." (Schmidt 1998, 445–446)

Pluralism provided both an empirical and normative theory of international politics and supported the positivist approach to international law. The study of international law during the interwar period was particularly significant in these early years of the international relations discipline. Similar to the way that pluralism was being positioned as an alternative framework for understanding the political development and organization of both national and international society, legal positivism was being extended from its domestic incarnation to an international conception.

Brian Schmidt writes, "According to the international lawyers who were attempting to extend legal positivism to the international realm, the claim put forth by juristic theorists that international law lacked the essential characteristic of law was not only theoretically erroneous but contrary to the practices that could be observed taking place among states. Just as there was a system of positive law domestically, the international legal positivists insisted that, contrary to Austin, there was also a body of internationally recognized rules that had the status of law. The positivist approach attempted to demonstrate that even without a centralized world authority it was, nevertheless, possible for international law to regulate effectively the external affairs of states." (Schmidt 1998, 448) The controversy surrounding the question of international law as law was not put to rest by Borchard and other positivists in this initial period of modern international relations. In fact, international legal scholars even today sometimes find it necessary to defend international law and its efficacy to world order against those who contend that it is too weak, vague, and inchoate, unenforceable, or infantile to be operational in the real world. (Ku and Diehl 1998, Part 1)

The Problem of International Organization

Another important characteristic of early twentieth century IR writings was the immense interest in the problem of international organization. Unlike earlier proposals for congresses of nations, international courts, and leagues of peace that were highlighted in the last chapter, the study of international organization became an overarching concern for international relations scholars in the first half of the twentieth century.

But international organization as a scholarly concern was not exclusive to the academy. Peace societies in Europe and the United States had been actively promoting the idea of international organization since at least the nineteenth century. The two Hague Conferences (1899 and 1907) were focal points for both activists of internationalism and scholars of politics and law. Before and after each, a flurry of conferences and meetings trained the attention of politicians and statesmen, publicists and journalists, lawyers and businessmen, and scholars on myriad proposals and schemes for world federation and government, international arbitration, world courts, and leagues of peace. Despite the failure of the Hague system to avoid World War I, the popular interest in international organization seemed to gain momentum, particularly when President Woodrow Wilson embraced the idea of a league of nations in 1916, becoming the leader of the movement for a league by 1918 and the chief architect of the Covenant of the League of Nations. The founding of the League of Nations in 1919 and Wilson's role in its creation (but failure to get Senate approval of the treaty and U.S. membership in the League) became the subject of intense study during the interwar years. (Kuehl 1969)

The Realists

The run up to and through World War I (or the Great War, as it is also called) witnessed considerable deliberation among scholars about the nature of the international system, particularly the role of the state, and a concern about "the ever greater menace that conflict posed to the international system—as World War I, then in course, showed." (Osiander 1998, 419) By the time World War II plunged the world into another global conflict, the first of many debates between idealists and realists was in full swing. It came to a head near the end of the interwar period when E. H. Carr published his "highly influential 1939 polemic, *The Twenty Years' Crisis.* For Carr, the 'science of international politics' arose as a reaction to the terrible experience of World War I, and the 'passionate desire' to prevent such disasters in the future caused the exponents of this new branch of enquiry to privilege wishful thinking over 'critical analysis.' Carr presents a view of Idealism (or utopianism as he calls it) as a naive, voluntarist progressivism based on overly sanguine and outdated tenets of nineteenth-century liberal doctrine, such as, in particular, the fundamental harmony of interest of all states or the benevolent force of public opinion. In this view, a neglect of the 'issue of power' is also characteristic of Idealism." (Osiander 1998, 410) Carr's denigration of the so-called idealists of the early twentieth century is strikingly similar to the political right or conservatives in American politics "smearing" their opponents with the dreaded "L" word (or liberal) in the 1990s. Unfortunately, the dismissal of the idealist school of thought by the realists on the grounds that it was utopian, simplistic, and naive misrepresents the significant contribution of this group to international thought as well as the continuity between the idealist approach and that of the realists to the study of international relations.

The realist critique of the idealists and liberal internationalism that emerged in the late 1930s and 1940s was a reaction (perhaps an overreaction) to the shortcomings of the discipline during the interwar years that had made international organization or international law (with their obvious moralistic or reformist bent) its central focus. "By the early 1940s, it was apparent that the field of international relations was undergoing a transition, which was best exemplified by the argument that the study of international politics should replace international organization as the central focus of the field. Those who identified themselves with the theory of realism, such as E. H. Carr, Hans J. Morgenthau, Frederick Sherwood Dunn, Frederick L. Schuman, Nicholas J. Spykman, and John Herz, sought to direct attention away from the study of international law and international organization and toward international politics where the enduring and endless quest for power and survival was preeminent." (Schmidt 1998, 452) This shift in focus characterizes the great debate within international relations (a debate that realists argue they ultimately won in the postwar period), as well as the transition from the first to the second period of the development of modern international theory.

The realists' challenge of the purported dominance for nearly forty years of the idealists gained momentum after World War II. The massive migration of European intellectuals to the United States before and during World War II was a major contributor to the realist school's invigoration of American international relations. According to Kenneth Thompson, "No other field or discipline profited more from this migration of talent than international studies and certain related sectors of political thought. One group constituted the most important figures in political philosophy: [Leo] Strauss, Hannah Arendt, [Hans] Jonas, and Eric Voegelin. Another included major theorists of comparative government: Carl Joachim Friedrich, Franz and Sigmund Neumann, Otto Kirchheimer, former German chancellor Heinrich Brüning, and Waldemar Gurian. International law received new impetus from Leo Gross and Hans Kelsen. Other legal scholars remained in England, including George Schwarzenberger and Hersch Lauterpacht, and still others chose to continue their work in Spain and Switzerland. History, sociology, economics, and literature claimed their share of leading European thinkers such as Jacob Viner, Friedrich A. von Hayek, Karl Mannheim, and Joseph A. Schumpeter. It would be difficult to find a comparable migration of human talent in all of intellectual history." (Thompson 1992, 46–47) This infusion of European thinkers into American higher education naturally reoriented American scholarship more towards the European view of international society and traditional political philosophy and away from the Wilsonian reformist view of international relations that maintained that international law and organization could (or should) replace power politics. This is part of a pattern throughout the twentieth century, according to Kenneth Thompson—"The twentieth century is a history of one established intellectual discipline following another in successive attempts to make thinking in international relations more coherent and relevant. International law and organization studies supplanted diplomatic history as the dominant approach in the 1930s and 1940s, and international politics and theory came into its own in the postwar period. Much as governments hailed the study of politics, with its focus on the political process within the nation-state, as an advance over constitutional law, postwar students of international politics announced that power, its determinants, and the normative and political constraints on power were essential for understanding the international political process. Domestic and international politics sought an organizing principle and found it in interest and power, however defined. In national politics, the focus is on political parties and interest groups. For international relations, it is the national interest and national power and prestige." (Thompson 1992, 52)

Hans J. Morgenthau's work on power and politics in international relations, particularly his classic text *Politics Among Nations: The Struggle for Power and Peace* (1948), defined the new field of international political studies and the postwar realist school of international thought. His influence is legion within the discipline of international relations and by the 1950s, he and other prominent realists, such as Reinhold Neibuhr, John H. Herz, and Sir Herbert Butterfield, succeeded in establishing realism and international politics as the dominant approach for the study of international relations. The post–World War II realists (and later the revisionist neorealists) resumed the discipline's focus on the state and state system. John A. Hall and T. V. Paul argue that:

> The main tenet of *realism* (whether classical or neo-realist) is that states live in an anarchical system, one which lacks the central governing authority familiar to us in the domestic sphere. In this competitive system, self-help is taken for granted with every state being responsible for its own security and economic welfare (Waltz 1979). States, seen as rational entities, seek to maximize their national interests, but worry about the losses and gains they make relative to other actors, friends, or foes. Wars and conflict are natural outcomes of this state of affairs as states seek power, territory, and resources, sometimes at the cost of other states. The temptation to dominate other states increases with the growth of power capabilities. Cooperation is rare and it is anyway likely to be evanescent given the inevitability of changes in national interest. While classical realists and neo-realists agree on these basics, the latter give importance to system structure, defined in terms of the distribution of power among major power actors, in determining war and peace. A bipolar structure with nuclear-armed superpowers is favored by the latter, while multipolar power structures are viewed as likely to occasion war (Waltz 1979; for classical views, see Morgenthau 1967). The major prescription for both types of realism for creating and sustaining order is through the attainment of a balance of power, both internationally and regionally. The mechanisms for obtaining balance vary, but states are held to ally together in the face of a rising power with hegemonic pretensions. Balance of power is predicated on the assumption that peace is preserved only when an equilibrium of power exists among great powers as well as among regional powers, otherwise the strong will be tempted to attack the weak. Countervailing power is essential in curtailing the power aspirations of a threatening state. Parity in power capabilities preserves peace, as the aspiring state cannot achieve its objectives militarily and would therefore desist from using force even if the opportunity arose. (Paul and Hall 1999, 4–5)

Michael Mastanduno argues that there are four assumptions that are central to the intellectual and scholarly work of realists.

> First, the most important actors in international politics are 'territorially organized entities'—city-states in antiquity, and nation-states in the contemporary era (Keohane 1986; Gilpin 1986, 304–5). Nation-states are not

> the only actors on the current world scene, but realists assume that more can be understood about world politics by focusing on the behavior of and interaction among nation-states than by analyzing the behavior of individuals, classes, transnational firms, or international organizations. . . . Second, realists believe that relations among nation-states are inherently competitive. Nation-states compete most intensely in the realm of military security, but compete in other realms as well, in particular in economic relations. . . . Competition is a consequence of anarchy, which forces states ultimately to rely on themselves to ensure their survival and autonomy. . . . Third, realists emphasize the close connection between state power and interests. States seek power in order to achieve their interests, and they calculate their interests in terms of their power and in the context of the international environment they confront. . . . The key point for realists is that in defining the so-called national interest, state officials look "outward," and respond to the opportunities and constraints of the international environment. . . . Fourth, realists assume that state behavior can be explained as the product of rational decision-making. As Robert Keohane puts it, for the realist "world politics can be analyzed *as if* states were unitary rational actors, carefully calculating the costs of alternative courses of action and seeking to maximize their expected utility, although doing so under conditions of uncertainty" (Keohane 1986: 165). (Mastanduno 1999, 21–22)

But as the postwar period progressed beyond the 1950s, it became quite clear that the so-called idealist/realist debate among scholars and theorists in international studies was not as definitive or clear-cut as some had argued. Both Martin Wight's tripartite classification of the traditions of international thought and the three dominant approaches to the study of international relations suggest that a symbiotic relationship existed among the different schools of thought for modern international relations, while at the same time allowing for fundamental differences that often made them contentious with each other. In other words, the simple dichotomy of realism versus idealism was never really accurate nor did it reflect the dynamism in international thought of the post–World War II era.

Perhaps the most important accomplishment of this "great debate" was that it tempered the more extreme views within the scholarly community and stimulated critical analysis of modern international life. Within this intellectual space new and revisionist theories proliferated. It is important to note that international organizations and their role in postwar international relations were more or less considered important by scholars and IR writers, even essential, as actors in the international order, but the prominence that the study of international organizations once enjoyed within academic circles during the early part of the twentieth century was considerably diminished.

Contending Theories of a World Politics and International Order

The proliferation of international theories during the postwar period is indicative of the profound changes that have occurred in the world since 1945. The postwar era was a transformative period for the world, both in terms of ideas and reality. As historian David Reynolds describes in the introduction to his book *One World Divisible*:

> The striking feature of recent decades has been the dialectical process of greater integration *and* greater fragmentation—the two being interrelated. If this book has a grand narrative, therefore, it is deliberately contrapuntal—*One World Divisible*. And that narrative is constructed mainly, but by no means exclusively, around what I take to be the central, political mechanism of the dialectic. This is the process of state building.
>
> Since 1945, the membership of the United Nations has more than tripled to 185 states. Most of them were born out of the death of empires, from Japan's in 1945 to Russia's in 1991, and particularly from the demise of European colonialism in Asia, Africa, and the Middle East. The emergence and attempted consolidation of new states has generated much of the friction of this last half-century—both destructive and creative. From this has arisen endemic conflicts, such as those surrounding the state of Israel, and also innovative cooperation, notably the European Union. States have imploded in civil war in Africa and the Balkans; they have also forged alliances, voluntary and involuntary, such as NATO and the Warsaw Pact. All have struggled to regulate their relations within the arena of the UN. States are objects as well as actors. The revenue, resources, and weaponry at their disposal have been contested by rival social groups, from Peronist Argentina to Christian Democratic Italy. Although not every member of the UN figures in these pages, an emphasis on the pro-

> liferation and interplay of states may act as an antidote to the tendency of books of broad history to subsume local variety in global teleology. . . .
>
> Within this framework of the state, I pay particular attention to two themes, both stemming from the challenges to liberalism and capitalism that precipitated the Second World War. One was whether liberal traditions of representative government could cope with democracy—with universal adult suffrage. The "vanguard democracy" of the Soviet Union was one challenge to liberalism; the militarized mass democracy of Nazi Germany was another. Both were exported across the developing world after World War II, as new states experimented with a single mass-party and/or military government. The other question, posed sharply by the depression of the 1930s, was whether the management of modern industrial economies could be left to market forces, at home and abroad. The Soviet model of a planned, autarkic economy seemed to have been vindicated by victory in World War II, and it was taken up, to varying degrees, by developing states from Latin America to India. On the other hand, the American philosophy of private ownership and open trade was gradually (and patchily) adopted in Western Europe and East Asia. . . .
>
> Another theme of the period is the growing prominence of what political scientists call "transnational" forces, those transcending the politics of national states. Multinational corporations existed in the first half of the century, but they came into their own when barriers to commerce and capital began to fall in the 1950s and 1960s. Initially, most of these companies were based in North America and Western Europe, but multinationals from Japan and the Asian tigers soon became major players as well. Even more significant was the growth of transnational capital. By the 1970s, economic growth and financial deregulation had produced a large and turbulent pool of private capital, exceeding all government reserves and sloshing around in search of speculative opportunities." (Reynolds 2000, 4–5)

The dynamics of postwar international relations could not possibly be explained adequately by either the realists and the traditional international political approach or the idealists and the international organization and law approach of the interwar period, providing considerable room for a variety of alternative paradigms and approaches to emerge and actually take root within the discipline of international relations.

Perhaps the most significant influence on postwar international relations theory was the onset of the Cold War and forty-year rivalry between the two superpowers—the United States and the Soviet Union. The East-West conflict shaped and defined the ideological and strategic perspectives on international politics for both scholars and policymakers. "The ideological perspective focuses on the doctrinal differences between East and West and on the different 'ways of life' that presumably shape how events, actions, and modes of economic and political organizations are to be interpreted. The strategic perspective, on the other hand, views the world in terms of military balances and of the relative equilibrium of weapons systems. It sees the future hinging on the quantitative and qualitative balance of destructive power and considers the national security policies most appropriate to deal with these global circumstances." (Kegley and Wittkopf 1981, 26–27)

Another conflict that subsequently emerged during the Cold War was the North-South conflict (the Have's versus the Have-not's) that reflected the disparities in global incomes and standards of living. This conflict was brought on when decolonization created newly independent nation-states in Africa and Asia in the 1960s and 1970s. These new members of the international community were relatively poor and their foreign policy objectives were focused on economic issues and changing the international economic order. According to Charles Kegley and Eugene Wittkopf, "Related to these developments has been a resurgent interest in the intellectual forerunner of political science, *political economy*. Political economy focuses on the interaction of economic and political forces and how these forces coalesce to allocate goods. In the context of international political inquiry, political economy specifically challenges the distinction between *high politics* (military-strategic issues) and *low politics* (economic issues). This distinction, reinforced by historical events since World War II, led political scientists to devote almost exclusive attention to political matters at the expense of economic ones (just as economists largely ignored political issues; see Spero, 1977). Reflecting the changing global environment, the political economy perspective seeks greater integration of politics and economics." (Kegley and Wittkopf 1981, 28) Beginning in the 1980s, the international political economy approach has grown considerably stronger within international relations, largely because of its analytical focus on what has become the most dynamic feature of the international system—economic globalization and the transformation of the world economy to a global market economy.

The Challenge of Behavioralism

Another important influence on the study of international relations after World War II was the behavioral movement, which emerged within the social sciences during the late 1950s and 1960s and embroiled the discipline in what Donald Puchala characterizes as the "second of the great debates" (Puchala 2000, 136–137). Charles Kegley and Eugene Wittkopf point out:

> Often called the scientific approach, behavioralism represented a challenge to preexisting modes of studying human behavior, and, more specifically, to the basis upon which truth-claims were derived by previous researchers, who came to be called "traditionalists." What ensued as this paradigm-shift occurred was an extensive and often heated debate over the principles and procedures most appropriate for investigating international phenomena. The debate centered on the meaning of theory, on the requirements for adequate theory, and on the methods best suited for testing existing propositions. . . .
>
> The behavioral paradigm sought nomothetic or lawlike generalizations about international phenomena, that is, statements about patterns and regularities presumed to hold across time and place. Science, behavioralists claimed, is first and foremost a generalizing activity. The purpose of scientific inquiry therefore is to discover recurrent patterns of interstate behavior. From this perspective (a view incidentally consistent with that of many "traditional" realists and idealists), a theory of international relations should entail a statement of the relationship between two or more variables, specify the conditions under which the relationship(s) holds, and explicate why the relationship(s) should be expected to hold. To uncover such theories, behavioralists leaned to comparative cross-national analyses rather than to case studies of particular countries at particular points in time. They also acknowledged the necessity of systematically gathering data about the characteristics of nations and about how they interact with one another. Hence, the behavioral movement spawned, and is often synonymous with, the quantitative study of international relations. . . .

> Armed with new tools for analyzing international relations, newly generated data for testing competing hypotheses that had been voiced over decades of traditional speculation, and sometimes with generous research support from governments and foundations, the behavioral paradigm commanded much of the attention in international relations research. Its early efforts were enthusiastic, and a generation of scholars was trained to study international relations with powerful new conceptual and methodological tools. (Kegley and Wittkopf 1981, 22–24)

In just over a decade, the behavioral movement fundamentally transformed the study of international relations, giving scholars powerful new quantitative methodology and analytical tools. Yet, by the 1970s the criticism voiced both from within and outside of the movement ultimately undermined its claim to be the "postrealist" paradigm for the discipline of international relations. Nevertheless, the behavioral approach has not been discarded by international relations scholars and continues to be employed in contemporary studies of international relations.

As the discipline debated over methods, scholars continued to develop alternative theoretical models and frameworks for analyzing and explaining the "new world order" and international problems. One group of theories is now commonly known as liberal international thought. Under this rubric, a constellation of approaches have been developed—functionalism (and neo-functionalism), international regimes theory, interdependence theory, theory of public goods, liberal institutionalism, multilateralism, transnationalism, and so on. Marxism, particularly the Marxist-Leninist framework and neo-Marxist theories, is another.

Marxist-Leninist and Neo-Marxist Theories

Before highlighting the different approaches within liberal international thought in the postwar period, let's take a look at Marxism and neo-Marxist thought, since it stands between the theories of realism and liberalism on international order. Marxism in the twentieth century was driven largely by the thinking and success of Vladimir Lenin and his Bolshevik Revolution in Russia in 1917. Marxist-Leninist writers did not find much value in the West's conception of a pluralistic community of states tied together through networks of voluntary associations for organizing the world. (Jacobson 1979, 74) They had a different vision of world order, an "utopian" alternative grounded in the promise of the *Communist Manifesto* and world revolution.

Marxist thinkers in the postwar period did little to alter Marxist-Leninist dogma—the primacy of horizontal (class) affiliations over vertical (national) affiliations in their worldview and the inevitable classless society born out of revolution. Yet, the international relations of Stalin's Soviet Union and the USSR's satellite communist states after World War II were not much different from their noncommunist counterparts. This is pointed out by Harold Jacobson—"In view of the extent to which the basic positions found in early Marxist writings have been repeated, it is striking how little they have affected the practice of communist states. In 1934 the U.S.S.R. joined the League of Nations. At that point, despite its earlier attack on the League, membership was important for the conduct of relations with non-communist states. And in its desire to gain security against Germany, the Soviet Union became one of the foremost advocates of joint action through the League. When it became apparent that this would not occur, the Soviet Union switched to the strategy of negotiating a bargain with Germany, and after its attack on Finland in 1939, the U.S.S.R. was expelled from the League. But when a new universal membership, general purpose organization, the United Nations, was created, the Soviet Union was among its founders, and despite repeated rebuffs within the organization in the 1940s and 1950s and rumors of withdrawal, the U.S.S.R. remained a member of the U.N. Moreover, given the opportunity of membership, no other communist state has chosen to remain outside of the U.N." (Jacobson 1979, 77)

Marxism did influence thinking about international political economy during the postwar period. It offered many newly independent countries in Africa and Asia alternative political and economic systems to that of their former colonial masters and established a separate international economic order for the communist states. Neo-Marxist thinkers, such as Antonio Gramsci and Herbert Marcuse, argued for even greater emphasis on struggle against "managerial capitalism" and the oppression of the proletariat, particularly in less developed countries, by the international capitalist order dominated by the United States and the affluent Western states (See Box 4.1). Marxist and Neo-Marxist thinking was indeed influential during the Cold War era and informed such theoretical approaches

BOX 4.1

Other Marxist Approaches

Many Marxist revisionists tend toward anarchism, stressing the Hegelian and utopian elements of his theory. The Hungarian György Lukács, for example, and the German Herbert Marcuse, who fled from the Nazis to the United States, have won some following among those in revolt against both authoritarian "peoples' democracies" and the diffused capitalism and meritocracy of the managerial welfare state. Lukács' *Geschichte und Klassenbewusstsein* (1923; Eng. trans., *History and Class Consciousness*, 1971), a neo-Hegelian work, claims that only the intuition of the proletariat can properly apprehend the totality of history. But world revolution is contingent, not inevitable, and Marxism is an instrument, not a prediction. Lukács renounced this heresy after residence in the Soviet Union under Stalin, but he maintained influence through literary and dramatic criticism. After Khrushchev's denunciation of Stalin, Lukács advocated peaceful coexistence and intellectual rather than political subversion. In *The Meaning of Contemporary Realism* (trans. 1963), he again relates Marx to Hegel and even to Aristotle, against the Stalinist claim that Marx made a radically new departure. Lukács' neo-Marxist literary criticism can be tendentious, but his neo-Hegelian insights, strikingly expressed, have appealed to those anxious to salvage the more humane aspects of Marxism and to promote revolution, even against a modified capitalism and social democracy, by intellectual rather than by political means.

Marcuse also reached back to the more utopian Marx. Now that most of the proletariat has been absorbed into a conformist managerial capitalism or has been regimented into bureaucratic peoples' democracies, freedom, argues Marcuse, is in retreat. In Western affluent societies most employers and workers are equally philistine, dominated by the commercialized mass media, or "cogs in a culture machine." The former Soviet Union had reverted to an even more philistine monolithic repression, distorting art and literature. This enslavement of man by his own industrial productivity had been clinched by the colossal power of governments, which rendered the old brief and brisk class warfare a romantic, impracticable idea. Marcuse attacked all establishments and transferred the redeeming mission of the proletariat to a fringe of alienated minorities—radical students and the exponents of the "hippie" way of life—as well as to Viet Cong guerrillas and Black Power militants. Such groups, he declared, could apparently form liberating elites and destroy the managerial society. Thus reappeared the old Marxist-Hebraic pattern of redemption through struggle by a chosen people.

The Italian Communist Antonio Gramsci deployed a vivid rhetorical talent in attacking existing society. Like Marcuse, Gramsci was alarmed that the proletariat was being assimilated by the capitalist order. He took his stand on the already obsolescent Marxist doctrine of irreconcilable class war between bourgeois and proletariat. He aimed to unmask the bourgeois idea of liberty and to replace parliaments by an "implacable machine" of workers' councils, which would destroy the current social order through a dictatorship of the proletariat. "Democracy," he wrote, "is our worst enemy. We must be ready to fight it because it blurs the clear separation of classes."

Not only would parliamentary democracy and established law be unmasked, but culture, too, would be transformed. A workers' civilization, with its great industry, large cities,

(continues)

and "tumultuous and intense life," would create a new civilization with new poetry, art, drama, fashions, and language. Gramsci insisted that the old culture should be destroyed and that education should be wrenched from the grip of the ruling classes and the church.

But this militant revolutionary was also a utopian. He turned bitterly hostile to Stalin's regime, for he believed, like Engels, that the dictatorship of the workers' state would wither away. "We do not wish," he wrote, "to freeze the dictatorship." Following world revolution, a classless society would emerge, and mankind would be free to master nature instead of being involved in a class war.

Since World War II, Gramsci's notions have enjoyed a minor revival. They appeal to the fringe of revolutionaries who admire Marcuse and detest the embourgeoisement of an idealized proletariat. But, in a civilization in which, if total war can be avoided, material prospects are good, the destruction of the old culture out of rage, envy, and naïve idealism appears to be a pointless program. Like Marcuse's doctrine, it is a cry of pain, typical of the 1920s in Italy.

From "Political Philosophy," Encyclopædia Britannica (2000), *http://www.britannica.com/eb/article?eu=11539 [author: John Edward Bowle, Professor of Political Theory, College of Europe, Brugge, Belgium]*

as dependency theory and liberation theology in the 1970s and 1980s. But in the end, most scholars of international relations see it as a failed or fatally flawed school of thought. As Michael Novak points out:

> The greatest of all Marxist theoreticians of the twentieth century, Leszek Kolakowski, has concluded that, in essence, Marxism is neither a practical nor a scientific theory but an expression of mystical will.
>
> "The influence that Marxism has achieved, far from being the result or proof of its scientific character, is almost entirely due to its prophetic, fantastic, and irrational elements. Marxism is a doctrine of blind confidence that a paradise of universal satisfaction is awaiting us just around the corner. Almost all the prophecies of Marx and his followers have already proved to be false, but this does not disturb the spiritual certainty of the faithful, any more than it did in the case of chiliastic sects: for it is a certainty not based on any empirical premises or supposed 'historical laws', but simply on the psychological need for certainty. In this sense Marxism performs the character of a religion, and its efficacy is of a religious character. But it is a caricature and a bogus form of religion, since it presents its temporal eschatology as a scientific system, which religious mythologies do not purport to be." (Kolakowski 1978, 525–526, in Novak 1986, 179–180)

The Institutional Approach and Rationalist Theories

Rationalist theories were among the first to appear within the postwar liberal international school, starting with functionalism, which came into vogue in the late 1950s and the 1960s. Functionalism was posited as an alternative to or substitute for theories about federalism, which had been prevalent in the now discredited "idealist" proposals of regional and global federations, such as the League of Nations, for organizing the international political system. Functionalism argues that "two basic and observable trends in modern history are of crucial importance in shaping the domain and scope of political authority; they are the growth of technology and the spread and intensification of the desire for higher standards of material welfare." (Jacobson 1979, 67)

Functionalists such as David Mitrany (1966 and 1975) and neo-functionalists like Ernst Haas (1958) sought to develop general principles that would explain why states join together or integrate. According to Friedrich Kratochwil, "In its starkest version, functionalism posits that the opportunities provided by large markets create incentives to abolish trade barriers and harmonize regulatory frameworks. Implicit in this argument is the view that economic cooperation will also foster political cooperation. Functionalists often suggest that integration is achieved 'by stealth,' that is, by relying on the dynamics of the integration process instead of basing it on explicit political undertakings that pose frontal challenges to sovereignty. . . . The other approach, neo-functionalism, is less sanguine about the automaticity of the integration process and more attentive to political factors, but it still shares many important assumptions with the functional model. For neo-functionalists, solutions to global problems can rarely be arrived at with recourse only to technical rationality and expertise, since questions of competing values and trade-offs are involved in most political choices. Thus the technical experts emphasized by classical functionalism must also be adept *political leaders* in the neo-functionalist framework." (Kratochwil and Mansfield 1994, 283–284)

Interest in studying integration was spurred by the creation of supranational organizations and institutions (for example, the European Coal and Steel Community, EURATOM, and the European Economic Community) in Western Europe. The European movement was an explicit application of functionalism by Jean Monnet and Robert Schuman, the original architects of what is now the European Union and the intellectual founders of neo-functionalism, and it continues to be a popular subject, both as a theoretical focus and an object of analysis, among international relations scholars.

Some of the shortcomings of functionalism, particularly its inability to explain why international economic or social institutions or organizations were not established or did not develop in a uniform way, were addressed by the theory of public goods, which became popular in the early 1970s and spawned the rational-choice approach to the study of international institutions. As Harold Jacobson points out, "The theory [of public, or collective, goods] deals with a seeming paradox: contrary to the assumption that rational self-interest would lead members of a group having a common interest to organize and act collectively to promote their common interest, this does not happen. The explanation expounded with particular clarity by Mancur Olson [1968] relates first to the hiatus between individual efforts and collective action. If the group is large, individual efforts will seem inconsequential and incapable of achieving the overall objective; hence the individual will concentrate on more proximate objectives even though their achievement may be counterproductive in terms of the group goal. . . . A second part of the explanation concerns the nature of the services that would result from collective action. Some services have the character of being public goods; that is, if they are available to anyone, they must be available to everyone. Thus, with respect to large organizations, individual efforts will have no noticeable effect on the organization, and the individual will receive the benefits of the organization whether or not he contributes." (Jacobson 1979, 72–73)

Another rationalist theory that is closely related to functionalism and the rational-choice approach is regime theory. Stephen Krasner, one of the leading scholars of regime theory and a neorealist, argues that "regimes can be defined as sets of implicit or explicit principles, norms, rules, and decision-making procedures around which actors' expectations converge in a given area of international relations. Principles are beliefs of fact, causation, and rectitude. Norms are standards of behavior defined in terms of rights and obligations. Rules are specific prescriptions or proscriptions for action. Decision-making procedures are prevailing practices for making and implementing collective choices." (Krasner 1994, 97) Whereas functionalism focused on collaboration problems, regime theorists saw other impediments to international cooperation—distributional, coordination, or bargaining problems—that are easier to resolve through institutions than collaboration problems. (Martin 1999, 82)

Regime theory emerged on the academic scene in the 1970s in an effort to explain why governments did not respond with "beggar-thy-neighbor" behavior to the "relative decline of U.S. hegemony: the achievement of nuclear parity by the Soviet Union; the economic resurgence of Europe and Japan; the success of OPEC [Organization of Petroleum Exporting Countries] together with the severe international economic dislocations that followed it. Specific agreements that had been negotiated after World War II were violated, and institutional arrangements, in money and trade above all, came under enormous strain. . . . Neither systemic factors nor formal institutions alone apparently could account for this outcome." (Kratochwil and Ruggie 1994, 7)

With such importance attached to norms, regime theory has drawn both realists (particularly its application of hegemonic stability theory to international institutions) and neoliberals to a common agenda. According to Edward Mansfield:

> Regime theorists typically argue that international interactions depend on the expectations of actors, and that the norms and rules of a regime help to shape and stabilize expectations. Since regime theorists attach such importance to norms, it is useful to discuss briefly their role in international relations. Realists view norms as reflections of power, or what Hobbes referred to as the "command of the sovereign." Thus, realists often argue that norms in international relations reflect the interest of hegemonic states. In their opinion, regimes are created and maintained by hegemons because regimes yield benefits for these states. Regimes weaken when a hegemon's power declines. These explanations therefore focus on the conditions under which regimes are most likely to be *supplied*.
>
> Many neoliberals, in contrast, focus on the conditions under which the *demand* for regimes is likely to be greatest. In their opinion, norms are not only reflections of power. Regimes are likely to be demanded regardless of whether or not a hegemon exists, because norms enable states to calculate costs and benefits of actions more accurately than would be possible in their absence. Norms help us to interpret the behavior of

> states and to determine whether their behavior is in accord with agreed-upon standards. By preventing cheating and free riding, norms allow states to acquire the necessary information to enforce agreements within the context of their ongoing relationships. (Kratochwil and Mansfield 1994, 95)

The rationalistic theories, highlighted above, concentrate on international institutions and are often discussed as part of the institutional approach to the study of international relations. They also represent the progressive shifts in analysis of international organization as a field of study during the postwar period. Kratochwil and Ruggie identify "four major analytical foci" for the study of international organization, which since World War II was most concerned with how to conceptualize the phenomenon of international governance:

> 1. the formal institutional focus—international governance is whatever international organizations do and one need only study their charters, voting procedures, committee structures, and so on to comprehend what it is these organizations do;
> 2. the institutional or decisionmaking processes focus—this perspective emerged in response to the obvious discrepancies between organizations' constitutional design and practices, eventually developing a more generalized research agenda that explored patterns of influence shaping organizational outcomes;
> 3. the organizational-role focus—this perspective shifted scholars' attention to the actual and potential roles of international organizations in three broad areas, a) the roles of organizations in the resolution of substantive international problems; b) institutional adaptation to the failure of states and existing international organizations to solve substantive problems; and c) a general concern with how international institutions reflect, modify, and/or magnify the characteristic features of the international system; and
> 4. the international regime focus—this perspective was thought to express the parameters and the perimeters of international governance and returned the field of international organization to its traditional analytical core on international governance. (Kratochwil and Ruggie 1994, 5–7)

Other approaches that began to appear in the 1970s and 1980s that have gained a foothold in international relations include Richard Falk's "World Orderism" and the World Order Models Project (WOMP) (see Falk 1975 and 1991); peace studies (see Klare and Thomas 1989 and 1991); and Immanuel Wallerstein's world-system theory (1974).

The second period (1945–1989) of the development of modern international theory is obviously very rich in its diversity, despite the contentious disagreements and heated debates that occured throughout. As Donald Puchala points out: "Despite all of its differences and debates, the discreteness of our discipline is in the objects of our attention, and our unity is in our research agenda. Scholars in the discipline of International Relations seek to identify and explain phenomena that result from encounters among states and peoples, and in particular to contemplate the uniqueness of such phenomena. We seek to identify and understand what happens when states encounter one another, when other organizations operating across political or cultural boundaries encounter one another, when peoples as cultural communities encounter one another, and when entities of all of these varieties encounter all others. Such encounters involve agents that need to be identified, processes that need to be tracked, and outcomes that need to be inventoried and explained. As a result of the efforts of several generations of scholars, our discipline has made considerable progress toward building a sophisticated understanding of encounters among states. We now have a rather comprehensive inventory of outcomes and reasonable understandings of when, how, and why such outcomes occur." (Puchala 2000, 141)

Modern International Theory after the Cold War—Reflectivism, Social Constructivism, and the Challenge of Globalization

The end of the Cold War in 1989 had a profound impact on international relations, altering the political, economic, and social landscape of the world. The breakup of the Soviet Union and the rise of ethnic and religious conflicts within states, rather than between them, has encouraged scholars to revisit their approaches to and perspectives on international politics, international order, and international institutions. Similarly, globalization, which started to build momentum in the 1980s, is now radically transforming the international economy into a global economy, giving further impetus to the revival of the international political economy approach within the discipline and spawning a new concentration on the processes of globalization. These tumultuous changes in the real world have challenged the ideologies and orthodoxies of modern international theory, making it possible for new approaches and frameworks to emerge.

Donald Puchala argues that the discipline has, once again, become embroiled in a new "great debate" between the "mainstreamers" (scholars who remain committed to the application of science to the study of international relations) and "dissidents" (scholars who are critical of science as applied to the study of international relations and skeptical of the assumptions that have underpinned the scientific effort). The "mainstream" includes the positivistic rationalist approaches that have been discussed earlier; while the "dissidents" can be broken down into two camps—postmodernists and social constructivists. (Puchala 2000, 137–140)

Steve Smith similarly sees the current situation of international theory divided into three main theoretical clusters. "First there is *rationalism*, containing the bulk of neorealist and neoliberal, as well as some Marxist, work on international theory (see Baldwin 1993). Second, there is *reflectivism*, which broadly consists of post-positivist approaches of critical theory, postmodernism, and feminist and gender theory (see Smith 1997). Third, there is *social constructivism* (see Wendt 1992), which attempts to bridge the gap between rationalism and reflectivism, basically by adopting the ontology of the former and a very 'thin' version of the epistemology of the latter. I think that the current state of theory is that rationalist approaches continue to dominate the mainstream, reflectivist approaches are gaining powerful sets of adherents, and that social constructivism will be 'flavor of the month' theory-wise within a year or two." (Smith 1999, 100). The tension of this debate between the advocates of science as applied to the study of contemporary international relations and those who are exploring other paths is likely to further broaden and deepen the discipline's scope and capacity to explain the dynamic relationships of the world we live in.

While there is a burgeoning literature of postmodernism, it remains to be seen if this school of thought for international relations provides students of international organizations any new insights into the subject. According to Donald Puchala, "The postmodern project reduces knowledge about international relations (or anything else) to subjective prejudice, and while it can evoke skepticism about science, as it surely has, it nevertheless offers no alternative. In postmodernism there is no research agenda for International Relations, save deconstruction, because there can be no attainable knowledge." (Puchala 2000, 139) Yet, we should not simply dismiss the postmodernists or the other reflectivist thinkers as irrelevant or without merit. Reflectivists do challenge the foundational meanings and assumptions of the Western philosophical account of the world and provoke important questions about the political and social realities of today's globalized or globalizing world. "The merit of postmodern thinking about the incremental and epochal changes in train is that it does offer an intimation of the limits of modernity and a 'symptomatology' of its ills." (Axford 1995, 208)

A broader perspective on international relations is being crafted by the Social Constructivist school. As a school of thought it is still in its infancy and, by its own admission, a work in progress. According to John Ruggie (1998): "Social Constructivism in international relations has come into its own during the past decade or so, not only as metatheoretical critique but increasingly in the form of empirical evidence and insights. Constructivism addresses many of the same issues that neo-utilitarianism has addressed, though typically from a different angle, but also some that neo-utilitarianism treats by assumption, discounts, ignores, or simply cannot apprehend within its ontology and/or epistemology. Constructivists seek to push the empirical and explanatory domains of international relations theory beyond the analytical confines of neorealism and neoliberal institutionalism in all directions: by problematizing states' identities and interests; by broadening the array of ideational factors that affect international outcomes; by introducing the logically prior constitutive rules alongside regulative rules; and by including transformation as a normal feature of international politics that systemic theory should encompass even if its empirical occurrence is episodic and moves on a different time line from everyday life." (Ruggie 1998, 27) It is a framework that captures the essence of the global reality of human affairs and focuses scholarly attention on important issues that had been previously ignored or deemed irrelevant. As an approach to the study of international relations, the Constructivist project is particularly useful to and largely embraced by many scholars whose primary research interest is and has been in international organizations and global governance.

As we move into the new millennium, international theory is being forced to grapple with a broader and more complex reality, one that has surpassed the narrow parameters of interstate relationships and structures. There is a compelling need for scholars of international relations to cast their nets widely, entertaining other perspectives from other disciplines, to see what new insights can be gleaned that help identify and more fully explain post–Cold War international relationships, structures, and encounters. As Puchala points out, "With regard to other kinds of inter-organizational encounters, our discipline has some way yet to go, and with regard to inter-cultural encounters, which we have neglected for far too long, we have not yet reached the point of identifying exactly what happens, or may happen, when cultural communities meet in either space or time. There is, therefore, a great deal of work still to be done. . . . The third debate, however, may turn out to be salutary by establishing that there are multiple pathways to knowledge about international relations, and this at least should open the way to the incorporation of the insights of the Humanities into our discipline." (Puchala 2000, 141) Indeed, the contributions of history, literature, philosophy, religion, and the arts to the study of international relations are important and can enhance the theoretical and conceptual efforts of international relations in regards to explaining post–Cold War international or global phenomena.

PART TWO

Manifestations of International Order

5

From the World of Ideas to the Real World

International organizations are manifestations of the ideas and strands of international thought discussed in the previous section. In this section we turn our attention away from the world of ideas to the real world and examine international organizations in greater detail.

International organizations come in many shapes and sizes. There are numerous classification systems for international organizations, but very few are comprehensive. The most comprehensive is the annual four-volume *Yearbook of International Organizations* that is put out by the Union of International Associations, which is headquartered in Brussels and an international organization itself. Traditionally, international organizations are categorized by scholars on a range of features that may include membership, purposes, functions, structure, and/or geography. Harold Jacobson, for example, argues in his classic text, *Networks of Interdependence*, that "all international organizations are alike in having participants from more than one state, but beyond this, differences abound." (Jacobson 1979, 4) He created a simple typology for categorizing international organizations (Figure 5.1) which utilizes two dimensions—manifest purposes and membership. "The first dimension concerns the manifest or stated purposes of the organization. A simple distinction can be made between organizations with mandates in specific fields and those with general mandates. . . . The second dimension involves the membership of the organization. Again a simple distinction can be made between organizations in which membership is limited to a particular group of states, or to individuals or associations from these states, and organizations in which membership is open to all states, or to individuals or associations from all states." (Jacobson 1979, 13)

Membership	Manifest Purposes	
	Specific	*General*
Limited	1 Pan American Health Organization Asian Broadcasting Union	2 Organization of African Unity European Movement
Universal	3 World Health Organization International Broadcasters Society	4 United Nations World Federation of United Nations Associations

Source: *Networks of Interdependence: International Organizations and the Global Political System* by Harold K. Jacobson (New York: Alfred A. Knopf, 1979), p. 13. Copyright © 1979. Reprinted by permission of the Institute for Social Research, The University of Michigan.

FIGURE 5.1 A Typology of International Organizations

The traditional categories of international organizations are useful in so far as they help us make fundamental distinctions among them. As we will see, international organizations are complex entities and few fit neatly into one or another of these schemes. International organizations are human creations and embody people's ingenuity in response to a variety of circumstances. There is always a human factor that often undermines efforts to systematize political, economic, and social organizations. Furthermore, international organizations are not static or unchanging; they adjust and adapt to the environment. In essence, each international organization is unique. Yet, it is impractical to analyze the tens of thousands of international organizations one by one, even if they merit individual attention. Therefore, it is important to keep in mind that there are always exceptions to the way international organizations are defined and distinguished, as well as the trends and generalizations about them.

With nearly a century of intense scrutiny of international organizations under our belt, we can now confidently conclude that there are three essential characteristics of international organizations. First, all international organizations have a membership from two or more states. Second, they share a fundamental aim to pursue the common interests of its members. And, third, they have a formal structure of a continuous nature that has been established by an agreement like a treaty or constitutional document. (Archer 1983, 34–35) Other distinctions that are commonly made among international organizations are based on geography—regional (or limited) and global (or universal) international organizations—and on the character of membership—governmental, non-governmental organizations (NGOs), and hybrid (governments and NGOs) international organizations. (Willetts 1996, 7–8)

Also, international organizations play three major roles—as an arena, an instrument, and an actor. (Archer 1983, 130–152) The first two roles are universal while the last one is not. International organizations are first and foremost a place (arena) within which action occurs, a locus for the action of its members. And they are established in order to achieve particular ends of its members, a tool (instrument) that is used by members to implement their decisions or actions. These two roles are basic features of every international organization. But it is less common for an international organization to be or become an actor. This requires that an organization have capacity that is distinguished from its members, a modicum of independence. Such capacity, whether it be financial, legal, or operational, is often denied or tightly circumscribed by the members. However, international organizations can and do acquire miens of this capacity over time, and depending on the type and structure of an international organization—private or public, governmental or nongovernmental, transnational or multinational—it may be constituted with this capacity from the outset, such as transnational corporations, or at a later stage in its development.

Perhaps a more meaningful way of identifying and distinguishing international organizations is to define them according to the three pillars of global governance discussed in the first chapter of this text—political international organizations, economic (or commercial) international organizations, and socio-cultural international organizations. These groupings are not exclusive of each other; rather they interact with each other and with the general external environment to produce governance of the world. Global governance is the nexus of all international organizations. In addition, international organizations are creatures of both historical and environmental circumstances. What needs to be governed is the most significant reason for the establishment of an international organization and this is determined, in large part, by the social sensibilities of societies at a particular time. In other words, international organizations are never created or operate in a vacuum. We must always put them in their proper context—the time, the place, and the people involved—in order to understand and analyze them fully.

Evolution of International Organizations

If we examine the evolution of international organizations, we can identify two stages in their development. The first stage, 1845–1945, marks the start-up phase of international organizations and coincides with the rise of people's "international" consciousness as well as the initial structuration of a nascent international system. The second stage, 1945–present, is the maturation phase of international organizations as the density and scope of the international system's structuration increased. The patterns of development for each of the governance domains during these two stages are different, but also interrelated in that a natural, though rough, equilibrium appears to be maintained among the three domains. For example, at one point in time economic governance needs may be greater or of higher importance than socio-cultural or political governance needs, and that results in the formation of international organizations to manage the economic domain. This would, in turn, highlight or expose deficiencies in how the socio-cultural and political domains are governed, thereby creating governance needs and the formation of international organizations to manage these domains. The cycle is continual within and between the domains, as well as stimulated by environmental events and conditions.

Stage One—The Start-Up Phase

It is generally accepted that international organizations began to take shape in the nineteenth century. Although there are earlier and ancient examples of international-like organizations, such as the Delian League (478 B.C.–404 B.C. and 378–377 B.C.–338 B.C.) in ancient Greece and the Hanseatic League (eleventh century–seventeenth century) in northern Germany, the first "modern" international organizations had to await the globalization of the sovereign nation-state system, which had become rooted in Europe by the seventeenth century. During the eighteenth and nineteenth centuries, the extension of the secular sovereign nation-state to the rest of the world started to displace other political systems that existed in Asia (China and India) or the Near East (the Ottoman Empire), forcing non-European societies to ultimately abandon their particular system and be absorbed into the European system. While large territorial pockets of societies (predominantly in Africa and Asia) were not to join the nation-state system until the mid-twentieth century, the colonial systems established by the European powers effectively tied these societies to the international system and predetermined that the sovereign nation-state was the only future for them.

Managing the Problems of War and Peace. As we know from European history, the development of the nation-state system in Europe was fraught with conflict and insecurity. The competition for power and land within and between the fledgling territorial political entities often ended up in wars, which would disrupt commerce, cause major environmental destruction, and create massive social dislocations. It could be argued that the European state system is the product of war. Two defining events in the evolution of state system in Europe were the Peace of Westphalia of 1648, which ended the Thirty Years War and marked the undoing of the Holy Roman Empire, creating the initial group of secular sovereign states; and the Treaty of Utrecht of 1713, which ended the War of Spanish Succession (1688–1713) and dashed the imperial aspirations of France's Sun King, Louis XIV, furthering the creation of additional sovereign states and enlarging the international nation-state system. As Hedley Bull points out, "War appears as a basic determinant of the shape the [international] system assumes at any one time. It is war and the threat of war that help to determine whether particular states survive or are eliminated, whether they rise or decline, whether their frontiers remain the same or are changed, whether their peoples are ruled by one government or another, whether disputes are settled or drag on, and which way they are settled, whether there is a balance of power in the international system or one state becomes preponderant." (Bull 1995, 181)

Charles Kegley and Gregory Raymond argue that the Napoleonic Wars at the beginning of the nineteenth century had a "system-transforming" effect on the international nation-state system.

> The Napoleonic Wars, which ravaged Europe from 1803 to 1815, were undertaken to establish a new international order, one that would impose

political unity on the Continent and reform the way European leaders ruled their tributary states. Napoleon sought to establish a single code of law, a public school system, and to implant liberal ideals in constitutions of the countries he conquered. His reforms generated several movements for national unification and republican administration. However, his methods were at times ruthless, and victory on the battlefield sometimes led him to violate many of the liberal principles that he espoused. . . .

Napoleon's Grand Empire reached its zenith in 1810 (see Map 5.1). Beyond France (which included Belgium and the lands on the left bank of the Rhine) were layers of dependent states and political allies. The former encompassed what is today the Netherlands, Spain, Switzerland, Western and Southern Germany, most of Italy, and parts of Poland. The latter included Austria, Prussia, Denmark, Sweden, and Russia. All of these countries were part of Napoleon's Continental System, a mechanism designed to crush Great Britain by prohibiting the importation of British goods into Europe. By interrupting this trade flow, Napoleon hoped to dry up a major source of London's revenues and establish France as the economic hub of Europe. Since its naval victory over the French in the 1805 Battle of Trafalgar, Britain had been able to retain control of seaborne commerce, thwarting Napoleon's military ambitions outside of Europe.

Napoleon's pursuit of hegemony stalled after 1811. The economic sacrifices demanded by the Continental System bred resentment from Zeeland on the North Sea to the distant shores of the Baltic Sea. Simultaneously, France began to suffer serious military setbacks [in Spain and then in Russia]. . . . Napoleon's empire finally collapsed after the Waterloo Campaign of June 12–18, 1815, but its fate had been sealed in defeats France suffered in the preceding three years. Following a series of treaties and armistice agreements, the victors met in Vienna to craft a peace settlement with France.

Napoleon's defeat at Waterloo concluded a period that had battered Europe for almost a quarter century and left over 2.5 million combatants dead. When measured by battle deaths per population, the toll exceeded all previous wars fought during the preceding three centuries. The carnage inspired pity in people of compassion and horror in people of prudence. It galvanized a consensus among the victors who met at the Congress of Vienna about the need to prevent another great-power death struggle from again erupting. (Kegley and Raymond 1999, 105–110)

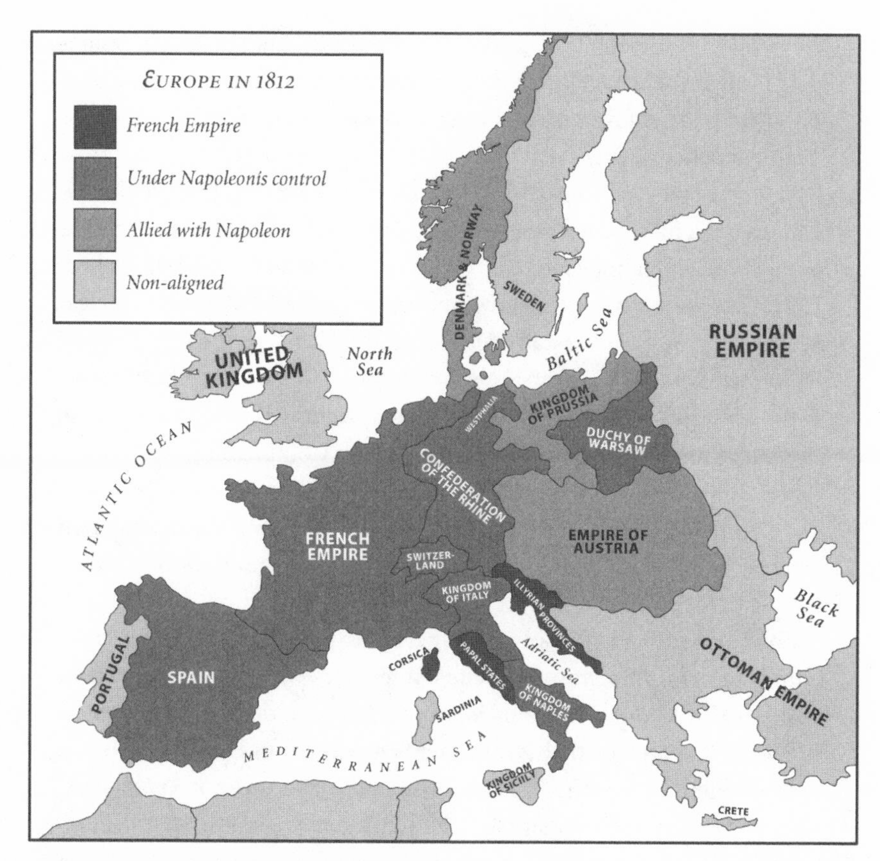

MAP 5.1 Europe in 1812

Napoleon's quest for hegemony and his vision of a new international order clearly re-shaped the international system, but it is the aftermath of Napoleon's defeat, in particular the Congress of Vienna, that marks the starting point in the evolution of international organizations as governance mechanisms of the international system. According to Michael Schechter,

> the conferees' primary goal in Vienna was the liquidation of unsettled political problems that had accumulated from years of warfare. This included restoring or disposing of those territories in Poland, Italy, Germany, the Netherlands, and Switzerland that Napoleon had overrun. To ensure that such political settlements were handled fairly, the negotiators had set up a statistical commission, which had made a complete census of

> the territories in dispute. The success of this fact-finding activity established a precedent that present-day states follow—that is, turning over authority to intergovernmental organizations to gather, collate, and disseminate policy relevant data.
>
> The conferees in Vienna also wrestled with a number of socioeconomic problems. For example, they declared that in the future the slave trade should be abolished. But no specific timetable was established. They dealt more definitively, however, with issues related to river navigation. For example, for the Rhine, they drafted a treaty providing for an elaborate international central control commission, the first such statute in the history of modern international organization. In fact, international rivers commissions, modeled after the Rhine Commission, were established throughout the 19th century. Some of these still exist today. More important, perhaps, the river commissions also served as important precedents for other transportation accords as industrialization spread in the 19th century.
>
> Coming out of Vienna was also what came to be called the Concert of Europe, a commitment to convene conferences when tensions arose or hostilities broke out. The significance of this proliferation of conferences lies in the experience that governments gained from consulting in war and peacetime. Of course, the commitment to talk was not always present, nor was the commitment to talk identical to a commitment to compromise. Many of the conferences failed to achieve their ends. (Schechter 1998, 6)

The Concert of Europe, while not an international organization in contemporary terms, was an important innovation in how the institution of diplomacy and international relations was organized. Building on the experience gained from previous peace settlements arranged through diplomatic conferences and congresses, the Concert's series of congresses that were convened over a fifty-year period (1815–1870) established a mechanism—a loosely organized alliance system that was designed to preserve an equilibrium among the great powers (Austria, Russia, Prussia, Great Britain, and France)—for states to manage their political and security relationships through consultation and negotiations. This balance-of-power system was effective from 1815 to 1849 in that disputes among the great powers did not escalate into war, but after 1849 the commitment to the system and to Austrian chancellor Prince Klemens von Metternich's great-power collective security approach began to wane and more than half the serious disputes between great powers resulted in war. (Kegley and Raymond 1999, 116–117) Over the 100 years that the Concert was in effect, the congresses developed some of the basic structural elements that now exist in contemporary international organizations, such as committees and conference secretariats.

The Hague Peace Conferences in 1899 and 1907 marked another important step forward in the development of international organizations in the political domain. These conferences were convened at the request of Tsar Nicholas II of Russia to address an arms race that was gaining significant momentum and involving costs that were becoming too heavy to bear. Even though these conferences did not alter the shape of or divisions within the international system, they were remarkable for two things—the participation of non-European states in these conferences and the conferences' objective to stop the arms race through some measure of general disarmament.

It is no small matter that invitations to these diplomatic confabulations were sent to states in the Americas and Asia and that six (the United States, Brazil, China, Japan, Persia, and Siam) were represented at the first conference in 1899. Twenty-four non-European states (out of forty-four delegations) were present at the second conference in 1907. The inclusion of states outside of Europe at these events was an indication of an expanded notion of the international society and who the relevant players are in the world. The objective of these conferences, disarmament on a global scale, was not necessarily common fare of diplomatic gatherings of the time and it should be of no great surprise that little was achieved. However, these conferences did make some progress in the fields of international law and organization. In international law these peace conferences updated the Laws of War, producing a string of conventions and agreements that sought to ban or control several new and future weapons (such as gas, balloons, bombardment, and soft-nosed bullets) and to regulate the conduct of armed conflict "so as to make it less rather than more unpleasant." (Best 1999, 625) The Hague Conference of 1899 also established for the first time a multilateral (that is, general versus bilateral or trilateral) approach to arms control, a tradition that remains with us to this day. Despite the limitations and weaknesses of this approach at that time and ever since, the fact that the Conferences of 1899 and 1907 engendered the universalization of debates on international security issues laid the foundation for subsequent institutionalization of international politics within formal international governmental organizations such as the League of Nations Assembly and the United Nations General Assembly.

In the field of international organization, the 1899 conference took a bold step by adopting the Convention for the Pacific Settlement of International Disputes. "In other and more common words, a multilateral treaty for arbitration between states. What was new and striking about it was not the idea of arbitration as such but its institutionalization, its installation in the foundation of an improved world order." (Best 1999, 628) Geoffrey Best points out:

> This excellent Convention of 1899 approached the goal of "obviating, as far as possible, recourse to force in the relations between states" by four different routes. First, they were urged to seek and to accept the "good offices" of friendly powers; so touchy did states tend to be about their sovereignty status, it was stipulated that no good offices etc. should be regarded as an "unfriendly act". Next, there was an ingenious suggestion that states in dispute should for a few weeks cease to deal directly with each other while they put their causes into the hands of trusted neighbours; just as prospective duellists used to communicate through "seconds". Third: "in differences . . . involving neither honour nor vital interests, and arising from a difference of opinion on points of fact", the difficulty could be settled by a Commission of Inquiry, a plain and simple fact-finding mission. And fourth, there was to be established at The Hague a Permanent Court of Arbitration, ready to handle all international business voluntarily entrusted to it.
>
> How shall we evaluate this pioneer legislation? The first thing to note is that everything in it was optional. Arbitration enthusiasts had hoped that the use of it would be obligatory. The Great Powers were not having that! Nor, for that matter, were most lesser ones. (Those in the Balkans were particularly unhappy even about the Commission of Inquiry, I don't know why.) Germany, well to the fore in declamations about national honour etc., took the lead in objecting to the obligatory principle, and insisted on the removal of even a very small bit of it in relation to minor

> disputes about matters in which, really, points of honour or national interest could scarcely be imagined. But that was how things were. And that essentially is how things still are. What states agree shall be arbitrated about or adjudicated on, can so be dealt with. What they decline to submit to such genial processes, cannot. . . .
>
> The great days of The Hague's Court of Arbitration were over by 1914. That is not to say that arbitration has ceased to figure in the affairs of states, only that it goes on in other forms; also that some of the causes that used to be thought appropriate for it were able to go, after 1919, to The Hague's other permanent court, the International Court of Justice (ICJ) established by the League of Nations in 1919, and re-established almost unchanged by the United Nations in 1945. (Best 1999, 629–630)

The first World War (1914–1919) ended the Concert system and reconfigured the international political system. The failure of the Concert to avert the conflict (despite the added tools developed at The Hague peace conferences) demonstrated the inherent weakness of the Concert's balance-of-power system. "Many historians contend that, in addition to an unrestrained arms race, the **polarized** system of alliances, and counteralliances (the Triple Alliance of Germany, Austria-Hungary, and Italy versus the Triple Entente of Russia, Britain, and France), engendered a chain reaction following the 1914 Austrian reprisal against the Sarajevo assassination [of Archduke Ferdinand], where prior commitments pulled one European state after another into a continental war." (Kegley and Raymond 1999, 149) (See Map 5.2.) It wasn't long before the war had become global, drawing in first Japan, which complied with its alliance commitments to Britain; then the Ottoman empire and Bulgaria, which joined the side of Germany and Austria-Hungary to form what was called the "Central Powers" (Italy remained neutral and eventually shifted to the Triple Entente Alliance); and then Rumania, China, and many other countries, which joined the expanding coalition of the Triple Entente Alliance and became referred to as the "Allies." Ultimately, thirty-two countries on six continents were at war. (Kegley and Raymond 1999, 150)

The Treaty of Versailles was the peace settlement reached between the victors—the Allied and Associated Governments—and the defeated Central Powers of World War I. As was the case in 1815, the settlement focused primarily on redefining the political landscape and the power configura-

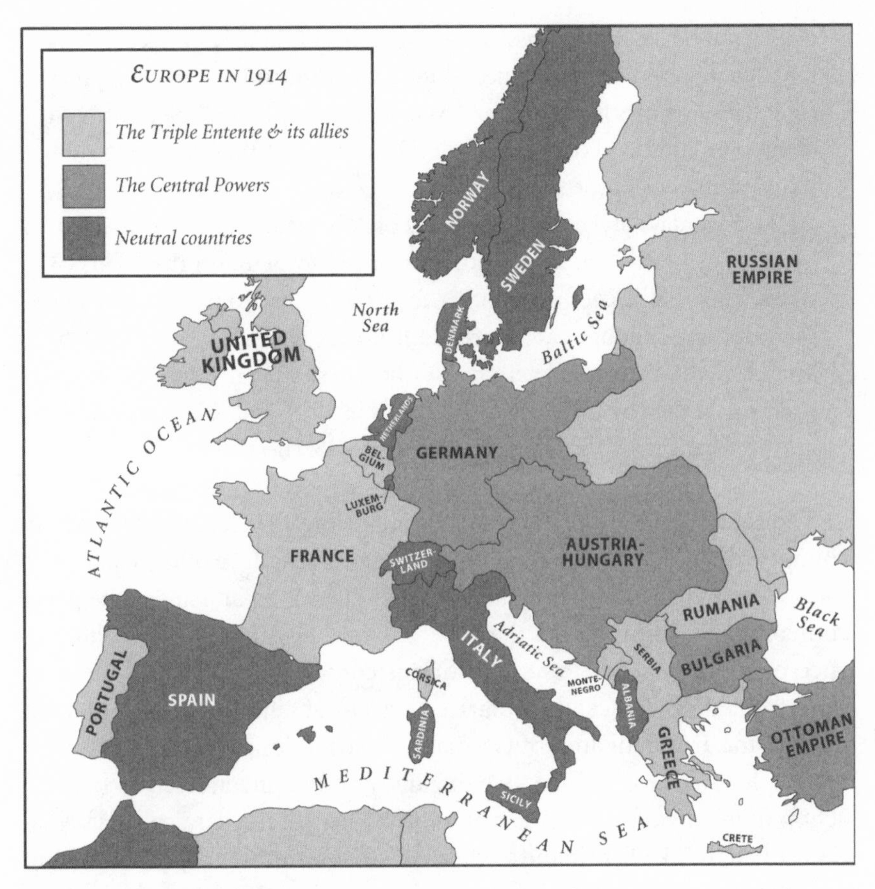

MAP 5.2 Europe in 1914

tion in the world, as well as stripping Germany of its status as a great power. (However, unlike the Congress of Vienna, the defeated powers—Germany and its allies—were excluded in the negotiations on the central issues of the final settlement and were forced to accept the burdensome terms of the peace, thus sowing the seeds for the next world war.) Territorial boundaries were redrawn and three major empires, the Hapsburg, Romanov, and Ottoman, were dismantled, creating several more nation-states in the process. By 1939, the international community grew to almost seventy states, including a new type of political system—the communist regime of the Union of Soviet Socialist Republics (USSR). (See Map 5.3)

The first article of the Versailles Treaty established the League of Nations, an ill-fated but bold attempt to institutionalize collective security to

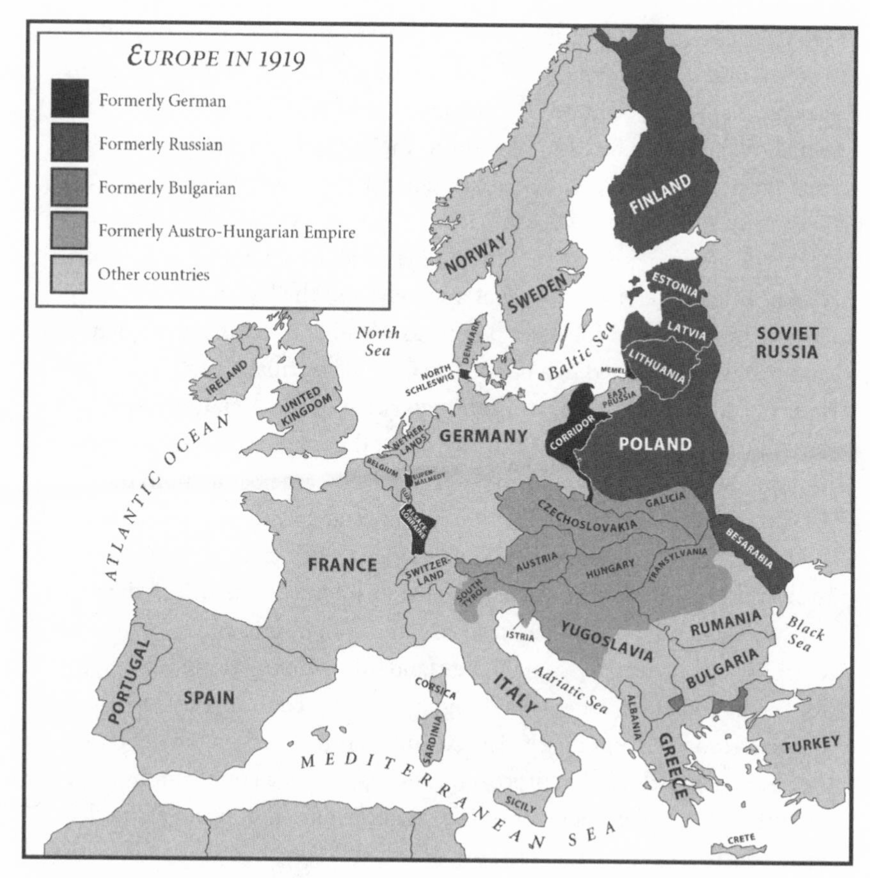

MAP 5.3 Europe in 1919

keep the peace. The war demonstrated the terrible consequences of an international order managed through secret diplomacy, alliances, and power politics, exposing the inherent instability of the Concert's "balance of power" system.

> In 1919 in the aftermath of the first "war to end all wars," it was apparent that a better means was needed to prevent widespread interstate violence. From the Versailles Peace Conference arose the League of Nations Convenant (or "constitution") on January 20, 1920, but the League ultimately proved unsuccessful in its quest to preserve the peace. However, its experiences provided lessons later about how to structure a collective-security system. Under Article 10 of the League's Convenant, members pledged

> "to respect and preserve as against external aggression the territorial integrity and existing political independence of all Members of the League." This language was the main target of critics in the U.S. Senate, which ultimately refused to consent to the convenant in spite of the fact that President Woodrow Wilson had championed the League.
>
> Articles 11 through 17 contained the germ of a collective-security system. The two main organs of the League were the Assembly, which contained all member states and met annually, and the less universal Council, which always had the great powers as members, met more frequently, and could be convened in a crisis. The Council normally dealt with matters that threatened the peace, although some of these matters came before the Assembly. The lack of clarity about the roles of the Assembly and Council was a weakness; all problems regularly came before both bodies.
>
> Voting mechanisms reflected the traditional practices of multilateral diplomacy. Although majority voting existed in principle for some issues, a sovereign state could not be compelled to submit to the will of the majority when, in its own interpretation, its national interests were threatened. Hence, unanimity came to be standard operating procedure except for inconsequential issues. The League relied on commitments by states not to use force except in self-defense until a process of pacific settlement had been completed. That process was to begin with a complaint by a disputant or by another member of the League. In essence, members undertook a legal obligation to use the organization if they themselves could not end a dispute. At least on paper, the League's covenant embodied a working system of security. (Weiss, Forsythe, and Coate 1997, 23–25)

The creation of a permanent secretariat as one of three principal organs of the League (the other two were the assembly and the council) was an important step forward in the structural design of international political organizations. Although the idea of a secretariat was not new (there were secretariats created for the Hague Peace Conferences and the diplomatic conferences of the Concert of Europe, as well as for international public unions discussed below), the significance of the League's secretariat was its truly international character, as developed by Sir Eric Drummond, the first secretary-general of the League. While Drummond and his successor, Joseph Avenol, were careful not to challenge the authority of the member states that rested in the assembly and the council, the administrative competence and effectiveness of the League's secretariat, particularly in nonmilitary security matters such as narcotics control, refugee assistance, and codification of international law, gave the League its distinctive profile as the first universal international political organization.

Managing Industrialization and an Internationalizing Capitalist Economy. Another important factor in the evolution of international organizations was the Industrial Revolution and the economic transformation of communities from predominantly agrarian societies to urban industrial societies. Industrialization "started in the nineteenth century in Britain, spread to Western Europe, then to North America, Australia, Japan, and New Zealand, and after that to Eastern Europe." (Jacobson 1979, 221) According to David Landes, the Industrial Revolution involved three important developments:

> (1) the substitution of machines—rapid, regular, precise, tireless—for human skill and effort; (2) the substitution of inanimate for animate sources of power, in particular, the invention of engines for converting heat into work, thereby opening an almost unlimited supply of energy; and (3) the use of new and far more abundant raw materials, in particular, the substitution of mineral, and eventually artificial, materials for vegetable or animal substances. These substitutions made the Industrial Revolution. They yielded a rapid rise in productivity and, with it, in income per head. This growth, moreover, was self-sustaining. In ages past, better living standards had always been followed by a rise in population that eventually consumed the gains. Now, for the first time in history, both the economy and knowledge were growing fast enough to generate a continuing flow of improvements. Gone, Malthus's positive checks and the stagnationist predictions of the "dismal science"; instead, one had an age of promise and great expectations. The Industrial Revolution also transformed the balance of political power—within nations, between nations, and between civilizations; revolutionized the social order; and as much changed ways of thinking as ways of doing. (Landes 1999, 186–187)

From the mid-nineteenth century onward, there was a dramatic increase in the commercial interaction of nation-states as new sources of energy (oil and electricity), new devices for communications (telegraph and telephone), and new or improved means of transportation (steamships, railroads, and automobiles) came online, enabling swifter and more efficient economic transactions to occur. At the same time, the social dislocations and change brought on by industrialization were particularly acute during the initial spread of the industrial economic model around the world and elevated concerns about people's welfare, particularly those most affected (for example, the rural cottage weavers and spinners in the textile industry, the city and town guilds of trained journeymen and masters in the industrial crafts, and the landlords in agriculture) or most vulnerable (women and children, factory laborers). The profound and global effect of the Industrial Revolution on the international system and its organization is highlighted by historian Eric Hobsbawn:

> It is true that the "world market", that crucial pre-condition and characteristic of capitalist society, had long been developing. International Trade [i.e., the sum total of all the exports and imports for all the countries within the purview of European economic statistics at this period] had more than doubled in value between 1720 and 1780. In the period of the Dual Revolution (1780–1840) it had increased more than threefold—yet even this substantial growth was modest by the standards of our period [1848–1875]. By 1870, the value of foreign trade for every citizen of the United Kingdom, France, Germany, Austria and Scandinavia was between four and five times that it had been in 1830, for every Dutchman and Belgian about three times as great, and even for every citizen of the United States—a country for which foreign commerce was only of marginal importance—well over double. . . .
>
> In thirty-five years, the value of the exchanges between the most industrialized economy and the most remote or backward regions of the world had increased about sixfold. Even this is of course not very impressive by present standards, but in sheer volume it far surpassed anything that had previously been conceived. The net which linked the various regions of the world was visibly tightening. . . .
>
> There is no doubt that the bourgeois prophets of the mid-nineteenth century looked forward to a single, more or less standardized, world where all governments would acknowledge the truths of political economy and liberalism carried throughout the globe by impersonal mission-

> aries more powerful than those Christianity or Islam had ever had; a world reshaped in the image of the bourgeoisie, perhaps even one from which, eventually, national differences would disappear. Already the development of communications required novel kinds of international coordinating and standardizing organisms—the International Telegraph Union of 1865, the Universal Postal Union of 1875, the International Meteorological Organization of 1878, all of which still survive. Already it had posed—and for limited purposes solved by means of the International Signals Code of 1871—the problem of an internationally standardized "language". Within a few years attempts to devise artificial cosmopolitan languages were to become fashionable headed by the oddly named *Volapük* (—"world-speak") excogitated by a German in 1880. (None of these succeeded, not even the most promising contender, *Esperanto*, another product of the 1880s.) Already the labour movement was in the process of establishing a global organization which was to draw political conclusions from the growing unification of the world—the International.
>
> Nevertheless international standardization and unification in this sense remained feeble and partial. Indeed, to some extent the rise of new nations and new cultures with a democratic base, i.e. using separate languages rather than the international idioms of educated minorities, made it more difficult, or rather, more circuitous. . . . Whatever the long-term prospects, it was accepted by contemporary liberal observers that, in the short and medium term, development proceeded by the formation of different and rival nations. The most that could be hoped was that these would embody the same type of institutions, economy and beliefs. The unity of the world implied division. The world system of capitalism was a structure of rival "national economies". The world triumph of liberalism rested on its conversion of all peoples, at least among those regarded as "civilized". No doubt the champions of progress in the third quarter of the nineteenth century were confident enough that this would happen sooner or later. But their confidence rested on insecure foundations. (Hobsbawn 1996, 50 and 65–66)

By the end of the nineteenth century, the incessant conflicts between the rulers of Europe, the spread of industrialization, and the social consequences of both war and economic transformation were to eventually yield the first international organizations. As already pointed out, the precursor of international organizations for the political domain was the Concert of Europe. It had most of the core features of a modern international organization, lacking only the "formal structure of a continuous nature." The experiences accumulated from the Concert were to greatly influence future architects of international organizations, especially the severe limitations that the all-important notion of state sovereignty imposed on international organizations for managing inter-state relations. Where such limitations were less problematic was in the economic and socio-cultural domains. As the Industrial Revolution transformed people's ways of thinking and ways of doing, the clear linkage of industrial advance to power was not lost upon government leaders. International commerce and trade filled the coffers of state treasuries while the foundries that churned out tons of steel, more powerful engines, and new weapons of greater destructiveness added to the firepower and mobility of national armies. Still, as a matter of policy states largely left business alone to pursue profits, the classic laissez-faire approach to commerce. The relationship between the state and the fledgling industrial economy was indeed intimate—states did finance, partially or fully, certain industries (railroad construction, steelworks, telegraph), protected many industries and commercial enterprises from foreign competition through tariffs and customs duties, and gave legal and political support to international cartels. But, economic growth could not be achieved in isolation. To realize greater national wealth and increase their power, states found it necessary to cooperate, but cooperation was confined to specific technical or administrative activities such as coordination of postal services or telegraphic communications. This form of cooperation was the first to be institutionalized in formal international governmental organizations.

The international organizations of the nineteenth century included the Central Commission for the Navigation of the Rhine (1815), *Conseil superieur de santé* (1838), the European Commission for Control of the Danube (1856), International Telegraph Union (1865), International Meteorological Organization (1873), Universal Postal Union (1874), International Office of Weight and Measures (1875), Union for the Protection of Industrial Property (1883), the Intergovernmental Organization for International Carriage by Rail (1890), Comité Maritime International (1897). They "developed at a time when central governments were expanding their administrative competence, both relative to provincial governments and, most relevantly, in terms of issue areas within which they exercised jurisdiction (i.e., aspects of social and economic lives previously within the private sphere were now part of the public domain). These early organizations—the so-called public international unions—served as collection points and clearinghouses for information, centers for decisions of problems common to governments, instruments for the coordination of national policy and practices, and agencies for promoting the formulation and acceptance of uniform or minimum standards in their respective fields. Some—like the river commissions—had regulatory, administrative, supervisory, and adjudicatory responsibilities." (Schechter 1998, 10) The public international unions were important precedent-setting organizations on procedural and decisionmaking for later international governmental organizations.

These international organizations were the products of international treaties or agreements. For example, in 1865 a comprehensive international convention for regulating and establishing uniformity of telegraph services was reached, creating the International Telegraph Union (now called the International Telecommunications Union), and less than ten years later, in 1874, the Conference of Berne reached an international agreement on regulating postal services, establishing the Universal Postal Union to administer this accord. This pattern was repeated in other areas—transportation (railroads and sea shipping), health (sanitation and disease control), science and industry (intellectual property, weights and measures, agriculture), and economics (finance and trade)—that increasingly fell within the expanding jurisdiction and/or administrative competence of central governments.

The initial impetus for establishing administrative and regulatory agencies on the international level was the obvious need to ease or eliminate constraints on commercial transactions between sovereign jurisdictions. For states, all of which jealously guard their sovereign prerogatives, creating these international organizations was a pragmatic and practical response to the challenges posed by technological developments and economic change. But states were also careful not to vest international bodies with too much authority, limiting their scope, function and tasks to specific purposes and technical matters. This preference is consistent with the general outlook of governments' role in society. Public administration even on the national level was relatively undeveloped throughout this period. However, the breakdown of the international economy which brought on the Great Depression in the 1930s and the shift to Keynesian economic thinking among the more advanced industrialized countries marked the beginning of a more interventionist posture for governments in economic affairs, both nationally and internationally. After the end of World War I, governments expanded the size and scope of their own domestic agencies considerably, which was mirrored on the international level with similar administrative agencies.

Coordinating International Social, Humanitarian, and Cultural Issues. Driving much of the early development of international organizations were private associations and organizations. According to Geoffrey Best, the world was swiftly "internationalizing" as people's consciousness of the world's "one-ness" grew each year during the final years of the nineteenth century and throughout the twentieth century.

> The word "globalization" was unknown and the expression "human rights" was not yet in use, but both concepts were (so to speak) in the air, seeking institutional embodiment. This movement of opinion was most evident in the mass of organizations and associations whose regular assemblies brought delegates and devotees together from all over the almost passport-free world and whose publications and star speakers had transnational followings. Several of these networks were intensely interested in [the 1899 Hague Peace Conference]. Most obviously so, the peace societies and the Inter-Parliamentary Union, which had been coming together in international peace congresses almost annually since the 1880s. Prominent in the peace movement and in proto-human-rights movements generally were many eloquent and indomitable women; the number of their associations being legion, I simply sum them up as forerunners of the Women's International League for Peace and Freedom, to flower in 1915. Then there were all the professional people (including since the 1870s, international lawyers)—all of them by the end of the [nineteenth] century well accustomed to get together across frontiers. And, to complete my sketch of this humming transnational civil society, every few years there were great international exhibitions—really big events in those days; though whether the causes of war or peace were better served by them would be matter for re-

> search. I suspect they served to some extent as arms fairs. The two big ones between which [the 1899 Hague Conference] was sandwiched were the Chicago's Columbian Exposition of 1893 and the Exposition Universelle in Paris on 1900. (Best 1999, 620)

The proliferation of private, nongovernmental international organizations since the late 1800s coincided with a "dramatic growth in the middle classes and a consequent increase in the numbers of people with the time, education and resources to take part in associations." (Seary 1996, 17) In most cases, private nongovernmental international associations and societies were initially formed on a national level to address social concerns, like starving children or the indigent, and to provide humanitarian assistance to refugees and casualties of war or civil strife—areas in which governments have always been less active (at least until the mid-twentieth century). The International Committee of the Red Cross (ICRC) is one of the earliest private international organizations to be established and its formation came about in a fairly typical way: "One person had identified a need and had collected a small group to campaign for an organisation to answer that need. The group had inspired the establishment of similar ones in other countries." (Seary 1996, 16)[1] Furthermore, the increased mobility and ease of long-distance communications, due to improvements in roads and rail services and to the rapid spread of telegraphic services, enabled greater interaction among national professional, commercial, scientific, and cultural societies and associations. This naturally led to the formation of international organizations, such as the International Publishers Association (1896), the International Chamber of Commerce (1919), World Confederation of Labor (1920), International Federation of Business and Professional Women (1930), Interna-

[1]The ICRC is not typical of most INGOs at the time, however, due to its unique status in international law and close association with the military medical institutions of national governments. The ICRC is assigned a particular role within the Geneva Conventions and Protocols, while the national Red Cross Societies was specifically recognized in Article 25 of the Covenant of the League of Nations, which reads: "The Members of the League agree to encourage and promote the establishment and cooperation of duly authorised voluntary national Red Cross organizations having as purposes the improvement of health, the prevention of disease and the mitigation of suffering throughout the world." Few other private international organizations were able to garner this much influence in international relations as the ICRC and the Red Cross and Red Crescent Movement.

tional Literary and Artistic Association (1878), International Pediatric Association (1910), and International Council of Scientific Unions (1919). Since these groups were not encumbered by the legal doctrine of sovereignty, their ability to mobilize individuals or associations was much easier than mobilizing states. This, in large part, explains why the population of private nongovernmental international organizations has been and remains the largest contingent of international organizations.

By the end of the first stage in the development of international organizations there were in place significant concentrations of international governmental organizations (IGOs) and international nongovernmental organizations (INGOs) for all three governance domains. The greatest number of international organizations created during this period were INGOs. It is estimated that over 150 had been founded by the end of the nineteenth century and by 1939 there were over 1,000. There were only 24 IGOs founded by the turn of the century and fewer than 100 by 1939.[2] (See Table 5.1.)

Most international organizations were founded in Europe and their headquarters were likely to be in Paris, Brussels, London, or Geneva, demonstrating the Euro-centric nature of international relations and the international order during this stage. But as the Appendix shows, there was a significant development of international organizations in the Americas and the beginnings of a similar development in Africa, Asia, and the Middle East. The concentration of organizations in Europe is to be expected since the international community was largely made up of European states.

The array of international organizations in the international system mirrored the institutions of modern national societies, which encouraged the "domestic analogy" approach to analyzing international organizations. There were international organizations that looked similar in structure and function to public institutions of central governments (for ex-

---

[2]It is difficult to get an accurate count of all international organizations created during the start-up phase. This is due to the fact that efforts to document and classify international organizations did not start until 1908 when the Central Bureau of International Organizations was established in Brussels by Henri La Fontaine and Paul Otlet, directors-general of the International Bibliographical Institute, and the first compilation of a comprehensive list of international organizations was published. The Union of International Associations, which was the successor organization to the Central Bureau, continued to compile this information and in the 1950s began publishing annually the *Yearbook of International Organizations,* which is the standard source for vital statistics about international organizations.

TABLE 5.1A Classification of International Organizations, 1924

I.	La vie internationale publique, en général		13
II.	La vie internationale privée, en général		10
III.	La vie internationale publique et privée, en particulier		620
	A. La vie physique	61	
	B. La vie économique	90	
	C. La vie sociale	135	
	D. La vie juridique	31	
	E. La vie politique et administrative	55	
	F. La vie scientifique	177	
	G. La vie esthétique	14	
	H. La vie sportive, touriste et distractive	25	
	I. La vie morale	4	
	J. La vie spirituelle et religeuse	28	

Source: Paul Otlet, Tableau de l'Organisation Internationale (Extract from: Rapport général à la Conférence des Associations Internationales, Genève, 1924). Bruxelles, Union des Associations Internationales, 1924. (UAI publication 114). Union of International Associations, *Yearbook of International Organizations*, 37th edition, Volume 3: Subject Volume. "Appendix 3: Table 3 – Classification of international organizations, 1924," p. 1662.

ample, the League of Nations, the International Labor Organization, and the public international unions), and many more that had the characteristics of private civic and commercial institutions (such as Rotary International, Women's International League for Peace and Freedom, Save the Children, and the International Chamber of Commerce).

International organizations had developed, by the end of their first stage, government-like structures and functions—legislative bodies (such as the assembly and council of the League of Nations), administrative bodies (the secretariat of the League and the bureaus and commissions of the international public unions), and judicial bodies (the permanent International Court of Arbitration and the permanent International Court of Justice). While the structure and function of IGOs may look similar to national governments, the IGOs did not have anywhere near the power, authority, or resources of their national counterparts. The private international nongovernmental organizations, on the other hand, more closely resembled their national counterparts in that they are organized to address particular concerns or interests and direct their activities toward influencing or changing public governmental institutions and public policies (in this they resemble special interest or pressure groups and lobbies).

TABLE 5.1B Number of International Organizations Founded from 1863 to 1954, in Five-Year Periods

	International Non-Governmental Organizations		*International Governmental Organizations*	
Period	*# Founded*	*Now in Activity*	*# Founded*	*Now in Activity*
1693–1849	5	5	1	1
1850–1854	1	1	0	0
1855–1859	4	1	2	0
1860–1864	6	3	1	0
1865–1869	9	4	5	3
1870–1874	8	6	3	1
1875–1879	17	9	2	2
1880–1884	11	6	3	2
1885–1889	29	16	2	1
1890–1894	35	19	3	3
1895–1899	38	20	2	1
1900–1904	61	22	5	2
1905–1909	131	42	4	1
1910–1914	112	38	4	3
1915–1919	51	31	8	3
1920–1924	132	102	11	6
1925–1929	163	101	12	9
1930–1934	128	83	5	5
1935–1939	97	61	6	5
1940–1944	46	28	13	10
1945–1949	306	264	53	42
1950–1954	319	308	33	32
Total	1,709	1,170	178	132

Source: Union of International Associations (1957) *The 1,978 International Organizations Founded Since the Congress of Vienna, Document No. 7* (Brussels: Union of International Associations), p. VIII.

The "domestic analogy" provides, at best, an approximation of how the constellation of international organizations is organized, but to go beyond that is misleading.

International organizations did not evolve systematically. In general, each was created without much regard for other organizations that had been established before. The obvious lack of organic connections between and among international organizations was an obvious structural defect of the international system. However, it should be noted that there was a generally uniform structure of international organizations. As Pitman

Potter points out in his 1948 text, *An Introduction to the Study of International Organization*:

> The core of international administration is an agency deputized for that function by the members of a union of states. In practice the agency may be called a bureau or commission or board or council or by any one of a dozen names. It may also vary in personnel from one person on part time to several hundred or even several thousand persons on full time, although the average agency may be thought of as consisting of twenty or thirty persons. At times, though rarely, the agency will maintain branches outside of its central core; and of course the larger agencies (United Nations Secretariat, for example) will be subdivided and organized internally in a very complicated way. . . .
>
> Just above the agency there may be stationed a supervisory body to watch over its operations on behalf of the member states; such is the Governing Body of the International Labor Organization, which also acts as the executive council for the union; in most cases supervision is relegated higher up—to the conference of the union or the member states themselves. Next in the ascending scale come one or more representative bodies or conferences which form the legislative and constituent organs; in most unions there will be only one such body. The formation of policy and exercise of leadership reposes on this level, which is really not a phase of administration but legislation, though very important for the success of the former; it is very necessary at the beginning and may be useful later also . . . .
>
> The objectives of international administration are chiefly the concern of states establishing this actively, but the personnel called upon to carry out the activities of the institution may, and indeed must, give some attention to this question. . . . The benefit or welfare of the member states may be set down as the general objective of international administration; from the texts of scores or hundreds of international instruments it is abundantly clear that this is the object of international administration rather than anything more abstract or altruistic. . . . International administration also may and does serve both the spiritual (in the broadest sense of the term) and the material welfare of its beneficiaries. It deals with practical economic interests but also with science and art; the former appeared somewhat earlier in the history of this activity and the impression

> is commonly held that such subjects constitute the whole of the field but that is far from the case . . . international administration ranges over the whole gamut of human life from astronomy to zoology; and touches upon some seventy or eighty other miscellaneous items in between. In any such analysis of subject-matters much overlapping and duplication will be observable. One of the most striking differences among international organizations is that between the organization with general jurisdiction (as to subject matter) and the highly specialized agency. The occurrence of numerous methodological items (which could as easily be transferred to other groups) will also be noted, and the eternal problem of political and non-political subjects. A statistical and historical summary of these matters . . . would reveal that both the oldest and the most numerous agencies are to be found in the field of communications, the least numerous and newest in law and government—although again the two areas are not entirely discrete . . .
>
> The activities of the international agencies can be grouped under two broad headings, those performed chiefly within the agency itself and those performed on the outside (toward member states or others). Under each heading will be found numerous items which can again be grouped in one case under three rubrics, namely custodial work, secretarial work, and the management of persons and plant, and, in the second, under informational, advisory, and executive action, the last item including, along with the characteristic element of enforcement measures, a certain amount of judicial action (the taking of decisions) and even of legislative action (adoption of regulations). The internal activities are not wholly confined within the agency—correspondence is not, for example—and some of the external activities call for a good deal of internal work both in their preparation and their execution. It is further noticeable that the first group of procedures is more nearly ministerial or non-discretionary in character, the second somewhat broader in the matter of policy. All agencies have a great deal of the former type of work to do; only a few rise to the true executive level. . . . (Potter 1948, 132–142)

Most INGOs are structured along the same lines as the IGOs described by Potter. INGOs are governed by periodic assemblies and executive bodies such as councils, steering committees, or boards that meet more often and have administrative bodies with professional staff who manage the day-to-day operations. The only significant differences are that the membership of INGOs are not states and that INGOs are not established by intergovernmental agreement. Of course, INGOs during this period did not aspire to govern the world themselves. Their ambitions were more limited and respected the boundary that separates the private from the public.

By the time World War II erupted, international organizations had become firmly established in international affairs and progressively more structured. The procedures and functions were increasingly standardized and the roles to be played between and among public and private international organizations more defined. So when the international order was destroyed by the second world war, international organizations had developed enough to survive and subsequently thrive.

Stage Two—Maturation Phase

World War II brought the curtain down on the "old" international order and in its wake the curtain was raised on a "New World Order." The war devastated the international economy; spurred incredible technological innovations in transportation (for example, aircraft and missiles), communications (radar and wireless radio), and energy (atomic energy); and weakened the hold of European states over their far-flung colonial empires. The immediate postwar era was a time of international reconstruction and, in many ways, a renewed opportunity to correct the shortcomings of the old international order. It was also abundantly clear that the great powers of a global international community were no longer solely European states, as evidenced by China's inclusion among the big powers and by the United States's having taken over the preeminent power position.

However, the new world order of 1945 did not rid the world of power politics or great power competition. The cooperation among the Allies quickly dissolved after the war was over, which ultimately turned into the Cold War between the Soviet Union and its satellite communist states in the East and the United States and its Western European allies in the West. The East-West conflict was both an ideological rivalry and a strategic contest of military might. It also created competing international political and economic systems which managed to coexist. The Cold War was an undercurrent that affected all international activities, including the development of international organizations, throughout the second half of the twentieth century.

Structuring a "Permanent" Peace. According to Charles Kegley and Gregory Raymond, planning for a postwar peace began almost from the beginning of the war through a series of conferences among the "Big Powers" (this group included initially the United States, Great Britain, and the USSR; later China and France were added) ultimately producing a blueprint for a new world political and economic order (see Table 5.2). The amazing thing about this process is not so much that the leaders of the Allies worked out the fundamental principles and doctrines for peace while the war was raging, but rather that they had decided from the beginning that an international organization was necessary to manage the postwar international order. One would think that the experience with the League of Nations would have put off Franklin D. Roosevelt, Winston Churchill, Joseph Stalin, Charles DeGaulle, and Chiang Kai-shek on such an approach. But, it appears that these men were sufficiently convinced that the League and other international organizations were not the reason for the war and that the best hope for a *permanent* peace was to formalize their wartime cooperation in a new international organization. (This was true even though the League was unable to effectively respond to challenges to the peace—the 1931 Japanese invasion of Manchuria, Italy's invasion of Ethiopia in 1935, or Germany's union with Austria and annexation of part of Czechoslovakia in 1938—that led to World War II.)

This was the main premise for the establishment of a new and improved collective security organization—the United Nations—to replace the League of Nations. It was widely believed that the shortcomings of the League were not all of its own making and that there was much to be commended to its basic design. "The League of Nations provided both positive examples that its successor organization, the UN, chose to emulate (such as a truly international secretariat, the potential utility of convening conferences on pressing issues where the existing international institutional machinery was found wanting, and the value of having a world court that could reach decisions in contentious cases and give advisory opinions) and negative examples—that is, procedural innovations that did not work all that well and from which the UN's founders could learn. Included in the latter are such things as (1) the necessity to have all great powers as members, even if that meant deviating from the League of Nations's egalitarian principles of unanimity in decision making and making it difficult for countries to leave the organization on their own volition;

TABLE 5.2 Postwar Planning During the War: Declarations and Doctrines

Date(s)	*Conference/Declaration*	*Key Doctrinal Principle(s)*
January 14–24, 1943	Casablanca Conference (French Morocco)	Roosevelt and Churchill issue declaration pledging that the war would end only with the unconditional surrender of the Axis states
October 1943	Moscow Foreign Ministers Conference (Four Power Declaration)	Allied unity and establishment of a global organization to maintain peace and security
November 28–December 1, 1943	Tehran Conference	Allied unity to preserve order, with U.S. air and naval support for Soviet and British soldiers for peace keeping in postwar Europe
July 1–22, 1944	Bretton Woods system (United Nations Monetary and Financial Conference)	Rules and institutions created near the end of World War II to govern international economic relations in the postwar world capitalist economy under U.S. leadership; this conference resulted in the creation of the International Monetary Fund (IMF) and the International Bank for Reconstruction and Development
August–September 1944	Big Four (including China) Conference at Dumbarton Oaks (Washington, D.C.)	Draft for negotiations to create the United Nations
September 1944	Quebec Conference	Roosevelt and Churchill agree on goal of reducing Germany to an agricultural economy, without any "war-making industries"
February 4–11, 1945	Yalta Conference (Crimea, Soviet Union)	Confirmed policy of unconditional surrender and complete demilitarization of Germany, division of Germany into four zones of occupation (U.S., British, French, Soviet) under unified control commission in Berlin, war crimes trials of Nazis, and study of reparation question. Secret agreements also accepted veto system for voting in future UN Security Council and for the Soviet Union to enter the war against Japan within three months of Germany's surrender (with

(continues)

		territorial concessions pledged to the Soviet Union for its participation)
April 25–June 1945	San Francisco Conference	Design of United Nations Charter; Big Four responsibility for preserving postwar order, with China's inclusion; dismemberment and disarmament of Germany, which would be de-Nazified through occupation
July 17–August 2, 1945	Potsdam Conference/ Potsdam Declaration of July 26	Four powers discuss new procedures for disarming Germany and preventing its resurgence as a military power; all former German territory east of the Oder and Neisse Rivers transferred to Polish and Soviet administration; the level of possible reparation payments and policies were considered, and a Council of Foreign Ministers was created to evaluate a peace settlement, as well as the Allied Control Council to administer it. In addition, Japan was given the ultimatum of choosing between unconditional surrender or total destruction, and the Soviet Union promised to enter the Pacific War once Germany was subjugated

Source: Charles W. Kegley, Jr. and Gregory A. Raymond, *How Nations Make Peace*, 1st Edition (New York: Wadsworth Publishers, 1999), 176–177. Copyright © 1999. Reprinted with permission of Wadsworth, a division of Thomson Learning: www.thomsonrights.com. Fax: 800–730–2215.

(2) the need to give the secretary-general greater constitutional powers; (3) the need to have a more readily accessible military force of its own; and (4) the need to have provisions to encourage independence in former colonial possessions (the consequences of which were a UN trusteeship system that was much more proactive than had been the League's mandate system)." (Schechter 1998, 11)

The structural refinements that were built into the UN Charter were rather modest and in practice still inadequate for the organization to function effectively. The UN's collective security machinery was often bypassed by the big powers, especially the United States and the USSR, and certain institutional provisions, like the Military Staff Committee of the Security Council, were never made operational. The lack of "organic connection" between and among international organizations was only partially addressed in the UN Charter. Chapters VIII–X establish the formal relationship between the United Nations and "Regional Arrangements" and "Specialized Agencies". On paper, these provisions created a system of international organizations, but in practice the system rarely functioned as such. Even though the practice often did not match the design, it would be wrong to conclude that the structure of the UN system was unsound. In fact, the UN structure has proven remarkably adaptable to the polarized international political environment because of the innovative leadership of the UN's secretariat, who were able to develop creative roles for the United Nations (for example, peacekeeping) in the Cold War and to shift the organization's resources and activities toward economic and social development in response to the new majority of developing countries in the UN's membership.

As the World War II alliance broke up into two camps, other international organizations were created to manage the military and political affairs of the two camps. The institutionalization of alliances in formal organizations was an innovation on the historical practice of creating military alliances to enhance security. The North Atlantic Treaty Organization (NATO) was the first, established in 1949 by twelve states (the United States, Canada, Belgium, Denmark, France, Iceland, Italy, Luxembourg, the Netherlands, Norway, Portugal, and the United Kingdom). NATO was set up to be a deterrent to Soviet expansionism and to demonstrate that the United States had permanent interests in the political future of Europe. When West Germany was permitted to join NATO a few years later, the Soviet Union established a similar organization—the Warsaw Treaty Organization—in 1955 with Albania, Bulgaria, Czechoslovakia, the Democratic Republic of Germany (East Germany), Hungary, Poland, and Romania. These two organizations were the most prominent throughout the Cold War, though the United States tried to organize similar alliances in other regions with less success (for example, the South East Asian Treaty Organization, or SEATO). The structure of NATO and the Warsaw pact, as well as other regional organizations like the Organization of American States (OAS), the Council of Europe, the Organization of African Unity (OAU), and the Association of South East Asian Nations (ASEAN), is similar to most international governmental organizations. All have "a general assembly (e.g., the NATO Assembly) in which all states enjoy voting power, and a smaller council (such as the OAS Permanent Council or the OAU's Commission of Mediation, Conciliation, and Arbitration) designed to act on behalf of the whole membership on important or urgent security matters, as well as secretariats to service the organization's activities."(Karns and Mingst 1991, 269). Regional security organizations added a second layer of international governmental organizations and often substituted for the inoperative collective security mechanisms of the UN Security Council.

The political landscape of the postwar international order was to become more complex when the colonial empires began to dissolve. Beginning in the mid-1950s, new nation states were born in Africa and Asia at a dizzying pace. In the span of less than twenty years, the international community added nearly ninety sovereign states to its ranks. The nation-state system had finally become global. As to be expected, decolonization also contributed to the creation of new international organizations. According to one study, decolonization opened up "opportunities for creating limited-membership IGOs . . . Organizations could be created both among new states and among new and old states. International bodies could make possible the continuation and extension of activities that were organized within the framework of a single sovereignty in the colonial era." The study points out that the limited-membership organizations established during the postwar period reflect three groupings of states based on broad political and economic alignments: "those that are members of the Organization of Economic Cooperation and Development (OECD), those that are members of the Warsaw Treaty Organization (WTO), and those that do not belong to either of these organizations, a group for this reason is called 'Other.' . . . The members of the OECD are those that are customarily referred to as the 'West,' and the members of WTO are those that are usually referred to as the 'Soviet bloc' or group. The residual category of 'Other' includes those states that are referred to as the Third World." (Jacobson, Reisinger, and Mathers 1986, 62) (See Map 5.4.)

Of the 563 IGOs for which membership information is available, 103 were comprised exclusively of states that were members of OECD; 28 ex-

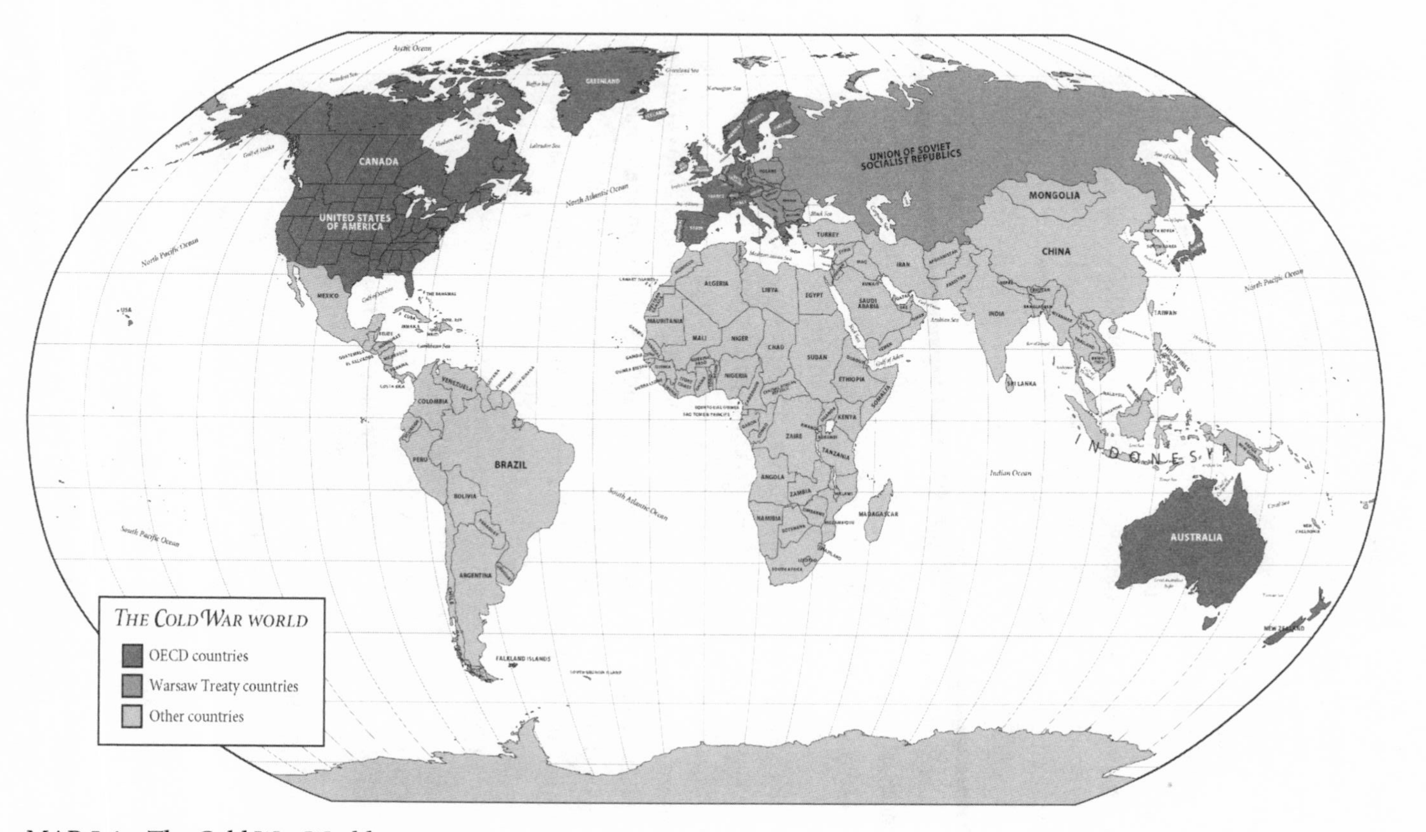

MAP 5.4 The Cold War World

> clusively of states that were members of WTO; and 178 exclusively of other states. Most of the Western IGOs were the basic agencies and offshoots of: the OECD, the North Atlantic Treaty Organization, the European communities, and the Nordic Council. Beyond the Warsaw Treaty Organization itself, the 28 Soviet-group IGOs were primarily derivatives of the Council for Mutual Economic Assistance (CMEA). CMEA includes three non-European states, Cuba, Mongolia, and Vietnam, that for most purposes of this analysis are included in the 'Other' category. In 1981 there were 38 IGOs comprised exclusively of CMEA members; these included the 28 comprised exclusively of WTO members.
>
> The IGOs that were comprised exclusively of states in the category 'Other' were less likely to be derivatives of other organizations than those comprised exclusively of OECD and WTO states. . . . The economically more advanced Western and Soviet-group states have been refining their existing relationships through establishing additional organizations, albeit often subsidiary ones, while Third World states have been establishing relatively more new relationships and consequently more new primary organizations. (Jacobson, Reisinger, and Mathers 1986, 63)

An important trend in the development of international organizations during the maturation phase was greater differentiation in their mandates. This trend towards specialization in political institutions started with security organizations in the 1940s and 1950s—13.5 percent of the total IGOs established during this time had security mandates. Starting in the 1960s, a growing number of international organizations were created with economic and social mandates (over 90 percent) while only 3.1 percent were established in the security field, indicating that the post–World War II political order had become relatively stable by this time (see Table 5.3).

Organizing International Economic Relations. State intervention in economic and social affairs on the national level had become near total after World War II. The dividing line between public and private was almost erased by the war, which opened the door to the realization of the welfare state. Martin van Creveld argues that:

> the move toward the welfare state started during the war itself. Both Churchill and Roosevelt were well aware that the efforts made by workers

TABLE 5.3 Distribution by Function of IGOs Comprised Exclusively of Members of Particular Political-Economic Groups Established from 1960 through 1981 (in percentages)

		Group(a)	
Function	*OECD*	*WTO*	*Other*
General	4.5	0	3.8
Economic	47.0	96.0	73.7
Social	47.0	4.0	18.8
Security	1.5	0	3.8
	100.0	100.0	100.1
No. of cases	66	25	133

Chi Square = 29.28
Cramer's Phi = .26
Sig. = .00

Note: (a) OECD = Organization for Economic Cooperation; WTO = Warsaw Treaty Organization.

Source: *The Politics of Global Governance: International Organizations in an Interdependent World*, edited by Paul F. Diehl (Boulder, CO: Lynne Rienner, 1997), p. 64. Copyright © 1997 by Lynne Rienner Publishers. Reprinted by permission of the publisher.

on behalf of their state would have to be compensated; when they signed the "Atlantic Charter" of early 1942, they officially declared "freedom from want" to be one of the Allies' principle objectives. To bring it about, contemporaries pointed to the enormous increase in production which had been brought about by mobilization and the harnessing of all resources to the military effort. It was suggested that, if only a small fraction of those resources could be retained in the hands of the state and used for public purposes, it should be possible to solve or at least alleviate some of the most pressing social problems, such as poverty, unemployment (both of them very conspicuous during the years of the Great Depression), inadequate health care, and insufficient access to secondary and tertiary education as a way toward a better life. . . . Broadly speaking, two series of steps were necessary to carry out this program. On the one hand, it was a question of concentrating much greater resources in the hands of the state—if not to the extent that this had been done during the war itself, than at any rate in comparison with the years before 1939. On the other, it was a question of devising new mechanisms for distrib-

> uting those resources to those groups and those people who appeared to need them most. Both sides of the problem had this in common that, if they were to be tackled and solved, the number of those working for the state would have to be greatly increased with all that this entailed for career opportunities, promotions, and sheer power over society as a whole. From the beginning, in other words, the proposed reforms commanded a constituency in the form of the state bureaucracy and all its manifold organs—one which, over the next three decades, would prove capable of pressing its demands for greater state intervention in virtually all fields of life almost independently of the electorate's wishes. (van Creveld 1999, 354–355)

As state power and control over economic and social activities of society gained momentum during and after World War II, the same could be observed on the international level. The plans of a postwar international economic order, according to Harold Jacobson, reflected an "expanded vision" of states' goals in economic and social affairs which included promoting economic growth, income stability through full employment, and greater equity through redistribution of wealth. In addition, it had become conventional wisdom that economic conditions were linked to national and international security. (Jacobson 1979, 231–234) Therefore, the blueprint for a new international economic order that was crafted during the war at the Bretton Woods Conference in 1944 mirrored the expanding role of the state in the economy. The conference created the International Monetary Fund (IMF) and the International Bank for Reconstruction and Development (the World Bank) which, along with a proposed international agency in the area of commercial policy, were the cornerstones of what was conceived as a global free-market economy.

> IMF's central purpose is to contribute to the expansion and growth of international trade by promoting exchange liberalization; that is, currencies that would be freely convertible and would have relatively stable values. In the original conception, states were to set the exchange rate of their currencies in consultation with IMF and not change the rate without engaging in prescribed discussions with the organization. In turn, IMF was assigned an amount of money that it could lend to member states so that they could engage in open-market operations to support the value of

their currencies. IMF can be seen as an international agency created to assist governments that found themselves in temporary balance-of-payments difficulties, and it was mandated to work toward the elimination of exchange restrictions and toward making currencies freely convertible. It was an attempt to avoid both the domestic costs of the gold standard and the uncertainties of a system of freely fluctuating exchange rates. Its function was to allow countries having temporary deficits on their accounts a period of time to attempt to correct these deficits—to see whether fundamental adjustments were truly necessary. IMF functioned according to the original conception until 1971. Since then, although IMF's objective has continued to be to promote exchange liberalization, its role with respect to exchange rates has been altered. . . .

The International Bank for Reconstruction and Development (IBRD), which was also created at Bretton Woods, was to deal with longer-term issues, as its name implies. Membership in IMF was a condition of membership in IBRD, or the World Bank as it is often called. Paragraph iii of Article I of IBRD's Articles of Agreement summarizes the bank's purposes:

"To promote the long-range balanced growth of international trade and the maintenance of equilibrium in balance of payments by encouraging international investment for the development of the productive resources of members, thereby assisting in raising productivity, the standard of living and conditions of labor in their territories."

The events of the 1930s, the currency devaluations and the defaulting on loans, had undermined the confidence of international investors, yet international investment was assumed to be essential to the long-term growth of the world economy. IBRD was assigned funds that it could use for loans to member states and, more importantly, to guarantee loans that it would arrange for member states through the usual investment channels, that is, through private capital markets.

The third specialized agency envisaged in the original scheme, that dealing with commercial policy, was stillborn. But a less elaborate and less powerful and extensive organization, the General Agreement on Tariffs and Trade (GATT), emerged from the effort to create an international trade organization. The General Agreement was originally envisaged primarily as a code of conduct for commercial policy. It commits contracting parties to maintain most-favored-nation treatment toward one another; that is, to grant all contracting parties the most favorable

> treatment extended to any country with respect to tariffs and other obstacles of trade. Using this basic obligation as the framework, GATT came to sponsor several negotiations in which bilateral bargains about mutual reductions in tariffs were extended to all contracting parties. Some exceptions to most most-favored-nation treatment are permitted under the General Agreement, but in principle these must be justified before the contracting parties. In the event of violations of the code, the General Agreement permits affected contracting parties to engage in retaliation by imposing higher tariffs or other sanctions against the violator. (Jacobson 1979, 235–236)

These international organizations were attached loosely to the United Nations as part of its decentralized system of autonomous specialized agencies (for example, the successors or continuation of the international public unions like the ITU, UPU, ILO, World Meteorological Organization, International Maritime Consultative Organization, and World Intellectual Property Organization, and new IGOs such as the Food and Agricultural Organization, United Nations Educational, Scientific, and Cultural Organization, World Health Organization, International Civil Aviation Organization, and the International Atomic Energy Agency). These organizations' central purpose was to facilitate international communications, transportation, and trade by minimizing obstacles to the fullest use of new technologies in these fields. Furthermore, they represented the intergovernmental infrastructure of international trade.

Regional Economic Structures. However, the Cold War was to divide the global economy into competing international economic systems—a liberal multilateral market system led by the United States and a system centered on the Soviet Union and its economy based on central planning. As pointed out above the majority of new limited-membership international organizations were established to manage these two economic systems. In the West, the OECD (the successor of the 1948 Organization for European Economic Cooperation which was established to implement U.S. Marshall Plan assistance for reconstruction of Europe) became the framework for cooperation among the industrialized states with market economies. In 1949, the communist states of Eastern Europe formed their own organization, the CMEA or Comecon, which organized the international economic cooperation of states with centrally planned economies. It should be noted that these two economic systems were considered mutually exclusive and rarely did they interact except through modest levels of trade and within the context of the United Nations system. This situation did not change fundamentally until the late 1980s when the Soviet Union made an attempt to integrate into the international market economy of the West through Mikhail Gorbachev's *perestroika* and *glasnost* policies. Of course, Gorbachev's policies failed and the USSR broke apart, taking with it into history the CMEA, the Warsaw Treaty Organization, and the other economic institutions (such as the International Bank for Economic Cooperation (IBEC) and the International Investment Bank (IIB)) created for the Soviet bloc.

Another important development in the postwar period was the emergence of another category of international organizations—blocs and supranational institutions. Martin van Creveld points out:

> If, on the one hand, modern technology has done much to encourage the founding of international organizations that do not have territory and are not states, on the other it has forced and still is forcing states to join together into blocks whose territory is larger than that of individual members. To date, the best-known and most successful of these blocks is the European Union, which provides a tangible expression of the fact that the economic relationships generated by modern technology are on too large a scale to be dealt with by individual countries. Originally the European Common Market had only six members and constituted no more than a free trade zone for coal and steel. Later the agreements were extended to other products as well, and common tariffs *vis-à-vis* the rest of the world were established . . . .
>
> From the start the EEC represented more than a mere temporary arrangement between sovereign states. Like the other type of international organization just discussed, it was intended to be permanent. Like them, it has its own legal persona and institutions. Over the years it has developed its own legislature (the European Parliament, located in Strasbourg), its own high court, and its own executive. All three, but the last named one in particular, still fall far short of what one would expect from a unified sovereign state. Yet since 1963, when Community law was declared to be directly binding on the member states, all three have cer-

tainly made their influence felt in the daily lives of people in all the member countries . . . .

[However], development toward a single European superstate is hampered by the existence of other international organizations, whether smaller ones, such as the Nordic Council, or larger ones such as the North Atlantic Treaty Organization. Having established no fewer than 112 Nordic institutions, and counting 450 "Nordocrats" (1985), the Nordic Council forms an organization inside an organization. In practice it has put few obstacles in front of European integration; but in principle its continued existence (and that of similar groupings among other countries) within the context of a closer European Union is no more acceptable than, say, a formal alliance between Virginia, North and South Carolina, and Georgia would be in the United States. . . . one might perhaps conclude that the obstacles which individual states such as Britain put in front of European unity are significant enough. However, in the long run even greater opposition is likely to come not from states but from other international organizations whose membership and purposes do not overlap.

Whatever the future of the European Community, its economic success has encouraged states in other parts of the world to create similar organizations. To date, none of them has progressed nearly as far as their model in creating common institutions and imposing a common law. On the other hand, multilateral arrangements aimed at reducing obstacles to trade, eliminating tariffs, achieving integration (as, for example, between the US and Canadian electricity grids and telephone networks), setting up common economic front *vis-à-vis* the rest of the world, and dealing with ecological problems now number in the dozens and may be found in every continent. To list some of the most important ones only, 1959 saw the establishment of EFTA (European Free Trade Association) all of whose members later joined the European Union. In 1960 this was followed by LAFTA (the Latin American Free Trade Association, which incorporates Mexico and all Latin American countries except Guyana) as well as CACM (the Central American Common Market). UDEAC (Union douanière et économique de l'Afrique centrale, with Cameroon, the Central African Republic, Congo, and Gabon as its members) was founded in 1966, ASEAN (Association of South East Asian Nations, made up of Indonesia, Malaysia, the Philippines, Thailand, and Singapore) in the next year. An Andean Common Market (ACM), with Bolivia, Chile, Colombia, Ecuador, Peru and Venezuela as its members, has existed since 1969 and was later followed by MERCOSUR which includes Brazil, Bolivia, Paraguay, Uruguay, Argentina, and Chile. In 1975, the Economic Community of West African States (ECOWAS) was founded by Benin, Gambia, Ghana, Guinea, Guinea-Bissau, Ivory Coast, Liberia, Mali, Mauritania, Niger, Nigeria, Senegal, Sierra Leone, Togo, and Upper Volta. In 1994 the ratification of the North American Free Trade Agreement (NAFTA) by the United States, Canada, and Mexico showed that not even the largest and most productive economy in history can exist in isolation. (van Creveld 1999, 385–388)

The North-South Divide. Decolonization created a second dimension in international economic relations. "The consequences of tripling the number of independent states in the system have been manifold: the agendas of international organizations became much more heavily tilted toward issues of economic development and relations between the developed countries of the industrial North and the less developed countries (LDCs) of the South. The ideological leanings of the LDCs toward a heavy governmental role in economic development and redistribution of wealth shaped programs and activities of many IGOs. Indeed, in 1974 these states championed a new international economic order (NIEO), marshalling support in the UN General Assembly for the Declaration on the Establishment of a New International Economic Order and the Charter of Economic Rights and of States Duties. The developing countries argued that the existing international economic order was structured to their disadvantage by weighted voting systems in institutions such as the World Bank and International Monetary Fund and by adverse terms of trade. The proposed norms and principles were reiterated in numerous meetings and resolutions. The NIEO dominated and polarized debate in a number of forums during the 1970s, at times making agreement on both economic and security issues impossible to achieve." (Karns and Mingst 1991, 275–276) Clearly, the North-South conflict arose out of the economic asymmetry between the industrialized countries in Europe and North America and the newly independent developing countries in Africa and Asia and focused on areas of disagreement about how the multilateral economic system should be managed. (Since the "Soviet bloc" countries had established a separate international economic system among themselves, they were not significant players in this conflict except perhaps as provocateurs fueling the conflict or as a possible alternative economic model for the newly independent states to adopt.)

This infusion of LDCs into the system also gave impetus to creation of additional international organizations dedicated to closing the gap between the rich and poor countries of the international community. In the 1960s, the United Nations Conference on Trade and Development (1964), the United Nations Development Program (1965), and the United Nations Industrial Development Organization (1966) were formed to improve trading conditions, to accelerate economic growth through transfer of technical knowledge and stimulating capital investment, and to mobilize greater resources for industrialization of LDCs. In addition, a number of regional development banks were established—the European Investment Bank (an EEC institution), the International Bank for Economic Cooperation and the International Investment Bank (for CMEA countries), the Inter-American Development Bank, the African Development Bank, the Asian Development Bank, the Central American Bank for Economic Integration, the West African Development Bank, the Caribbean Development Bank, and the Andean Development Corporation—to promote economic development in poor areas of their respective regions. (Jacobson 1979, 240)

The population of international governmental organizations by the 1990s had grown considerably, with economic and technical bodies being the largest contingent. The UIA had a count of 118 IGOs in 1954, which grew to 1,820 organizations by 2000 (see Table 5.4). Also, one can see that the system had become quite stratified by 1981—the bottom layer consisted of the 171 LDCs or the Third World, in the middle were the nine centrally planned economies of the communist countries or the Second World, and the top layer was made up of the twenty-four industrialized countries or the First World. The distribution of IGOs also mirrored the economic stratification of the international community in that there is an inverse proportional concentration or density of organizations for each strata. The greatest density of IGOs is among the top strata, with more than four IGOs for each state, followed by the middle layer with more than three IGOs for each state. At the bottom is the Third World with only slightly more than one IGO for each state (Jacobson et al. 1986, 63).

In the 1980s and 1990s, this picture began to change. First, some countries in Latin America and Asia were able to rise out of the bottom layer and were dubbed Newly Industrialized Countries (NICs), creating a second tier to the top layer. Second, the breakup of the Soviet Union in 1992 increased the number of countries in the middle stratum from nine to over twenty and changed the economic character of this level from centrally planned economies to "economies in transition" towards liberal market economies. However, several of these countries actually moved into the bottom layer. Finally, the end of the Cold War altered the fundamental division of the world economy from competing political-economic systems (free-market system versus centrally planned system) to the level of economic development of countries within basically the same economic system. Now that there is a single economic system for the planet, the institutions of the international economic order are more compatible with each other and have become more instrumental to the management of the global economy.

International Business Organizations. Private profit-making international organizations—Multinational and Transnational Corporations—have become another prominent element to the institutional structure of the international economy since 1945. Different forms of international cooperation among private commercial enterprises have emerged since the Industrial Revolution. In the twentieth century two forms are of significance to the institutional infrastructure of world economy. The first form was the cartel. Cartels were most prevalent in the years between the world wars. According to Tony Porter, "In the period between World Wars I and II, firms joined international private formalized collaborative arrangements of an unprecedented number and complexity. In industry after industry cartels were set up that were governed by highly specific market-sharing commitments and were often consolidated by license sharing, formal international organization, joint production facilities, and mechanisms for monitoring and enforcing compliance. Estimates placed the proportion of goods sold under cartel control in 1939 in the United States—hardly the center of cartel activity—at 87 percent for mineral products, 60 percent for agricultural products, and 42 percent for manufactured products. In many industries virtually all international trade was controlled by cartels." (Porter 1999, 266) The actual numbers of interna-

TABLE 5.4 International Governmental Organizations by Year, 1954–2000

Year	*# of IGOs*
1954	118
1966	199
1976	252
1981	1039
1988	1702
1992	1609
2000	1820

Source: Appendix 3: Table 2, Union of International Associations, *Yearbook of International Organizations*, Vol. 3: Subject Volume, 37th Edition, p. 1661.

tional cartels that had been formed during this period is hard to pinpoint, though estimates of several hundred are common (see White 1951).

After World War II, international cartels came under attack for their anti-competitive affects on markets and monopolistic tendencies in international trade. A successful drive by the United States to break up cartels in the early postwar period transferred the management of industries to an American form of industrial organization—namely, the large hierarchical structure of U.S. corporations that are characteristic of today's Multinational Corporations (MNCs) and Transnational Corporations (TNCs). These organizations, now numbering in the thousands, are largely concentrated in the advanced industrial countries in North America and Western Europe, but have a global reach through tens of thousands of subsidiaries and associates. "The number of firms that have become transnational has risen exponentially over the past three decades. In the case of 15 developed countries, that number increased from 7,000 at the end of the 1960s to some 40,000 in the second half of the 1990s. The number of parent firms worldwide is now in the range of 60,000. These parent firms form a diverse universe that spans all countries and industries, and include a large and growing number of small and medium-sized enterprises. More and more TNCs hail from countries that have only recently begun to undertake international production—witness the growth of TNCs from some developing countries and economies in transition." (UNCTAD 2000, 8)

The growing density of TNCs and the complex networks of private arrangements for inter-firm cooperation/collaboration, such as joint ventures and strategic partnerships or alliances, that have been established in the last ten to twenty years demonstrate that an impressive international structure of private organizations for the global economy is present. The significance of these private international organizations to the international system's institutionalization and organizational development will be explored more in the next chapter.

Diversification of International Nongovernmental Organizations

The steep rise in establishing international governmental organizations after World War II also occurred among international nongovernmental organizations (INGOs). In the postwar period, the number of INGOs in the world grew over tenfold, from 1,008 in 1954 to over 15,000 in 2000 (see Table 5.5). A study of INGOs in 1997 found that:

> Not-for-profit international organizing grew rapidly in the latter part of the nineteenth century, with about 10 new organizations emerging each year during the 1890s. The population burgeoned after the turn of the century, reaching a peak of 51 foundings in 1910. The severe collapse after that point led to a low of four foundings in 1915. Swift recovery after World War I yielded a period of fairly steady growth followed by some decline during the 1930s that preceded another steep fall going into World War II.
>
> Following the war, international organizing exploded. By 1947 over 90 organizations a year were being founded, a pace that was maintained and even surpassed through the 1960s. The pattern for dissolved INGOs is similar, indicating a generally steady proportion of INGOs that eventually dissolved, but revealing peaks of fragility among organizations founded just before each of the wars.
>
> INGOs foundings and dissolutions thus match the general "state of the world" rather well, rising in periods of expansion and declining rapidly in times of crisis, with declines beginning shortly before the outbreaks of the world wars. (Boli and Thomas 1997, 263)

The rapid growth of INGOs since World War II is attributable to the dramatic increase in the needs of post-war societies. The INGOs established before the war were well situated to address the social and economic conditions in Europe and the western hemisphere. There were clusters of organizations for specific subject matters—humanitarian and relief organizations, international labor and business organizations, international professional and scientific organizations—which reflected the mainstream

TABLE 5.5 International Nongovernmental Organizations by Year, 1954–2000

Year	*# of INGOs*
1954	1008
1966	2830
1976	5155
1981	9396
1988	16325
1992	12457
2000	17364

Source: Appendix 3: Table 2, UIA (2000) *Yearbook of International Organizations*, Vol. 3: Subject Volume, 37th Edition, p. 1661.

transnational activities during the start-up phase. But, conflicts during the postwar years were dominated by wars of liberation and anti-colonial insurgencies in Africa and Asia, which caused massive movements of refugees into neighboring countries that had neither the infrastructure nor the resources to accommodate such large influxes of poor people. These humanitarian crises were markedly different from those that earlier characterized European emergencies. As decolonization brought the newly independent states of Africa and Asia into the international community during the 1960s and 1970s, very severe socioeconomic problems were revealed; circumstances that are now clearly (and perhaps perpetually) associated with the Third World—namely, social and economic underdevelopment, mass illiteracy, overpopulation, and grinding poverty—which required different operational strategies and approaches to overcome.

The urgent nature of these longer-term problems spurred the creation of a new cluster of private organizations with a specialization in economic and social development. This cluster focuses on one or more specific development areas—agricultural, social, medical, educational, and so on. In addition to implementing development projects throughout the developing world, development organizations have become deeply involved in the policy-formation process, both as critics of international agencies and as advocates for alternative development policies. Many of the development organizations, like International Planned Parenthood Federation, the World Council of Churches, Community Aid Abroad, CARE International, and Coopération internationale pour le développement et la solidarité, complement the humanitarian relief groups. Increasingly the operational aspects of development and humanitarian assistance organizations have blended to constitute today's extensive international network of private voluntary organizations, which now number in the tens of thousands.

> Relief NGOs frequently specialise in one or more of the five activities that are commonly understood to compose the relief discipline: food distribution, shelter, water, sanitation and medical care. To this may be added the rehabilitation efforts to bring a society traumatised by a complex emergency to minimum self-sufficiency: animal husbandry, agriculture and primary health care. Perhaps half of these NGOs perform relief work exclusively, whereas the other half work in both relief and development. The larger development NGOs (CARE, Catholic Relief Services, World Vision, Save the Children, and Oxfam/UK) have the added advantage in many emergencies of having had development programmes and staff to run them in the countries before the onset of the emergency. This advantage gives them a familiarity with the culture, ethnic groups and development programmes of the country as well as with indigenous staff.
>
> Since the Ethiopian famine of 1985—a watershed event for most of the 10 major NGOs that work in relief—a quiet revolution has taken place in doctrine and practice between relief and development. Traditional relief efforts were commodity-driven and logistically-based, with little programmatic, economic or developmental thought given to how the relief effort might be more than simply pushing down death rates and saving lives. Most NGOs, as a matter of policy, will now try to integrate into their relief work developmental components particularly focused in agriculture, microenterprise, primary health care, reforestation and road construction. This is done through food or cash for which recipients are assigned a specific project that community leaders have determined is of longer-term importance in the area. Much more effort now is spent on examining the economics of what is happening in famine, with the major food NGOs conducting household, food price and market surveys as a regular part of their relief interventions. A recent study of the USAID/OFDA [US Agency for International Development/Office of Foreign Disaster Assistance] effort in the Somalia emergency showed that 50% of its relief grants to NGOs contained developmental interventions. (Natsios 1996, 69)

During the last quarter of the twentieth century, a gradual convergence of purpose and action has occurred among three clusters of international nongovernmental organizations—human rights organizations, environmental organizations, and development and humanitarian organizations. Human rights groups, like Amnesty International and Human Rights Watch, often collaborate with development and humanitarian organizations such as Save the Children or ICRC in pressuring governments and intergovernmental organizations to give greater legal protection to vulnerable groups (for example, minorities, children, women, refugees) and victims of torture, genocide, political persecution, and religious intolerance. Operationally, the two communities are quite distinct in that human rights organizations work on developing or improving legal and judicial machinery on the national and international levels.

The other cluster of INGOs to emerge as a major force in international relations is environmental groups. These organizations started to gather momentum in the 1970s when environmental problems were first politicized internationally at the UN's Conference on the Human Environment in 1972. The environmental organizations fall into two basic groupings—those that are structured and operate as traditional international entities (for example, federations of national organizations that work through national and international governmental structures) and those that are protest or activist global movements. The best known of the traditional group include International Union for Conservation of Nature and Natural Resources—World Conservation Union, World Wide Fund for Nature (WWF), and the World Resources Institute. The best known of the latter are Friends of the Earth, Greenpeace, and the Rainforest Action Network. After the Stockholm Conference in 1972, the number of organizations dealing with a wide range of environmental issues (for example, deforestation, global warming, climate change, air and water pollution, and protection of endangered species) expanded at an incredible pace and were to dominate the international NGO scene. Environmentalists also found common cause with the other clusters as the notion of humanitarianism became multifaceted and complex in the 1980s.

As the constellation of international nongovernmental organizations grew more dense and their respective capabilities improved, the rough division of labor between private and intergovernmental organizations that had developed (mainly a contractual relationship with the private organizations in a subordinate role to the inter-governmental agency) began to change. Most notably, the deference given to national and international authorities by private organizations had weakened or was totally disregarded. Many INGOs, particularly those established in the 1960s and 1970s, were simply no longer willing to countenance governmental or intergovernmental foot-dragging on urgent problems or to be closed out of the decisionmaking processes. For many, experiences in the field convinced them that project work was only mitigating symptoms of problems, that getting at the root causes required systemic change, and that to get systemic change they needed "to speak truth to power." The extreme forms of this shift to advocacy are the theatrical spectacles sometimes put on by Greenpeace and Médecins sans Frontières and the direct action campaigns of the Rainforest Action Network.

The turning point in the relationship between public and private came about in the 1990s when a growing number of failed states in Africa, the Balkans, the Middle East, and the former Soviet Union created very complex emergencies almost simultaneously, stretching the capacity and resources of the international community to respond. It was quite clear that interventions in complex humanitarian emergencies could not be successfully undertaken by the United Nations alone, and the technical expertise and on-the-ground experience of the private relief and development organizations were critical assets in meeting such a challenge. In addition, a series of world conferences that were convened by the United Nations during the 1990s on education (1990), children (1990), the environment and development (1992), human rights (1993), population and development (1994), social development and women and development (1995), and food and shelter (1996) have further altered the relationship between IGOs and INGOs. Jacques Fomerand points out:

> Until the 1970s, NGOs played a relatively modest role in UN conferences. Their presence has grown by leaps and bounds in recent years and has now been virtually institutionalized under various modalities. "Forums" are held concurrently with intergovernmental meetings or with highly colorful and visible related events that frequently overshadow the more restrained deliberations of government officials. As early as the 1975 Mexico City meeting, NGO forums became an integral part of UN conferences on women. Ten years later, the Nairobi conference concluded the first UN Decade for Women. More than 15,000 persons were in atten-

> dance on that occasion. Approximately 35,000 persons convened in Beijing during the first week of September 1995. Some 1,300 organizations were accredited at the social development summit. This figure does not include those that have consultation status with the ECOSOC and the Commission on Sustainable Development. . . . NGOs from Third World countries have become increasingly visible at UN conferences. Close to two-thirds of NGOs present at the social development summit came from developing countries. (Fomerand 1996, 123)

The mounting pressure for change and the reality of post–Cold War humanitarian crises did in the end produce some results that garnered for INGOs, particularly humanitarian and development organizations, more respect from governments and the secretariats of IGOs, as well as a seat at the conference table now and then. By the end of the twentieth century, it was safe to conclude that INGOs had succeeded in becoming partners with governments and intergovernmental organizations in managing the crises and more long-term social problems of the world.

However, there remains considerable differences within and between the three main clusters of INGOs. The fortunes for each cluster have seesawed over the years, improving as their issues or functions were high on the international agenda and declining when the world's attention waned or was distracted by something else. Sharp divisions and strong disagreements among INGOs are all too common, which make it difficult (if not impossible) for them to establish connective structures of greater permanence than the ad hoc coalitions and alliances that enable at least minimal levels of cooperation when interests, issues, or events converge.

The universe of international organizations is much more complex and diverse today than in the nineteenth century. Over the last fifty years, international organizations have matured in how they are structured and operate, particularly for the earliest organizations that have survived the various changes in the international system and remain in operation. The initial questions about the legitimacy and authority of international organizations have largely been answered, though they resurface now and then, especially in times of major upheaval in international affairs. Even more important is their growing capacity to be actors in international relations, most notably among transnational corporations and international nongovernmental organizations.

There is an obvious cumulative effect in the evolution of international organizations, as demonstrated by the growth of the population of international organizations and the widening scope of their activities. International organizations are heaped on top of each other as the architects of the international order see the need or the environment presents something new that existing international organizations do not address. This has led to considerable overlaps and redundancies within and among the burgeoning population of international organizations. It is common to see clashes and conflicts among two or more international organizations that are competing for attention, resources, position, and/or power. While competition may be expected among the tens of thousands of transnational corporations and brings about certain efficiencies and lower costs in production, this is not so for international governmental or nongovernmental organizations, which are supposed to foster cooperation to effectively solve international problems or achieve common goals.

Not all international organizations are created equal and the many asymmetries in authority, legitimacy, and capability among them reflect to the jumbled or hodgepodge manner in which they were established. There are some broad trends and general patterns in the development of international organizations as highlighted in this chapter. But, it should be obvious that there is a foundation upon which the international system has been built and a faint outline of a basic structure for an emergent global system. Whether or not today's international organizations are the key mechanisms for governance of the global system is difficult to determine with any certainty, but there is little doubt that they have become an essential ingredient to the transition of the world from the international to the global.

6

Architects of International Order: States, Markets, and Civil Society

The international order we have today is the result of the interactions between and among states, markets, and civil society as they respond to environmental circumstances (such as war, technological innovations, and/or social needs) throughout the twentieth century. The international order that emerged after World War II was for the most part designed by the United States and reflected the American view of order. According to G. John Ikenberry, "the order that was envisioned for postwar relations among the industrial democracies—and hopefully for the larger world system—was inspired by liberal sentiments, an economic theory of war, and lessons drawn from the 1930s. . . . a postwar order that would ensure 'economic peace' based on free trade and investment, rules and mechanisms of joint economic management, and political institutions to facilitate the peaceful settlement of disputes." (Ikenberry 1999, 24) The institutional framework that was designed by the major powers, particularly the United States, for the postwar international system sought to re-constitute a world order along familiar lines—to that of a modern democratic society. It gave states and their organizations the lead role in establishing and managing the order, but it also recognized that market actors (international business enterprises) in the private sector, and nongovernmental and private voluntary organizations in the civil society sector, had a role in building the organizational infrastructure of the international system.

As it is on the national level, the international system is roughly divided between public and private spheres. The primary actors in the public sphere are states, while non-state actors constitute the private sphere. International institutions, particularly international organizations, closely mirror the relationships found in nation-states between the public and private spheres. However, the international level lacks a single or central global authority with the power to govern the system in the same way as the state on the national level; it is this characteristic that defines the way organizations of the international system have been designed and structured. The historical circumstances that permitted international organizations to emerge as outlined in the last chapter indicate that international order is the work of three inter-related societal groupings—nation-states and their governments, markets and businesses, and civil society (nongovernmental organizations and private voluntary organizations). Each group played a role in the organizational design and structure of the international system. Through reacting to and interacting with each other, an array of international economic, political, and social institutions have been constructed—including formal ones like laws and regulations, explicit contracts, and market exchange rules, and informal institutions such as common values, norms, customs, ethics and ideology. All "set the constraints within which tangible and non-tangible resources are used" and, in the end, enable things to get done in the world. (United Nations 2000, 210)

The 1945 architecture of the international order differentiated three sectors—a public sector (states and their governments), a private sector (markets and businesses), and a civil society sector (nongovernmental and private voluntary organizations)—that closely mirrored the model of the modern welfare state. The architects of the new world order anticipated that each sector would develop the international institutions and organizations to structure the interactions among the actors within their respective parts of the international system, and that these institutions and organizations would reflect the organizing principles that were identified with each of these sectors on the national level. Therefore, international governmental organizations (IGOs) were designed and act on the same imperatives of public administration as do national governmental bodies; international commercial enterprises are subject to the same market principles as national firms; and international nongovernmental organizations are structured to embody the same set of social values and to meet human needs as are their local counterparts. Governance of the international system was to be achieved through an overlapping latticework of international institutions and organizations that were built by each sector.

States, the Principal Architects of World Order

The principal architects of international order are states. And it was states that put together the original blueprint for the post–World War II international system—the Atlantic Charter of 1941. (See Box 6.1) The charter's eight principles provided the normative basis for international organizations that were to manage postwar international political and economic relations. At the time, states claimed exclusive representation on the international level of the interests and well-being of their societies. Therefore, the interests of businesses and commercial enterprises and of nongovernmental and private voluntary organizations were to be aggregated on the national level and channeled through states to the international level.

The planners of the postwar order were dominated by Americans who approached the design of the international system similar to the way the Roosevelt administration went about reforming the U.S. government through the New Deal. According to Anne-Marie Burley, "The original blueprint for the postwar international order was drawn up by American policymakers who projected the philosophy, substance, and form of the New Deal regulatory state onto the world. Many of the same people who had taken responsibility for reshaping American domestic government now took responsibility for the world. They adopted the same generic solution for the world's problems as for the nation's: government intervention through specialized administrative organizations. The specific types of organization proposed to solve different specific regulatory problems varied over the same range, both domestically and internationally. . . . Although the final structure and details of all these entities required extensive multilateral negotiation, with results that often departed significantly from the proposals developed by U.S. planners, the U.S. plans remained the basic blueprint for a system of global economic, political, social, and cultural regulation." (Burley 1993, 130, 142) However, the plans for the postwar international system did not produce a strong central governing authority over this decentralized regulatory system, opting to loosely link the specialized international organizations for economic or other functions (the so-called functional organizations) by attaching them to a general international organization with nominal power to coordinate their activities, thus preserving the power and political control of states over the international system.

BOX 6.1

Atlantic Charter
August 14, 1941

The President of the United States of America and the Prime Minister, Mr. Churchill, representing His Majesty's Government in the United Kingdom, being met together, deem it right to make known certain common principles in the national policies of their respective countries on which they base their hopes for a better future for the world.

First, their countries seek no aggrandizement, territorial or other;

Second, they desire to see no territorial changes that do not accord with the freely expressed wishes of the peoples concerned;

Third, they respect the right of all peoples to choose the form of government under which they will live; and they wish to see sovereign rights and self government restored to those who have been forcibly deprived of them;

Fourth, they will endeavor, with due respect for their existing obligations, to further the enjoyment by all States, great or small, victor or vanquished, of access, on equal terms, to the trade and to the raw materials of the world which are needed for their economic prosperity;

Fifth, they desire to bring about the fullest collaboration between all nations in the economic field with the object of securing, for all, improved labor standards, economic advancement and social security;

Sixth, after the final destruction of the Nazi tyranny, they hope to see established a peace which will afford to all nations the means of dwelling in safety within their own boundaries, and which will afford assurance that all the men in all lands may live out their lives in freedom from fear and want;

Seventh, such a peace should enable all men to traverse the high seas and oceans without hindrance;

Eighth, they believe that all of the nations of the world, for realistic as well as spiritual reasons must come to the abandonment of the use of force. Since no future peace can be maintained if land, sea or air armaments continue to be employed by nations which threaten, or may threaten, aggression outside of their frontiers, they believe, pending the establishment of a wider and permanent system of general security, that the disarmament of such nations is essential. They will likewise aid and encourage all other practicable measure which will lighten for peace-loving peoples the crushing burden of armaments.

Franklin D. Roosevelt
Winston S. Churchill

The backbone of the international system's infrastructure is international law. Authority, legitimacy, and effectiveness of the system and its institutions are eventually enshrined within legal codes that define the structural aspects of institutions, as well as the environment within which institutions operate. Therefore, it can be anticipated that IGOs will be legally defined and constituted (much in the same way that national governments are) and that their primary source of authority and legitimacy is derived from international law, particularly the multilateral treaties that create them.

As Table 6.1 shows, there has been impressive growth in the number of multilateral treaties and treaty subjects during the twentieth century, especially during the 1926–1950 and the 1951–1975 periods. But it should be noted "that of the 6,000 multilateral treaties, only 30% are general multilateral treaties, that is, open to all states for participation. Seventy percent are plurilateral treaties that are limited in participation by geographic region or subject matter. Explosive as these numbers are, multilateral treaties are only 10% of all treaty activity in the world." (Ku 2001, 5) Table 6.2 shows the number of multilateral treaties that created an international organization as well as those that address some aspect of an IGO other than to create it. Although the vast majority of multilateral treaties are not linked to an IGO, there were significant growth spurts in the number of treaties creating or linked to an international organization during the 1926–1950 and 1951–1975 periods. Again, it is important to note that the growth in number of treaties creating an international organization is very modest relative to overall treaty activity.

Key Structural Features of IGOs—Function, Decisionmaking, and Secretariats

IGOs have similar structures and practices to that of public sector organizations on the national level (see Armstrong 1982, chapters 3–6). Hence, international organizations that are created by and for states have encompassed more or less the same competencies and functional characteristics as the state. States' competencies and authority can and do expand and contract over time. For example, the world has moved from the "limited government" concept that was prevalent in the nineteenth century to the "welfare state" concept in the twentieth century and is now moving back towards "limited government" at the start of the twenty-first century. IGOs established during these time periods reflect these characteristics. The international system during the nineteenth century created only a handful of IGOs, which were meticulously structured along administrative lines with small bureaucracies. The international system of the twentieth century expanded the subject matter under public management, reflecting the expansion of the state's role on the national level to the

TABLE 6.1 Multilateral Treaty Subjects by Period,* 1648–1995**

	1648–1750		1751–1850		1851–1899		1900–1925		1926–1950		1951–1975		1976–1995	
	#	%	#	%	#	%	#	%	#	%	#	%	#	%
Political/Diplomatic	72	84%	64	64%	162	48%	249	38%	292	25%	508	25%	315	19%
Military	13	18%	8	8%	17	8%	55	8%	99	8%	80	4%	59	4%
Economic	1	1%	13	13%	143	42%	241	36%	546	46%	885	43%	719	44%
Human Welfare			13	13%	11	3%	68	10%	144	12%	158	8%	111	7%
Cultural			1	1%			7	1%	17	1%	34	2%	24	1%
Environment			1	1%	3	.8%	20	3%	56	5%	134	7%	209	13%
Other					2	.6%	23	3%	29	2%	248	12%	182	11%
Period Total	*86*	*100%*	*100*	*100%*	*338*	*100%*	*663*	*100%*	*1,183*	*100%*	*2,047*	*100%*	*1,619*	*100%*

* These data were provided by the Comprehensive Statistical Database of Multilateral Treaties (CSDMT), a project of the Honors Programs at Pennsylvania State University. It originated in 1998 with a review by Prof. John Gamble of Christian L. Wiktor, *Multilateral Treaty Calendar, 1648–1995* (Dordrecht: Martinus Nijhoff Publishers, 1998) prepared for the *American Journal of International Law* (v. 93, pp. 565–6, 2000). Since then, Wiktor and other sources have been used to develop a comprehensive listing of all multilateral treaties from 1648–1995. The emphasis of CSDMT is breadth and statistical data. Initially, this included these variables: signature date, laterality, three topic categories, and relationship to IGOs. Currently, the project is being expanded to include length, number of articles, selected parties, dispute settlement, termination clauses and official languages.

** *Time periods were selected to balance natural chronological breaks and adequate amounts of data for each period so that conclusions are reasonable.*

Source: Global Governance and the Changing Face of International Law by Charlotte Ku (New Haven, CT: Academic Council on the United Nations System, 2001), p. 4. Copyright © 2001 by ACUNS. Reprinted by permission of the publisher.

TABLE 6.2 Multilateral Treaties and International Organizations, 1648–1995

Time Period	*Total # of Treaties*	*Breakdown Number*	*Percent of Total*
1648–1750	86	No link: 86	100%
1751–1850	100	No link: 100	100%
1851–1899	338	No link: 324	96%
		Creates an IO: 3	1%
		Some link to an IO: 11	3%
1900–1925	663	No link: 588	91%
		Creates an IO: 30	5%
		Some link to an IO: 3	4%
1926–1950	1183	No link: 1001	91%
		Creates an IO: 58	5%
		Some link to an IO: 44	4%
1951–1975	2047	No link: 1580	79%
		Creates an IO: 165	8%
		Some link to an IO: 253	13%
1976–1995	1619	No link: 1459	90%
		Creates an IO: 100	6%
		Some link to an IO: 60	4%

Note: These data were provided by the Comprehensive Statistical Database of Multilateral Treaties (CSDMT), a project of the Honors Programs at Pennsylvania State University. It originated in 1998 with a review by Prof. John Gamble of Christian L. Wiktor, *Multilateral Treaty Calendar, 1648–1995* (Dordrecht: Martinus Nijhoff Publishers, 1998) prepared for the American Journal of International Law (v. 93, pp. 565–6, 2000). Since then, Wiktor and other sources have been used to develop a comprehensive listing of all multilateral treaties from 1648–1995. The emphasis of CSDMT is breadth and statistical data. Initially, this included these variables: signature date, laterality, three topic categories, and relationship to IGOs. Currently, the project is being expanded to include length, number of articles, selected parties, dispute settlement, termination clauses and official languages.

Source: *Global Governance and the Changing Face of International Law* by Charlotte Ku (New Haven, CT: Academic Council on the United Nations System, 2001), p. 23. Copyright © 2001 by ACUNS. Reprinted by permission of the publisher.

welfare state. This led to a proliferation of international bureaucracies of increasing size and complexity. At the end of the twentieth century came a resurgence of the limited government concept, as states placed greater confidence in market forces to provide the services and needs of society. This largely halted the establishment of new IGOs within the international system. (This trend is captured in the last time period of Table 6.2, where there is a decline in the number of multilateral treaties generally and in the number of IGOs created by multilateral treaties.)

Purposes and Functions. The IGOs of the international system in the post-World War II era can be divided into three broad categories—political, economic, social/cultural—that reflect the purpose(s) of an organization. Among these three categories, there is a pecking order of importance. The political gets the most attention and shapes the other two, because it involves the fundamental and overarching focus that states have on national interests and security, as well as human rights and justice issues. These more sensitive concerns of states, especially security, are not easily organized as they are often at the core of the state's authority and power over the people and territory it claims to govern. States are more reticent when it comes to empowering or structuring an IGO to oversee these issues. In this regard, states are extremely careful not to sacrifice any power to an international body. Therefore, these IGOs—particularly multi-purpose international organizations such as the United Nations, the Organization of American States, Organization for Security and Co-operation in Europe, the League of Arab States—are weaker, structurally, than their counterparts in the economic and social/cultural domains.

Friedrich Kratochwil argues that IGOs always have shown a "curious organizational design that bolted together various organizational forms familiar from domestic politics. The assemblies of these organizations concerned with the definition of 'problems' are held together by little more than a yearly schedule to discuss and thereby legitimate and delegitimate issues of concern. Precisely because the domains of these organizational efforts are barely specifiable or of unquestioned legitimacy, only the weakest form of institutionalization is possible: the debate. Topics have to be attended to sequentially and all members ought to pay attention. The organizational economies that are available are schedules (forcing an end to debate), consensus procedures, reduction of participants (committees), and limited delegation (to produce, e.g., a draft agreement). 'Councils' are formally empowered to make decisions on certain issues and represent some weak form of authority based on some notion of representation. Only seldom is the actual formal, hierarchically organized bureaucracy entrusted with the administration of programs." (Kratochwil 1993, 467) Nevertheless, states have institutionalized their political and strategic relationships in a variety of multilateral organizations. While some are believed to be more capable, such as the North Atlantic Treaty Organization and the Organization of Security and Cooperation in Europe, others are far less so (for example, the Commonwealth of Independent States (CIS), ASEAN Regional Forum (ARF), the Organization of African Unity (OAU), which was renamed the African Union in 2002, the League of Arab States, the Gulf Cooperation Council, the U.N. Security Council and General Assembly).

The collective security architecture was initially designed with the U.N. Security Council at the apex of the system. Regional arrangements or agencies were to be subordinate and supplementary mechanisms for resolving interstate conflicts. Chapter VIII of the U.N. Charter outlines the relationship that is supposed to exist between the two levels:

> Article 52. 1. Nothing in the present Charter precludes the existence of regional arrangements or agencies dealing with such matters relating to the maintenance of international peace and security as are appropriate for regional action, provided that such arrangements or agencies are consistent with the Purposes and Principles of the United Nations.
>
> 2. The Members of the United Nations entering into such arrangements or constituting such agencies shall make every effort to achieve pacific settlement of local disputes through such regional arrangements or by such regional agencies before referring them to the Security Council.
>
> 3. The Security Council shall encourage the development of pacific settlement of local disputes through such regional arrangements or by such regional agencies either on the initiative of the states concerned or by reference from the Security Council. . . .
>
> Article 53. 1. The Security Council shall, where appropriate, utilize such regional arrangements or agencies for enforcement action under its authority. But no enforcement action shall be taken under regional arrangements or by regional agencies without the authorization of the Security Council, with the exception of measures against any enemy state, as defined in paragraph 2 of this Article, provided for pursuant of Article 107 or in regional arrangements directed against a renewal of aggressive policy on the part of any such state, until such time as the Organization may, on request of the Governments concerned, be charged with the responsibility for preventing further aggression by such a state.
>
> 2. The term enemy state as used in paragraph 1 of the Article applies to any state which during the Second World War has been an enemy of any signatory of the present Charter.

> 3. The Security Council shall at all times be kept fully informed of activities undertaken or in contemplation under regional arrangements or by regional agencies for the maintenance of international peace and security.

This language was purposely vague, thereby "allowing governments the flexibility to fashion instruments to foster international peace and security" which "could include treaty-based organizations that pre- or post-date the United Nations or ad hoc mechanisms created to deal with a specific concern"(Weiss, Forsythe, and Coate 1997, 38). The notion of regional institutions handling conflicts in their area would appear to be simple common sense, but the reality of postwar international politics, particularly the superpower competition during the Cold War that revived the "balance of power," stunted the development of an integrated multilateral security system for the world. This was especially the case in the non-Western parts of the world, which often became the fields of battle between the United States and the Soviet Union as they jockeyed for influence. Regional arrangements that were developed at the end of the 1940s, namely NATO and the Warsaw Treaty Organization, intentionally avoided being placed within the scope of Chapter VIII, while classic regional organizations like the OAS and the OAU have never enjoyed the capacity or resources to effectively deal with outbreaks of conflict in their areas. To this day, the architecture of collective security remains inchoate, despite recent efforts to strengthen the capabilities of both the United Nations and regional organizations. No new grand design for an integrated global security system has been put on the table nor is it likely to be in the near future with the international system overwhelmingly dominated by the United States.

Next is the economic area. The role of the state in the economy (nationally and internationally) has grown a great deal since 1945. For much of the post-war era there were competing economic models, which advocated more or less state intervention (for example, the market economies of the West with limited government intervention and the command economies of the East with total government control). Although there is considerable debate among scholars and policymakers as to the appropriate level of state intervention in the economy, there is a fundamental consensus on the necessity of public oversight and regulation of the economy through state institutions and an agreement that these institutions provide the framework for economic activity to occur. (See Sassen 1996; Greico and Ikenberry 2003) This consensus clearly informed the design and structure of the postwar international economic order that would ensure stable currencies, orderly cross-border trade, sufficient food supplies, and economic development.

As was noted in the previous chapter, states have always found it more practical (or possible) to establish IGOs to administer technical issues such as health, transportation, trade, and communications. Therefore, the architects of the postwar international system came to early agreement on forming technical organizations (so-called functional organizations) such as the World Bank and the International Monetary Fund (the Bretton Woods Institutions) in 1945, the Food and Agriculture Organization (FAO), 1945, the International Civil Aviation Organization (ICAO), 1945, the World Health Organization, 1946, and the Intergovernmental Maritime Consultative Organization, 1948. At the same time, existing technical institutions were reconstituted, such as the International Labor Organization (ILO), 1919; the International Telecommunications Union (ITU), 1865; Universal Postal Union, 1874; World Meteorological Organization, 1873; and the Bank for International Settlements (BIS), 1930. These organizations deal with matters that pose little threat to states' domestic control over their respective territory or population and where the coordination of policies are obviously (if not clearly) in the states' interests.

While negotiations are often long and tedious on what a treaty or convention addressing technical or economic matters should include, the resistance to reaching an agreement that delegates basic powers to a "collective body" for supervising, coordinating, and/or administrating the implementation of such treaties or conventions is considerably less. For the most part, states have not challenged the legitimacy or authority of this type of international organizations—which now includes the U.N. Specialized Agencies, the World Trade Organization, regional and sub-regional multilateral development banks (Inter-American Development Bank, Asian Development Bank, African Development Bank, West African Development Bank, Eastern Caribbean Central Bank, the Inter-American Development Bank, the Islamic Development Bank), the Organization of Economic Cooperation and Development (OECD), Association of South East Asian Nations (ASEAN), Asia Pacific Economic

Cooperation forum (APEC), the South Asian Association for Regional Cooperation (SAARC), the original European Communities, the Organization of Petroleum Exporting Countries (OPEC), International Whaling Commission, Economic Community of West African States, Southern African Development Community, Mercado Común del Cono Sur—Southern Cone Common Market (MERCOSUR), and the North American Free Trade Agreement. While the politics is less divisive about and within such organizations, there are politics involved nonetheless, since even the most technical organization does impinge on the autonomy of states and their prerogatives over such matters.

The architecture of the international economic system with its overlapping yet distinct groupings of IGOs along functional lines (finance, trade, transportation, telecommunications, health and economic development) is more coherent and effective than that of the collective security system. These IGOs have been instrumental to the successful incorporation of more and more national economies into the international economic system. They have proven their worth and value as intermediaries among an expanding number of countries with considerable economic asymmetries in size, capacity, and form. Indeed, economic IGOs have played a key role in fostering and managing the growing complexity of economic interdependence and an expanding international economic agenda.

However, this decentralized structure of autonomous administrative and regulatory agencies has run up against the increasing complexity of international economic relations under the torrent of globalization. The growing web of economic ties among nations has bundled traditionally separate economic activities like finance and trade, pushing countries to deepen their integration with the international economy and to increase coordination of their policies through regional and international institutions. While these new circumstances have placed considerable stress on the architecture of the international economic order, governments have not shown any desire to overhaul the existing institutional infrastructure or to create new organizations. As one international economic official observed, "Contemporary changes have taken place within the framework of existing institutions, but the creation of new ones has not yet seemed necessary. With the exception of the formalization of the GATT into the WTO, the times are characterized by the adaptation of existing institutional frameworks to the new circumstances. Perhaps further down the road the consensus will emerge to sustain a major institutional overhaul. Meanwhile, those changes that have taken place are in the form of marginal adaptation of existing institutions." (Cohen 1999, 90).

Finally, the social/cultural area is still largely defined and applied at the domestic level, and states have approached this area instrumentally on the international level, either to buttress the power of the state or to reinforce the role of the state in the economy. States have also established international organizations based on common religious, cultural, and linguistic heritages. Some of the more prominent IGOs for these dimensions include the United Nations Educational, Scientific and Cultural Organization (UNESCO), the Organization of Islamic Conference (OIC), the Commonwealth, Community of Portugese-Speaking Countries, Organisation internationale de la Francophonie, and the Agence de Coopération Culturelle et Technique (ACCT). These organizations constitute another form of connection among societies that is important to the state's authority and legitimacy. Solidarity created by formalizing religious or cultural values that are shared transnationally through IGOs reinforces the political foundation of the states involved.

Decisionmaking. Decisionmaking mechanisms and processes are another structural feature that have been copied from national structures. Decisionmaking in IGOs is conducted in a similar fashion to national parliaments and congresses in that the assemblies, councils, and committees of IGOs are considered "public" deliberative bodies with quasi-legislative powers. This feature varies from organization to organization. Generally, IGOs follow a procedure of "one state, one vote" to reinforce the international system's underlying principle of sovereign equality of states. Only a few organizations have deviated from this axiom and have devised various weighted voting formulas, as in the World Bank and the IMF, where the voting power of member states is commensurate to their financial contribution, or in the Council of Ministers of the European Union, where each member state is given a certain number of votes based on its population. Architects of the postwar international order did make one important change in the way decisions are determined in IGOs—replacing the unanimity rule with a simple or qualified majority rule. One of the weaknesses of pre–World War II international organizations was an explicit requirement for all decisions of the organization to be unanimous, which gave each member state a "veto." This proved disastrous for producing collective action on obvious and acute problems. It should be noted, however, that international decisionmaking is a long drawn-out process and fraught with qualifications. The principle of sovereign equality, the special status accorded major powers (for example, the veto of the five permanent members in the U.N. Security Council), and the politicization of economic and social issues have all contributed to the elongated and cumbersome decisionmaking process that has become characteristic of IGOs.

While states have regularly sought to improve the effectiveness and efficiency of inter-governmental decisionmaking largely through procedural manipulations, reduction of participants, and/or cutback of agenda items, only marginal improvements have been achieved. In fact, more energy has been devoted to reforming the administrative and management structures of IGOs, the secretariats, as a way to overcome institutional ineffectiveness and inefficiency. A major reason why so little has changed in the inter-governmental decisionmaking process of formal international organizations is the significant constitutional hurdles such changes often need to clear. For example, removing the veto of the five permanent members of the U.N. Security Council requires that member states agree to a change in Article 27(3)[1] of the U.N. Charter, deleting the phrase "including the concurring votes of the five permanent members" (hurdle 1), and then adopt this amendment to the Charter "by a vote of two thirds of the members of the General Assembly and ratified in accordance with their respective constitutional processes by two thirds of the Members of the United Nations, *including all the permanent members of the Security Council*"(Article 108, emphasis mine) (hurdle 2). In other words, decisionmaking mechanisms, once established through an international treaty, convention, or charter, are extremely difficult to change. International politics has not evolved to the extent that radical change of inter-governmental decisionmaking is perceived as either more efficient or effective in terms of protecting or advancing the interests of states, particularly the major powers.

---

[1]Article 27(3) reads: "Decisions of the Security Council on all other matters shall be made by an affirmative vote of nine members including the concurring votes of the permanent members; provided that, in decisions under Chapter VI, and under paragraph 3 of Article 52, a party to a dispute shall abstain from voting."

Secretariats. The secretariats of IGOs are an essential part of these organizations' design. "Originally, [secretariats] were created to service conferences—to make necessary physical arrangements, record debates and decisions, prepare documentation, and provide translation services. Although these and similar activities remain an important part of the duties of secretariats, in some international organizations their responsibilities have become much broader." (Jacobson 1979, 96) IGO secretariats vary considerably in size and structure, largely determined by the manifest purposes of the organization. Therefore, multi-purpose organizations like the United Nations have elaborate and differentiated bureaucracies with several thousand employees recruited from different countries and regions, while specific-purpose organizations like MERCOSUR have quite small secretariats with a much smaller payroll and have mainly administrative responsibilities (for example, documentation and communication services that support the work of inter-governmental bodies). In all cases, secretariats are headed by a single individual—the secretary-general, director-general, or executive director—elected to the post by one or more of the organization's inter-governmental bodies for fixed terms of four or more years. Other high-level officials are usually appointed and serve at the discretion of the executive head. The rest of the bureaucracy consists of people who possess the various skills and competencies needed to fulfill the tasks and duties of the organization.

There is a built-in tension between the secretariat and the other parts of the organization. On paper, secretariats are often characterized as an administrative institution with clear and limited responsibilities. (The U.N. secretary-general, for example, is specifically designated "chief administrative officer of the Organization" in Article 97 of the U.N. Charter.) In practice, however, secretariats are much more significant and, over the years, have assumed (or acquired) more institutional power vis-à-vis the intergovernmental bodies that technically control the organization. The old axiom "what the legislature decides, the executive does" has never accurately portrayed how public organizations operate in the real world. Government bureaucracies have always clashed with their political overseers, reflecting an inherent conflict between bureaucratic interests, which often seek to maximize autonomy, and the political controls of representative bodies, which constrain and, at times, thwart the imperatives of the bureaucracy. For international organizations the seemingly straightforward doctrine of an independent international civil service (borrowed in large measure from the British civil service tradition)—the idea that the secretary-general and staff impartially and loyally serve *all* member states (not any one state or group of states) and implement policies that are determined by the member states—has never been respected or fully realized. IGO secretariats are never immune from the political machinations of the member states (this was especially true during the Cold War) and have the added burden of blending conflicting bureaucratic cultures into an effective international administrative system. Furthermore, secretariats contend with a common chronic problem—insufficient and inadequate financial resources. It is often said, and rightly so, that an IGO is only as strong or effective as the weaknesses of its secretariat.

Although the actual number of IGOs created since 1945 is small compared to the international organizations of the private and nongovernmental sectors, it must be recognized that there is a qualitative difference between IGOs and other international organizations. The difference is largely that of importance. The power and reach of IGOs are considerable, despite the obvious problems of the international system's decentralized structure and fragmented institutional architecture. The state-centric international order, which has been forged by two world wars and the expanding powers of the state, has yet to escape the historical circumstances that have created it. The idea that public institutions are the sole providers of societal goods, services, and welfare had reached its peak in the twentieth century and only recently has such a view been seriously contested.

Markets

The private sector contribution to the architecture of the international order complements that of states. The organizing principle for this sector has been and continues to be the institution of the market. The market, in theory, is the place where producers and consumers interact and is a mechanism that orders the relationships among the factors of production (capital, labor, and raw materials). It is self-correcting through competition, which, in turn, produces efficiency. Market competition disciplines the private sector in three fundamental ways. "First, exchanges among those who want to buy and sell set the *level of production*. The demand of buyers balances the supply of sellers. Transactions among them set an equilibrium for production. . . . Second, . . . markets *minimize costs.* Competition opens the door to suppliers who think they might be able to underprice goods or provide goods superior to those already in the market. Such competition keeps the market honest and restrains price increases. . . . Third, . . . market forces *regulate quality.* Producers who sell inferior goods and services will soon find themselves losing business to competitors who make better products." Furthermore, a competitive market "depends on *arm's-length transactions among large numbers of buyers and sellers for relatively undifferentiated goods*" (Kettl 1993, 14–15).

The market is a place or space, not a thing. It is an institutional framework composed of atomistic, competitive firms through which economic transactions are made. The so-called "invisible hand" of the market, according to Adam Smith, is supposed to guide people's selfish interests towards the common good. The virtues/benefits of market competition are now conventional wisdom within business circles around the world and have become the main policy objectives of governments. Markets are embedded in a domestic or national framework. Governments, to a lesser or greater extent, regulate markets in response to a broader set of public interests, such as employment, equitable income distribution, social welfare, and political stability. Markets are differentiated by industry and sector—so, there are capital markets, labor markets, agricultural, industrial, energy, and high-tech markets, and many more. Although markets are not, in the strict sense, international organizations, they are the cornerstone of today's global economy and shape the institutions and organizations that populate the private sector.

Models of Economic Systems

For the most part, the private sector operates within the context of national economies, which can be divided into three models of economic systems: the American regulated free-market model, the European social-market model, and the Japanese coordinative corporate model. According to Mihály Simai, each model represents "specific patterns of development with differences in innovative capacities, resource allocation, production and consumption patterns, international competitiveness, and attitudes toward globalization and interdependence. These models were not rationally conceived in advance of events; rather, they evolved as events unfolded, social learning progressed, innovations appeared, and the international demonstration effect exerted its influence. Social and economic theories like Keynesianism and liberalism also shape the models. Although the interconnectedness of national economies has engendered similarities in organizational forms and policies, national historical, cultural, social, and institutional environments have markedly influenced the development and performance of these economic models."(Simai 1994, 137–138)

The American model's fundamental characteristics include "a more limited role for the state in the economy than the state is permitted in other industrial countries; a foundation in risk-taking and flexible entrepreneurship; a symbiosis of small, medium, and large firms; the simultaneous protection of competition and competitors; a sophisticated and competitive money market; a profit-oriented business perspective; and a mass-consumption orientation . . . ." The social market model that has evolved in Western Europe is "a variant of a social market economy combined with the remnants of the post–World War II welfare state. In some countries, like the Benelux nations and France, the model has preserved many elements of the welfare state. In other countries, and especially in Germany, the model has become a corporate version of the social market economy, which combines the advantages in efficiency of decentralized economic guidance with the benefits of central corrective mechanisms for dealing with market failures." Finally the Japanese model has "several important characteristics, some of recent origin, others rooted in Japan's history. The historical element is especially influential in the development of high standards of education, a strong work ethic, and a diligent labor force. The emphasis placed on long-term development in the Japanese model has been widely recognized as another key element . . . . The Japanese have long understood that the dynamism of a market economy in a world of strong competitors is not created by textbook competition between independent producers, but by the application of the most up-to-date technology by firms wielding extremely strong market power. To the government and nongovernmental actors of Japan, modern competition is a prolonged, comprehensive battle in which education, technical development, resource accumulation, competitive pricing, quality manufacturing, and market penetration strategies are all important weapons." (Simai 1994, 138, 143, and 149)

These three market models indicate the fundamental importance of private firms to the economic order and characterize the economies of the industrialized (and newly industrialized) countries in the world. The rest of the world (the developing countries in Africa, Latin America, and Asia) had developed a "hybrid" economic model that had elements of the various market economy systems and some parts of central planning, the only alternative economic model, which was used by the Soviet Union and other communist countries such as China, Cuba, and those of Central/Eastern Europe from the post–World War II period until the collapse of the Soviet Union in 1991. "The central planning model enshrined the ideological principles and practices of state ownership in a hierarchical economic system, where development goals, priorities, and output and distribution targets were defined by the central authorities. Economic information was communicated to producers and consumers through central directives. The model was inward-looking and sought to maximize economic growth in physical terms, based on quantitative targets. International economic cooperation was considered merely a balancing item in economic plans . . . and rarely went beyond relatively simple forms of trade relations." (Simai 1994, 155) Obviously, the model of central planning did not have a role for private enterprise and ultimately failed. While remnants of this model can still be found in the economic systems of some developing countries, the trend since the disintegration of the Soviet Union and the global collapse of communism after 1992 has been for all countries to adopt market system economies and to develop a private sector.

Private International Commercial Organizations Before 1945

Private for-profit firms have a long history of international cooperation and have built private international organizations to facilitate such cooperation. The need to organize the relationships between and among an expanding number of private commercial enterprises in the world could not be met simply by the market. The diversity of interests of private actors and the built-in competition mechanism of the market system pushed market actors to form various kinds of cooperative institutions on the international level. In the early part of the twentieth century, the dominant form of international organization for private companies was the cartel, which is a formal or informal organization "between three or more producers to coordinate their output and prices." (Cutler, Haufler, and Porter 1999, 12)

> The economic literature has identified a number of factors that are associated with the formation of cartels. According to economists, cartels form where there is a high concentration of production, high barriers to entry, a small set of 'fringe' producers that are large enough to affect the market but too small to be part of the cartel, a product for which there are no substitutes, and barriers to the ability to compete on nonprice factors while maintaining uncompetitively high prices. Under these circumstances, firms perceive it to be in their interest to cooperate in order to reap superprofits and are able to create and maintain a cartel to do so. Thus, the structure of the market situation explains cooperation. (Cutler, Haufler, and Porter 1999, 7)

According to Heinz Schmidt (1950), most cartels are based on verbal agreements, or "gentleman's agreements." Members are committing themselves to a manner of conduct as opposed to definite measures, hence many did not formulate or record structural plans, policies, or procedures. Furthermore, Schmidt identified four basic types of cartels:

1. Term Cartels/Price Cartels—terms of the cartels are prices related to commerce, banking, or transportation. In these cartels, members must adhere to certain set prices.
2. Profit-Distributing Cartel—occurs when income flows to one destination and is divided among the members based on the amount that each member participated in the production of the product.
3. Order Cartel—based on territorial division of the markets. This cartel accepts orders and distributes them to members based on their location.
4. Patent Cartel—not only based on a cartel agreement, but also on a patent that is granted and protected by the state.

Cartels were particularly prevalent in Europe, where such industrial organizations were generally accepted as natural economic phenomena, as demonstrated by an Inter-Parliamentary Union resolution adopted at its XXVIth Conference in London in 1930:

> Cartels, trusts and other analogous combines are natural phenomena of economic life towards which it is impossible to adopt an entirely negative attitude. Seeing, however, that those combines may have a harmful effect both as regards public interests and those of the State, it is necessary that they should be controlled. This Control should not take the form of an interference in economic life likely to affect its normal development. It should simply seek to establish a supervision over possible abuses and to prevent those abuses.
>
> An efficacious means of fighting such abuses and a basic condition for eventual control is to be found in publicity, which implies the obligation for cartels and similar combines to announce their existence and to register in the books of the State. To this should be added a stipulation making compulsory written agreements for such combines.
>
> Conventions which have not been made in writing, or which have not been communicated and submitted to the competent authority within the given time, should not be entitled to claim legal protection.[2]

This view was at odds with the long-standing antipathy towards monopolies and trusts in the United States, which had prohibited any monopolization of trade and commerce and made such practices and organizations illegal through the 1890 Sherman Antitrust Act. This fundamental difference in perspectives between the United States and Europe gradually changed after World War II, when European governments started to adopt antitrust legislation and competition policies that were more in line with American antitrust practices (see Boserup and Schlichtkrull 1962). Indeed, the reconstruction of the international economy after the war was heavily influenced by the United States, which "vigorously used antitrust policy to delegitimize cartels, opening the field for the mode of socioeconomic organization associated with its leading firms, the oligopolistic but relatively autonomous multinational corporations." (Porter 1999, 259) The multinational corporations (MNCs) followed the familiar domestic pattern of oligopolistic inter-firm cooperation that was characteristic of modern industrial capitalism on the international level.

---

[2] Union Interparlementaire, *Compte rendu de la XXVIe Conférence*, Génève: Payot et Cie, 1931, pp. 33–34. Quoted in Miller 1962, 59.

Multinational Corporations and the Post-World War II International Economy

After 1945, the American model of industrial organization—the multinational corporation—replaced cartels as the dominant form of international business organization of the private sector. The internationalization of the American corporation was aided and abetted by the international liberal economic order that was constructed at the Bretton Woods Conference in 1944, which established the World Bank and the International Monetary Fund. Big corporations within the U.S. domestic economy were well positioned to benefit from the post-war international economy. U.S. multinational corporations through their "powerful international intrafirm hierarchies, with head offices centralized territorially under U.S. jurisdiction, provided the new source of private authority for industry after industry [after the second World War]."(Porter 1999, 271) Likewise, the MNC was "a new and powerful form of international investment." (Spero 1981, 102) Joan Edelman Spero describes this phenomenon as follows:

> A multinational corporation is a firm with subsidiaries which extend the production and marketing of the firm beyond the boundaries of any one country. . . . Multinational corporations are among the world's largest firms. . . . These corporate giants also tend to be oligopolistic. They are able to dominate markets because of their size, their access to financial resources, their control of technology, or their possession of a special differentiated product. . . .
>
> Foreign subsidiaries are directly owned by the parent either through sole ownership or through joint venture with public or private groups. . . . Decision making for multinationals tends to be centralized, though management structures vary from company to company, and policy control emanates from the parent company when the international aspects of a firm's business become important. The classic pattern of international investment has been from semi-independent foreign operations to the integration of international operations within a separate international division to the integration of international operations within the total company. . . . Production may take place in different stages in several different countries, and the final product may be mar-

> keted in still other countries. Integrated production and marketing reinforce the need for central decision making and central planning and are made possible by central control and central management.
>
> Multinationals in many cases are mobile and flexible. Some are tied to specific countries by the need for raw materials or by a large capital commitment. Others, however, are able to shift operations across national boundaries for the purposes of company profits, markets, security, or survival. Mobility and flexibility are related to the central decision-making structure and to the vast resources of the company.
>
> The centralized, integrated organizational structure reinforces the tendency of multinational corporations to make decisions with concern for the firm and the international environment and not with concern for the particular states in which it is operating. Their vast size, centralized organization, and integrated production and marketing are powerful resources which firms can use to follow their international goals or policies. (Spero 1981, 103–104)

By the 1970s, the power and influence of multinational corporations were evident in international affairs. As Phillip Taylor pointed out in 1984: "It should be obvious that, by economic indicators alone, MNCs are powerful international nonstate actors. For example, were it possible to equate the annual gross sales of MNCs with the gross national products of nation-states, one could have concluded in 1972 that General Motors was larger than Switzerland, Pakistan, and South Africa; that Royal Dutch Shell was bigger than Iran, Venezuela, and Turkey; and that Goodyear Tires was larger than Saudi Arabia. Moreover, nearly 75 percent of the world's production is controlled by 200 MNCs. In some Western European markets, 70 to 90 percent of those markets is controlled by as few as four large corporations." (Taylor 1984, 205)

The proliferation of the multinational corporation was particularly pronounced in the developed market economies of North America, Western Europe, and Japan, where the "development of communications, transportation, and techniques of management and organization have made possible centralization, integration, and mobility. The computer, telecommunications, and the development of corporate organization, which to a great extent came from the United States and were used by U.S. firms, have been important factors in the dominance of U.S. corporations. The managed but less restrictive international economic system provided a favorable setting for multinational expansion in the postwar era. The elimination of restraints on capital flows and trade provided the possibility for expansion of direct investment." (Spero 1981, 107) While most of the foreign direct investment (FDI) since World War II has been within and between firms in the developed market economies, MNCs also saw new business opportunities within the fledgling economies of newly independent developing countries that emerged from the decolonization process during the 1960s and 1970s. Although many developing countries feared and often resisted foreign domination of their underdeveloped economies by MNCs, the alternative of pressing for larger levels of official development assistance (ODA) from developed countries as the primary means for economic development failed to produce sufficient capital to generate economic growth. Increasingly, these countries have had to rely on FDI for developing their economies and for stimulating growth, despite the power and influence MNCs would have over national economic goals and welfare. The oligopolistic structure of most industries in the international economy has never truly been challenged during the postwar era. Only modest efforts were made by states and international governmental organizations to regulate oligopolistic market behavior and related restrictive business practices (for example, the 1976 "Guidelines for Multinational Enterprises" adopted by the OECD).

Transnationalization of International Business Enterprises

An outgrowth of the "multinationalization of production and competition" during the last quarter of the twentieth century was the transnational corporation, or TNC (the successor to the MNC in terms of how a firm is organized and operated). According to Simai, TNCs "are directly involved in the interpenetration of national economic structures by international ownership, production, and employment, through which corporations not only share markets with host country firms but also increasingly integrate those firms into the corporations' international networks." (Simai 1994, 233–234) International business organizations have developed horizontal structures, in contrast to the hierarchical and vertical structures of the earlier MNCs, increasing interfirm cooperation in the forms of alliances, strategic partnerships, and "knowledge-based networked oligopolies."

TABLE 6.3 The World's Top 10 TNCs in Terms of Transnationality, 1998

Ranking 1998 by					
Foreign Assets	*TNI**	*Corporation*	*Country*	*Industry*	*TNI**
34	1	Seagram Company	Canada	Beverages/Media	94.8
57	2	Thomson Corporation	Canada	Media/Publishing	94.6
10	3	Nestlé SA	Switzerland	Food/beverages	94.2
82	4	Electrolux AB	Sweden	Electrical /electronics	92.7
69	5	British American Tobacco Plc	UK	Food/tobacco	91.0
62	6	Holderbank Financière Glarus	Switzerland	Construction materials	90.5
12	7	Unilever	Netherlands/UK	Food/beverages	90.1
15	8	ABB	Switzerland	Electrical equipment	89.1
71	9	SmithKline Beecham Plc	UK	Pharmaceuticals	82.3
98	10	SCA	Sweden	Paper	80.8

*TNI is the abbreviation for "transnationality index", which is calculated as the average of three ratios: foreign assets to total assets, foreign sales to total sales and foreign employment to total employment.

Source: UNCTAD/Erasmus University database, Table III.7 in UNCTAD 2000, 79.

According to the United Nations Conference on Trade and Development (UNCTAD), TNCs currently number 63,000 parent firms with 630,000 foreign affiliates and multitudes of inter-firm arrangements. TNCs are the driving force in the expansion of international production in today's world economy. This expansion is captured in UNCTAD's transnationality index of TNCs—an average of three ratios: foreign assets/total assets, foreign sales/total sales, and foreign employment/total employment—which measures the foreign dimension in a firm's overall activities. In its *World Investment Report 2000*, the average transnationality index of the world's top one hundred TNCs rose from 51 percent in 1990 to 54 percent in 1998. Leading the index in 1998 are firms from countries with small domestic markets (see Table 6.3), while firms in the food and beverage industry were at the top and trading firms were at the bottom (see Table 6.4).

This structural transition of international business is demonstrated by the recent trends in cross-border merger and acquisitions (M&As). There are three types of cross-border M&As: horizontal (between competing firms in the same industry), vertical (between firms in client-supplier or buyer-seller relationships), and conglomerate (between companies in unrelated activities). UNCTAD points out that the "balance between these

TABLE 6.4 Industry Composition of the Top 100 TNCs, 1990 and 1998

	Number of entries		*Average TNI* per industry (percentage)*	
Industry	*1990*	*1998*	*1990*	*1998*
Electronics/electrical equipment/computers	14	17	47.4	52.6
Motor vehicle and parts	13	14	35.8	49.0
Petroleum exploration/refining/distribution and mining	13	11	47.3	52.7
Food/beverages/tobacco	9	10	59.0	74.3
Chemicals	12	8	60.1	58.5
Pharmaceuticals	6	8	66.1	64.3
Diversified	2	6	29.7	38.0
Telecommunications	2	6	46.2	40.4
Trading	7	4	32.4	24.6
Retailing	–	3	–	52.0
Utilities	–	3	–	26.0
Metals	6	2	55.1	45.5
Media	2	2	82.6	86.7
Construction	4	1	58.8	90.5
Machinery/engineering	3	–	54.5	–
Other	7	5	57.6	69.9
Total/average	100	100	51.1	53.9

*TNI is the abbreviation for "transnationality index", which is calculated as the average of three ratios: foreign assets to total assets, foreign sales to total sales and foreign employment to total employment.

Source: UNCTAD/Erasmus University database, Table III.6 in UNCTAD 2000, 78.

types of M&As has been changing over time. The importance of horizontal M&As has risen somewhat in recent years: in 1999, 70 per cent of the value of cross-border M&As were horizontal compared to 59 per cent ten years ago. Vertical M&As have been on the rise since the mid-1990s, but staying well below 10 per cent. In the late-1980s M&A boom, conglomerate M&As were very popular, but they have diminished in importance as firms have tended increasingly to focus on their core business to cope with intensifying international competition. They declined from a high of 42 per cent in 1991 to 27 per cent in 1999." (UNCTAD 2000, 101)

The growth of cross-border M&As as a mode of entry for international expansion reflects a shift in the preference of TNCs. It also represents a significant vehicle for restructuring markets, industries, and firms, globally and regionally. "The current wave of unprecedented global and regional restructuring through cross-border M&As reflects a dynamic interaction between the various basic factors motivating firms to undertake M&As and changes in the global economic environment, in the pursuit of strategic corporate objectives. . . . Cross-border M&As are growing so rapidly in importance precisely because they provide firms with the fastest way to acquiring tangible and intangible assets in different countries, and because they allow firms to restructure existing operations nationally or globally to exploit synergies and obtain strategic advantages. In brief, cross-border M&As allow firms rapidly to acquire a portfolio of locational assets which has become a key source of competitive strength in a globalizing economy. In oligopolistic industries, furthermore, deals may be undertaken in response to the moves or anticipated moves of competitors. Even firms that would not want to jump on the bandwagon may feel that they have to, for fear of becoming targets themselves." (UNCTAD 2000, xxi)

Besides cross-border M&As, firms are also turning to nonequity vehicles—international alliances and collaboration agreements—to achieve a global presence. "These arrangements may be horizontal, linking firms in different industries, or vertical, linking firms at different stages of production in the same industry. . . . These agreements can take a variety of forms ranging from joint ventures to licensing deals to research consortia to supply arrangements." (Reinicke 1998, 22) Alliances are particularly popular in technology-intensive industries (such as telecommunications, aerospace, computers, and pharmaceuticals). Lynn Mytelka and Michel Delapierre argue that knowledge-based networked oligopolies are today's new global business organizations. They have emerged out of the growing knowledge-intensity of production and the shortening product life cycles since the 1980s, which pushed firms to widen their market share overseas and to penetrate overseas markets that were often highly regulated and dominated by public monopolies. The subsequent deregulation of markets and privatization of public monopolies spurred the globalization of competition and encouraged a wave of mergers and acquisitions as a means to consolidate the market positions of leading firms domestically and to increase access to markets internationally. Mytelka and Delapierre argue that these new oligopolies share three characteristics:

1. They are knowledge-based, that is, involve collaboration in the generation of, use of, or control over the evolution of new knowledge.

As a result, the new knowledge-based oligopolies are dynamic, seeking to organize, manage, and monitor change as opposed to rigidifying the status quo.

2. They are composed of networks of firms rather than of individual companies. Alliances thus form the basic structure and building-blocks of the global oligopoly.
3. In terms of their organization, the new oligopolies can form within or across industry segments and sometimes do both at the same time. They are moving and reshaping themselves much as an amoeba would, stretching out its "foot" to include new actors when the assets they bring to the network are complementary and eliminating others whose resources are no longer critical. (Mytelka and Delapierre 1999, 132–133)

These complex global arrangements (see Box 6.2) have outrun much of the legal and regulatory mechanisms of states (as well as intergovernmental organizations), thereby limiting the abilities of states to manage or direct either their own economies or the global economy. TNCs shape the terms on which competition in the global economy will take place and have incredible influence on how the global economy is managed and structured. This has led to conflicts with states and other societal actors, particularly when the interests and goals of TNCs do not coincide or are not consistent with the broader social goals and objectives of these other groups. Indeed, the clout of today's transnational corporations is increasingly seen as "a threat to national sovereignty and democratic accountability. For example, countries may feel that their freedom to set taxes as they wish is threatened by the ability of multinationals to shift profits, or operations, from one country to another." (*The Economist*, January 29, 2000, p. 21)

International Trade and Business Associations

Economic globalization has placed a spotlight on TNCs and the various international business organizations that they join and form. Trade associations and industry-specific organizations are not new on the international scene, however they grew both in numbers and significance in the latter half of the twentieth century. The phenomenal increase in the numbers of small, medium, and large firms engaged in international trade has

BOX 6.2

Biopharmaceuticals and the Emergence of a "Health Care Industry"

Like information technology, biotechnology is highly knowledge-intensive. On average, $240 million is required to bring a new drug to market. Also like information technology, biotechnology has wide applicability across many industries. However, in contrast to information technology, these applications markets are still quite distinct and different kinds of biotechnology processes and products are taken up by seed companies, new materials firms, the chemical and the pharmaceutical industries. Within the latter, moreover, traditional oligopolies had developed within therapeutic categories and these have remained strong although there is evidence that the new gene sequencing and genetic engineering techniques will enable large networked firms to cross over from one therapeutic category to another. What is most remarkable about the transformation of the pharmaceutical industry into a biopharmaceutical industry, however, and what differentiates it from the data-processing industry, is the speed with which the large pharmaceutical firms captured and managed this process.

A number of factors account for the role of large pharmaceutical firms in the ongoing transformation of this industry. The relationship of these large pharmaceutical firms to the smaller dedicated biotechnology firms (DBFs), who pioneered these new techniques, and the relationship of the large pharmaceutical firms to each other are critical elements here. Unlike the star performers in the semiconductor industry, the newer DBFs were initially too small and specialized to become dominant players on this new potentially important horizontal market segment. Their ability to grow and strengthen an independent biopharmaceutical segment, moreover, was limited by the long period of research and clinical testing that was required before biotechnology products began to teach the market. The knowledge and experience of the larger pharmaceutical firms in clinical testing and certification by the Food and Drug Administration and the substantial financial resources they could apply to these activities as well as to research, put them at a clear advantage when compared to the smaller DBFs. Genentech and Chiron, two of the top biotechnology firms in the emerging biopharmaceutical industry are not Intel or Motorola, as we shall see below. Indeed, with the notable exception of Amgen, few of the major dedicated biotechnology firms have survived as independent players into the 1990s.

During the decade following the discovery of rDNA techniques, large pharmaceutical firms entered into a period of intense competition. Firms have appeared and disappeared in rapid succession among the top ten. From 1982 to 1989 Bristol-Myers, for example, moved from 10th to 2nd place after its acquisition of Squibb, Glaxo moved from 19th to 3rd place, Bayer dropped from 2nd place to 6th, Ciba-Geigy from 5th to 8th, and Pfizer from 6th to 11th. Between 1989 and 1992, however, this process started to slow down as only two of the top ten firms changed: American Home Products dropped from the list and Hoffman-La Roche moved from 16th to 9th. Amongst the top five, Ciba-Geigy replaced SmithKline Beecham in fifth place. Although calculated differently, the Fortune 500 shows the same degree of stability at the top between 1990 and 1995, with all of the top ten firms simply jockeying for position among themselves.

(continues)

Advancing within the top ten during the 1990s has largely taken place through a process of concentration with two spectacular in-country mergers and acquisitions that strengthen core firms in the global knowledge-based network oligopoly. In the United Kingdom, Glaxo acquired Wellcome PLC in 1995 propelling the former into first place and in Switzerland, the merger of Sandoz and Ciba-Geigy in 1996 moving the Novartis, as they will now be called, into second place worldwide.

Within the pharmaceutical industry, evidence is accumulating that, alongside the mergers and acquisitions, a networked, knowledge-based biopharmaceutical oligopoly is emerging. Over the 1980s biotechnology inputs came to play an increasingly important role in the pharmaceutical industry, especially in diagnostics. By the end of that decade, the top ten pharmaceutical forms, had begun to solidify their position in biotechnology through a rash of acquisitions and alliances. This was made easier by the financial difficulties of small dedicated biotechnology firms who faced not only high costs for research but for product development, clinical testing, and marketing. Genentech, the second largest dedicated biotechnology firm by sales, and Syntex, another innovative biotechnology firm, were both acquired by Hoffmann-La Roche. Chiron, the fourth largest DBF, acquired Cetus in 1991 but was itself taken over by Ciba-Geigy and later merged into Novartis. Glaxo-Wellcome acquired Affymax; Rhone-Poulenc-Rorer acquired Institut Merieux, Cannaught Bio Sciences, and 37 percent of Applied Immune Sciences. American Home Products took over the Genetics Institute, American Cyanamid acquired Immunnex in 1992 and was itself taken over by American Home Products in 1994, and Hoescht acquired Mario-Merrell-Dow and the U.S. diagnostics firm Syva in 1995. Only Amgen, the top independent DBF, was able to solidify its position in biopharmaceuticals through the acquisition of Synergen.

When not acquiring DBFs outright, the top twenty pharmaceutical firms were engaging in strategic partnerships. In the newer areas of emerging 'health care industry' diagnostics, therapeutics, and drug delivery, strategic partnering activity developed rapidly in the 1990s. Total biotechnology alliances of the top twenty pharmaceutical firms increased from about 150 in 1988–90 period to over 350 in the 1994–96 period.

Some of these partnerships link large pharmaceuticals to each other in traditional oligopolistic fashion—through cross-licensing, distribution, and marketing agreements. Most of these partnerships, however, link a large pharmaceutical company to a network of smaller dedicated biotechnology forms whose research is increasingly financed by the larger pharmaceutical firm and whose results are licensed on an exclusive basis to that company (outlicense). SmithKline Beecham, for example, claims to have more than 140 such partnerships worldwide, including its links to university research institutes. Glaxo has more than ten strategic partnerships with American DBFs and fifty with universities in the United States alone. Research on new gene therapies to deal with retroviruses and cancer, is exclusively done by Rhone-Poulenc-Rorer (RPR), through Gencell, its network of sixteen American DBFs in which RPR holds a minority interest. Through these alliances, pharmaceutical firms, once exclusively rooted in chemical processes, are now quite at home in biotechnology.

Competition among the large pharmaceutical firms, moreover, is increasingly based on these knowledge-based networks. Thus Merck (U.S.) is collaborating with Celltech (U.K.) in the development of an asthma drug that Celltech invented, as well as with Astra (Sweden), a member of the traditional oligopoly in asthma drugs headed by Glaxo, itself allied

(continues)

with the small American biotechnology firm ICOs in the development of a rival asthma drug. Strategic partnerships, as this example illustrates, can be used to reinforce the traditional oligopolies within therapeutic categories. In the $23 billion market for antibiotics, traditional oligopolists are forming partnerships with gene-sequencing firms. By identifying the genetic structure of bacteria, researchers can work on treatments that attack genes essential for its survival. Pfizer has worked closely with Microcide and Incyte on such products. Building networks of alliance partners is yet another strategy currently being employed by the more aggressive of the large pharmaceutical firms. As gene therapies develop, biopharmaceutical firms are beginning to establish closer links to medical delivery systems—managed health care units and clinics.

In sum, alliance formation has intensified and this emerges most clearly if we take a dynamic perspective. Thus, in the early 1980s, few of the big pharmaceutical companies had formed R&D partnerships. For top-ranking firms such as Hoechst, Bayer, and Hoffmann-La Roche alliances were marginal. A few companies, Ciba-Geigy and Eli Lilly, for example, had a small number of alliances with U.S. DBFs and only Sandoz had formed R&D partnerships with smaller pharmaceutical firms. In the mid-1980s several large pharmaceutical companies became involved in technology partnerships but principally the linkages between them were in marketing. Their R&D ties were primarily to the small dedicated biotechnology firms, while their earlier links to universities began to decline. By the mid-1990s, all of the largest pharmaceutical companies were involved in technology partnerships and much of the competition in the growing diagnostic market, in vaccines, and in therapeutics was based on knowledge-based networks that linked large pharmaceutical firms to a host of small DBFs.

Equally important for the reconfiguration of this industry and the emergence of a networked knowledge-based oligopoly within it, is the way in which biotechnology is serving to break down the walls between therapeutic categories and build links across new horizontal segments within the emerging industry. The rules of the game in clinical diagnostics, for example, have been changing along these lines, as has the role of human genetics and gene therapies. Core biopharmaceutical firms such as Bayer, Johnson & Johnson, SmithKline Beecham, and Hoechst have diagnostic divisions, while SmithKline Beecham and Hoffmann-La Roche have recently concluded alliances with companies that specialize in gene sequencing. To the extent that these trends in concentration and alliance formation continue, there is a danger that alliances, which have created new opportunities for small and medium-sized enterprises, will be transformed into new barriers to entry as the biopharmaceutical firms become major actors in health care delivery.

From Private Authority and International Affairs *by A. Claire Cutler, Virginia Haufler, and Tony Porter (eds.) (Albany, NY: State University of New York Press, 1999) pp. 140–143.*

produced a commensurate rise in the number of international associations, which are technically not-for-profit organizations of "for-profit" organizations, for every industry and sector. For example, the International Council of Marine Industry Associations (ICOMIA) was formed in 1965 to bring together in one global organization all the national boating federations and other bodies involved in the recreational marine industry and to represent them at international level. ICOMIA, according to its own literature, aims to provide for its members a forum in which to consider issues of common concern, to collect relevant data and to formulate agreed policy; to seek to break down all barriers to trade, including the removal of unnecessary or unviable legislation; to promote awareness of the recreational marine industry's requirements and objectives, including the improvement of boating safety; to maintain close dialogue with international bodies, national governments, and other regulatory authorities on behalf of its members; to support its members "in every way possible" and to give recommendations and guidance on compliance with new international standards and regulations; to publish its opinions and recommendations, to formulate draft international standards and codes of practice; to promote the concept of recreational boating as being in harmony with a clean and attractive marine environment; and to assist in the promotion of recreational boating as being fun and available for all. (See ICOMIA's website www.icomia.com.) This and countless other business and industry associations that have sprung up in the last fifty years have contributed to the institutional infrastructure of the international economic order.

Globalization of the world economy, which is spurred on by the information technology revolution, has catapulted many private sector leaders (chairmen and/or chief executive officers) into high-profile roles (some even to the ranks of a global celebrity) within the international economic and political systems. While these men and women have always been influential, due to their position at the top of large business organizations and their command over the enormous resources (both financial and human) of such organizations, it is relatively recently that they have become active players on the international stage, dealing with issues that are not necessarily directly related to their business. Therefore, starting in the last decade of the twentieth century a number of private international organizations have been established by corporate leaders as instruments of and arenas for them to be directly involved in pressing international social and political issues and problems. These organizations include the World Economic Forum, the World Business Council for Sustainable Development, the Prince of Wales International Business Leaders Forum, CSR Europe (formerly the European Business Network for Social Cohesion), Business for Social Responsibility, and the Global Business Council on HIV & AIDS.

International business and trade organizations are very similar in design to the international nongovernmental organizations that make up civil society (see below). They purportedly represent the collective interests and common concerns of individual companies and/or national industry associations to other international entities, especially regulatory or governmental agencies and bodies on the international level that affect the structure and operations of markets. TNCs, as well as medium and small national firms, use these international organizations in much the same way as states use IGOs—as vehicles for cooperation and coordination among a diverse and increasingly competitive group of members. While the organizations may be structured and function like INGOs of civil society, they do have some important features that are distinctive. First, most international business organizations are clearly defined by industry (accounting, pharmaceutical, banking, and so on) and/or sector (such as agriculture, services, finance, or manufacturing). Second, these international organizations are more akin to private clubs with substantial membership fees, a tendency toward cartel behavior, and a history of strict separation from the public sector. Third, they are important sources of private international commercial and trade law. They, along with individual merchants and corporations, "have been intimately involved in creating and enforcing merchant laws for over a millennium, although their authority has weakened at times. Merchant laws have operated authoritatively in gaining the trust, the general perceptions of legitimacy and a high degree of compliance from the merchant community." (Cutler 1999, 300) A few of these organizations include formal private dispute settlement bodies (most notably, the International Court of Arbitration of the International Chamber of Commerce) and have established mechanisms for private regulation of industry and trade. While not all private business associations are wealthy and powerful, they all play an important role in today's global market economy.

Civil Society

Civil society (non-governmental organizations or NGOs) is another influential non-state actor that has been involved in the design of the international order. It has steadily grown in size and importance since the end of World War II. Unlike states or markets, civil society is less structured and more fragmented as a group. Inter-organization relations are extremely fluid and, in recent years, civil society organizations have increasingly organized themselves internationally in non-permanent networks and coalitions, which are managed virtually through the Internet rather than through traditional permanent organizational structures such as bureaucracies and offices. The NGO phenomenon is clearly not something new to the international arena, but the power and influence of NGOs in international political and economic affairs today is. This change in status of NGOs has prompted greater interest in them among both policymakers and scholars that has provided a much clearer picture of how these groups are organized and what roles they play in the structure and organization of contemporary international relations.

According to Leon Gordenker and Thomas Weiss, NGOs have several defining characteristics:

> Apart from the function of representing people acting of their own volition, rather than by some institutional *fiat*, NGOs have other defining characteristics. They are formal organisations that are intended to continue in existence; they are thus not *ad hoc* entities. They are or aspire to be self-governing on the basis of their own constitutional arrangements. They are private in that they are separate from governments and have no ability to direct societies or to require support from them. They are not in the business of making or distributing profits. . . . [They] have transnational goals, operations or connections . . .
>
> Not every organisation that claims to be an NGO exactly fits this definition of a private citizens' organisation, separate from government but active on social issues, not profit making, and with transnational scope. At least three significant deviations from these specifications can be identified. The first of these is a GONGO—government-organised nongovernmental organization. They achieved notoriety during the Cold War because many so-called NGOs owed their very existence and entire financial support to communist governments in the Soviet bloc or authoritarian ones in the Third World. There were also a few such "NGOs" in the West, particularly in the USA, where they were often a front for administration activities. Although the Western species may have been more nongovernmental than their Soviet or Third World counterparts, they were not created for the classic purposes of NGOs. . . .

> The second special type of NGO is QUANGOs (quasi-nongovernmental organisations). For example, many Nordic and Canadian NGOs, a handful of US ones, and the International Committee of the Red Cross (ICRC) receive the bulk of their resources from public coffers. The staffs of such organisations usually assert that as long as their financial support is without strings attached and their own priorities rather than those of donor governments dominate, there is no genuine problem. . . . Their services aim at internationally-endorsed objectives and their operations are distinct from those of governments, even if their funding is public. . . .
>
> The third mutant type—the donor-organised NGO (DONGO)—is also distinguished by its source of funds. "As donors become more interested in NGOs, they also find themselves tempted to create NGOs suited to their perceived needs." (Brown and Korten 1989, 22) Both governments and the UN system have "their" NGOs for particular operations and purposes.(Gordenker and Weiss 1996, 20–21)

Furthermore, Weiss and Gordenker identify four types of inter-organizational mechanisms that increase the effectiveness and efficiency of NGOs—formal bridging groups (coalitions), federations, UN coordinating bureaus, and connections to governments. Formal NGO coalitions such as the Asian NGO Coalition for Agrarian Reform and Rural Development or the International Council of Voluntary Agencies help member organizations develop common positions on issues or policies and, in the case of development or humanitarian operations, assist with coordination of activities. These coalitions act as bridging organizations and function as "a conduit for ideas and innovations, a source of information, a broker of resources, a negotiator of deals, a conceptualiser of strategies and a mediator of conflicts." Most of the large NGOs, particularly in the development and humanitarian assistance field, are structured in the more traditional form of a federation. "Organisational members of a federation share an overall image and ideology. For example, Oxfam's ideology sets out a grassroots development orientation that all its national affiliates employ. But the national groups are responsible for their own fundraising and projects. Although members of such federations meet periodically at both the management and working levels to discuss common problems, each national member remains autonomous." (Gordenker and Weiss 1996, 27, 28)

The final two mechanisms—the UN coordinating bureaus and connections to governments—have only recently become more institutionalized. Development and humanitarian agencies of the UN system (for example, UNICEF, UNDP and UNHCR) and other IGOs (such as the Organization of Security and Cooperation in Europe, the European Union, and regional development banks) have been compelled to improve cooperation with and coordination of NGO activities due to the increase of complex emergencies in the 1990s. However, IGO efforts to coordinate NGOs in the field have not been always welcome or successful. Yet, when complementary tasks exist between NGOs and IGOs, cooperation appears to come more easily. "For example, in election monitoring within UN-orchestrated operations in El Salvador and Cambodia, NGOs could more easily make public pronouncements about irregularities than could the civilian or military staff of the UN Observer Mission in El Salvador (ONUSAL) and the UN Transition Authority in Cambodia (UNTAC). In such circumstances, rather than rivalry, a sensible division of labour appeared between NGOs and IGOs. For some of the same reasons, discernible complementarity has developed between Amnesty International or Human Rights Watch and the United Nations. Because NGOs can push harder and more openly for drastic changes, which can then be codified over time by the UN, a 'symbiotic' relationship has developed in the context of establishing new human rights standards and implementing existing ones." (Gordenker and Weiss 1996, 29)

Similarly, NGO relations with governments have changed in recent years. All governments regulate activities of NGOs (both domestic and international groups) through domestic legislation and administrative procedures. Depending on the purpose of the NGO, the relationship with a government may be either cooperative or contentious, involving a range of activities from lobbying for change of government policies to providing public services that had once been managed by the government. Since the end of the Cold War, the expectations of NGOs and their role in national society have grown considerably, especially in societies transitioning to democracy after years of oppressive authoritarian regimes or in countries where the government system has collapsed altogether. "Previously, NGO-government relationships were often ones of benign neglect at best, or of suspicion and outright hostility at worst." (Gordenker and Weiss 1996, 30)

Perhaps the best indicator of the changes in civil society is the area of finance. "Once little more than ragged charities, non-governmental organisations (NGOs) are now big business," argued a special report of *The Economist.* Tens of thousands of NGOs in the world are predominantly small domestic groups (two million groups are estimated to have been founded in the United States since the 1960s, and at least 65,000 NGOs in Russia have been formed since the breakup of the USSR). "Most of these are minnows; some are whales, with annual incomes of millions of dollars and a worldwide operation. Some are primarily helpers, distributing relief where it is needed; some are mainly campaigners, existing to promote issues deemed important by their members. The general public tends to see them as uniformly altruistic, idealistic and independent." Governments have increasingly turned to NGOs as they privatize their aid programs, preferring "to pass aid through NGOs because it's cheaper, more efficient—and more at arm's length—than direct official aid." (*The Economist*, January 29, 2000, pp. 25–28) This has ballooned the budgets of several humanitarian and development NGOs, turning them into multi-million-dollar enterprises. For example, one quarter of Oxfam's revenues of $162 million in 1998 came from the British government and the EU; World Vision US received $55 millions from the U.S. government; and 46 percent of Médecins Sans Frontières' income is from government sources.

The amount of resources now put in the hands of civil society groups automatically changes the way many of these organizations are managed and operated. Experts on operational humanitarian and development NGOs point out that such changes are most noticeable in the way these organizations are governed.

> It happens that the tumultuous changes and crises of the 1990s coincided with the approaching "middle age" of several of the oldest and largest relief and development organizations. These organizations, established in the wake of World War II or before, now found themselves with large and growing bureaucracies, outdated operational systems, and a perceived alienation from their original values. The reengineering and restructuring processes many went through, or are going through still, represent a genuine, deep introspection on the part of these organizations. Some have undergone major overhauls of their financial, human resources, and information systems. The furthest reaching of these changes, however, are reflected in how the organizations are governed.

> The individual organizational evolutions of the NGOs are each unique, and too complex to be labeled as simply "centralization" or "decentralization" of authority. Yet, broadly, for the largest, multi-country NGOs, there seems to be a convergence toward more coordinated, global forms of governance with stronger representation and participation from developing countries. NGOs having separate national entities of the same name, such as Save the Children and MSF, which at one time operated as independent national organizations under loose umbrella structures, have over the years moved toward a confederated model with a greater degree of central coordination. At the opposite end of the spectrum, NGOs such as CARE and World Vision have moved from a highly centralized, unitary corporate model to various forms of federation, where the national affiliates have more autonomy and a voice in the overall governance of the organization. (Lindenberg and Dobel 1999) World Vision's "global bumblebee" structure seeks to devolve decision-making authority to local affiliates while binding them under a single, coherent global mission strategy. The changes in governance reflect at once the need for tighter coordination and policy coherence among affiliates and the desire to increase southern participation. The language of inclusion and partnership has long been a part of the NGOs' mission statements, but decision-making for many years remained squarely in the north, as manifested in primarily northern boards of directors. Most of the large and longstanding relief and development NGOs now strive for mixed boards, projects that are locally initiated and designed, resource acquisition in both north and south, and multiple partnerships and affiliates around the world. (Lindenberg and Dobel 1999) Some NGOs, notably CARE, have begun to actively seek out (or create, when necessary) local NGO partners to mentor and support until such time as they are able to join the federation as equal members. (Forman and Stoddard 2002)

The larger NGOs have adopted global management practices like those of TNCs, which is indicative of the increasing similarities that can be found between civil society organizations and international business: "As they get larger, NGOs are also looking more and more like businesses themselves. In the past, such groups sought no profits, paid low wages—or none at all—and employed idealists. Now a whole class of them, even if not directly backed by businesses, have taken on corporate trappings. Known collectively as BINGOs, these groups manage funds and employ staff which a medium-sized company would envy. Like corporations, they attend conferences endlessly. Fund-raisers and senior staff at such NGOs earn wages comparable to the private sector. Some bodies, once registered as charities, now choose to become non-profit companies or charitable trusts for tax reasons and so that they can control their spending and programmes more easily. Many big charities have trading arms, registered as companies. One manufacturing company, Tetra Pak, has even considered sponsoring emergency food delivery as a way to advertise itself." (*The Economist*, January 29, 2000, p. 28)

Until recently, the institutional infrastructure of civil society was dominated by organizations headquartered and managed in the advanced industrial countries of the North. This is due to the fact that many private voluntary organizations have their origins in Europe or the United States and the financial resources for underwriting the activities and programs of these organizations are more readily available in these countries. However, the telecommunications revolution has played a significant role in the emergence of robust NGO communities in developing countries of the South. Most of these newer organizations are local or national, small, and poor. Yet, today's telecommunications technology has helped Southern NGOs overcome many of their disadvantages, especially the meager resources that are at their disposal, and to be taken seriously in the international alliances and coalitions in which they participate. For example, it would have been impossible for the Jubilee 2000 debt relief campaign and the International Campaign to Ban Landmines, each a broad global coalition of NGOs all pursuing a simple central concern, to have been organized or informed without the Internet. (Peel 2001, 7)

Structural Convergence in the International Order

The distinct structural features of international organizations for each of the societal groups we have examined are now showing signs of convergence and integration. Globalization has intensified the symbiotic relationship among private and public international organizations. It is no longer practical to subordinate institutions and organizations that have been created by non-state actors in the structure of the international order. In fact, civil society organizations and TNCs are reshaping the landscape of international relations in ways that were not possible as recently as the 1980s. The legal, institutional, and functional barriers that once divided the three sectors are being lowered as the international system adjusts to the tremendous changes in the international environment. Each sector is experiencing a consolidation of institutional resources in response to the global restructuring of the international order.

While a robust debate continues to be waged within academic and policy circles on the dimensions of globalization and the impact it is having on states and the international system, other societal actors—the private sector and civil society—have begun to assert themselves in the practical matters of governance. In the 1990s, non-state actors (TNCs and NGOs) seem to have burst onto the international stage. "Civil society organizations as well as corporations have successfully reorganized themselves on a transnational scale, using various forms and varying degrees of influence to make their interests count in international politics. In some cases, transnational non-state interests have managed to almost fully transcend control of nation-states, demonstrated most vividly by the emergence of terrorist networks such as 'Al Qaeida' or transnational networks of organized crime. As a result, states are no longer the sole determinants of the international system." (Witte, Reinicke, and Benner 2002, 4) Obviously, the roles and relationships within and between sectors are changing and this is having a profound impact on the international system's architecture.

Because international commercial enterprises and civil society organizations are less encumbered by legal or political strictures that are commonly imposed on international governmental organizations, they appear to adapt more readily to changing circumstances and to adjust their operations accordingly. Increasingly TNCs and NGOs are expanding the space they occupy within the international order and challenging the state-centered hierarchical structure of the international system. States and IGOs, on the other hand, seem hard-pressed to adjust to the changing conditions created by rapid globalization. As a senior British diplomat recently pointed out:

> States are organized essentially on military lines and the core of the state remains its monopoly on force. . . . As military values decline, commercialisation is in the ascendant. Little escapes it today: religion, charity, friendship (via dating agencies), sport—all are organised commercially. But while markets represent a form of organisation different from that of the state, they are not an alternative. Markets require regulation, a legal system and a

medium of exchange, which requires monetary policy. Above all markets need security. . . . We still live in a world of sovereign states but sovereignty is expressed more often through negotiation than through military action. In domestic politics, sovereignty rests with the people; internationally it belongs to the state. The primary concern of governments is to satisfy electorates, not to reach compromises in international institutions. Thus, we live in a world in which co-operation is increasingly necessary but is made extremely difficult. Everything else may become global—markets, currencies, corporations—but the state remains stubbornly territorial. . . . Unable to operate effectively outside its borders, the state may give way to organisations better designed for global operations and co-operation. The corporate sector will set many international standards on its own. Transnational corporations may even work out international procedures for arbitration themselves. One effect of globalisation is to make the state an important part of the network rather than the top of a hierarchy. (Cooper 2002)

However, IGOs are trying to respond to change and are increasingly open to innovation. "Reinvention" is a common refrain among policymakers who are actively pushing institutional change on both the national and international levels. Borrowing and adapting ideas and methods from the private sector, IGOs have taken some steps to streamline their operations, to increase productivity, and to improve inter-organizational coordination and cooperation. For example, U.N. Secretary-General Kofi Annan launched an ambitious reform process in 1997–1998. This "quiet revolution at the United Nations" involves "fundamental, not piecemeal, reform" of the culture and management structure of the UN system:

The fundamental objective of this reform effort is to narrow the gap between aspiration and accomplishment. It seeks to do so by establishing a new leadership culture and management structure at the UN that will lead to greater unity of purpose, coherence of efforts, and agility in responding to the pressing needs of the international community. The major source of institutional weakness in the United Nations is the fact that over the course of the past half century certain of its organizational features had become fragmented, duplicative, rigid, in some areas ineffective, in others superfluous. The Cold War and the system of bloc politics that was its consequence made it extremely difficult and in some cases impossible for the organization to implement the Charter conceptions of its many roles, especially in the area of peace and security. In this hostile environment, the numerous new initiatives that the UN was able to launch throughout the Cold War years all too often were simply layered onto previous activities. Even previous reform efforts were constrained by these same forces. Often they produced parallel mechanisms or created additional bodies that were intended to coordinate, rather than instituting effective management structures.

Once the Cold War ended, the United Nations rushed and was pushed to respond to a vast increase in demand for its services. We made many mistakes, often because the means given to the organization did not match the demands made on it. Now that the frenzy of the immediate post–Cold War years has passed, we can and must step back to reassess which are the most effective means to realize the UN's enduring goals.

We know, for example, that over the course of the next generation a majority of the world's most rapidly growing economies will be located in what is now the developing world, while many of the least developed countries risk being bypassed by this process of economic expansion. We know that most of the policy issues in which the UN is involved have become, or are now better understood to be, intersectoral or transsectoral in character. We know that information age technologies have transformed the temporal context of policymaking, putting a premium on agility and flexibility of any organization that operates within it. Finally, we know that the institutional context in which all international organizations now operate is much more densely populated by other international actors, both public and private, than it was in the past. Today intergovernmental organizations at all levels number in the thousands. The resources of several of these organizations far exceed those of the United Nations. Moreover, the expanding transnational network of nongovernmental organizations (NGOs) encompasses virtually every sector of public concern, from the environment and human rights to the provision of microcredit, and is active at virtually every level of social organization, from villages on up to global summits. And the private sector continues to expand transnationally.

These developments demand, first, that the UN focus within its overall Charter mission on those intersectoral activities, or on those aspects of activities, that it does better than others, and, second, that we devise effective means by which to collaborate with other international organizations and

> institutions of civil society, thereby amplifying the effect of its own moral, institutional, and material resources. In sum, the very organizational features that are now most demanded by the UN's external context in some respects are in shortest supply: strategic deployment of resources, unity of purpose, coherence of effort, agility and flexibility. The current reform effort aims at redressing this imbalance. (Annan 1998, 128–129)

Much progress was made in reorganizing the U.N. secretariat after 1997, when the secretary-general started putting his plan into effect. The secretariat's work program is now divided into five core mission areas—peace and security, economic and social affairs, development cooperation, humanitarian affairs, and human rights—with executive committees over each of four areas (human rights is a "cross-cutting focus" and participates in the other core areas). A senior management group has been established, consisting of the conveners of the executive committees and other senior officials, that functions like a cabinet. The secretary-general also integrated and rationalized a number of departments, consolidated U.N. operations at the country level, and overhauled the U.N.'s human resources policies. The General Assembly established a new senior post of deputy secretary-general to enhance the managerial capability of the programs and operations across the U.N. system and to ensure intersectoral and interinstitutional coherence of U.N. activities. The assembly also rationalized some responsibilities in the area of humanitarian affairs, establishing a segment of the Economic and Social Council dedicated to humanitarian affairs and designating the emergency relief coordinator as the U.N. humanitarian assistance coordinator. However, the more fundamental reform proposals that require member states' action did not make much headway. These included reducing the items on the assembly's agenda, establishing a ministerial-level commission to review the legal relationship between the United Nations and the specialized agencies, and transforming the Trusteeship Council into an intergovernmental mechanism for managing the global environment and commons (as well as the reform proposals that have been developed by the assembly's five working groups since 1992).

Perhaps more important is the emphasis in this U.N. reform exercise on the principles of "good governance" (such as the rule of law, legitimacy, trust, and accountability) and "partnership." The U.N. Millennium Declaration (see Box 6.3) adopted at the fifty-fifth General Assembly in

BOX 6.3

Resolution adopted by the General Assembly
[*without reference to a Main Committee (A/55/L.2)*]
55/2. United Nations Millennium Declaration

The General Assembly
Adopts the following Declaration:

United Nations Millennium Declaration

I. Values and principles

1. We, heads of State and Government, have gathered at United Nations Headquarters in New York from 6 to 8 September 2000, at the dawn of a new millennium, to reaffirm our faith in the Organization and its Charter as indispensable foundations of a more peaceful, prosperous and just world.

2. We recognize that, in addition to our separate responsibilities to our individual societies, we have a collective responsibility to uphold the principles of human dignity, equality and equity at the global level. As leaders we have a duty therefore to all the world's people, especially the most vulnerable and, in particular, the children of the world, to whom the future belongs.

3. We reaffirm our commitment to the purposes and principles of the Charter of the United Nations, which have proved timeless and universal. Indeed, their relevance and capacity to inspire have increased, as nations and peoples have become increasingly interconnected and interdependent.

4. We are determined to establish a just and lasting peace all over the world in accordance with the purposes and principles of the Charter. We rededicate ourselves to support all efforts to uphold the sovereign equality of all States, respect for their territorial integrity and political independence, resolution of disputes by peaceful means and in conformity with the principles of justice and international law, the right to self-determination of peoples which remain under colonial domination and foreign occupation, non-interference in the internal affairs of States, respect for human rights and fundamental freedoms, respect for the equal rights of all without distinction as to race, sex, language or religion and international cooperation in solving international problems of an economic, social, cultural or humanitarian character.

5. We believe that the central challenge we face today is to ensure that globalization becomes a positive force for all the world's people. For while globalization offers great opportunities, at present its benefits are very unevenly shared, while its costs are unevenly distributed. We recognize that developing countries and countries with economies in transition face special difficulties in responding to this central challenge. Thus, only through broad and sustained efforts to create a shared future, based upon our common humanity in all its diversity, can globalization be made fully inclusive and equitable. These efforts must include policies and measures, at the global level, which correspond to the needs of developing countries and

(continues)

economies in transition and are formulated and implemented with their effective participation.

6. We consider certain fundamental values to be essential to international relations in the twenty-first century. These include:

• *Freedom.* Men and women have the right to live their lives and raise their children in dignity, free from hunger and from the fear of violence, oppression or injustice. Democratic and participatory governance based on the will of the people best assures these rights.

•. *Equality.* No individual and no nation must be denied the opportunity to benefit from development. The equal rights and opportunities of women and men must be assured.

• *Solidarity.* Global challenges must be managed in a way that distributes the costs and burdens fairly in accordance with basic principles of equity and social justice. Those who suffer or who benefit least deserve help from those who benefit most.

• *Tolerance.* Human beings must respect one other, in all their diversity of belief, culture and language. Differences within and between societies should be neither feared nor repressed, but cherished as a precious asset of humanity. A culture of peace and dialogue among all civilizations should be actively promoted.

• *Respect for nature.* Prudence must be shown in the management of all living species and natural resources, in accordance with the precepts of sustainable development. Only in this way can the immeasurable riches provided to us by nature be preserved and passed on to our descendants. The current unsustainable patterns of production and consumption must be changed in the interest of our future welfare and that of our descendants.

• *Shared responsibility.* Responsibility for managing worldwide economic and social development, as well as threats to international peace and security, must be shared among the nations of the world and should be exercised multilaterally. As the most universal and most representative organization in the world, the United Nations must play the central role.

7. In order to translate these shared values into actions, we have identified key objectives to which we assign special significance.

II. Peace, security and disarmament

8. We will spare no effort to free our peoples from the scourge of war, whether within or between States, which has claimed more than 5 million lives in the past decade. We will also seek to eliminate the dangers posed by weapons of mass destruction.

9. We resolve therefore:

• To strengthen respect for the rule of law in international as in national affairs and, in particular, to ensure compliance by Member States with the decisions of the International Court of Justice, in compliance with the Charter of the United Nations, in cases to which they are parties.

• To make the United Nations more effective in maintaining peace and security by giving it the resources and tools it needs for conflict prevention, peaceful resolution of dis-

(continues)

putes, peacekeeping, post-conflict peace-building and reconstruction. In this context, we take note of the report of the Panel on United Nations Peace Operations and request the General Assembly to consider its recommendations expeditiously.

• To strengthen cooperation between the United Nations and regional organizations, in accordance with the provisions of Chapter VIII of the Charter.

• To ensure the implementation, by States Parties, of treaties in areas such as arms control and disarmament and of international humanitarian law and human rights law, and call upon all States to consider signing and ratifying the Rome Statute of the International Criminal Court.

• To take concerted action against international terrorism, and to accede as soon as possible to all the relevant international conventions.

• To redouble our efforts to implement our commitment to counter the world drug problem.

• To intensify our efforts to fight transnational crime in all its dimensions, including trafficking as well as smuggling in human beings and money laundering.

• To minimize the adverse effects of United Nations economic sanctions on innocent populations, to subject such sanctions regimes to regular reviews and to eliminate the adverse effects of sanctions on third parties.

• To strive for the elimination of weapons of mass destruction, particularly nuclear weapons, and to keep all options open for achieving this aim, including the possibility of convening an international conference to identify ways of eliminating nuclear dangers.

• To take concerted action to end illicit traffic in small arms and light weapons, especially by making arms transfers more transparent and supporting regional disarmament measures, taking account of all the recommendations of the forthcoming United Nations Conference on Illicit Trade in Small Arms and Light Weapons.

• To call on all States to consider acceding to the Convention on the Prohibition of the Use, Stockpiling, Production and Transfer of Anti-personnel Mines and on Their Destruction, as well as the amended mines protocol to the Convention on conventional weapons.

10. We urge Member States to observe the Olympic Truce, individually and collectively, now and in the future, and to support the International Olympic Committee in its efforts to promote peace and human understanding through sport and the Olympic Ideal.

III. Development and poverty eradication

11. We will spare no effort to free our fellow men, women and children from the abject and dehumanizing conditions of extreme poverty, to which more than a billion of them are currently subjected. We are committed to making the right to development a reality for everyone and to freeing the entire human race from want.

12. We resolve therefore to create an environment—at the national and global levels alike—which is conducive to development and to the elimination of poverty.

13. Success in meeting these objectives depends, *inter alia*, on good governance within each country. It also depends on good governance at the international level and on trans-

(continues)

parency in the financial, monetary and trading systems. We are committed to an open, equitable, rule-based, predictable and non-discriminatory multilateral trading and financial system.

14. We are concerned about the obstacles developing countries face in mobilizing the resources needed to finance their sustained development. We will therefore make every effort to ensure the success of the High-level International and Intergovernmental Event on Financing for Development, to be held in 2001.

15. We also undertake to address the special needs of the least developed countries. In this context, we welcome the Third United Nations Conference on the Least Developed Countries to be held in May 2001 and will endeavour to ensure its success. We call on the industrialized countries:

• To adopt, preferably by the time of that Conference, a policy of duty- and quota-free access for essentially all exports from the least developed countries;

• To implement the enhanced programme of debt relief for the heavily indebted poor countries without further delay and to agree to cancel all official bilateral debts of those countries in return for their making demonstrable commitments to poverty reduction; and

• To grant more generous development assistance, especially to countries that are genuinely making an effort to apply their resources to poverty reduction.

16. We are also determined to deal comprehensively and effectively with the debt problems of low- and middle-income developing countries, through various national and international measures designed to make their debt sustainable in the long term.

17. We also resolve to address the special needs of small island developing States, by implementing the Barbados Programme of Action and the outcome of the twenty-second special session of the General Assembly rapidly and in full. We urge the international community to ensure that, in the development of a vulnerability index, the special needs of small island developing States are taken into account.

18. We recognize the special needs and problems of the landlocked developing countries, and urge both bilateral and multilateral donors to increase financial and technical assistance to this group of countries to meet their special development needs and to help them overcome the impediments of geography by improving their transit transport systems.

19. We resolve further:

• To halve, by the year 2015, the proportion of the world's people whose income is less than one dollar a day and the proportion of people who suffer from hunger and, by the same date, to halve the proportion of people who are unable to reach or to afford safe drinking water.

• To ensure that, by the same date, children everywhere, boys and girls alike, will be able to complete a full course of primary schooling and that girls and boys will have equal access to all levels of education.

(continues)

• By the same date, to have reduced maternal mortality by three quarters, and under-five child mortality by two thirds, of their current rates.

• To have, by then, halted, and begun to reverse, the spread of HIV/AIDS, the scourge of malaria and other major diseases that afflict humanity.

• To provide special assistance to children orphaned by HIV/AIDS.

• By 2020, to have achieved a significant improvement in the lives of at least 100 million slum dwellers as proposed in the "Cities Without Slums" initiative.

20. We also resolve:

• To promote gender equality and the empowerment of women as effective ways to combat poverty, hunger and disease and to stimulate development that is truly sustainable.

• To develop and implement strategies that give young people everywhere a real chance to find decent and productive work.

• To encourage the pharmaceutical industry to make essential drugs more widely available and affordable by all who need them in developing countries.

• To develop strong partnerships with the private sector and with civil society organizations in pursuit of development and poverty eradication.

• To ensure that the benefits of new technologies, especially information and communication technologies, in conformity with recommendations contained in the ECOSOC 2000 Ministerial Declaration, are available to all.

IV. Protecting our common environment

21. We must spare no effort to free all of humanity, and above all our children and grandchildren, from the threat of living on a planet irredeemably spoilt by human activities, and whose resources would no longer be sufficient for their needs.

22. We reaffirm our support for the principles of sustainable development, including those set out in Agenda 21, agreed upon at the United Nations Conference on Environment and Development.

23. We resolve therefore to adopt in all our environmental actions a new ethic of conservation and stewardship and, as first steps, we resolve:

• To make every effort to ensure the entry into force of the Kyoto Protocol, preferably by the tenth anniversary of the United Nations Conference on Environment and Development in 2002, and to embark on the required reduction in emissions of greenhouse gases.

• To intensify our collective efforts for the management, conservation and sustainable development of all types of forests.

• To press for the full implementation of the Convention on Biological Diversity and the Convention to Combat Desertification in those Countries Experiencing Serious Drought and/or Desertification, particularly in Africa.

• To stop the unsustainable exploitation of water resources by developing water management strategies at the regional, national and local levels, which promote both equitable access and adequate supplies.

(continues)

• To intensify cooperation to reduce the number and effects of natural and man-made disasters.

• To ensure free access to information on the human genome sequence.

V. Human rights, democracy and good governance

24. We will spare no effort to promote democracy and strengthen the rule of law, as well as respect for all internationally recognized human rights and fundamental freedoms, including the right to development.

25. We resolve therefore:

• To respect fully and uphold the Universal Declaration of Human Rights.

• To strive for the full protection and promotion in all our countries of civil, political, economic, social and cultural rights for all.

• To strengthen the capacity of all our countries to implement the principles and practices of democracy and respect for human rights, including minority rights.

• To combat all forms of violence against women and to implement the Convention on the Elimination of All Forms of Discrimination against Women.

• To take measures to ensure respect for and protection of the human rights of migrants, migrant workers and their families, to eliminate the increasing acts of racism and xenophobia in many societies and to promote greater harmony and tolerance in all societies.

• To work collectively for more inclusive political processes, allowing genuine participation by all citizens in all our countries.

• To ensure the freedom of the media to perform their essential role and the right of the public to have access to information.

VI. Protecting the vulnerable

26. We will spare no effort to ensure that children and all civilian populations that suffer disproportionately the consequences of natural disasters, genocide, armed conflicts and other humanitarian emergencies are given every assistance and protection so that they can resume normal life as soon as possible.
We resolve therefore:

• To expand and strengthen the protection of civilians in complex emergencies, in conformity with international humanitarian law.

• To strengthen international cooperation, including burden sharing in, and the coordination of humanitarian assistance to, countries hosting refugees and to help all refugees and displaced persons to return voluntarily to their homes, in safety and dignity and to be smoothly reintegrated into their societies.

• To encourage the ratification and full implementation of the Convention on the Rights of the Child and its optional protocols on the involvement of children in armed conflict and on the sale of children, child prostitution and child pornography.

(continues)

VII. Meeting the special needs of Africa

27. We will support the consolidation of democracy in Africa and assist Africans in their struggle for lasting peace, poverty eradication and sustainable development, thereby bringing Africa into the mainstream of the world economy.

28. We resolve therefore:

• To give full support to the political and institutional structures of emerging democracies in Africa.

• To encourage and sustain regional and subregional mechanisms for preventing conflict and promoting political stability, and to ensure a reliable flow of resources for peacekeeping operations on the continent.

• To take special measures to address the challenges of poverty eradication and sustainable development in Africa, including debt cancellation, improved market access, enhanced Official Development Assistance and increased flows of Foreign Direct Investment, as well as transfers of technology.

• To help Africa build up its capacity to tackle the spread of the HIV/AIDS pandemic and other infectious diseases.

VIII. Strengthening the United Nations

29. We will spare no effort to make the United Nations a more effective instrument for pursuing all of these priorities: the fight for development for all the peoples of the world, the fight against poverty, ignorance and disease; the fight against injustice; the fight against violence, terror and crime; and the fight against the degradation and destruction of our common home.

30. We resolve therefore:

• To reaffirm the central position of the General Assembly as the chief deliberative, policy-making and representative organ of the United Nations, and to enable it to play that role effectively.

• To intensify our efforts to achieve a comprehensive reform of the Security Council in all its aspects.

• To strengthen further the Economic and Social Council, building on its recent achievements, to help it fulfil the role ascribed to it in the Charter.

• To strengthen the International Court of Justice, in order to ensure justice and the rule of law in international affairs.

• To encourage regular consultations and coordination among the principal organs of the United Nations in pursuit of their functions.

• To ensure that the Organization is provided on a timely and predictable basis with the resources it needs to carry out its mandates.

• To urge the Secretariat to make the best use of those resources, in accordance with clear rules and procedures agreed by the General Assembly, in the interests of all Member States,

(continues)

by adopting the best management practices and technologies available and by concentrating on those tasks that reflect the agreed priorities of Member States.

• To promote adherence to the Convention on the Safety of United Nations and Associated Personnel.

• To ensure greater policy coherence and better cooperation between the United Nations, its agencies, the Bretton Woods Institutions and the World Trade Organization, as well as other multilateral bodies, with a view to achieving a fully coordinated approach to the problems of peace and development.

• To strengthen further cooperation between the United Nations and national parliaments through their world organization, the Inter-Parliamentary Union, in various fields, including peace and security, economic and social development, international law and human rights and democracy and gender issues.

• To give greater opportunities to the private sector, non-governmental organizations and civil society, in general, to contribute to the realization of the Organization's goals and programmes.

31. We request the General Assembly to review on a regular basis the progress made in implementing the provisions of this Declaration, and ask the Secretary-General to issue periodic reports for consideration by the General Assembly and as a basis for further action.

32. We solemnly reaffirm, on this historic occasion, that the United Nations is the indispensable common house of the entire human family, through which we will seek to realize our universal aspirations for peace, cooperation and development. We therefore pledge our unstinting support for these common objectives and our determination to achieve them.

8th plenary meeting
8 September 2000

2000 outlined an ambitious set of priorities, including precise, time-bound development goals (or the Millennium Development Goals, MDG) for future U.N. activities and reform. This list of priorities and goals is remarkable in that it reflects an important shift in attitude towards both the United Nations and how the United Nations should be restructured to meet the immense challenges of globalization. Furthermore, the declaration explicitly calls for a change in the relationship between the United Nations and non-state actors—an area that the secretary-general began building up in 1997.

The secretary-general put great stock in the idea of "partnership" between the United Nations and civil society and between the United Nations and the private sector for realizing the MDG as well as contributing to the other core mission areas of the organization (see United Nations

2002, 23–26). Although the shape of these partnerships is still evolving, the relationships between the United Nations and international actors from civil society and the private sector are increasingly institutionalized.

Emergent Forms of Complex Global Cooperation

The pluralization of international relations is one of the more important consequences of globalization. Economic and political liberalization has enabled transnational private interests to emerge and increased non-state actors' influence on the international agenda. Yet, most mechanisms for international decisionmaking are still dominated by or strictly exclusive to states, who, in theory, represent the interests of their citizens on the international level, relegating non-state actors to the corridors and back rows at international gatherings addressing their concerns and interests. This arrangement has been under increasing attack from both civil society and the private sector whose international activities have outpaced states' efforts to retain control over the international environment and international governmental institutions' "rule-setting" functions. Transnational corporations now dominate trade, investment, and technology, and in emerging areas of the global economy (for example, the Internet) where governments are either too slow or unable to act, TNCs are creating their own rules and standards.

Civil society organizations have become powerful international players too. They have developed sophisticated transnational structures that enable them to coordinate efforts in advocacy, service-delivery, and policy development. Increasing numbers of NGOs have crowded in at international governmental conferences on the environment, disarmament, trade, development, housing, and so on, fundamentally changing the way of doing international politics. "What we can observe in the 1990s is the emergence of a supranational sphere of social and political participation in which citizen groups, social movements, and individuals engage in dialogue, debate, confrontation, and negotiation with each other and with various governmental actors—international, national, and local—as well as the business world. . . . The number of organisations and individuals that are part of global civil society has probably never been bigger, and the range and type of fields in which they operate never been wider: from UN conferences about social welfare or the environment to conflict situations in Kosovo, from globalised resistance to the Mutual Agreement on Investments to local human rights activism in Mexico, Burma, or Timor, and from media corporations spanning the globe to indigenous peoples' campaigns over the internet." (Anheier, Glasius and Kaldor 2001, 4) The international system is increasingly caught up in a whirlwind of competing and clashing interests as state and non-state actors jockey for position and control—an inevitable consequence of a widening "participatory gap" (or "democratic deficit") of traditional international organizations and institutions.

As operational and participatory gaps in the international system's institutional infrastructure grow, new and innovative institutional arrangements for managing globalization are emerging. The new organizational forms, at this stage of development, vary widely in size, composition, and functional capacity. Some have been instigated by the private sector, others by civil society, and still others are the creation of states and international organizations. They go by a variety of names—global public policy networks (see Reinicke and Deng et al. 2000), private sector initiatives (see Stern and Hicks 2000), public-private partnerships, and global alliances and coalitions.

The recent history of the Internet's development captures the dynamics of how structures of international cooperation are changing. Rapid advances in information technologies in the 1990s have created a new global common space called cyberspace. The creation and rapid technological development of the Internet—"a global network of computer networks which operates using a set of open technological protocols of which the Transmission Control Protocol (TCP/IP) suite is the most important" (Naughton 2001, 148)—has revolutionized the communications environment. As John Naughton points out: "The facilities [the Internet] provides for accessing information, communicating, publishing, and organizing evince a tremendous democratising potential. The network appears to promise the realisation of Thomas Paine's dream of a society in which everyone has a voice: a true Jeffersonian market in ideas. If this dream is ever to be fully implemented, however, a fundamental problem will have to be addressed and solved. This is the issue of inequality of access to the Internet: the so-called 'digital divide', the term popularly used to describe the gap between the 'information rich' and the 'information poor'. If the benefits and facilities are available to a selected few, then its democratising potential, not to mention its economic potential, will never be realized." (Naughton 2001, 157) Unlike the natural physical global commons, cyberspace today is open, free, permissive, and uncontrolled (at least in "information rich" industrialized countries). Yet, the various utilities of the Internet are not always compatible (e-commerce versus scientific research) or socially desirable (cyber-terrorism and pornography).

While the early users of the Internet—predominantly, civil society groups and academics—thought that the "Net" was beyond the reach of governmental regulation and commercial control, the rules and norms they had established to govern users' behavior on the Net could not ultimately stop governments or businesses from entering the space. Once governments and businesses joined in, the online community changed "to include a much more diverse population and a host of explicitly commercial enterprises. Under these circumstances, the old rules no longer make sense. Accordingly, the rules of the Internet are now rapidly evolving, pulled and prodded by the often-conflicting interests of business entities, governmental agencies, and traditional Net users. In general, governments have tended, initially at least, to approach the Internet as if it were any other realm of public activity: they presume some authority to control certain kinds of speech, or to prohibit the sale of restricted goods, or to stem the flow of information deemed damaging to the state. At the same time, traditional users have clamored to maintain the old rules of interaction: to keep cyberspace a realm of open communication and universal access, removed from any form of governmental intervention. The business community, by contrast, has been relatively quiet, with managers avoiding public debate as they concentrate on the more immediate tasks of staking a claim in cyberspace. Yet merely by staking a claim and securing their position, firms have already changed the Internet's rules. In particular, just by concentrating on their commercial requirements, firms have begun to establish, on their own and from the ground up, three distinct sets of rules: rules of property, rules of currency, and rules of enforcement. Together these rules and their makers constitute a powerful, if still emerging, source of private authority and private international governance." (Spar 1999, 36–37) The successful commercialization of cyberspace suggests that the private sector has emerged victorious, at least for the time being. Yet, it is important to note that the outcome of the process is not a new hierarchy but rather a "more fluid and heterogeneous policy architecture in which states and a hyper-empowered global business community cooperate and compete in a wide range of forums to devise market-enabling rules." (Drake 2001, 26)

Governance of the Internet involves two arenas, management of the underlying infrastructure and management of communications and commerce conducted over the infrastructure. The private sector has built elaborate collective mechanisms for the first arena to coordinate technical projects and company policies related to infrastructure issues and development, such as the Internet Engineering Task Force and the Internet Architecture Board. One of the institutional innovations to emerge is the Internet Corporation for Assigned Names and Numbers (ICANN), which is a private, not-for-profit corporation registered in California. According to William Drake, "ICANN represents a new hybrid form of international organization. Its semicorporatist organizational structure includes a president and chief executive officer, a secretariat, and a board of directors, the latter of which has ultimate decision-making authority; a Domain Name Supporting Organization, an Address Supporting Organization, and a Protocol Supporting Organization, each comprising various industry factions; and an At-Large Membership of Internet users around the world that elects five of the board's nineteen directors. In addition, ICANN has a Government Advisory Committee comprising representatives (usually from communications ministries) of dozens of governments." (Drake 2001, 42) International regime development for the second arena remains incipient and largely within traditional institutional arrangements such as the International Telecommunications Union, the World Intellectual Property Organization, the U.N. Centre for Trade Facilitation and Electronic Business, and the World Trade Organization.

Another, yet similar, institutional innovation is the Global Reporting Initiative (GRI), which was inaugurated at the United Nations in New York on April 4, 2002. The GRI is a permanent, independent international sustainability reporting institution put together by the Coalition for Environmentally Responsible Economies in collaboration with the United Nations Environment Programme (UNEP). "The GRI was established to develop, promote, and disseminate a generally accepted framework for sustainability reporting—voluntary reporting on the economic, environmental, and social performance of corporations and other organisations. Its mandate as an international standards body is to make sustainability reporting as routine as financial reporting while achieving the highest standards of consistency and rigour. . . . The GRI involves the active participation of thousands of representatives from business, accountancy, investment, environmental, human rights, and labour organisations world-wide in designing a common framework called the Sustainability Reporting Guidelines. More than 110 pioneering companies from around the world have already undertaken sustainability reporting using the GRI Guidelines—including BASF, British Telecom, Bristol-Myers Squibb, Canon, Co-operative Bank, Danone, Electrolux, Ford, GM, Interface, KLM, NEC, Nike, Novo Group, Nokia, Shell, and South African Breweries." (GRI Press Release, April 4, 2002; see the GRI website www.globalreporting.org) The GRI appears to be using a similar structure to that of ICANN—it has a board of directors comprised of representatives from all continents and "numerous stakeholder constituencies," a chief executive officer, a permanent secretariat headquarters in Amsterdam, and plans for regional offices in the United States, Latin America, Asia, and Africa.

Other organizational experiments that are being developed for a range of global issue areas are so-called public-private partnerships. "Partnership" is the label in vogue these days for a vast array of informal and formal public-private arrangements, which have become ubiquitous for addressing a wide range of global issues. The structure of public-private partnerships on the international level varies considerably depending on the partners and the partnerships' objectives. A number of partnerships have been formed between the private sector and environmental nongovernmental organizations to manage sustainable development and the environment and they have worked reasonably well in bridging traditionally adversarial positions in this conflicted arena. The success of civil society-business partnerships has produced a set of standard mechanisms for transnational cooperation and a model that is being employed in other issue areas.

Partnering with the private sector and civil society organizations on sustainable development projects and programs became a favorite tool of several agencies of the U.N. system beginning in the 1990s, particularly the U.N. Development Program, the U.N. Environment Program, the World Health Organization, and the World Bank. Many of the partnerships are a contractual agreement between an international agency, NGOs, and a company or companies that outlines commitments of resources and assets of the parties towards delivering a service or pursuing a joint venture. For example, UNDP and Coca-Cola formed a partnership to focus on innovative use of information and communications technology (ICT) for youth education and development in Asia. The goal is to help local communities gain access to ICT to help overcome socio-economic disparities.

The U.N.'s Global Compact is another example of international public-private cooperation.

> The GC [Global Compact] engages the private sector to work with the UN, in partnership with international labor and NGOs, to identify, disseminate, and promote good corporate practices based on nine universal principles. These are drawn from the Universal Declaration of Human Rights, the International Labour Organization's (ILO) Fundamental Principles and Rights at Work, and the Rio Declaration on Environment and Development. . . . Specifically, companies are asked to undertake three commitments:
>
> 1. To advocate the GC in mission statements, annual reports, and similar public venues . . .
> 2. To post on the GC Website at least once a year concrete steps to act on any or all of the nine principles, discussing both positive and negative lessons learned . . .
> 3. To join with the UN in partnership projects to benefit developing countries largely marginalized by globalization, particularly the least developed.
>
> Companies initiate participation by having their chief executive officer send a letter to the secretary-general expressing their commitment, a step that typically requires board approval. (Ruggie 2001, 371–372)

The Global Compact has spawned numerous regional, national, and sectoral public-private partnerships around the world. (In February 2002, for example, the New Partnership for African Development, or NEPAD, was announced and it secured private sector commitments at the UN Conference on Financing for Development in Monterrey, Mexico, in March.) Through its network approach, the Global Compact has enhanced the U.N.'s operational capacity in directing or guiding foreign direct investment (FDI) and other private sector resources towards poverty reduction projects and sustainable development strategies in developing countries.

The Global Compact and other international public-private partnerships exhibit key characteristics of what John Ruggie calls interorganizational networks (IONs):

> IONs are formed by autonomous organizations combining their efforts voluntarily to achieve goals they cannot reach as effectively or at all on their own. They rest on a bargain, not coercion. . . .
>
> IONs typically come into being to help their participants understand and deal with complex and ambiguous challenges. They are inherently experimental, not routine and standardized. . . .
>
> IONs "operate" as shared conceptual systems within which the participating entities perceive, understand, and frame aspects of their behavior. . . .
>
> IONs must be guided by a shared vision and common purpose. . . .
>
> IONs are a loosely coupled organizational forms, resting on non-directive horizontal organizing principles. Its participants meet when and in formats required to conduct their work. (Ruggie 2001, 375)

According to Jan Martin Witte, Wolfgang Reinicke, and Thorsten Benner, these networks are representative of "horizontal governance systems" that have started to proliferate on the global level. "Multisector networks create bridges on a transnational scale among the public sector (national, regional or state, and local governments as well as inter-governmental groups), the private sector and civil society. They (a) reflect the changing roles and relative importance among them; (b) pull diverse groups and resources together; and (c) address issues that no group can solve by itself." (Witte et al. 2002, 10) Global public policy networks borrow heavily from the private sector in both design and operation. Generally, these networks, such as the World Commission on Dams, the Roll Back Malaria campaign, and Medicines for Malaria Venture, are built on the open-sourcing model and "manage knowledge from the bottom up," reflecting many of the management approaches currently in fashion within knowledge-intensive industries such as communications and pharmaceuticals.

It is probably too early to pass judgment on these experiments of complex global cooperation, and only time will tell whether they can withstand the turbulence created by globalization. Public-private partnerships and multisector networks have, in some cases, been effective in bringing the private sector into the business of providing global public goods, but they have not necessarily changed the architecture of the international system. Indeed, these emergent forms of global cooperation build upon the traditional institutional infrastructure and strengthen the existing system. They appear to be more like a provisional measure or interim step in the process of reconfiguring sectoral jurisdictions and boundaries, rather than the new structure of global governance. However, the change in the relationships between states, markets, and civil society brought about by these arrangements are clearly significant. The rigid hierarchical bureaucratic structures and institutions of the international system are being dismantled or reinvented and this process has opened space to non-state actors and private institutions. There is greater mutual respect and appreciation of each sector's contribution to effective management of complex global issues. Adversarial and confrontational attitudes are less pronounced. The tripartite network approach has increased the contributions of each sector to the provision of global public goods and therefore are an important innovation in the way global issues are governed.

7

International Organizations and the Management of International Change

The incredible rate of international institution-building during the twentieth century, particularly the latter half, has resulted in significant institutionalization of world politics, whereby "institutional rules govern more of the behavior of important actors—more in the sense that behavior previously outside the scope of particular rules is now within that scope or that behavior that was previously regulated is now more deeply regulated." But as we know, international institutions vary considerably on many dimensions—for example, "the WTO [World Trade Organization] and the international regime for the protection of polar bears are both institutions, but they differ according to the scope of their rules, the resources available to the formal organizations, and their degree of bureaucratic differentiation." (Goldstein, Kahler, Keohane, and Slaughter 2000, 387) Nevertheless, the increasing density of international organizations managing key societal functions—economy, law, technology and science, the environment, and security—indicates the fruition of a functioning international society.

International organizations provide a framework for states and nonstate actors to work out differences and to peacefully manage shifts in relationships that occur when the international political and economic landscape changes. International organizations are both an arena where the rules and regulations that govern international society are set and an instrument of international society for implementing them. They were "set up to perform a variety of tasks: keeping the peace, promoting economic development, allocating the radio frequency spectrum, reducing obstacles to trade, ensuring that technology is used only for peaceful purposes, and facilitating the maintenance of stable exchange rates—to name only a few. . . . Whatever their specific tasks and fields of activities, international organizations can be divided into two broad categories according to the way in which they perform these tasks. Some organizations are established to provide a forum or framework for negotiations and decisions, others to provide specific services. . . . In reality, of course, many international organizations fall into both categories. ILO, for example, has an extensive technical assistance program, but also provides a framework for the negotiation of International Labor Conventions. Similarly ITU, UNESCO, WHO, IAEA, and IMF execute services in their own right and at the same time provide frameworks for discussions and negotiations among their member states." (Cox and Jacobson 1997, 75–76). States and non-state actors have come to rely more and more upon international organizations to manage the complex dynamics of transnational activities on a broadening range of issues.

Robert Cox argues that there are "two main functions of international organization: one, to respond effectively to the pressing problems of the present; the other, to be concerned with longer-term questions of global structural change and with how international organization—or we can use the broader term 'multilateralism'—can help shape that change in a consensually desirable direction." (Cox 1996, 525) These two functions entail that international organizations be competent in operational management as well as possess sound political and diplomatic skills.

Furthermore, international organizations have evolved toward greater autonomy through their operational activities. According to Jan Klabbers, "Lawyers usually insist, and arguably have to insist, that organizations are more than mere vehicles for the aggregate will of their member states. Instead, they are considered to have a will of their own, a *volonté distincte*, which renders it conceptually feasible to distinguish them from other forms of inter-state cooperation, and to lift them beyond the mere sphere of cooperation. The international organization, in this view, is not merely a forum for cooperation, but it is something more than that: it is an actor in its own right, with its own agenda, its own goals, and its own role to play." (Klabbers 2001, 226) Although this view is not without its critics and skeptics who rightly point out that there is scant empirical evidence of such an independent will of international organizations, the fact that international organizations perform an expanding list of tasks—many being determined and implemented by the organizations themselves—demonstrates that they have considerable autonomy and a growing operational capacity distinct from other players on the international stage. However, the process of moving from arena and/or instrument to actor has not been easy for international organizations. The line between these different roles has never been clear-cut and many organizations have to perform these roles simultaneously.

The agency of international organizations is qualified by three factors—managing the different and often conflicting expectations and interests of states and of a burgeoning collection of non-state actors; meeting the needs and problems of people on the local, national, regional and international levels; and developing and implementing processes and mechanisms for effectively dealing with changes in the international system without adequate funding, political support, and/or resources. According to Dennis Dijkzeul and Leon Gordenker, international organizations "operate simultaneously in two arenas: a strategic arena, in which goals are set and decisions are being made; and an implementing arena, in which these goals and decision should be translated into action in order to help people. Ideally, the latter happens in close cooperation with these people. The international organizations form the link between those two arenas; they are intermediary organizations." (Dijkzeul and Gordenker 2003, 320) These two arenas entail distinct and sometimes contradictory functions for international organizations, which makes linking the two arenas a very complex and difficult task.

In the strategic arena, international organizations contend with an increasingly crowded and complex international political process that is still jealously guarded by states. While the secretariats of international organizations support and have some influence on international decisionmaking, the organizations themselves are traditionally outsiders in the process and have little, if any, control over who participates or the outcomes of the process. Their influence is largely that of special expertise on the issues or the problem being addressed (without an overt political agenda or a special interest bias) that helps guide the process towards decisions or facilitates compromise and cooperation on politically sensitive and contentious issues.

In the implementing arena, international organizations take on a different function—namely, translating the decisions taken in the strategic arena into effective and efficient services and programs. In this regard, international organizations have to move from a political role to a management role. "For international organizations this means programming for delivering services, training, technology transfer, and advocacy, with the ultimate aim of building national and local capacities for self-reliance. To be successful in these operational tasks, management has to eschew ambiguity. Directness, as well as clear guidance and goals from the actors in the strategic arena, facilitate program management, but this occurs only infrequently. Internally, accountability requires explicit goals, clear lines of authority, and unambiguous delineation of responsibility, as well as strong evaluation and follow-up. This is based on a managerial logic that emphasizes the values of authenticity (managers mean what they say) and sincerity (managers really do what they say they will do). Without these values implementing organizational change or programs will at first be haphazard and later it will become harder, if not impossible." (Dijkzeul and Gordenker 2003, 323-324) Balancing the political necessities imposed by the strategic arena with the managerial requirements in the implementing arena is no easy feat, especially since international organizations operate simultaneously in several strategic and implementing arenas (local, national, regional, and international) that intensify both the complexity and the contradictions with which they have to contend, and many fail to do so. Unfortunately, the many shortcomings of international organizations, which are regularly pointed out by their critics, are due to their inability to manage the contradictions of their different roles.

During the Cold War most international organizations were paralyzed between the two superpowers. The international agenda was focused on the ideological and strategic rivalry of the superpowers, the "high politics" issues of security and deterrence. Only on the margins were international organizations able to perform the tasks originally assigned to them in this area. The Cold War, however, did not curtail the operational development of international organizations in other areas such as international trade and finance, economic development, and the environment, while regional organizations with mandates for managing "low politics" (for example, economic integration and technical cooperation) flourished. International organizations were compelled to eschew activities that could be characterized as supranational or a direct challenge to states' sovereignty and to limit their role to that of service providers, expert centers, and advocates. But even within these limitations, international organizations played an important role in the survival of the international system throughout the Cold War period, and beyond that were able to ameliorate many of the problems that were either being ignored or aggravated by states. They have been instrumental in the development of international law, expanding its scope and content, and the universalization of human rights; in limiting inter-state armed conflict, promoting arms control and disarmament, and enlarging the notion of international security from its narrow definition of "national security" to a broader one of "human security"; in putting the environment onto the international agenda and devising international policies that protect against environmental degradation and promote sustainability of the ecosystem; and in the internationalization of the world market economy and easing the integration of developing countries and the former socialist economies in the global economy through extensive economic and social development and technical assistance programs.

Regulations, Norms, and International Law

International governmental organizations are the backbone of an increasingly elaborate international regulatory system and an international legal order that has redefined the division of responsibilities between states and the international community. Since the creation of the United Nations, the scope of international law has widened considerably, incorporating more policy fields that were previously approached on a purely national basis, such as human rights and the environment. The rapidly growing number of IGOs exemplifies the increasing legalization of the international system in the sense that international institutions "bind states through law: [states'] behavior is subject to scrutiny under the general rules, procedures, and discourse of international law, and, often, domestic law" (obligation); "demonstrate a high degree of precision, meaning that their rules unambiguously define the conduct they require, authorize, or proscribe" (precision); and "legal agreements delegate broad authority to a neutral entity for implementation of the agreed rules, including their interpretation, dispute settlement, and (possibly) further rule making." (delegation) (Goldstein et al. 2000, 387). The degree to which international institutions are legalized varies along these three dimensions (see Figure 7.1), producing several forms as shown in Table 7.1.

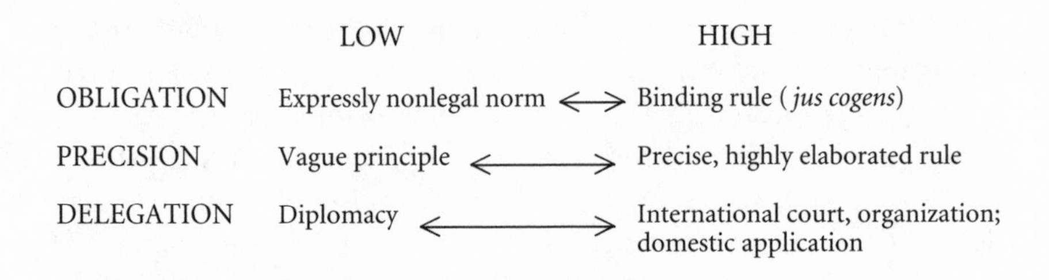

Source: Kenneth W. Abbott, Robert O. Keohane, Andrew Moravcsik, Anne-Marie Slaughter, and Duncan Snidal, "The Concept of Legalization," *International Organization*, 54:3 (Summer, 2000), p. 404. Copyright © 2000 by the IO Foundation and the Massachusetts Institute of Technology. Reprinted by permission of the publisher.

FIGURE 7.1 The Dimensions of Legalization

Setting Rules and Standards of the International System

Since 1945 states have granted more and more authority to IGOs for developing the rules and standards of the international system, and IGOs through their various activities have operationalized the many norms of the international legal order.

> Like domestic administrative agencies, international organizations are often authorized to elaborate agreed norms (though almost always in softer ways than their domestic counterparts), especially where it is infeasible to draft precise rules in advance and where special expertise is required. The EU Commission drafts extensive regulations, though they usually become binding only with the assent of member states. Specialized agencies like the International Civil Aviation Organization and the Codex Alimentarius Commission promulgate technical rules—in coordination situations. In cases like these, the grant of rule-making authority typically contains (in Hart's terms) the rule of recognition; the governing bodies or secretariats of international organizations may subsequently develop rules of change. At lower levels of delegation, bodies like the International Labor Organization and the World Intellectual Property Organization draft proposed international conventions and promulgate a variety of nonbinding rules, some for use by private actors. International organizations also support interstate negotiations.
>
> Many operational activities serve to implement legal norms. Virtually all international organizations gather and disseminate information rele-

TABLE 7.1 Forms of International Legalization

Type	*Obligation*	*Precision*	*Delegation*	*Examples*
Ideal Type: Hard law				
I	High	High	High	EC; WTO-TRIPs; European human rights convention; International Criminal Court
II	High	Low	High	EEC Antitrust Art. 85–6; WTO-national treatment
III	High	High	Low	US-Soviet arms control treaties; Montreal Protocol
IV	Low	High	High (moderate)	UN Committee on Sustainable Development (Agenda 21)
V	High	Low	Low	Vienna Ozone Convention; European Framework Convention on National Minorities
VI	Low	Low	High (moderate)	UN Specialized agencies; World Bank; OSCE High Commissioner on National Minorities
VII	Low	High	Low	Helsinki Final Act; Nonbinding Forest Principles; technical standards
VIII	Low	Low	Low	Group of 7; Spheres of influence; balance of power
Ideal Type: Anarchy				

Source: Kenneth W. Abbott, Robert O. Keohane, Andrew Moravcsik, Anne-Marie Slaughter, and Duncan Snidal, "The Concept of Legalization", *International Organization*, 54:3 (Summer, 2000), p. 406.

vant to implementation; many also generate new information. Most engage in educational activities, such as the WTO's training programs for developing country officials. Agencies like the World Health Organization, the World Bank, and the U.N. Environment Program have much more extensive operations. These activities implement (and thus give meaning to) the norms and goals enunciated in the agencies' charters and other agreements they administer. Although most international organi-

> zations are highly constrained by member states, the imprecision of their governing instruments frequently leaves them considerable discretion, exercised implicitly as well as through formal interpretations and operating policies. The World Bank, for example, has issued detailed policies on matters such as environmental impact assessment and treatment of indigenous peoples; these become legally binding when incorporated in loan agreements. The World Bank's innovative Inspection Panel supervises compliance, often as the result of private complaints. (Abbott, Keohane, Moravcsik, Slaughter, and Snidal 2000, 417)

The widening scope of international law is the result of an international "legislative process" that is conducted predominantly through IGOs, particularly the U.N. system. Over the course of the last fifty years, intergovernmental bodies like the U.N. General Assembly and the Economic and Social Council, the World Bank's Governing Board, and the World Health Assembly, have produced much of the "law" that currently governs international relations (both "hard" law, which is binding legal instruments—such as treaties, customary law, general principles of law, international administrative law, and judicial decisions and authoritative teachings—and "soft" law, which consists of non-binding instruments such as conference declarations, resolutions, and even model laws and guidelines). Moreover, IGOs themselves have contributed to the body of international law, as Paul Szasz explains:

> Aside from making political recommendations or taking other types of decisions through their representative organs, most IGOs engage in particular activities. Indeed, for some organizations this is the principle means of manifesting themselves. The United Nations, for example, engages in peacekeeping operations, succors refugees, gives technical assistance, registers and acts as a depository of treaties; financial institutions make loans and grants; others promote health, or agriculture, or education by giving or arranging for technical assistance, carrying out research, convening meetings, and so forth.
>
> All these activities by international entities may, just like the activities of states, create international law if carried out—as is usual for organizations created by international law and subject to the scrutiny of many states—in a regular manner and in the conviction that even if not re-

sponding to positive requirements of international law they are at least authorized by and in conformity with such law.

Most IGO activities involve the conclusion of agreements—between the IGO and states, and sometimes among IGOs. Such massive participation in the conclusion of treaties cannot but influence the law and the practices relating thereto. Furthermore, as IGOs have become the predominant depositories of multilateral treaties, the rules for carrying out these functions are increasingly those set by the organizations. Finally, since most multilateral treaties are now developed under the aegis of an IGO, the practices relating to the format of these instruments are in the first instance determined by these organizations.

Aside from the formalities relating to treaty-making, the substance of an increasing number of treaties, particularly bilateral treaties between an IGO on the one hand and a state on the other, displays an understandable regularity (because an IGO cannot wantonly discriminate between states), which through a consistent repetition of certain legal obligations may tend to establish legal norms. These obligations include those relating to privileges and immunities of the organizations, the settlement of disputes with them, the conditions for granting technical, financial or other assistance, and the arrangements for international meetings.

Going beyond these legal provisions, many IGOs have established patterns of carrying out certain functions: the granting of fellowships, the assignment and control of experts, the protection of refugees, the delivery of supplies, and the stationing of military forces. Taken together with the rules deriving from the bilateral agreements just referred to, these multifarious activities can be said to have created numerous pockets of IGO-related customary law. (Szasz 1997, 43–44)

International Human Rights as a Benchmark

International human rights and humanitarian law have been a major focus of international organizations since the end of World War II. The inclusion of "human rights" in the UN Charter (Articles 1 and 55) gave the United Nations the mandate to "elaborate a strong set of explicit and fairly detailed international human rights standards. In particular, the Universal Declaration of Human Rights, unanimously adopted by the U.N. General Assembly on December 10, 1948, and the 1966 International Human Rights Covenants provide an authoritative statement of international human rights norms." (Donnelly 1994, 204) However, the problem before international organizations was not setting human rights standards ("promoting" human rights), but rather in implementing these norms ("protecting" human rights).

> When the Universal Declaration of Human Rights was adopted in 1948 as a "common standard of achievement for all peoples and nations," virtually all governments said the standards were not to be legally binding upon them. At that time, no specific human rights violations, apart from slavery, genocide, and gross abuses of the rights of aliens, were effectively proscribed. Virtually all states shielded themselves happily behind Article 2(7) of the UN Charter in arguing that human rights was strictly an internal affair for the state concerned. While a UN Commission on Human Rights was set up, governments entirely dominated its work. Independent experts were accorded no role whatsoever and NGOs were restricted, in formal terms, to stiff, cameo appearances. The Commission's mandate was largely confined, in practice, to the drafting of new treaties and other legal instruments. Governments wasted no time in declaring in 1947, that the Commission had "no power" whatsoever to respond in any way to violations of human rights. They did, however, agree to establish a procedure that would channel the thousands of complaints the United Nations received annually. This bureaucratic maze was subsequently dubbed by John Humphrey (who struggled valiantly as the head of the UN's human rights Secretariat) as "the world's most elaborate waste-paper basket.". . .
>
> Today, however, [more] than fifty years after the adoption of the UN Charter, significant progress has been made. The standards contained in the Universal Declaration are, in practice, applicable to every state, whatever its formal attitude to their legal status. The view that human rights violations are essentially domestic matters, while still put forward in an almost ritual manner from time to time, receives very little credence from the international community. A vast array of international standards, the most important of which are the six "core" human rights treaties, supplements the Universal Declaration. In addition to the six expert treaty bodies created by the United Nations to supervise the compliance of states parties with their obligations under those treaties, regional human rights conventions and implementing machinery have been set up in Europe,

> the Americas, and Africa. The United Nations has also created a complex array of other, additional monitoring mechanisms. . . .
>
> In brief, the international human rights system has developed to an extent that was inconceivable by the vast majority of observers in 1945. Even at the time of the first World Conference on Human Rights, held in Teheran in 1968, not a single treaty monitoring body was in existence. Moreover, no procedures existed for investigating violations, other than for Southern Africa and the Occupied Territories in the Middle East. States were simply not held accountable, except when outrageous violations coincided with the short-term political interest of at least two of the three geopolitical blocs. Indeed, during the past twenty-five years the United Nations system has made immense progress. Of course, it is by no means sufficient and we must acknowledge the enormous inadequacies as well. (Alston 1994, 355–357)

The human rights system has also been bolstered and further developed through the activities of numerous human rights NGOs. They have played a strategic role in many of the breakthroughs in the international human rights regime, including the advancement of the rights of children and women through their advocacy and participation in the preparations of the U.N. Convention on the Elimination of Discrimination Against Women (CEDAW) and the U.N. Convention on the Rights of the Child and strengthening international human rights machinery and procedures through their lobbying of governments and international organizations for creation of the U.N. High Commissioner for Human Rights and the establishment of the International Criminal Court. Indeed, NGOs working in the area of human rights have paved the way for an expanded role of other civil society organizations in international relations. "Voluntary networks have also demonstrated their power to influence states in the monitoring of state conduct in the treatment of their own citizens. '*Principled issue networks*,' as agents for change in state behavior and even in international standards, are a force for social change that appear to have emerged from the increased level of private transnational activity. Made possible through resources provided by foundations, spurred on by the commitment of individuals, and held together by new technologies, these transnationally linked organizations have had some notable achievements particularly in the protection of human rights." (Ku 2001, 31)

The norm-making activities of international organizations have been instrumental for managing the changes in the international system. The intergovernmental processes and procedures that have been developed within IGOs, and the growing participation of business and civil society organizations in these processes, give substance to the idea of an international society and an international system governed by the rule of law, as well as a method that can effectively regulate the interaction between and among states and non-state actors. International organizations have fostered universalization of important social principles (such as human rights, democracy, equity in the global economy, sustainable development), reflecting a further shift in the international legal order from the traditional emphasis on state values (sovereignty) to a concern for human values and welfare. (Ku 2001, 26–27) This change in emphasis indicates the cumulative influence of IGOs, international business, and civil society groups on the international system and the broader role of international organizations (governmental and non-governmental) in upholding these values.

Human Security and the Management of Violent Conflict

International organizations have been actively involved in the management of violent conflict in international society. During the immediate postwar period and throughout the Cold War, international governmental organizations provided forums where intentions of states could be clarified and problems between states that might otherwise end up in armed conflict could be aired. IGOs and NGOs within civil society dealing with peace and security matters facilitate the exchange and availability of information, as in the annual general debate at the start of each regular session of the United Nations General Assembly, the open meetings of the Security Council where positions are explicated, or the data on military capabilities of states published by private research organizations like the Stockholm International Peace Research Institute (SIPRI) and the Center for Defence Information in Washington, D.C. Think tanks and other international affairs NGOs have played an important role in opening lines of communication between states in what has become known as "Track II" diplomacy (for example, United Nations Associations, New York Council on Foreign Relations, Moscow State Institute of International Relations, Shanghai Institute on International Studies, Carnegie Endowment for International Peace, Center for Strategic and International Studies, International Peace Academy, and many more). Exchange visits and international conferences organized by these groups supplement official diplomatic channels, and in situations where diplomatic ties had become strained or had broken down (as was often the case between the superpowers during the Cold War), these unofficial diplomatic activities were important conduits for governments to signal their positions and intentions and to forestall further deterioration in their relations into armed conflict. In addition, IGOs were often brought into conflicts between states. A 1972 study of IGOs' management of international conflicts found that "roughly two-thirds of 104 disputes involving fatalities in the period from 1945 through 1970 were brought before one or more of five international governmental organizations—the United Nations, the OAS, the OAU, the Arab League, and the Council of Europe—and several disputes that did not involve fatalities were also brought before these bodies." (Jacobson 1979, 211) However, the same study also discovered that the IGOs were only successful in contributing towards a solution in half of the disputes brought before them.

Mediation and Conflict Prevention

International organizations also act as mediators after there is an outbreak of armed conflict between states, sending envoys into conflict areas to negotiate ceasefires, truces, and peace agreements and deploying peacekeeping troops to separate belligerents and protect civilian populations. In this regard IGOs have developed a formal diplomatic profile, which is distinct from that of states and of "collective representation" of states, in the management of inter- and intra-state conflict situations. This development is, in part, the result (or consequence) of an increasingly common practice among executive heads of IGOs (for example, the U.N. secretary-general) to deploy special representatives and/or envoys to conflict areas for a variety of political and diplomatic tasks. This practice was initiated by the first secretary-general of the United Nations, Trygve Lie, in 1948 with the appointment of Ralph Bunche as the "Personal Representative of the Secretary-General" to the UN mediator for the Middle East, Count Folke Bernadotte. After the assassination of Count Bernadotte, Lie appointed Bunche acting UN mediator for the Middle East. Bunche set the precedent for and established the fundamental characteristics of the function—"part diplomat and part manager." (See Rivlin 1990 and Fafo 1999.) From rather humble and uncertain beginnings, the role of the SRSG has both endured and expanded as an instrument of the secretary-general. The function, under a variety of titles—special envoy, special co-ordinator, personal representative, and representative—has also been employed by other international organizations (NATO, EU, OSCE, and others) as well as by states, international non-governmental organizations, and other non-state actors.[1]

The special representative of the secretary-general (SRSG) is one of many instruments the U.N. secretary-general has developed to overcome the limitations of the office and other institutional obstacles. "SRSGs are appointed only in exceptional circumstances, either when the 'normal' instruments available to the Secretary-General have proven insufficient or when the UN has been asked to play an exceptional political, peace-keeping or peace-building role. In a variety of situations and circumstances, SRSGs have been responsible for conducting supportive diplomacy and mediation related to conflict prevention and resolution, heading peace-keeping operations and verification missions, and co-ordinating peace-building activities. Within the UN system, the SRSG has often been at the centre of the operational relationships in the field among the UN Secretariat, the wider UN family of agencies, funds and programmes, other international organisations, the parties to the conflict and donor countries." (Fafo 1999, 23)

Since the end of the Cold War, the actual number of SRSGs deployed in the field has increased considerably, as has the scope of the position. Throughout the Cold War, the function was closely tied to peacekeeping operations that were mounted by the United Nations in response to interstate conflicts (so-called first generation or classical peacekeeping, of which there were only fifteen examples between 1948 and 1988). Since

---

[1]There are some important differences in the specific tasks or duties assigned to SRSGs as compared to those for special envoys and coordinators and personal representatives and representatives of the SG, but the distinctions are rather subtle. It is common for these different titles to be interchangeable, particularly SRSG and special envoy, in the media as well as in use by scholars and practitioners (for example, the Pearson Peacekeeping Centre decided to use the title "special envoys" rather than SRSG for a roundtable, "Special Envoys in the Twenty-first Century: Diplomacy, Leadership and Management," it conducted in October 2000).

1989, the number of UN peacekeeping operations has doubled (to close to thirty) and they have become much more complex, involving large contingents of both military and civilian personnel and a wider range of humanitarian and development responsibilities, in response to the rise in intra-state conflicts—so-called "second generation" peacekeeping (United Nations 1996, 3–9).

Civil society groups like the International Committee of the Red Cross and religious or church-based NGOs (such as the Quakers) have also been active in mediation, though they have come to this role from a different starting point. Civil society mediation and conciliation efforts evolved out of humanitarian relief operations, which placed these organizations in conflict zones and required that they negotiate with the warring parties to have access or free passage to bring food, medicine, and other relief to civilians and noncombatants caught up in the fighting. This experience led to a more prominent role of NGOs in mediation activities as intra-state conflicts became prevalent in the waning days of the Cold War and throughout the 1990s. Humanitarian and development NGOs like the International Rescue Committee, Médicins Sans Frontière, Catholic Relief Services, Save the Children, Oxfam, and CARE often had field experience or operations in places where fighting had broken out as well as intimate knowledge of the place, culture, and the people. This naturally made these groups interlocutors between fighting factions in inter-ethnic conflicts within countries. A good example is the role played by the Community of Sant' Egidio in Mozambique:

> The Rome-based Community of Sant' Egidio, founded in 1968 by a group of students intent on 'spreading the truth of the Gospel' (Hume 1994, 15), ended up involved from 1989 to 1992 in helping to mediate the Mozambican peace process between Joaquim Chissano of the Frente de Libertação de Moçambique (FRELIMO) and Afonso Dhlakama of the Resistência Nacional Moçambicana (RENAMO). For a number of years, members of the Sant' Egidio community had worked in Mozambique in a humanitarian capacity. Their members were one of the very few groups that worked among and were trusted by people and leaders on both sides of the conflict.
>
> By 1989, both parties to the conflict acknowledged a military stalemate and agreed that a negotiated settlement was the only viable solution. Al-

> though the sides could not agree on a number of potential mediators, both agreed to work with the Sant' Egidio community to resolve their conflict and develop a new relationship. The negotiations were long and arduous, stalling on a number of occasions; they involved mediation efforts by outside governments, including Zimbabwe, Botswana, South Africa, and Italy, as well as by Lonrho, a British investment firm. Sant' Egidio was there at the beginning and at the concluding Rome Accord of October 4, 1992. (Mayotte 1999, 170)

In the 1990s, conflict prevention and conflict resolution NGOs formed at an amazing pace, turning into a vibrant cottage industry. Groups like Search for Common Ground, the Carter Center and the International Crisis Group have become important players in almost all the trouble spots around the world (for example, the Middle East, the Balkans, the Great Lakes Region and Sub-Saharan region of Africa, the Korean Peninsula, Central America, and Southeast Asia). However, the success rate of Track II diplomacy and nongovernmental mediation in preventing or resolving conflicts is not much better than that of IGOs or states.

Disarmament and Arms Control

Another traditional security area in which international organizations are active is disarmament and arms control. Starting with The Hague Peace Conferences of 1899 and 1907, states and NGOs took up disarmament as a means to prevent wars and to limit the use of weapons that cause "unacceptable levels of human suffering." The premise of the traditional disarmament agenda is the idea that armaments increase the likelihood of war and therefore, reducing or eliminating the instruments of war will impede both the appetite and capacity of states to use force in their relations. Absent the weapons, armies and navies, and other war-making materiale, states will have no alternative than to resolve their differences "peacefully" (that is, by negotiation, arbitration and/or adjudication). This view was (and still is) considered impractical at best and dangerously utopian at worst by policymakers and realists who argue that power is the prevailing and determining factor in international relations and security. Despite the fact that general and complete disarmament is improbable, the international community has always renewed efforts toward disarmament after a major international conflict that clearly demonstrates the grave risks posed by unconstrained arms races to world peace and human survival, especially after the development of weapons of mass destruction (nuclear, biological and chemical).

IGOs have been the venue for many of the multilateral negotiations on disarmament (such as the 1932 First World Disarmament Conference under the auspices of the League of Nations, the U.N. Commission on Conventional Armaments, and U.N. Disarmament Conference) and have been assigned particular responsibilities for monitoring or verifying compliance with disarmament and arms control conventions or treaties. For example, the ICRC and other humanitarian organizations monitor the 1981 Convention on Conventional Weapons, the IAEA administers the 1968 Non-Proliferation Treaty, and the Organization for the Prohibition of Chemical Weapons was created to administer the 1992 Chemical Weapons Convention. But, the activities of IGOs have been severely limited and often questioned by states, all of whom consider a well-armed military essential to national defense and security and are always reluctant to open up their military facilities and weapons programs to outside scrutiny or inspection. Even after the Cold War ended and the disarmament and arms control discussions shifted away from preventing a nuclear third world war between the United States and the USSR to disarming states and ethnic groups, paramilitaries, and irregular forces in the various intrastate conflicts, the constraints on IGOs' efforts continued. (See Spear 2001 and Bernauer 2001.)

Civil society organizations, particularly humanitarian organizations, have pushed along disarmament and arms control in a variety of ways—campaigns, "shaming," confidence- and security-building measures (CSBMs), and research and analysis—but always as outsiders. Their influence in this arena has proven to be most effective in renewing states' interest in and commitment to disarmament and arms control through "recontextualizing the issues" in non-security terms:

> For example, the ICRC played a crucial role in having certain weapons banned and in developing international law for the conduct of war. The ICRC was largely responsible for putting excessively injurious conventional weapons on the agenda, and it played a considerable role in doing the same for land mines. Indeed work on land mines initially grew out of efforts to develop humanitarian law. A key basis of the claim for the

> ICRC to act on the issue was its framing as a humanitarian concern. The Arms Transfer Project of Human Rights Watch and other NGOs subsequently picked up the land mine campaign. NGOs staked their claims for involvement through recontextualizing the issue. As noted by Price, "It reflects an effort on the part of civil society to alter the conduct of violence by redefining it as a humanitarian concern, which is a realm where civil society and the NGO community often have special claims to expertise and authority." (Price 1998, 638)
>
> A similar level of NGO involvement was displayed in the establishment of a European Code of Conduct for Arms Transfers. Here too the issue is framed in a manner that deflected attention from security issues. For example, emphasis was placed on the human rights consequences of weapons transfers to undemocratic regimes. The NGO attempt to get a global UN code of conduct for arms transfers also focuses on the nonsecurity aspects of such a code. Once issues are framed in security terms NGOs take a back seat. (Spear 2001, 587–588)

For decades a great deal of effort and energy has been devoted to disarmament and arms control with only marginal results. The concepts of self-defense and deterrence have remained the guiding principles of states and their governments for meeting their fundamental duty to protect and defend their people and territory against all threats and have justified the maintenance of large national military establishments. Perhaps more telling of the strict control that states maintain over this area are the many negotiation forums, other than IGOs, that they have established. Nuclear disarmament was and remains largely a bilateral affair between the United States and the Soviet Union (and now Russia), and the nuclear weapon states (the United States, Russia, France, Great Britain, China, India, and Pakistan) have resisted any multilateralization of negotiations for reducing nuclear arsenals and have purposively kept the issue out of the Non-Proliferation Treaty's process, a U.N. framework. Export control regimes—such as the Zangger Committee and the Nuclear Suppliers Group for nuclear materials, the Wassenaar Arrangement for conventional weapons and dual-use technologies, the Australia Group for chemical and biological weapons materials, and the Missile Technology Control Regime—are predominantly informal intergovernmental groupings of countries through which states negotiate with little to no involvement of non-state actors.

Humanitarian Intervention and Global Terrorism

Despite the challenges and difficulties that international organizations face in the field of peace and security, their contribution to managing violent conflict in the world is important and continues to grow. Both IGOs and NGOs are in the forefront in developing tools and institutional mechanisms (like the "second generation" peacekeeping operations) for addressing the complex dynamics of armed conflicts within "failed" states that dominate the post–Cold War security field. As Andrew Natsios points out:

> In Africa, the Balkans, the Middle East, and the former Soviet Union, the growing number of failed states has produced a widening level of chaos to which NGOs and the UN have tried to respond. However, even the most charitable assessment must conclude that their responses have had mixed results. These complex humanitarian emergencies are defined by five common characteristics: the deterioration or complete collapse of central government authority; ethnic or religious conflict and widespread human rights abuses; episodic food insecurity, frequently deteriorating into mass starvation; macroeconomic collapse involving hyperinflation, massive unemployment and net decreases in GNP; and mass population movements of displaced people and refugees escaping conflict or searching for food. This instability does not respect national boundaries and frequently spills over into neighbouring countries, many of which are themselves unstable. The spreading chaos does not appear to be subsiding and presents the international community with a major challenge. (Natsios 1996, 67)

This rather gloomy picture of the immense humanitarian tasks confronting international organizations was compounded when terrorists from Osama bin Laden's al-Qaeda organization attacked the United States on September 11, 2001, destroying the World Trade Center in New York, which killed thousands, and striking the Pentagon in Washington, D.C., which killed hundreds more.

International organizations' response to the 9/11 terrorists attack was swift. Within twenty-four hours, the North Atlantic Council of NATO adopted a resolution that invoked the collective self-defense provisions of Article 5 of the North Atlantic Treaty—the first time the alliance had ever taken such action—while "the United Nations Security Council met at the call of its president, Jean-David Levitte of France, and considered a resolution his colleagues had drafted overnight that would chart the course for the international response to the terrorist attacks. Within in an hour the Council approved it unanimously—including the votes not only of Russia and China but also of the Council's Muslim members, Bangladesh, Mali, and Tunisia. . . . The resolution described 'terrorist attacks'—and not just the attacks on the World Trade Center and Pentagon—as posing a 'threat to international peace and security,' bringing them under the umbrella of Chapter VII of the U.N. Charter and thus raising the possibility of enforcement action. It called on the world community 'to combat by all means' these threats to peace and security, a euphemism well understood by Council members to embrace possible use of military force. The resolution also declared that states have an obligation to help 'bring to justice' the organizers and sponsors of these atrocities and warned that those harboring the terrorist networks 'will be held accountable.'" (Laurenti 2002, 21–22) International terrorism jumped to the top of the world security agenda after languishing for thirty years on the margins of the international agenda. September 11 demonstrated a frightening new reality: Terrorism was no longer a localized irritant to international peace and security, it was truly global with capabilities to project devastating destructive power, including weapons of mass destruction, anywhere, anytime. International organizations are indispensable to the complex task of coordinating and managing international action against international terrorism, especially the peace-building operations that follow the military campaigns and focus resources on addressing the root causes (like political injustice) of terrorism.

Terrorism and the humanitarian emergencies of post–Cold War conflicts have caused a serious reexamination of the meaning of security in the world. International organizations have been instrumental in transforming the meaning of security from its traditional "national security" emphasis to a broader context of "human security." "Security traditionally has focused on the state because its fundamental purpose is to protect its citizens. Hobbled by economic adversity, outrun by globalization, and undermined from within by bad governance, the capacity of some states to provide this protection has increasingly come into question. . . . Human security today puts people first and recognizes that their safety is integral to the promotion and maintenance of international peace and security. The security of states is essential, but not sufficient to fully ensure the safety and well-being of the world's peoples." (Axworthy 2001, 19–20) Although the concept of human security is still in its infancy, it has gotten some traction as a new normative basis for international intervention in conflicts. Human security is being pushed by IGOs, the private sector, and civil society because it recognizes that today's conflicts, especially within states, are more likely to break out in places where human rights are violated, economic and social development is stymied, and/or the environment is severely degraded (all areas where international organizations have considerable experience and expertise) and that lasting solutions to such conflicts cannot be achieved without addressing these fundamental issues. Not only does this new paradigm for international security reflect the changes in the security environment in the wake of the Cold War and the tragedy of September 11, but it also represents a more refined normative framework for international peace and security, linking traditional security with nonsecurity concerns.

Sustainable Development

Poverty, hunger, infectious diseases, illiteracy, population growth, and pollution have been major causes of social, economic, and political instability in and between countries for hundreds of years. While these issues of human welfare (and survival) are matters to be managed and satisfied by national authorities, they have all been elevated to the international agenda over the course of the last century. International organizations have been particularly active in this arena, especially after countries across Asia, Africa, and Latin America and the Caribbean gained their independence during the postwar period and swelled the ranks of the international community—tripling the membership of the United Nations by 1980 (see Table 7.2). These former colonies were "under-developed" (or "economically poor") and as their numbers grew, their economic and social development became a focal point of most international organizations, particularly the United Nations (see Emmerij, Jolly and Weiss 2001, chapters 1 and 2).

TABLE 7.2 Decolonization and Growth in UN Membership, 1945–2000

	YEAR										
	1945	*1950*	*1955*	*1960*	*1965*	*1970*	*1975*	*1980*	*1990*	*1995*	*2000*
Total UN Membership	51	60	76	100	118	127	143	153	160	185	189

Source: UN, *United Nations Member States* (New York: UN, 2000).

Notes: The first two decades of the UN are marked by the admission of new states that achieved independence in the decolonization process. In September 1960 alone seventeen newly independent states, sixteen from Africa, joined the UN. This was the biggest increase in membership since the establishment of the UN. In the late 1960s half of the member states had achieved independence since 1945, and more than one-fourth had been independent for less than five years.

In the 1990s the disintegration of the USSR, Czechoslovakia, and the Republic of Yugoslavia led to the admission of nineteen new independent states to UN membership: the eleven states of the Commonwealth of Independent States (CIS), with the membership of the Soviet Union being continued by the Russian Federation; three Baltic states (Estonia, Latvia, and Lithuania); and Bosnia and Herzegovina, Croatia, Slovenia, the former Yugoslav Republic of Macedonia, and Slovakia.

Meeting Basic Needs

Traditionally, these problems are viewed largely in economic terms (a product of market failure) or as humanitarian concerns (a result of human or natural disasters). Overcoming these problems—meeting basic needs—had become a primary function of government as part of the welfare state's expanding obligations to its citizens. But the spillover of these problems across national borders was a powerful reason why states needed to cooperate with each other. A government unable to provide sufficiently for the welfare of its citizens was not only a risk to itself, but also a risk to its neighbors. In principle, it is in the interest of states to provide aid and assistance to those states that are wanting in meeting the basic needs of their citizens, both as a preventive strategy and on ethical grounds. This principle was incorporated into the founding documents of many post–World War II international governmental organizations—the preamble and Article 55 of the U.N. Charter, preamble and Article 1 of the FAO Constitution, preamble and Chapter 2 of the WHO Constitution, preamble and Article 1 of the UNESCO Constitution, and Articles 1 and 2 of the OECD Convention—and the meeting of basic needs "as a global right was stated in the Universal Declaration of Human Rights of 1948, which explicitly expressed the social dimension of human rights." (Simai 2001, 46) Mihály Simai points out:

> In the world after the Second World War, the Universal Declaration of Human Rights reflected an important recognition by countries about the role of welfare, democracy and human security in the sustainability of global peace. A fundamental place in the standard-setting activities of the United Nations was taken by the idea of social development. As early as 1954, the United Nations prepared an interesting report on the measurement of social progress, or as the title put it, "International Definition and Measurement of Standards and Levels of Living" (UN, 1954). This listed the perceived components of the level of living, resulting from the peculiarities of environmental conditions, cultures, values, economic, political and social conditions. It included (1) health, including demographic conditions, (2) food and nutrition, (3) education, including literacy, (4) conditions of work, (5) employment situation, (6) aggregate consumption and savings, (7) transportation, (8) housing and household facilities, (9) clothing, (10) recreation and entertainment, (11) social security, and (12) human freedoms. The report was a largely statistical exercise that advanced collective thinking in international organizations and countries and the development of the statistical indicators. Later, a number of social goals were included in the targets of Development Decades. Some UN agencies, such as Unicef, the WHO, the FAO and the ILO, tried to develop or recommend policies along the lines of the standards established in 1954, to redefine the goals of development. Thus the UN system was working for social progress in a number of areas, with the UNDP, the Unicef, the ILO and the Unesco leading the way. (Simai 2001, 47)

International organizations are not the primary agents of development assistance; multilateral aid represents only a small proportion of total Official Development Assistance (ODA) that flows to developing countries. The vast majority of ODA is bilateral and comes from the twenty-two member countries of the OECD Development Assistance Committee (DAC), with Japan and the United States providing nearly half of the

$53.74 billion in 2000 that was directed to 149 countries and territories (forty-eight Least Developed Countries, twenty-four Other Low Income Countries, forty-five Lower Middle Income Countries, and thirty-two Upper Middle Income Countries). International organizations have done more in shaping the ideas of and influencing donor policies for international development. Indeed, it can be argued that the work of "development economists" in the secretariats of the United Nations, OECD, the World Bank, and the European Union has been instrumental in developing strategies that went beyond the strict focus on economic growth, stressing the multidimensional character of the development process which emphasizes the importance of addressing basic needs of people such as food, housing, clothing, education, health, and employment. The basic-needs approach that emerged in the 1970s shifted the targets of aid and ODA, marking a partial departure from the Cold War geopolitical calculus of foreign aid. "And so the bulk of bilateral development assistance of the industrial countries was turned to basic-needs fulfillment as a top priority, including Washington's 'basic human needs.' The Development Assistance Committee (DAC) of the OECD issued policy papers on the theme, as did the organization's Development Centre. The World Bank joined the ranks of enthusiasts, in part because of the great interest taken by Hollis Chenery, who was then the chief economist and vice president. Mahbub ul Haq and Paul Streeten developed the basic-needs strategy further, and McNamara pushed his operational people to start making loans in this area. Chenery together with the [Institute of Development Studies] IDS in Sussex produced a seminal book, *Redistribution with Growth*, which was published by Oxford University on behalf of the World Bank. The UN family jumped on the bandwagon as well. For example, the WHO, FAO, and UNESCO produced policy papers on basic needs, showing how they were qualified to foster one or more of them." (Emmerij, Jolly, and Weiss 2001, 74) International organizations have been critical conduits through which foreign aid is increasingly channeled and coordinated towards improving standards of living in the developing world with impressive results:

> Largely due to foreign aid provisions, food production has outpaced population growth in the global South for the past four decades. India's food production, for example, has almost doubled since the 1960s. Seven times

> more people are literate in the developing world than in 1950. Infant mortality has dropped by more than half, from 180 deaths per 1,000 births to 69 deaths. Increased family planning has been one of aid's most notable successes. The most striking example is in Bangladesh, where in 1970 only 3 percent of women were using contraceptives, and in 1990, 40 percent were. Other significant advances have been made in health, such as the eradication of smallpox in 1977 and the widespread immunization of children for common childhood diseases. International aid also played an important role in supporting democratic reforms in countries such as South Africa, Namibia, Cambodia, Panama, and Haiti. In Africa, where droughts have taken the lives of hundreds of thousands, aid has provided early warning systems that have reduced the large-scale fatalities. Aid's contribution to the building of infrastructure and communications in developing countries is its most visible and controversial success. Thousands of roads, telephone lines, and hospitals now exist in countries where there was no access to markets and no communication or medical facilities, but many of these mega-projects have had disruptive and harmful effects on local populations, who were perhaps considered less important than the shining monuments of Northern aid. (Hoy 1998, 6–7)

International nongovernmental organizations have also been significant players in international development and are increasingly called upon by donor governments and IGOs to deliver relief and/or to implement development programs and projects. The larger development NGOs such as CARE, Catholic Relief Services, Oxfam/UK, Save the Children, and World Vision have a long and respectable track record in translating the basic-needs strategy into operational activities throughout the developing world. In addition, these and thousands of other groups have been outspoken advocates for economic and social development that focused on the people rather than on economic growth, per capita GDP, and large economic infrastructure projects (dams, power plants, and communications systems). In large measure, NGOs have pushed many major global issues (such as population, gender, children, education, shelter, health, the environment) onto the international agenda through their research, field projects and programs, and technical expertise.

More recently transnational corporations have also become involved in what the U.N. Development Program calls human development. However, private sector participation in social development is more self-serving than philanthropic. Although most major transnational corporations have now embraced the human development agenda and the basic tenets of corporate social responsibility, their conversion was often only after they became targets of NGO activism. For example, the Nestlé boycott in the 1970s and 1980s that was organized by NGO activists in the International Baby Food Action Network succeeded in ending direct advertising and promotion of infant formula to mothers by baby food companies (Nestlé was targeted because it was the largest producer) and caused the infant formula industry to significantly modify marketing practices in developing countries to be in accordance with the WHO/UNICEF corporate code of conduct for marketing of breast milk substitutes. This type of NGO activism has been instrumental in changing corporate practices and policies in developing countries and convincing private sector leaders that they too have a responsibility to contribute to the social welfare of people and communities where they do business. Indeed, the more "enlightened" TNCs have discovered that investing in the social sector is actually good business, producing tangible benefits such as greater productivity, increased consumption, and more markets. But for most corporations, human development is still considered to be the responsibility of the public sector and a "cost" that eats into the bottom line.

Environment Versus Development

By the late 1960s evidence was mounting that industrialization and human activity were significantly degrading the natural environment. Air and water pollution, desertification, deforestation, and other environmental problems threatened progress and development. It had become quite clear that "in a world where environmental damage and its social consequences ignore borders, substantial and effective international cooperation is essential." (Conca 1996, 103) The environment, historically, had been considered a fundamental prerogative of the territorial state and its management (exploitation, resource extraction, public/private use) was the sole concern of national governments. As Seyom Brown points out:

> Traditionally, where humans consumed, took possession of, or altered nature's "givens," these actions, although constrained by national or local

> community interests and laws, typically ignored the well-being of outsiders (human and non-human), especially those outside of the national community. Moreover, the international indifference was legitimized by the dominant norms and institutions of the world polity.
>
> Despite national variations in the amount of governmental regulation of private action and in the extent of devolution of regulatory authority to local subdivisions of government, countries the world over lodged ultimate responsibility for ensuring prudent private and community use of natural resources in their national governments. If countries got in each other's way in the use of natural resources, they would negotiate or fight to determine access or shares; and that, for the time being, would be that. But the traditional lack of continuing international monitoring and control of natural resources has become a luxury in the contemporary period, dangerous to the affluent as well as an unjust infliction on the poor.
>
> The required international monitoring and control regimes, if they are to be congruent with the natural commons, in many cases will need to traverse the territorial boundaries of the existing nation-states. This is obviously the case for the global ecological commons (the Earth's biosphere, its climate and weather systems, and the great world ocean). Transborder ecology regimes will also be required for many localized biotic, geologic, and atmospheric commons. (Brown 1996, 91–92)

International organizations have always been in the forefront on global environmental issues. The United Nations system took hold of the issue when the Economic and Social Council (ECOSOC) adopted a resolution in 1968 calling for a conference to address the problem of the human environment. This coincided with a similar appeal that came out of the 1968 Intergovernmental Conference of Experts on a Scientific Basis for a Rational Use and Conservation of the Resources of the Biosphere. The biosphere conference was the catalyst for the establishment of UNESCO's Man and the Biosphere Program in 1971, while the ECOSOC resolution brought about the 1972 United Nations Conference on the Human Environment in Stockholm. "The United Nations Conference on the Human Environment (UNCHE) pioneered a pattern for future conferences in that some NGOs were invited to participate as observers at the conference but many more attended simultaneous, parallel activities called the Environment Forum and the Life Forum. And the media were present in large numbers, so that events had a considerable impact on world opinion. Stockholm put environment firmly on the international agenda—a subject that has expanded to include development, sustainability, and global resources management . . . ." (Emmerij, Jolly, and Weiss 2001, 89) According to Margaret Keck and Kathryn Sikkink, "This first NGO forum parallel to a UN official conference pioneered a transnational process that would become absolutely central to the formation and strengthening of advocacy networks around the world. As it developed, the NGO forum format led to dialogue, conflict, creativity, and synergy. The face-to-face contact helped activists from different backgrounds and countries recognize commonalities and establish the trust necessary to sustain more distant network contacts after the conference was over." (Keck and Sikkink 1998, 123)

The Stockholm conference set the stage for the transformation of the international development paradigm. More so than human rights, the environment emerged in the 1970s and 1980s as the focal point for international cooperation as international organizations seized on a relatively strong consensus to integrate protection of the environment into international development strategies. "Following Stockholm, ministries of the environment were created so that the idea became embedded in governmental structures. Within the UN itself the UNEP was established to help ensure follow-up of its 106 recommendations. This new UN body, located in Nairobi, has disappointed many because of its small size, out-of-the-way location, lack of funds, and vague terms of reference. Nonetheless, it has published an annual report on *The World Environment* and commissioned a number of useful technical studies. Under the leadership of its first executive director, Mostafa Tolba, the UNEP also played a major role in preparations for the negotiations in Montreal of the protocol on ozone depletion." (Emmerij, Jolly, and Weiss 2001, 91–92) International environmental law exploded over the twenty years that followed the meeting in Stockholm and most of it was developed by international organizations. Ved Nanda points out:

> The United Nations system, comprising an array of specialized agencies in addition to the UN organs, is actively engaged in the development of international environmental law. At the inception of UNEP, several of these agencies already were engaged in activities with substantial environmental dimensions, and they continue to perform their environmental functions, often in conjunction with UNEP. These include the Food and Agricultural

Organization of the United Nations (FAO), the International Maritime Organization (IMO), UNESCO, the World Health Organizations (WHO), the World Meteorological Organization (WMO), the International Atomic Energy Agency (IAEA), and the World Bank, among others . . . .

It is worth noting that UNEP is responsible for twenty-three of the thirty-plus environmental accords on major marine regions. The process by which UNEP has operated begins with the accumulation and analysis of pertinent scientific data, in conjunction with the scientific community. This is followed by the preparation of a draft convention/protocol, which sets the stage for UNEP to convene an *ad hoc* working group of experts, both legal and technical, to review the draft and to make the necessary revisions.

UNEP then consults with those parties considered critical for political acceptance and eventual adoption of a proposed convention. These include governments, especially those of developing countries, to which it pays special attention; industrial and special interest groups; and nongovernmental organizations. Once it has built a consensus on the basic issues, UNEP convenes a diplomatic conference to consider the draft convention. If no binding legal instrument is contemplated, the revised draft guidelines or principles are presented to the Governing Council for its adoption. This process has been used successfully by UNEP both for reaching agreement on specific conventions and in the regional seas program.

UNEP's serious attention to stratospheric ozone depletion dates back to 1980, when its Governing Council decided that the agency should take measures for such protection. The next year, the Governing Council specifically opted for a convention, reiterating in 1982 its call that UNEP develop a convention to limit, reduce, and prevent activities that may have adverse effects on stratospheric ozone by building scientific, economic, and political consensus over a number of years. UNEP accomplished its goal partially in 1985, with the adoption of the framework Vienna Convention for the Protection of the Ozone layer (Vienna Convention), before moving nearer to its goal in 1987 with the adoption of the Montreal Protocol on Substances that Deplete the Ozone Layer (Montreal Protocol), and the 1990 London Amendments.

UNEP was also responsible for the negotiation and adoption of the Basel Convention on the Control of Transboundary Movements of Hazardous Wastes and Their Disposal (Basel Convention). UNEP's preparatory work for this Convention included its issuing of the 1985 Guidelines

> and Principles for the Environmentally Sound Management of Hazardous Wastes and its initial 1987 Draft Convention on the Transboundary Shipment of Hazardous Waste. As with the ozone convention, after an *ad hoc* working group of experts convened by UNEP prepared recommendations for the project, the final draft of the Basel Convention was presented. (Nanda 1997, 296–298)

International environmental law was further elaborated through the three U.N. Conferences on the Law of the Sea (1958, 1960, and 1973–1982), which produced the 1982 U.N. Convention on the Law of the Sea. "The Convention itself is the result of the most ambitious global institutional law-making effort ever undertaken. Its introduction of global compulsory arbitration, its conferral of quasi-legislative authority on a host of 'competent international organizations' in the environmental and safety fields, and its establishment of an international organization to regulate deep seabed mining are widely regarded as significant steps in strengthening global institutions in and of themselves, and as precedents." (Oxman 1997, 331) Throughout the 1980s environmentalism grew considerably, especially after publication in 1987 of *Our Common Future*, the report of the World Commission on Environment and Development (which is also known as the Brundtland Commission, named after the commission's chairperson, Gro Harlem Brundtland of Norway). This report marked an important shift in international environmental politics towards issues of sustainability, which seek to bridge the conflicting imperatives of environmental protection and economic development, and set the stage for the 1992 United Nations Conference on Environment and Development (UNCED) that was held in Rio de Janeiro, Brazil.

The UNCED process probably did more to change international politics than any other international event before or after. The process involved all sectors (states, business, and civil society) in a way that had not been possible earlier in international relations. The access and participation of civil society organizations before, during, and after the conference was a breakthrough for NGOs. "Compared to Stockholm, UNCED saw explosive growth in the scale and scope of NGO participation. The greater NGO presence at UNCED reflected the general growth in environmental NGOs during the 1980s, particularly in the South. The multistage, protracted nature of the 'UNCED process'—the Brundtland Commission activities, the

UNCED Preparatory Committee meetings, national reporting efforts and planning for the parallel Global Forum for NGOs—also played a key role in mobilising NGOs. UNCED also used accreditation rules that were loose by UN standards, establishing what may be an important precedent. By the end of the fourth and final PrepCom, 1,420 NGOs had been accredited in addition to those already accredited to ECOSOC. Nongovernmental organisations enjoyed not only an unprecedented presence at UNCED but also greater influence. . . . Accredited NGOs also gained access to PrepCom sessions and some albeit limited access to draft materials and working documents. This afforded the opportunity to at least comment and lobby during the PrepCom sessions, where much of the actual politicking took place. Five environmental NGOs—IUCN, Greenpeace, Environment and Development Action in the Third World, the Conservation Foundation, and the Environmental Defense Fund—were able to place a representative among the 120 individuals making up the working parties of the PrepCom sessions." (Conca 1996, 111) However, the access enjoyed by civil society groups in the run-up to UNCED was denied to them at the official sessions of the conference itself, except for those groups who were able to place a representative as a member on national delegations.

International business also became more engaged on international environmental policymaking in the run-up to UNCED. Peter Haas argues:

> MNCs were largely absent from international environmental politics until the creation of UNCED. Initially, most firms seemed to misjudge the depth of environmental concern and the potential influence of scientists and international institutions. Analysts suggest that MNCs are important forces for environmental improvement if they choose to use green and efficient technology and to develop new, cleaner products and production techniques. Institutionally, MNCs have helped to provide informational exchange about timely and valuable technologies.
>
> Many MNCs have guidelines and codes of conduct for environmental practices, ecological accounting procedures, and public environmental accounting, either through the International Standards Organization's ISO 14000 procedures for conducting environmental audits or through voluntary sectoral guidelines developed by industry groups. Some of the largest MNCs associated with the Business Council for Sustainable Development, an industry forum created before UNCED to facilitate input from MNCs,

> have called for global uniform environmental standards based on some of the most stringent national measures currently in force. For obvious reasons, the private sector prefers voluntary standards over regulation. Further, MNCs argue that they are more dynamic over the long run when they can avoid locking in premature or obsolete technologies into command-and-control-based policies. (Haas 2001, 325–326)

The unprecedented interaction among civil society, the private sector, and states and the subsequent international consensus that emerged on sustainable development in the 1990s put in motion a fundamental reconfiguration of the international political and economic landscape. The concept of sustainable development helped to transcend, at least in principle, a long-standing divide between developed and developing countries (the so-called North-South conflict), and to increase appreciation of the independent role international organizations can play. According to Paul D'Anieri:

> There are three reasons to believe [international organizations] can play a larger role as independent actors in environmental issues than in other areas.
>
> First, IOs in the environmental sphere are likely to have more autonomy than those in other areas because they are only tenuously linked to security (defined traditionally) on which states most closely guard their sovereignty. They are more closely linked to trade and economic development issues, but are still distinct. As the economic repercussions of environmental programs become more important, however, states are likely to pay more attention and limit the autonomy of IOs.
>
> Second, the nature of environmental issues plays to the strengths of international organizations. International organizations' primary independent role is in shaping agendas and debates. To the extent that environmental issues are new items on the international agenda, organizations have more room to influence how those issues and agendas are defined. In addition, the lack of scientific certainty on many questions means that neither state interests nor the international agenda are firmly set. Organizations that sponsor research and engage in public education will have a relatively open field in which to work.
>
> And third, at least in some areas, international organizations are likely to be more unified and goal oriented than those in other areas. Because envi-

> ronmental protection is perceived as a universal goal, there is a greater chance of staffers in environmental organizations coming to agreement on a common plan and putting that ahead of the narrower interest proposed by each of their countries. In addition, because many of the issues are seen as technical issues, there is a presumption that there is a best solution that can be found. There is less room for a perception of inherent conflict of interest on environmental issues. This will be particularly true when staffers and delegates to the IOs come from states' environmental ministries rather than their foreign ministries. (P. Haas, 1990). (D'Anieri 1995, 161–162)

Sustainable development has emerged in the post–Cold War period as one of the primary paradigms (along with human rights and human security) of the international order. The inter-sectoral, interdisciplinary character of sustainable development places international organizations in the driver's seat and gives primary responsibility to international organizations for managing the complex interdependencies of UNCED's Agenda 21—"a sweeping environmental policy to promote sustainability, with 2,509 specific recommendations applying to states, international institutions, and members of civil society." (Haas 2001, 329) It remains to be seen if international organizations will be able to successfully reconcile competing priorities—meeting human needs (and consumption), on the one hand, and ecological needs (and preservation) on the other. Although much progress has been made in international environmental policy since UNCED, the "new global policy network of environmental actors" that has emerged remains fragile and conflicted.

The Global Economy

Since the end of World War II, world economic growth and stability have been a major concern of several international organizations. The establishment of the Bretton Woods system entrusted to the International Monetary Fund and the World Bank significant responsibilities for managing the post-war economic recovery and financial stability, while the General Agreement on Tariffs and Trade (GATT) was the forum established to restore the international trade system and to manage reductions in tariffs and other trade barriers. The postwar international economic order relied on effective international institutions "to prevent a return to the 'beggar thy neighbor' policies of the 1920s and 1930s involving closed trading blocs and competitive exchange rates that were seen in retrospect as major contributors to depression and war." (Gwin 2001, 151) The international economic system that was put in place in the waning months of World War II reflected a basic consensus among Western governments that the international economy should be a liberal system, "one which relied primarily on a free market with the minimum of barriers to the flow of private trade and capital." (Spero 1981, 24)

International Finance

International finance deals with cross-border movements of capital. Financial institutions such as banks, mutual funds, and markets facilitate these movements as intermediaries channeling money from savers to investors. Economists generally agree a modern market economy and economic growth depend upon a strong financial infrastructure, which includes "sound financial institutions and well-functioning markets, the physical and intellectual capital on which both depend to operate, and an effective system of government oversight" (Litan 2001, 196), to provide financial stability and mechanisms for adjustments in the economy. On the national level, central banks and finance ministries govern this arena of national economies, while on the international level no such financial authority exists. Instead, the international financial architecture rested on the international organizations of the Bretton Woods system, with its fixed but adjustable exchange rates and limited controls on capital flows, which worked well in maintaining monetary stability and encouraging growth in international trade and investment, particularly among the developed market economies, for much of the postwar period. According to Joan Spero:

> The IMF was to be the keeper of the rules and the main instrument of public international management. Under the system of weighted voting, the United States was able to exert a preponderant influence in that body. IMF approval was necessary for any change in exchange rates. It advised countries on policies affecting the monetary system. Most importantly, it could advance credits to countries with balance-of-payments deficits. The IMF was provided with a fund, composed of contributions of member countries in gold and in their own currencies. The original quotas planned were to total $8.8 billion. In the event of a deficit in the current

> account, countries would be able to borrow up to eighteen months and, in some cases, up to five years from this fund.
>
> Despite these innovations in public control, the original Bretton Woods placed primary emphasis on national and market solutions to monetary problems. It was expected that national monetary reserves, supplemented when necessary by IMF credits, would finance any temporary balance-of-payments disequilibria. No provision was made for international creation of reserves. New gold production was assumed sufficient. In the event of a structural disequilibrium, it was expected that there would be national solutions—a change in the value of the currency or an improvement by other means of a country's competitive position. Few means were given the IMF, however, to encourage such national solutions. (Spero 1981, 35)

However, the IMF's modest credit facilities and the World Bank's conservative lending policy were easily overwhelmed by Europe's huge balance-of-payments deficits by 1947, putting the whole international economic system into crisis. The United States stepped in to shore up the system by providing liquidity in the form of massive outflows of U.S. dollars through aid programs like the Marshall Plan and Cold War military expenditures. American leadership of the system was critical to the ultimate economic recovery of Western Europe and Japan, but once these countries' economies were back on their feet in the 1960s the system was unable to manage the increasing monetary interdependence that the return to convertibility of West European currencies (at the end of 1958) and the Japanese yen (in 1964), the internationalization of banking and of production, and the creation of a market for Eurocurrencies facilitated. The resulting massive international capital flows, in particular the rise in speculation against exchange rate changes by multinational banks and corporations, was destabilizing. "The movement of billions of dollars or pounds or deutsche marks or francs from country to country in a few days or even a few hours during a currency crisis became common." (Spero 1981, 46–50) The Bretton Woods system of fixed exchange rates finally came to an end when the United States abandoned the "fixed gold parity" (a rate of $35 an ounce) of the dollar and let its exchange rate float in the early 1970s.

International financial institutions adapted to this fundamental change in the system, ultimately repositioning themselves as crisis managers. According to Robert Litan, "The IMF has transformed itself into a quasi lender of last resort for countries that have suffered bouts of financial crisis—and specifically, runs on their scarce holdings of foreign exchange. The IMF has justified this role as an effort to prevent financial contagion, while providing bridge financing to countries that agree to reform their economies as a condition for the loans. Such "conditionality," which was controversial at the outset of the fund, traditionally has taken the form of macroeconomic belt-tightening or reductions of government deficits and increases in domestic interest rates designed to encourage investors (domestic and foreign) to maintain holdings of domestic currency. In the Southeast Asian financial crisis [of 1997–98], the IMF broadened its conditions to include reforms in various domestic functions as well: financial regulations, bankruptcy regimes, and systems of corporate governance, among others." (Litan 2001, 208–209)

The World Bank and the regional development banks for Africa, Asia, Latin America, and eventually Eastern Europe also gradually shifted their lending activities from long-term project financing to countries, particularly the newly independent developing countries in Africa, Asia, and Latin America, that had difficulty accessing capital at reasonable interest rates to providing medium-term balance of payments support through "structural adjustment loans." "The division of labor [between the IMF and World Bank] further blurred when the Bank announced its program of structural adjustment lending in 1979. Responding to the second oil price shock, the Bank offered medium-term balance of payments support . . . . The Bank conditioned its structural adjustment loans (SALs) on measures that addressed the underlying, structural causes of members' balance of payments deficits. While there had been precedents in 'program' loans often designed to meet the immediate consequences of crises, and project loans had often carried conditions regarding output prices and other related variables, in their boldness and breadth the SALs represented a major policy shift. The Bank moved away from its nearly exclusive emphasis on discrete projects to the provision of non-project, balance of payments loans aimed at broader economic reform." (Feinberg 1988, 221) The conditionality of the IFI's lending policies has been a source of friction within the international economic system as it runs head-on into issues of national sovereignty and the prerogatives of states to determine their economic development. Yet, the ability of IFIs to impose these conditions on borrowing countries clearly demonstrates the incredible power they have accumulated over the last thirty years.

However, the role played by the international financial institutions in the development of a liberal international market economy during the 1980s and 1990s was particularly strong. The need for stabilization and external financial assistance was obvious as a response to the growing debt crisis of developing countries and high inflation and rising unemployment in developed countries, but the so-called "Washington Consensus," which directed the IMF, World Bank, and the regional development banks to push market-oriented remedies and economic liberalization in their structural adjustment programs, brought back laissez-faire—an economic and financial orthodoxy emphasizing financial balance and low inflation over employment creation and income distribution as the road to economic growth. Throughout the 1980s and 1990s, the IFIs' prescriptions supported a shift away from the state to the private sector for generating economic growth. This shift was evident in two major areas of policy:

- The establishment of a healthy base for growth through macroeconomic stabilization and austerity programs. This was seen as an important step on the road to the return of growth and prosperity. It included fiscal discipline to put an end to budget deficits, tight controls on public expenditure, and reliance on unified exchange rates in place of import controls and export subsidies.
- The restructuring of the economy toward export- and market-oriented activities through liberalization, deregulation, and privatization. The objective was to strengthen the private sector as the main actor of growth and development through tax reform, liberalization of trade and finance, privatization, deregulation, and strengthening of property rights. Countries should also be opened to foreign direct investment. (Emmerij, Jolly, and Weiss 2001, 126)

This neoliberal approach to international economic policy and the IFIs' role in enforcing it have been roundly criticized by NGOs for their disregard for the poor, the environment, women and children, and other social welfare issues. Even though the neoliberal indulgence of the private sector and the liberalization of capital markets did spur a dramatic increase in foreign direct investment (FDI) and private capital into developing countries and emerging markets reaching $255 billion in 1998, most private capital flows between developed countries (international trade follows a similar pattern) and the flows to developing countries is concentrated in only a few countries—"China, Brazil and Mexico account for almost one-half of the total [FDI going to developing countries]. Altogether, only twenty countries accounted for more than 90 percent of total net capital inflows to the South during the 1990s, whereas their shares were around 50 percent during the 1970s and 1980s. In other words, more than 100 developing countries now share the remaining 10 percent." (Emmerij, Jolly, and Weiss 2001, 178) The anticipated benefits of liberalization and integration with the world economy never materialized for many developing countries.

Another important outcome of the deregulation and liberalization of international finance in the 1980s and 1990s was the acceleration of globalization of markets and private financial institutions such as banks, mutual funds, and insurance companies. Absent inter-governmental supervision, the importance of globally operating private actors—particularly institutional investors (pension funds, insurance companies, and investment funds) and international rating agencies (such as Standard & Poor's and Moody's)—grew. However, empowering the private sector has not brought about greater stability in today's crisis-prone world economy. Indeed, these private actors contribute to financial crises, as Heribert Dieter argues:

> In 1995 [institutional investors] held capital investments amounting to US$20,950 billion. Putting this figure in relation to the economic output of the major industrialized countries, we see what enormous financial capacities are in their hands: in 1994 the GDP of the G7 countries amounted to US$17,150 billion. One striking fact is how rapidly the investments of investment funds have grown in the US and Canada since 1987. The investments of such companies rose by 405 per cent (in the US) and 868 per cent (in Canada) between 1987 and 1996.
>
> Roughly one third of the overall capital investments of institutional investors is held by pension funds (32 per cent), insurance companies (39 per cent), and investment companies (29 percent). However, differences emerge when we look at the countries of origin of these institutional investors. [The 1998 *Annual Report* of the Bank for International Settlements (p. 84) reported that in 1995, institutional investors in the US held 50 per cent of total investments amounting to $10,500 billion; in Japan—14 per

> cent, totaling $3,035 billion; in the UK—9 per cent, $1,790 billion; in France—6 per cent, $1,159 billion; in Germany—5 per cent, $1,113 billion; in Canada—2 per cent, $493 billion; and in Italy—1 per cent, $223 billion.]
>
> In theory, a variety of actors with different goals will provide for mutually complementary behaviors and ensure stability of both national financial markets and the global financial system. In practice, this is not the case. The regular rating of money managers' success and comparisons with the development of the overall market tend to favor 'herd behavior.' In practice, fear of a bad rating leads to risk-aversion on the part of pension and investment fund managers, especially when individual markets are suddenly regarded as critical.
>
> True, it is not only the investment strategies of fund managers but also the interplay of institutional investors and rating agencies (private firms that rate credit risks) that are responsible for pro-cyclical behavior on the part of the financial markets. Frequently, institutional investors, and especially pension funds, limit their investments to a given risk level. Here we see the development of the close interplay with the rating agencies. If a debtor is down-rated by a rating agency and the new rating is below the minimum standards of an institutional investor, a responsible money manager will liquidate these investments, even if he is convinced that their rating will improve over the medium term. The result is a self-reinforcing process: capital is withdrawn, which leads the rating agencies to downgrade the credit rating of debtor countries again, which in turn entails further outflow of capital: a vicious circle. (Dieter 2002, 71–73)

The financial crises of the 1990s (Mexico in 1994–1995, Southeast Asia in 1997–1998, Russia in 1998, and Brazil in 1999) have prompted calls from several quarters for "re-regulation" of the world economy and a "new international architecture" for global finance. But, as Robert Litan points out, "For the time being, there will be no radical changes in direction. . . . [A] policy of cautious incrementalism has emerged, one that seeks to reduce the likelihood and severity of future crises. This policy, to which a growing number of countries are subscribing, contains several elements: more intensive financial regulation by governments in emerging markets; a bias against supporting pegged exchange rates; the establishment of a Contingent Credit Line to insulate countries with well-designed economic policies from contagious currency runs (by providing an up-front line of credit to countries following sound policies but threatened with global financial instability); in the wake of the IMF's refusal to provide loans to Russia in the fall of 1998, a policy of 'constructive ambiguity' on crisis lending by the Fund, which should encourage more prudent economic policies from countries that can no longer count on IMF loans (beyond a country's quota) as a matter of right; and a continuation of some kind of policy loan conditionality, although the details of the conditions are likely to change as the Fund and member states gain more experience with them." (Litan 2001, 223–224)

International Trade

International trade in goods and services is the other cornerstone of the international economic order and is intertwined with international finance. It is a major factor that pushes countries and their economies towards integration and liberalization. International trade has contributed significantly to world economic growth, but it is also a conduit for disturbances of the world economy brought on by national policies, imbalances, and changes in competitive positions.

International and regional organizations have played an important role in the growth of international trade. Originally, an International Trade Organization was proposed as the counterpart to the Bretton Woods financial institutions, but this proposal failed to win U.S. congressional approval. A "temporary implementing treaty"—the General Agreement on Tariffs and Trade (GATT)—filled this institutional gap and was the key institution for regulating and liberalizing world trade for almost fifty years. Through a series of trade negotiations—called "rounds," GATT members succeeded in significantly reducing trade barriers and reaching consensus on free trade principles that have guided the development of international trade policy since the end of World War II. Over time, the GATT became more formalized, establishing a small secretariat to implement GATT rules and do preparatory work for trade negotiation conferences, and was eventually succeeded at the end of the Uruguay Round (1986–1993) by the establishment of the World Trade Organization (WTO). (See Box 7.1.) GATT was the "keeper of the rules" of the postwar multilateral trading system, which includes reciprocity, nondiscrimination, and prohibitions of quantitative restrictions, dumping, and subsidies, and managed the system through periodic rounds of multilateral negotiations.

BOX 7.1

GATT/WTO Role in Global Trade Development

As a trade institution, the GATT got off to a difficult start [in 1947], representing a stop-gap agreement among contracting parties—rather than a true international institution. The twenty-three GATT members negotiated a series of tariff concessions and free trade principles designed to prevent the introduction of trade barriers. Under the agreement, more than 45,000 binding tariff concessions were covered, constituting close to $10 billion in trade among the participating countries.

As the sole interim framework for regulating and liberalizing world trade, the GATT was highly successful at overseeing international trade in goods and progressively reducing trade barriers. Whereas the Annecy Round of 1949 resulted in 5,000 more tariff concessions and the entry of ten new GATT members, the Torquay Round of 1951 led to an overall tariff reduction of close to 25 percent and the inclusion of four new contracting parties. The 1956 Geneva Round that followed fostered further agreement of tariff reductions worth approximately $2.5 billion. Under the terms of the Dillon Round of 1960–1961, for the first time, a single schedule of concessions was agreed for the recently established European Economic Community (EEC), based on the Common External Tariff. Tariff concessions worth more than $4.9 billion in trade were also negotiated. In total, tariff reductions for the first five rounds amounted to 73 percent.

The Kennedy Round of 1962–1967 proved to be the most dramatic facilitator of trade liberalization. GATT membership increased to sixty-two countries responsible for more than 75 percent of world trade at the time. New tariff concessions surpassed 50 percent on many products as negotiations expanded from product-by-product approach to an industry/sectorwide method, while overall tariff reductions were 35 percent. In addition, an agreement establishing a Code on Anti-Dumping was also brokered. This period from 1945 until the end of the 1960s is often dubbed the golden age of trade liberalization, witnessing a dramatic reduction of border barriers. With the United States acting as the world's central banker, providing the major impetus for international trade liberalization and dominating manufacturing production, these two decades were marked by unprecedented economic growth and development.

By the 1970s, however, the Bretton Woods financial system faced severe challenges. A weakening dollar and balance-of-trade deficit throughout the decade prompted President Richard Nixon to take the United States off the gold standard and devalue the dollar. By the mid-1970s, the Organization of Petroleum Exporting Countries (OPEC) "oil shocks" produced stagflation and a rise in new domestic "inside the border" protectionism in the form of voluntary export restraints (VERs) and support for declining industries. Although the developed countries remained the dominant agenda setters, developing countries increasingly sought to become more influential in obtaining the benefits of international management. Finally, the liberal consensus had begun to erode, both among the advanced industrialized countries and the developing world. The United States continued to run large deficits but was unable to get Europeans or the Japanese to revalue their currencies. The most vocal critics of the trade and financial order came from the developing countries, which argued that the open monetary, trade, and financial system perpetuated their underdevelopment and dependence on the richer Northern countries.

(continues)

It is in this context of increasing complex interdependence that the next GATT round was negotiated. In the Tokyo Round of 1973–1979, a record ninety-nine countries agreed to further tariff reductions worth more than $300 billion of trade and an average reduction in manufacturing tariffs from 7 to 4.7 percent. In addition, agreements were reached on technical barriers to trade, subsidies and countervailing measures, import licensing procedures, government procurement, customs valuation, and a revised antidumping code. Yet for most participants, the Tokyo Round was a disappointment. With inadequate implementation and enforcement mechanisms in place, disputes involving nontariff barriers and agricultural and industrial subsidies remained relatively unsolved. Still, the Tokyo Round marked the first time that GATT dealt with significant nontariff barriers arising from domestic policies.

Following significant difficulties in setting the agenda for a new round, the Uruguay Round got under way in 1986, with the United States again taking the major initiative. The high level of contentiousness that threatened the conclusion of the round was unprecedented. In part, this reflects the changing balance of power among more actors in the system, the dissolution of the liberal consensus and inclusion of diverse interests, and the unwillingness of the United States to be the lender and market of last resort. The era of détente and the subsequent end of the Cold War also served to weaken the security arguments for continuing economic cooperation. Finally, the United States was no longer the undisputed hegemon of the system. In addition to a rise of a "fortress Europe" and a "Japanese miracle" replicated by the East Asian newly industrialized countries, the debt crisis of the 1980s led to power- and burden-sharing arrangements with Europe and Japan.

After several delays from the original target conclusion date of 1990, the Uruguay Round was finalized in 1993. Despite serious conflicts during the round, it succeeded in establishing the WTO. This new institution is equipped with both a Trade Policy Review Mechanism (TPRM) to increase transparency of trade laws and practices across borders, and a strengthened Dispute Settlement Mechanism (DSM). In addition, many issues that had previously been absent or not subject to GATT discipline such as services, trade-related investment, and intellectual property are now incorporated into the WTO. Market access for agricultural products has also been dramatically improved as countries have committed to transforming their quotas to tariffs and then implementing reductions.

Most recently, an effort to start a new round of global negotiations under the appellation of the "Millennium Round" was marred by unprecedented conflict surrounding the WTO ministers meeting in November 1999 in Seattle. Although dispute among the major powers on how best to move forward with a new round was hardly unprecedented, the active protests by environmentalists, labor activists, human rights activists, and many other self-styled antiglobalists were unanticipated.

In summary, despite recent problems, under the global trade regimes of GATT and the WTO, tariffs have been significantly reduced, and global trade has grown at an annual average of 6 percent from 1947 to the present. Still, although tariff rates have been drastically reduced, the decline of tariffs has been accompanied by a rise of various nontariff barriers.

Although GATT/WTO has clearly dominated the international trade system, regional organizations have also been key instruments for liberalizing trade among member countries. The implications of regional trade arrangements for the world trade order have been hotly debated since the establishment of the European Economic Community (EEC) in 1958. Some analysts contend that regionalism undermines the GATT/WTO global trade system, while others argue that it strengthens the system. Granted the regional integration projects that have been undertaken in Europe (European Union, European Free Trade Area) and in North America (North America Free Trade Agreement, Free Trade Area of the Americas) do contravene the nondiscrimination principle of GATT/WTO and have the potential of turning into closed trade systems or rival blocs, but to date these arrangements have not fragmented the world economy into regional trading blocs. Nor have those for other regions, namely the Latin American Free Trade Area, Caribbean Community and Common Market, Central American Common Market, the Andean Group, Mercado Común del Cono Sur, Economic Community of West African States, Southern African Customs Union, Southern African Development Community, Preferential Trade Area of Eastern and Southern Africa, Central European Free Trade Agreement, Association of Southeast Asian Nations, Asia-Pacific Economic Cooperation, South Asian Association for Regional Cooperation, Gulf Cooperation Council, the Maghreb Group, and the Arab Common Market. Indeed, these regional organizations promote trade liberalization, albeit more within a region than globally, which for some regions (such as Asia and Europe) has improved the international competitiveness of their members' economies, although others (for example, Africa) have yet to see any real gains or economic benefits from opening up their markets. Furthermore, most of the regional integration processes—defined as the gradual reduction of political and economic barriers between a specific group of nation-states, who transfer some of their sovereignty to a supranational organization—are still in the very early stages of development and few have ambitions to follow the path of the European Union.

Another significant development in the international trade system is intrasectoral or intraindustry trade. Mihály Simai points out:

> This trade has grown much faster than world trade; by the late 1980s, it constituted about one-half of total world exports. Its growth has been stimulated by the spread of transnational firms and their global sourcing

> strategies, which have contributed to the deepening division of labor while offering large reduction costs. Intraindustry trade will remain important in the future, especially among transnational corporations, interconnected as they are by ownership, strategic alliances, cross licensing, and long-term contracts. The ability to compete in the global economy will increasingly depend on a country's capabilities (meaning primarily the capabilities of its firms) to realize the potential gains derived from the globalization of supporting industries and to concentrate value-added aspects of industrial and service activities.
>
> The information revolution, as we have observed above, has dramatically decreased transportation and communication costs; facilitated the instant transmission of technology blueprints, fluctuations in stock prices, and changes in marketing strategies; and altered the traditional character of intraindustry trade. The informational revolution will also permit the future integration of output and sales through the use of computer systems. Although national governments can disrupt the integration process with protectionist measures and regulations, to do so would be to risk global chaos and incur losses (in terms of declining trade and output, shrinking incomes, rising unemployment, and so forth) on a far greater scale than protectionism brought in the past. On a regional level, the functioning of the single European market and the expansion of the EC toward Central and Eastern Europe, Japanese policies for the establishment of more structured relations with many Asian countries, and the development of the North American free trade area will help spread the new forms of intraindustry trade. Another factor in the expansion of world trade has been, and will remain, the increasing internationalization of the service sector and telecommunications. (Simai 1994, 223–224)

Clearly, there are significant imbalances in the international trade system, particularly between the advanced industrial countries and developing countries, that have not been corrected by economic liberalization and laissez-faire. Freer trade has not closed the gap between rich and poor countries and the asymmetric interdependence of the world economy. The North-South divide has widened, not narrowed. Poverty and social inequities have deepened in the South, while the North has prospered. The persistence of these glaring disparities in the global economy has fueled opposition to further trade liberalization and global integration. Anti-globalization coalitions consisting of human rights, labor, and environmental groups have pushed the primary international institutions of the liberal international economic order (the Bretton Woods institutions and WTO) to include a number of other issues on their agenda such as the environment, social issues, and women's issues. There has also emerged a trend towards closer cooperation between the Bretton Woods institutions and the UN specialized agencies and development programs. The relationship between the UN system with its emphasis on economic and social development and the World Bank, IMF, and WTO with their focus on economic growth have become less distant and contradictory. The World Bank, for example, has started to shift its priorities towards tackling the environmental and social problems in the developing world that endemic poverty causes and open markets and competition haven't overcome. This position is more in line with that being advocated by the United Nations Development Program, UNICEF, the UN Economic Commissions for Africa, Europe, and Latin America and the Caribbean, and the UN Conference on Trade and Development (UNCTAD) that have long been pushing the human dimension of economic development. However, even closer coordination of international organizations' economic and social policies has yet to demonstrate that international organizations can indeed control and direct the forces of globalization and respond to what is called the "new social question"—the intensification of old outstanding social problems of unemployment, poverty, and income distribution and the emergence of new elements such as "international criminality, growing urban dualism, new forms of international 'migration' very often linked to civil wars and lack of economic opportunity, and drugs, which itself has become a global industry." (Emmerij, Jolly, and Weiss 2001, 134–136). (See Box 7.2.)

International organizations have been swept up in the vortex of globalization. Globalization has rendered the Utopia of independent self-contained, self-sufficient, territorially bound societies increasingly an anachronism as it pushes all towards an inexorable political, economic, and social interdependence. Yet, the institutional infrastructure of international society has barely been able to cope with the complex changes of globalization. Under such circumstances, international organizations have struggled valiantly to stay abreast of events, maintain relevance, and recast themselves operationally and structurally as effective instruments for managing the uncertainty and turmoil in the world.

BOX 7.2

Eight Propositions about the "New Social Question"

(1) Globalization is private sector-driven; regionalization is public sector-driven. The growing globalization of markets for finance and goods is being realized by private firms that function increasingly worldwide. It owes very little, if anything, to governments. On the contrary, when in March 1957 the Rome Treaty creating the European Common Market was signed, there were six heads of state or prime ministers sitting around the negotiating table with no private-sector representatives in sight. The same can be said about the creation of the South American Common Market (MERCOSUR) and the North American Free Trade Agreement (NAFTA), although for the latter business was more visible. In a sense these parallel activities demonstrate that the public sector at present is running several laps behind the private sector, in spite of a head start.

(2) Globalization is sharpening the intensity of competition and competitiveness. Competition is increasingly being seen as the only solution for survival, as well as the panacea for many social problems. Countries compete for capital, and companies compete for markets. And people are often affected by the intensity of both forms. If there are high levels of unemployment, the response is to become more competitive. If poverty is widespread, growth enabled by increased competition is once again the answer. However, extreme competition diminishes diversity in a society and contributes to social exclusion. Individuals, enterprises, cities, and nations that are not competitive are marginalized or excluded from the global economy. As systems lose their variety in this way, the more they lose the capacity to renew themselves. The Latin root of the verb "to compete" (*competere*) means "to seek together." This is a far cry from what competition is becoming in the global era.

(3) Technology, one of the engines of globalization, cuts as a two-edged sword. There was a time when futurologists explained the wonders that technology would have in store for individuals, enterprises, and countries alike. Francis Fukuyama, in a burst of technological evangelism, emphasized the path to "limitless accumulation of wealth" and "an increasing homogenization of all human societies."* People would be able to produce more with less labor and earn more by putting in fewer hours of work—Utopia, many thought at the time. But Utopia is here today. Societal restructuring has not kept pace with economic and technological restructuring. Labor markets, educational systems, and pension and tax regimes are largely as they were thirty years ago, whereas the economy and technology have changed dramatically.

(4) Orthodox, neo-liberal policies have not solved the old, outstanding social problems of unemployment, poverty, and income distribution. In fact, they have frequently intensified them. Life expectancy and school enrollment rates have improved in the world as a whole (although Eastern Europe has gone in the opposite direction), and East and Southeast Asia have done better than other countries (until recently). However, with respect to crucial indicators like unemployment, poverty, and income distribution, the situation has deteriorated in an unacceptably high number of countries.

(5) A new social question has arisen, which has two components. The first is the intensification of the "old" social problems. The second is the emergence of "new" elements—

(continues)

including international criminality, growing urban dualism, new forms of international "migration" very often linked to civil wars and lack of economic opportunity, and drugs, which itself has become a global industry.

(6) The world has entered into a period of global wealth in the midst of increasing national and individual poverty. In spite of the hyperbole surrounding the increasing number of millionaires and even billionaires, almost half the world survives on the equivalent of less than $2 per day, and hundreds of millions of people are worse off today than they were ten or even twenty years ago. The absolute number of people living in poverty continues to increase in many parts of the world. Global enterprises are privately owned and in the business of profit making. They will, therefore, locate their multifarious activities in such a manner as to minimize costs (including paying taxes) and maximize profits. At the same time, the combination of neo-liberalism and globalization have given rise, as we have seen, to a growing social and economic vulnerability for a large part of the globe's population. It follows that while enormous global wealth is being created, the income of many governments is declining at the very moment that they require additional resources to pay for the increased financial outlays necessitated by the new social question. Globalization can be a very positive factor that contributes to the creation of wealth. Everyone is affected by it; many feel its negative aspects in their daily lives; and few really benefit. Globalization has given rise to a new distribution problem leading to social fragmentation and the loss of social cohesion.

(7) Mega-cities, particularly in the South, have become "Romes without Empires." Although rural exodus began long before globalization, the latter has exacerbated the problems of increased open unemployment and squattering. Mega-cities breed crime and waste resources, for instance, by travel to and from work. There has developed an urban question within the new social question, which has many dimensions—including poverty, housing, health, unemployment, slum areas, crime, drugs, street children, and quality of education. The urban question amounts to more than the sum total of the different problems just enumerated. It is difficult to calculate the "value added," but it certainly has a lot to do with the quality of life, or the lack of it, in urban settings. Common problems can be observed in urban conglomerates worldwide. The most important include growing inequalities, spatial and social fragmentation, and informalization leading to the phenomenon of "cities divided against themselves." The fundamentally social character of the urban problem is clear because poverty, social exclusion, and marginalization have become structural.

(8) There is no equivalent of social support at the regional and global levels. At the end of the nineteenth century capitalism had combined dynamic economic opportunity with persistent social problems at the national level. Extreme riches existed side-by-side with appalling poverty. It took strong and imaginative leadership from German Chancellor Otto von Bismarck (hardly a progressive) to start building a national welfare state to balance the power of the market, to construct an income floor below which no one was allowed to fall, and hence to ensure a more equitable distribution of income. States were strong, and decision making mattered in a world economy that was largely organized along national line. The private sector became somewhat less free, limited by social regulation.

(continues)

Now, a century later, globalizing markets are giving private enterprise the freedom that their national counterparts had at the end of the nineteenth century. Thus, at the beginning of the twenty-first century a paradoxical situation has arisen, but this time at the global level. An economy propelled by energetic and dynamic global enterprises is booming, while many states grow poorer and have to shrink the welfare fabric that has been patiently constructed over the past decades, particularly since World War II. In many respects, a countervailing power is required for the planet. Overlooking for the moment the man's more bellicose aspects, what is now needed is a "new Bismarck," acting on a global scale to redefine the economic responsibility of states and the social responsibility of the business community and to develop a vision steering these two entities toward cooperation instead of cutthroat competition.

* Francis Fukuyama, *The End of History and the Last Man* (New York: Free Press, 1992), xiv.

8

Conclusion: The "New World Order" and the Future of International Organizations

The breakup of the Soviet Union and collapse of the ideological and strategic rivalry between the superpowers in the early 1990s uncovered many weaknesses in the patchwork design of the international system's organizational infrastructure. Many international governmental organizations had become ossified as their machinery, reflecting the organizational design circa 1945, atrophied due to neglect or lack of use during the forty years of the Cold War. So, when the constraints and conditions of the Cold War were lifted, much of the international machinery desperately needed retooling, in the short-term, and a total overhaul in the long term. Private non-state actors—transnational corporations and civil society organizations—seized the opportunity to fill the political and economic space that states had abandoned or were failing to maintain control over. But, they too are struggling to overcome organizational and institutional weaknesses of their own, though adjusting and restructuring of private organizations' management and operations to the post–Cold War environment are being achieved faster than within public international organizations.

According to Jessica Mathews, the end of the Cold War caused a "power shift" within the international system that has had profound implications for the international order. "The absolutes of the Westphalian system—territorially fixed states where everything of value lies within some state's borders; a single, secular authority governing each territory and representing it outside its borders; and no authority above states—are all dissolving. Increasingly, resources and threats that matter, including money, information, pollution, and popular culture, circulate and shape lives and economies with little regard for political boundaries. International standards of conduct are gradually beginning to override claims of national or regional singularity. Even the most powerful states find the marketplace and international public opinion compelling them more often to follow a particular course." (Mathews 1997, 50) The world has definitely and irreversibly changed, leaving in tatters the post–World War II international order.

The new post–Cold War world order as proclaimed by President George H. W. Bush at the United Nations in 1990 was envisioned to be "a new partnership of nations that transcends the Cold War. A partnership based on consultation, cooperation, and collective action, especially through international and regional organizations. A partnership united by principle and the rule of law and supported by an equitable sharing of both costs and commitment. A partnership whose goals are to increase democracy, increase prosperity, increase peace, and reduce arms." (Bush 1990, 152) The United States, as the world's sole superpower with unparalleled global military and economic might, saw the end of the Cold War as an opportunity to establish (or reestablish) "a singular global vision of world order . . . a global order centred around issues of military security as identified by the UN Security Council, and especially by the United States", resuscitating traditional 'top-down' multilateralism of the state-centric international system. (Schechter 1999c, 7) But, this vision of a new world order has been difficult to implement for the simple reason that it underestimates the depth and breadth of the opposition to its imposition from "incoherent and weak collectivities uncomfortable with the dominant powers' choice of issues for the global agenda (for example, nuclear non-proliferation), the methods employed in choosing those issues (that is, privileging the Security Council and G-7 over the General Assembly and with the USA acting unilaterally when it cannot forge consensus on salient issues) and acting upon them (as in the Gulf area), as well as the disjunction between the power available to effectuate a hegemonic world order in a period where power (broadly defined) is widely dispersed." (Schechter 1999c, 20) Michael Schechter points out:

> The consequences for multilateralism of this effort have been portrayed as considerable. Issues, like asylum and arms sales, not on the dominant

> powers' agenda, are relegated to the periphery of international organizations' agendas, thus limiting those organizations' ability for innovation or task expansion or expanding their constituencies through re-legitimation of their activities and thus their ability to serve as agents of global change. Organizations, chief among them the UN system, perceived as conduits for resurgent American hegemony have been deligitimized in the eyes of multiple important collectivities, thus weakening the opportunities of those organizations to cope with those or other issues on the global agenda. Thus far they—like NATO and the EU—have proven incapable of accommodating to a world of competing world orders, with different global agendas. Steps undertaken by executive heads to reverse this trend have thus far been unsuccessful . . . . Innovations—especially those in the name of further democratization or decision-making—would, if allowed to go forward, possibly aid in the relegitimization of these organizations as independent and autonomous agents of global change. But the prospects for such innovations have been found to be minimal, as underscored by the UN's difficulties in the post-Gulf era. Almost any proposal perceived as having been initiated by 'the North' appears to be 'dead on delivery'. Partly as a consequence, an upsurge in aggressive unilateralism (as with VERs [Voluntary Export Restraints]) and alternative multilateralisms, including regionalism (for example, NAFTA) and 'bottom-up', 'new' mechanisms (as in the realm of humanitarian relief), has evolved. Thus far, however, alternative multilateralisms have been underdeveloped, underfunded and relatively ineffectual. Some, however, expect (or at least hope) that the [UN] Commission on Sustainable Development will set a new (reversed) pattern (that is, of organizations serving as agents of global structural change by successfully working at the interstices of multiple collectivities with seemingly conflicting preferred world orders). (Schechter 1999c, 20–21)

Early on in the post–Cold War period, many observers commented on the growing world "disorder" that was unfolding, especially the increasing number of intra-state conflicts and failed states that were heavily taxing the international system's capacity to respond. Globalization had already undermined state sovereignty and the states system and was contributing to a sense of uncertainty and chaos in the world. According to Harlan Cleveland, "The world of the 1990s and beyond is fundamentally different from anything in our cultural memory of international relations. No 'power' has the power to undertake on its own responsibility 'to make the world safe for diversity.' It is already apparent that a nobody-in-charge world will be more volatile and more crisis-prone than the potentially fatal yet eerily stable confrontation of nuclear-tipped superpowers glaring at each other from their hardened silos." (Cleveland 1993, 78) Clearly, the new world order is still "in a period of gestation, and its final form will not be visible until well into the [21st] century. Part extension of the past, part unprecedented, the new world order, like those which it succeeds, will emerge as an answer to three questions: What are the basic units of the international order? What are their means of interacting? What are the goals on behalf of which they interact?" (Kissinger 1994, 806) Globalization has certainly made it more difficult and much more complicated to reach an answer to these three questions, and exasperated many of the efforts to design a post–Cold War world order.

Globalization and the Transformation of the International System

Globalization is a complex phenomenon producing significant political, economic, and social effects. "The dynamics of globalization are bringing together societies and ecosystems that were once buffered from each other by physical, political, and cultural barriers. An international system composed of sovereign states is being transformed into a global one where national boundaries are much less important. A rapidly moving flow of people, pests, products and ideas across borders is producing a planetary mingling of species and cultures that will have uncertain consequences. . . . These rapid changes in the human condition are increasing many kinds of insecurity, ranging from bioinvasion to terrorism, and now represent a major discontinuity in ongoing evolutionary processes." (Pirages 2002, 2) The inability of policymakers on the national and international level to respond effectively to growing insecurities and uncertainties reveals the severe limitations of states to provide public goods and regulate public bads. (See Figure 8.1.) As we know, the international system is organized to handle "at the border" issues (for example, trade barriers) and inter-state concerns and is precluded from interfering with any matters ("behind the border" issues such as health, security, human rights, and poverty) claimed to be within the territorial boundaries of states and the

Goods	*Bads*
International peace	Inter-state armed conflicts/wars
Human security	Intra-state ethnic conflicts/civil wars/international terrorism
Disarmament	Weapons of Mass Destruction/Conventional weapons
Equity	Poverty/wage inequalities/foreign debt
Justice and human rights	Genocide/crimes against humanity/child labor/slavery
International law	Illicit narcotics trafficking/Organized Crime/aggression
Human health	HIV/AIDS and other infectious diseases
Environment	Climate Change/water and air pollution/deforestation
Outer Space	Space-based weapons/space junk
Oceans	Pollution/overfishing
Common heritage	Vandalization, neglect, and destruction of cultural artifacts
Economic development and growth	Poverty/macro-economic instability
Telecommunications	Digital divide
International trade	Tariff and non-tariff trade barriers

FIGURE 8.1 Select List of Global Public Goods and Bads

exclusive concern of the governing authorities of a sovereign state. The institutional architecture of the international system still reflects this jurisdictional divide between national and international for the provision of public goods. However, globalization has shifted many public goods from the domestic or national domain ("behind the border" issues) to the international or global level. The lines that once separated the global and the local have become blurred, while externalities and spillovers (negative and positive) are increasing and varied along both the private-public dimension and the local-national-regional-international-global dimension. (See Kaul, Grunberg, and Stern 1999.)

Globalization has also changed the way we see and understand security, economic development, the natural environment, and myriad other human concerns and activities. New paradigms, such as sustainable development, human security, and humanitarian intervention, have emerged that now frame an expanding list of "global public goods." However, the architecture of the international system is not designed along these lines and the new paradigms do not fit easily within established international policy frameworks. "Public policymakers (national and international alike) find themselves in an increasingly difficult position. Confronted with a broad range of complex challenges, they all too often discover that they lack the adequate knowledge and instruments to effectively tackle them." (Witte, Reinicke, and Benner 2002, 6) Retooling international governmental organizations to meet these concerns has proven to be a painstakingly slow undertaking. To date, reform efforts of international institutions and organizations have been incomplete and largely ineffective, creating a so-called "operational gap" as intergovernmental organizations struggle to adapt their operations to respond to the growing list of externalities, which can no longer be contained within national borders.

The Technological Revolution

Certainly, advances in technology and the information/communication revolution have had the greatest impact on the international system. As the driving force of globalization, technology has done more than anything else to transform the international system into a global one. The most obvious effect of technology has been in the economic domain. As Joseph Grieco and John Ikenberry point out:

> Technology, or the state of knowledge used in production, is clearly an important part of the story of the increasing globalization of the present-day world economy. At least three types of technological change are tightening the linkages across national economies. First, continuing improvements in transportation technology have reduced costs of international exchanges of goods, services, and technology itself. . . . Second, and perhaps even more important than cost-cutting improvements in transportation technology, advances in communications and computing technology have created new opportunities today for both trade and cross-national financial transactions. . . . Third, MNEs [Multinational Enterprises] have learned how to employ these advances in transportation, communications, and computing technologies in order to become more active in the world economy. Managers in MNEs have learned how to use cheaper telecommunications, increasingly powerful computers, and, during the past decade, the Internet to coordinate the operations of their subsidiaries and their independent suppliers across national borders and even around the world. Moreover, financial firms have learned to employ the new telecommunications and computing technologies to develop, price, and trade new international financial products, such as currency options, and to identify and monitor new and profitable investment opportunities in foreign markets. Thus, the interaction between

> improved communications and computing technologies, on the one hand, and advances in knowledge regarding management and investment, on the other, may be the most important technical driver of modern globalization. (Grieco and Ikenberry 2003, 220–221)

The technology revolution is also driving the globalization of international political and social relations. It has increased the number of international actors on the world stage, disrupted traditional hierarchies, and spread power and authority more widely. According to W. Andy Knight:

> Modern communications (in the form of television, radio, newspapers, telephones, fax machines, the internet and electronic mail, satellites, fiber-optics, and so on), appear to be uniting and fragmenting audiences, exacerbating social cleavages as well as bringing formerly disparate groups together, heightening existing antagonisms as well as providing a means through which such friction can be resolved, eroding national boundaries as well as propelling ultra-nationalist fervor, increasing political cynicism as well as raising the level of civil society's political consciousness. Individual citizens have been empowered as a result of the media's influence. At the same time, because of their adeptness with the utilization of communication systems, state leaders have also been empowered *vis-à-vis* civil society. Modern transportation has allowed people of formerly distant societies to interact more frequently. It acts as a conduit for bringing individuals from different countries with similar interests together.
>
> The overall effect of the above "double movement" has been a shrinkage in social, political, economic and cultural distances. As a consequence of this phenomenon, formerly dense and opaque frontiers are being dissolved, thus breaking down the Westphalian notion of inside versus outside. National boundaries are no longer able to divide friend from foe. Indeed, the technological revolution has the potential of creating in the minds of people around the world a sense of global citizenship which could result eventually in the transfer of individuals' loyalties from "sovereignty-bound" to "sovereignty-free" multilateral bodies. (Knight 1999, 277)

Advances in technology are the engines of change and innovation, creating what many scholars are now calling "complex interdependence." But, complex interdependence, as we now know, is full of asymmetries and inequities, problems that technology seems to intensify and magnify rather than mitigate. In other words, technology and innovation are not a panacea to the problems associated with complex interdependence because technology and access to it is unevenly dispersed within the international system and is clearly controlled by corporate and governmental interests of the advanced industrial societies, which benefit most from technology. But it can and does create powerful mechanisms of global cooperation through which some global issues are managed more effectively.

The transformational power of technology cannot be denied and, in recent years, considerable energy has been expended on closing the so-called "digital divide." A new "movement" has emerged within the field of economic and social development which advocates the uptake of information and communication technologies (ICT) in developing countries and the dedication of aid resources towards its rapid introduction in "digitally deprived" areas of the world. Mike Chege argues that ICTs and the Internet provide four obvious benefits for the poor: 1) economic benefits–providing business with access to real-time market information, greater internal efficiencies, and reduction in costs, as well as additional channels to market goods and services; 2) health benefits—providing healthcare professionals with fast and low-cost access and distribution of medical research and public health information, near instantaneous communications with peers and other experts in healthcare, and a more efficient ability to track diseases; 3) education benefits—giving educators an effective tool for delivering education and training to remote and impoverished areas and to a broader segment of the population; and 4) "e-government" initiatives—making available to citizens direct access to information and public services (which is supposed to foster greater transparency and accountability of governments and public administration). (Chege 2002). However, there is growing concern that the "ICT-for-development campaign" is being oversold. According to Robert Hunter Wade:

> ICT-for-development can be seen as a fad, a focal point for enthusiastic action by many kinds of actors concerned with development. The history of development thinking since the 1950s is full of fads: not only tractors in Africa in the 1960s and early 1970s but also "integrated rural develop-

> ment" (IRD) in the 1970s and environment-in-development in the 1980s and early 1990s. Fads are analogous to financial bubbles. They have advocates—who (by definition) have a solution looking for a problem, who skew information to favor their solution and disfavor alternatives, who build up alliances to promote their solution, who want action now, and who insulate themselves from discomfirming evidence. Fads can help development by channeling enthusiasm into action. But channeling enthusiasm into action may require poor decisionmaking in the sense of no serious consideration of alternatives—because serious consideration of alternatives might make consensus around one alternative more difficult. Better to claim that the route to the future is clear. Good decisions, on the other hand, require open-minded consideration of several goals and alternative paths and open-minded consideration of evidence for and against. But it is even more difficult to get consensus that one of the alternatives is the best and therefore more difficult to get concerted and enthusiastic action. The big worry about the ICT-for-development movement is that it reflects a rationality of *action* that is obstructing rational *decisions* about development investments. (Wade 2002, 461–462)

The "digital divide" may not be bridged by throwing computers and software at the problem, but by bringing ICTs to bear in development strategies and poverty reduction programs the gap will certainly be narrowed to the benefit of all. In the long run, a global ICT infrastructure, once in place, will be the backbone of the global system and the mechanisms through which the system will be governed.

Reform Versus Revolution

The search for new mechanisms of governance can be characterized as a duel between reform and revolution. The reformist position is epitomized by the "singular global vision of world order" dominated by the United States. It emphasizes slow incremental change of the international system and considers the current international architecture basically adequate for meeting the challenges and problems posed by globalization; existing international institutions and organizations only need a bit of tweaking to be more efficient, more capable, more effective. The revolutionist position is exemplified by the "nobody-in-charge" world order dominated by an amorphous global civil society. It advocates radical change of the international system and considers the international architecture antiquated, outmoded and unrepresentative of today's wired, transnationalized global society; existing international institutions and organizations need to be radically restructured and democratized, and new global organizations created. The reform outlook focuses on closing the operational gaps, while the revolution position emphasizes correcting the participatory gaps. The tension between these two positions highlights the complexity in dealing with an increasingly dynamic and diverse world order.

The fate of existing international organizations will be determined, in large part, by the side that ultimately prevails. Questions abound on the capacity and capability of international organizations to "govern" the complex global order of the twenty-first century. Structures appear to be in sufficient supply, but in many ways inadequate. The rapid changes in the political, economic, and social landscape have made adaptation and reform of international institutions extremely difficult. The slow pace at which IGOs have reformed the decisionmaking or inter-governmental machinery and the incompleteness of operational reforms suggest that the leadership within the political domain, which is essential to build the architecture of global governance, is still lacking. As Paul Diehl points out:

> The prospects for expanding the roles, functions, and powers of international organizations in global governance seemed bright at the beginning of the 1990s. Yet a series of events underscored the problems and limitations of international organizations as they approached the twenty-first century. The enhanced ability of the UN Security Council to authorize new peacekeeping missions did not necessarily translate into greater effectiveness in halting armed conflict or promoting conflict resolution. The United Nations was largely ineffective in stopping the fighting in Bosnia, could not produce a political settlement in Somalia, and was too slow to prevent genocide in Rwanda. Despite its successes, the European Union stumbled badly in its peace efforts toward Bosnia, and attempts to create a common currency as well as other integration efforts promise significant domestic and foreign political controversy. Other organizations, such as the North Atlantic Treaty Organization (NATO), now struggle with the new environment and the redefinition of their roles as their original purposes have been significantly altered or rendered obsolete. As we approach the twenty-first century, international organizations

> play a greater role than they ever have in history. Yet we are still reminded that state sovereignty and lack of political will by members inhibit long-term prospects of those organizations for creating effective structures of global governance. (Diehl 1997, 3)

It would then be expected that TNCs and private sector-driven international organizations would lead the way. In some ways, this came about. The economic domain of global governance clearly moved to the top of the global agenda. Commercialization or privatization of significant segments of the political and social domains has given global business and private-sector associations unprecedented power and authority in the global system. "Transnational corporations and investment funds have grown to such dimensions that in some cases they are regarded as greater powers than (most) nation states and that the latter can no longer afford to ignore them. . . . Private rating-agencies have come to occupy key positions [in international financial markets]. They are assessing the credit ratings not just of private debtors but also of sovereign nation states. Their ratings decide which countries have access to international financial markets and on what conditions. The fact that these agencies are not accountable to the public is all the more alarming because their assessments of country risks are not only narrowly economic in perspective but may actually be wrong and may exacerbate crises. This was demonstrated most dramatically by the Asian crisis. It has now been suggested that the assessment process for medium- and long-term ratings should involve trade unions and other elements of civil society. . . . Remarkably, reform proposals like these do not rely on 'more state' but on better control of (commercial) private entities by (more public-interest-oriented) private entities" (Hummel 2002, 7–8). Market-driven politics has dominated the post–Cold War world and the entrepreneurial rationality that guides most TNCs' management and operations has made significant inroads in the political and social-cultural arenas. Yet, the long-term preeminence of the economic pillar of the global governance model is far from certain, as the events on September 11, 2001, demonstrate and the dramatic erosion of confidence in and credibility of corporate leaders in the aftermath of the rash of big business scandals in 2002 that destroyed Enron, WorldCom, and Arthur Andersen. Could the burgeoning and fractious global civil society lead? Perhaps.

Social movements and nongovernmental organizations have demonstrated considerable influence in core global issue areas—human rights, sustainable development, gender, human security, and global health—and have shown remarkable tenacity in their efforts to change the system. They have waged and won important battles in the international arena—for example, the ban on landmines, a string of human rights accords from slavery to women and children to the International Criminal Court, and protection of the global environment including the atmosphere, the oceans, tropical forests, endangered species, and biodiversity. Their demands for greater transparency of and more participation in the decisionmaking in the international system are steadily being heeded and granted. But more "power to the people" does not guarantee good governance, human security, or social justice and is not a cure-all for the failings of states and the interstate system. Global civil society's strength is also its greatest weakness. Its resistance to institutionalization offers an alternative to the top-down hierarchical structure of social relationships, but the under-institutionalization of global civil society has kept it fragmented and conflicted, limiting the power it needs to effectively contend in global politics and dimming its aspirations and that of the socio-cultural domain to lead the way to global governance.

The tussle between the three pillars of global governance reflects both the disequilibrium of the international order and the dynamic character of the transformation process. It also indicates that the two biggest gaps in the international system—the operational deficiencies and the "democratic deficit"—have not been closed or even narrowed by the growing interaction of actors across the three governance domains. Reform and revolution of the international system are simultaneously at work, sowing uncertainty and confusion about the means and ends of the interaction among the primary actors (governments, markets, and civil society) within the system. At this stage in the development of a global order for the twenty-first century, "World politics has become like a three-dimensional chess game in which one can win only by playing vertically as well as horizontally. On the top board of classic inter-state military issues, the United States is likely to remain the only superpower for years to come, and it makes sense to speak in traditional terms of unipolarity or hegemony. However, on the middle board of inter-state economic issues, the distribution of power is already multipolar. The United States cannot obtain what it wants on trade, anti-trust or financial regulation issues without the co-operation of the European Union, Japan and others. It makes little sense to call this American hegemony. On the bottom board of transnational issues, power is widely distributed and chaotically organized among state and non-state actors. It makes no sense at all to call this a unipolar world or an American empire. And this is the set of issues that is now intruding into the world of grand strategy." (Nye 2002). Unfortunately, no one knows the duration of the gestational period before a new world order will be born.

International Organizations and the Future of Global Governance

It should be quite clear that the transformation process is fraught with danger and violence. It would appear that the world makes one step forward only to take two steps backward. The progress that has been made in so many areas on the international agenda—human rights, international law, sustainable development, non-proliferation, democratization, and so on—during the 1990s has in some areas stalled (for example, sustainable development and democratization), while in others reversed (such as non-proliferation). The new global capitalism has made a global market economy a fact and spurred an amazing expansion of wealth in the world. But, here too the vicissitudes of the marketplace and growing global disparities between rich and poor have provoked protests and increasing opposition (for example, the "Seattle Movement") as well as efforts to stop or roll back further economic liberalization. Even the most recent wave of "democratization" has seemingly crested already and in some places is on its way down (see UNDP 2002).

Perhaps the biggest and most challenging setback in the transition to a new global order is the emergence of global terrorism. The terrorist attacks of 9/11 have put strategic issues back on top of the global agenda and revived the waning fortunes of the state as the center of the international system. The response to the events of September 11, namely the American-led "war on terror", has significantly increased governmental powers and the "relegitimation" of central institutions as the state reclaims political, economic, and especially military responsibility for peace and security, domestically and internationally. The state in reasserting its power has again attempted to reimpose order and stem further fragmentation of the now globalized international system. (See Caraley 2002.)

As we move through this very precarious period in the development of a new world order, the facility of international organizations for bridging the political, economic, and social divisions in the world is needed more than ever before. International organizations' role as intermediaries between states, markets, and civil society on the global level is critical to managing the dilemmas of globalization and the multidimensional character of the global condition. The capacity of international organizations to meet the governance needs across the three domains of governance has to be strengthened with new resources so as to enable international organizations to serve as agents of global structural change. Arguably, contemporary terrorism and the other anti-systemic forces created by globalization are symptomatic of the institutional deficiencies within all three governance domains and are not likely to yield to traditional power structures of twentieth century international relations (no matter how much firepower the United States has and can project). Faster and deeper interaction of the three institutional pillars of global governance (see Figure 8.2) will move forward the integration of the governance domains and facilitate the development of new structures which will address the institutional deficiencies of global governance.

While the core characteristics of global governance outlined in the first chapter—multipolarity of power and decentralization of authority; transformed international institutions, regimes and organizations; and, a global system that is stable, responsive and ordered—are not fully evident in the world today, the path we need to take to realize them is. As Franz Nuscheler argues:

> There are also developments that show global governance to be more than an illusion: the establishment of a number of regimes that are deepening and codifying international cooperation in various policy fields; the establishment of the International Criminal Court to prosecute crimes against humanity throughout the world; a "policy of intervention" to improve human rights and to develop the rule of law by means of appropriate conditionalities and promotion instruments in development policy; the development of an international civil society that refuses to leave politics up to "the state"; the attempts undertaken by world

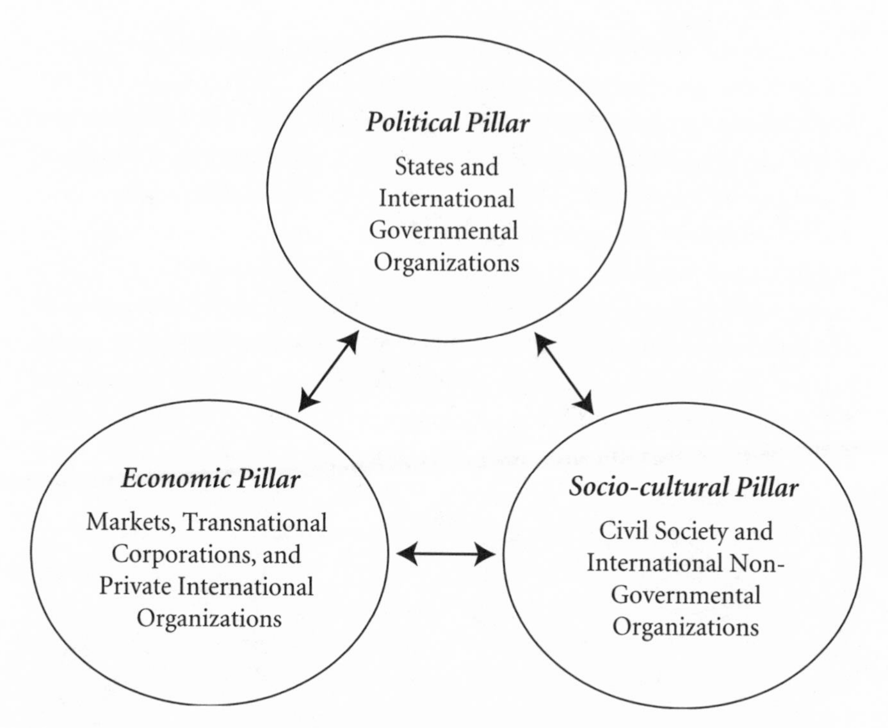

FIGURE 8.2 Intersectoral Processes Between the Three Pillars of Global Governance

conferences to work out cooperative solutions to the most pressing world problems. Under pressure generated by these problems as well as by the international NGO scene, the neoliberal "Washington consensus" is breaking down. The annual assembly of the IMF and World Bank in the fall of 1999 called on the two Bretton Woods institutions to devote more of their efforts to poverty reduction.

Numerous international organizations and negotiation processes provide forums in which to practice cooperative patterns of thinking and action and engage in learning processes that can flow back into national decision-making processes. The pressure of problems and the concomitant growing transaction costs imposed by efforts to come up with solutions without cooperation will also force global players to regulate the uncontrolled dynamics inherent in globalization and impel the 'lonely superpower' to engage in international cooperation, because the latter, alone or together with NATO, will prove unable to solve the problem of govern-

> ability of the world (see Huntington 1999). There is no future for hegemonic notions of world order in a polycentric and turbulent world.
>
> Global governance is not a romantic project aimed at a safe and tidy 'global neighborhood,' but a realistic response to the challenges of globalization and global risks. It is an evolutionary project, developing step by step. (Nuscheler 2002, 181–182)

As we move forward on this path towards global governance, international organizations of today and those yet to come will play an important part in overcoming the many obstacles along the way. International organizations are the building blocks of this "evolutionary project" and, in the final analysis, the architecture of global governance.

Appendix
List of International Organizations by Location and Year of Founding

Africa

1909 – East Africa Natural History Society
1922 – Men of the Trees
1935 – Marchoux Institute
1939 – Centre Muraz

Americas

South America

1907 – Pan American Railway Congress Association
1911 – Postal Union of Americas, Spain and Portugal
1916 – South American Football Conference
1917 – Latin American Odontological Federation
1918 – South American Athletics Conference
1925 – Pan American Highway Congress
1927 – Inter-American Children's Institute
1928 – Inter-American Commission of Women
1928 – Pan American Institute of Geography and History
1929 – International Federation of Pezota Vasca
1934 – Inter-American Commercial Arbitration Commission
1938 – Ibero-American Organization of Inter-Municipal Cooperation
1938 – Latin American Association of Communications Researchers
1939 – Inter-American Juridical Committee

1941 – Inter-American Council of Commerce and Production
1941 – Latin American Union of Ecumenical Youth
1941 – International American Academy of Comparative and International Law
1941 – International American Hotel Association
1942 – Inter-American Conference on Social Security
1944 – Latin American Pediatric Association

United States of America

1851 – International Organization of Good Templars
1869 – Phi Delta Phi International Legal Fraternity
1870 – Jehovah's Witness
1875 – Theosophical Society
1879 – Church of Christian Scientists
1883 – World's Women's Christian Temperance Union
1884 – Institute of Electrical and Electronics Engineering
1884 – Association of Official Analytical Chemists
1888 – International Council of Women
1889 – Astronomical Society of the Pacific
1890 – Organization of American States
1890 – General Federation of Women's Clubs
1891 – International Association of Refrigerated Warehouses
1893 – International Association of Chiefs of Police
1895 – Africa Inland Mission International
1895 – World's Christian Endeavor Union
1897 – International Jewish Labor Bund
1899 – Gideons International
1900 – International Association for Religious Freedom
1902 – Pan American Health Organization
1902 – International Alliance of Women
1904 – International Electrotechnical Commission
1905 – Rotary International
1905 – Care International
1906 – International Academy of Pathology
1909 – United Lodge of Theosophists
1910 – Armenian Relief Society
1911 – World Methodist Historical Society

1911 – International Association of Pupil Personnel Workers
1911 – International Star Class Yacht Racing Association
1912 – American Association of Port Authorities
1913 – Rockefeller Foundation
1914 – International Association of Industrial Accident Boards and Committees
1914 – International Association of Convention and Visitor Bureaus
1914 – International Ice Patrol
1914 – General Council of the Assemblies of God
1914 – American Jewish Joint Distribution Committee
1914 – International City Management Association
1915 – Helen Keller International
1917 – Lions Club International
1919 – Quota International
1919 – International Association of Women Ministers
1919 – Zonta International
1920 – Self Realization Fellowship
1920 – ASM International
1920 – Society of Economic Geologists
1920 – International Association for Dental Research
1920 – World Boxing Organization
1921 – Soroptimist International of the Americas
1921 – Commission on World Mission and Evangelism of World Council of Churches
1922 – International Association of Y's Men's Clubs
1922 – International Brotherhood of Magicians
1922 – Lucis International
1923 – Standing Committee on Commonwealth Forestry
1923 – American Management Association
1924 – International Society of Arboriculture
1924 – B'nai Brith Youth Organization
1924 – International Society of Sugar Cane Technologists
1925 – Battelle Memorial Institute
1925 – Pan American Medical Association
1926 – Central American and Caribbean Sports Organization
1926 – International Chiropractors Association
1927 – International Radio Consultative Committee

1928 – International Dragon Class Association
1928 – Pan Pacific and South-East Asia Women's Association
1929 – Pan Pacific Surgical Association
1929 – International Moth Class Association
1930 – Pan American Womens Association
1930 – World Convention of Churches of Christ
1930 – Econometric Society
1932 – Snipe Class International Association
1932 – Commonwealth Games Federation
1932 – International Bridge, Tunnel and Turnpike Association
1933 – International Rescue Committee
1935 – Alcoholics Anonymous World Services
1936 – International Correspondence Society of Allergists
1936 – Ford Foundation
1937 – Foster Parents Plan International
1938 – Inter-American Safety Council
1938 – Sierra International
1938 – International Training in Communication
1938 – International Advertising Association
1938 – International Council for Distance Education
1938 – International Institute of Ibero-American Literature
1939 – International Game Fish Association
1939 – International Lightning Class Association
1939 – Secular Institute of Plus X
1939 – World Federation of Methodist Women
1939 – Inter-American Travel Congresses
1940 – Inter- American Bar Association
1940 – Inter-American Statistical Institute
1940 – Pan American Association of Ophthalmology
1940 – International Surfing League
1941 – Inter-American Federation of Touring and Automobile Club
1941 – Institute of Internal Auditors
1941 – World Association of Estonians
1942 – Society of Plastics Engineers
1942 – Inter-American Press Association
1942 – Inter-American Defense Board

1942 – Inter-American Institute for Cooperation on Agriculture
1942 – International Society for General Semantics
1942 – United Seaman's Service
1943 – International Magnesium Association
1943 – International Oxygen Manufacturers Association
1943 – Catholic Relief Services
1944 – International Monetary Fund
1944 – Junior Chamber International
1944 – International Federation of Women Lawyers
1946 – Pan American Association of Rhino Laryngology

Asia

1897 – International Commission for Uniform Methods of Sugar Analysis
1931 – International Leprosy Association
1937 – International Wool Secretariat

Europe

Austria

1815 – Central Commission for the Navigation of the Rhine
1884 – International Ornithological Committee
1884 – International Ornithological Congress
1895 – International Friends of Nature
1921 – International Federation of Commercial, Clerical, Professional, and Technical Employees
1922 – International Association of Individual Psychology
1922 – International Society for Contemporary Music
1923 – Pan European Union
1923 – International Criminal Police Organization–Interpol
1926 – International Society for History of Pharmacy
1926 – Internationale des organizations culturelles ouvrieres
1926 – International Federation of Freight Forwarders Associations
1930 – Associated Country Women of the World
1936 – International Federation of Catholic Medical Associations

Belgium

1617 – International Association of Charities
1873 – Institute of International Law
1873 – International Law Association
1881 – International Gymnastic Federation
1884 – International Railway Congress Association
1885 – International Union of Public Transport
1890 – International Union for the Publication of Customs Tariffs
1890 – Miners' International Federation
1891 – International Federation of Building and Woodworkers
1895 – International Actuarial Association
1895 – International Federation for Information and Documentation
1897 – International Association for the Protection of Industrial Property
1897 – Comite maritime international
1898 – International Touring Alliance
1902 – International Society of Surgery
1903 – International Dairy Federation
1907 – World Federation of Diamond Bourses
1907 – Union of International Associations
1909 – European Construction Industry Federation
1910 – Council for International Congress of Entomology
1910 – World Union of Catholic Women's Organizations
1910 – International Federation of the Periodical Press
1911 – Federation cynologique internationale
1912 – International Institute of Physics and Chemistry
1912 – International Federation of Secondary Teachers
1913 – Labour Sports International
1913 – International Union of Radio Science
1913 – International Union of Local Authorities
1915 – Toc H
1919 – Central Bureau for Astronomical Telegrams
1919 – International Union of Geodesy and Geophysics
1919 – International Association of Geomagnetism and Aeronomy
1919 – International Association of Volcanology and Chemistry of the Earth's Interior

1919 – International Astronomical Union
1920 – Societe Internationale d'histoire de la medicine
1921 – Belgian Luxembourg Economic Union
1921 – World Federation of Clerical Workers
1922 – International Confederation of Midwives
1922 – International Geographical Union
1922 – International Co-operative Insurance Federation
1922 – International Union of Pure and Applied Physics
1922 – Union of International Motor Boating
1923 – International Spiritualist Federation
1923 – International Federation for Physical Education
1923 – Central Bureau of Compensation
1924 – European Golf Association
1925 – European Young Christian Workers
1925 – International Federation for Graphical Industries
1926 – International Office of Allotments Gardens Leagues
1927 – International Social Security Association
1927 – International Union of Lawyers
1930 – International Office of Military Medicine Documentation
1930 – International Federation of the Cinematographic Press
1930 – International Commission of Agricultural Engineering
1931 – International Institute for Sugar Beet Research
1932 – International Committee for Life, Disability and Health Assurance Medicine
1933 – Permanent Service for Mean Sea Level
1934 – International Special Committee on Radio Interference
1935 – International Union of Associations of Heating, Ventilating and Air Conditioning Contractors
1935 – International Centre for Studies in Religious Education
1935 – International Association for Hydraulic Research
1935 – World Organization of Gastroenterology
1937 – Inter-Cultural Association

Czechoslovakia

1921 – International Peasant Union
1921 – Nationless Worldwide Association

1924 – European Goods Trains Timetable Conference
1929 – International Puppeteers Union
1937 – International Association for Vegetative Science

Denmark

1920 – Nordic Forwarding Agents Association
1923 – Nordic Insulin Laboratory
1926 – Nordic Insulin Foundation
1928 – Northern Hydrographic Group
1929 – International Montessori Association
1936 – Nordic Numismatic Union
1944 – Scandinavian Herpetological Society

Finland

1883 – European Fellowship
1922 – Nordic Conference of Supervisors and Technicians
1936 – Central Council of the Nordic Farmers Association
1938 – Nordic Union of Hotel, Café and Restaurant Workers

France

1833 – Society of Saint Vincent DePaul
1855 – World Alliance of Young Men's Christian Associations
1860 – Alliance Israelite Universelle
1865 – International Telecommunication Union
1869 – Society of Comparative Legislation
1875 – International Congress of Americanists
1875 – International Bureau of Weights and Measures
1878 – International Federation of Surveyors
1878 – International Literary and Artistic Association
1881 – Pontifical Committee for International Eucharistic Congress
1883 – Alliance Francaise
1883 – International Union for Protection of Industrial Property
1886 – International Phonetic Association
1888 – Inter-Parliamentary Union
1890 – French Language Congress of Psychiatry and Neurology
1893 – International Institute of Sociology
1894 – International Olympic Committee

1894 – Permanent International Association of Navigation Congresses
1896 – International Publishers Association
1896 – International Transport Workers' Federation
1899 – Permanent Court of Arbitration
1900 – International Botanical Congress
1900 – International Dental Federation
1900 – International Technical Committee for the Prevention and Extinction of Fire
1900 – International Commission on Illumination
1905 – Universal Alliance of Diamond Workers
1905 – International Aeronautical Association
1907 – International Shooting Union
1908 – Exotic Pathology Society
1908 – International Ice Hockey Federation
1909 – International Federation of Esperantist Railwaymen
1909 – Permanent International Association of Road Congresses
1910 – International Union of Catholic Esperantists
1910 – International Pediatric Association
1911 – International French Language Congress of Forensic and Social Medicine
1911 – International Genetics Federation
1911 – Christian Esperanto International Association
1912 – International Pharmaceutical Federation
1913 – International Fencing Federation
1915 – Women's International League for Peace and Freedom
1919 – International Association for the Physical Sciences of the Ocean
1919 – International Academic Union
1919 – League of the Red Cross and Red Crescent Societies
1919 – International Union of Pure and Applied Chemistry
1920 – International Institute of Anthropology
1920 – East/West Committee
1920 – World Confederation of Labour
1920 – Service civil international
1920 – International Union Against Tuberculosis and Lung Disease
1920 – International Institute of Refrigeration
1920 – International Chamber of Commerce
1920 – Postal, Telegraph and Telephone International

1921 – International Federation for Sport Shooting
1921 – International Equestrian Federation
1921 – International Conference on Large High Voltage Electric Systems
1921 – World Education Fellowship
1922 – Federation internationale du sport automobile
1922 – International Federation of Human Rights
1922 – International Union of Railways
1923 – International Association of Horticulture Producers
1923 – International Bobsleighing and Tobogganing Federation
1923 – Association of Attenders and Alumni of the Hague Academy of International Law
1923 – International Confederation of Professional and Intellectual Workers
1923 – International Society of Classical Bibliography
1923 – International Court of Arbitration of International Chamber of Commerce
1923 – International Union Against the Venereal Diseases and the Treponematoses
1923 – European Industrial Gases Association
1924 – International Office of Epizootics
1924 – International Federation of the Seed Trade
1924 – International Committee of Sports for the Deaf
1924 – World Union of Jewish Students
1924 – International Sporting Press Association
1925 – Union for International Deposit of Industrial Designs
1925 – International Union of Producers and Distribution of Electrical Energy
1925 – Russian Nobility Union
1926 – International Diplomatic Academy
1926 – World Council of Management
1926 – International Philatelic Federation
1926 – Association of French-Language Writers
1926 – International Confederation of Societies of Authors and Composers
1927 – Association of Physiologists
1927 – International League Against Racism and Anti-Semitism
1928 – International Association of Department Stores

1928 – International Association of Juvenile and Family Court Magistrates
1928 – International Union for the Scientific Study of Population
1928 – International Exhibitions Bureau
1928 – International Catholic Organization for Cinema and Audiovisual
1928 – Permanent International Committee of Linguists
1929 – Latin Society of Otorhinolaryngology
1929 – International Bureau of the Societies Administering the Rights of Mechanical Recording and Reproduction
1929 – International Federation of Women in Legal Careers
1929 – International Wool Textile Organization
1929 – International Agency for the Prevention of Blindness
1930 – International Association of Rolling Stock Builders
1930 – International Committee for the Diffusion of the Arts and Literature Through the Cinema
1930 – International Commission for History of Art
1930 – International Esperanto Institute
1930 – Soroptimist International of Europe
1930 – Bank for International Settlements
1930 – International Committee on Systematic Bacteriology
1931 – International Milling Association
1931 – International Association of Wood Anatomists
1931 – World Federation of Foreign-Language Teacher's Association
1931 – St. John's International Alliance
1932 – International Union for Public Welfare
1932 – International Committee of Producers Cooperatives
1933 – International Korfball Federation
1933 – International Container Bureau
1933 – International Federation of Film Producers' Associations
1934 – International Commission for Food Industry
1934 – International Union of Therapeutics
1934 – International Association of Skal Clubs
1934 – International Society for Criminology
1934 – International Union Against Cancer
1935 – Henri Capitant Association for the French Legal System
1937 – Association of French Language Countries Nationless Esperanto Workers

1937 – International Association of Insurance and Reinsurance Intermediaries
1937 – Equipes Notre-Dame
1937 – International Society of Blood Transfusion
1937 – International Institute of Public Finance
1937 – Association of French Speaking Societies of Philosophy
1937 – International Institute of Philosophy
1938 – International Permanent Committee on Canned Foods
1938 – International Fiscal Association
1938 – International Federation of Film Archives
1939 – International Federation of Chief Editors
1944 – Group for Advanced Analytical Methods

Germany

1849 – International Kolping Society
1874 – International Union of Marine Insurance
1886 – Anatomical Society
1890 – International Federation of Ex Libris Amateur Societies
1891 – International Union of Forestry Research Organizations
1900 – New Bach Society International Union
1901 – International Association for Past and Present History of Art of Printing
1901 – International Federation Textile and Clothing
1903 – International Study Institution of Middle Classes
1904 – International Automobile Federation
1910 – International Association of Liberal Religious Women
1910 – World Union of Catholic Teachers
1912 – International Federation of Meat Traders Association
1917 – Permanent International Vinegar Committee
1920 – European Federation of Energy, Chemistry and Miscellaneous Industries
1922 – International Association of Theoretical and Applied Limnology
1923 – Christian Movement for Peace
1924 – European Authors Association Die Kogge
1925 – International Licensing, Innovation and Technology Consultants Association
1925 – Ladies Hairdressers International

1927 – International Federation of Grocers Association
1928 – International Federation of Periodicals
1928 – International Catholic Association for Radio, Television and Audiovisuals
1928 – International Federation of Catholic Dailies
1929 – Open Door International: For Economic Emancipation of Women Workers
1929 – International Association of Schools of Social Work
1930 – International Heinrich Schutz Society
1930 – International Federation of Employees in Public Service
1931 – World Hebrew Union
1932 – International Federation for Inner Mission and Christian Social Workers
1932 – International Federation of Social Workers
1938 – International Federation for Medical Psychotherapy

Hungary

1926 – European Swimming Federation

Italy

1563 – World Christian Life Community
1603 – Pontifical Academy of Sciences
1847 – Salesian Youth Movement
1891 – International Peace Bureau
1892 – International Rowing Federation
1909 – Pontifical Biblical Institute
1910 – Pontifical Institute of Sacred Music
1911 – International Association of Tariff Specialists
1912 – International Council of Jewish Women
1915 – Congregation for Catholic Education
1921 – Catholic International Union for Social Service
1924 – International Savings Banks Institute
1925 – Pontifical Institute of Christian Archeology
1926 – International Federation of Catholic Journalists
1930 – International Scientific Centre of Fertilizers
1931 – International Christian Union of Business Executives
1932 – International Confederation for Agricultural Credit

1933 – International Federation of the Phonographic Industry
1933 – International Commission on Glass
1934 – International Olive Oil Federation

Mediterranean

1910 – International Commission for Scientific Exploration of the Mediterranean Sea

The Netherlands

1892 – International Skating Union
1895 – International Commission on Zoological Nomenclature
1902 – International Old Catholic Bishop's Conference
1906 – International Service for Geomagnetic
1913 – International Federation for Housing and Planning
1919 – International Fellowship of Reconciliation
1921 – International Grail Movement
1921 – War Resister's International
1926 – International Federation of Teacher's Associations
1927 – International Congress of Carboniferous-Permian Stratigraphy and Geology
1923 – International Religious Fellowship
1935 – International Confederation of Art Dealers
1938 – International Bureau of Fiscal Documentation
1938 – World Organization of Young Esperantists
1938 – International Society of Phonetic Sciences
1938 – International Association of Plant Breeders for the Protection of Plant Varieties
1943 – International Federation of Magical Society

Poland

1908 – Universal Medical Esperanto Association
1912 – Agudath Israel World Organization
1925 – International Confederation of European Beet Growers

Russia

1880 – World ORT Union
1902 – Mizrachi Hapoel Hamizrachi Workers Organization

1934 – Baltic Entente

Scandinavia

1932 – Nordic Leather Chemists Society
1939 – Foundation for the ACTA Odontologica Scandinavia

Spain

1922 – International Association of Hydrological Sciences
1924 – International Radiation Committee
1928 – International Maritime Radio Association
1930 – International Institute of Administrative Sciences

Sweden

1866 – Scandinavian Dentists Association
1866 – Scandinavian Association for Dental Research
1869 – Nordic Postal Union
1872 – Scandinavian Industry Baptist Union
1875 – Letterstedt Society
1882 – Swedish Society Against Painful Experiment on Animals
1885 – Committee of Youth Hostel Organizations in Nordic Countries
1895 – World Student Christian Federation
1899 – Northern Shipowners Defense Club
1901 – Nordic Federation of Factory Workers Unions
1907 – International Temperance Union
1907 – Nordic Transport Workers Federation
1907 – International Council on Alcohol and Addictions
1907 – Northern Council of the Deaf
1909 – Scandinavian Jewish Youth Federation
1910 – Nordic Ships Officers Congress
1916 – Nordic Musicians Union
1918 – Scandinavian Agricultural Research Workers Association
1918 – Nordic Cooperative Wholesale Society
1919 – Nordic Engineer Officers Federation
1919 – Nordic Radiological Society
1919 – Nordic Housewives Association
1919 – Nordic Pool of Aviation Insurers
1919 – Nordic Poultry Science Association

1920 – Nordic Nurses Federation
1921 – Nordic Shooting Union
1922 – Scandinavian Neurological Association
1923 – Confederation of Nordic Bank Employees Union
1924 – Standing Committee for Nordic Ironmongers
1924 – International Canoe Federation
1924 – Council of the Wholesale Merchants Federations in the Northern Countries
1924 – Nordic Union of Food and Allied Workers
1925 – Scandinavian Society for Military Medicine
1927 – Nordic Union of Dispensing Chemists
1928 – International Commission on Radiological Protection
1928 – International Federation for Modern Languages and Literatures
1930 – Nordic Society for Rehabilitation
1931 – Nordic Delegation of Central Savings Banks Organization
1931 – Federation of Nordic Cereal Societies
1933 – Nordic Society of Obstetricians and Gynecology
1934 – Christian Templars Council of Nordic Countries
1934 – Nordic Council of Local Government Officers
1934 – Nordic Master Painters' Organization
1934 – Internationale des societes de surveillance
1934 – Nordic Society of Pharmacology
1935 – Nordic Road Association
1936 – Nordic Newspaper Publishers' Joint Board
1936 – Nordic Actors' Council
1937 – Nordic Association of Hairdressers
1937 – International Society for Chronobiology
1937 – Nordic Peoples Travel Organization
1938 – Nordic Temperance Council
1940 – Nordic Ecumenical Council
1942 – Salvation Army Students Fellowship

Switzerland

1863 – International Committee of the Red Cross
1873 – American Dental Society of Europe
1882 – International Conference for Railway Technician Unity

1886 – International Union for the Protection of Literary & Artistic Works
1890 – International Federation of the Blue Cross
1890 – Intergovernmental Organization for International Carriage by Rail
1892 – Union for the International Registration of Marks
1893 – Central Office for International Carriage by Rail
1893 – International Metalworkers Federation
1897 – Jewish Agency for Israel
1897 – World Zionist Organization
1897 – International Catholic Society for Girls
1901 – International Society for Business Education
1902 – International Council for the Exploration of the Sea
1904 – International Textile Manufacturers Federation
1905 – Baltic and International Maritime Council
1906 – International Esperantist Scientific Association
1908 – Universal Esperanto Association
1913 – International Trade Secretariat
1920 – League of Nations
1920 – International Labor Organization
1920 – World Organization of the Scout Movement
1920 – International Association of Applied Psychology
1920 – International Union of Food and Allied Workers Associations
1921 – Pax Romana, International Movement of Catholic Students
1921 – International Seed Testing Association
1921 – International Social Service
1921 – International Federation of Trade Unions of Transport Workers
1922 – International League of Religious Socialists
1923 – General Anthroposophical Society
1924 – Leading Hotels of the World
1924 – International Roller Skating Federation
1925 – International Association for Social Progress
1925 – International Bureau of Education
1926 – Quaker United Nations Office
1927 – Conference of International Catholic Organizations
1927 – International Committee of Foundry Technical Association

1927 – International Musicological Society
1927 – International Relief Union
1928 – International Red Cross & Crescent Movement
1928 – International Photobiology Association
1928 – World Association of Cooks' Societies
1928 – International Union for Quaternary Research
1929 – International Association for Bridge and Structural Engineering
1929 – Federation of Semiofficial and Private International Institutes in Geneva
1930 – International Federation of Associations of Textile Chemists and Colourists
1930 – International Federation of Business and Professional Women
1931 – International Union of Prehistoric and Protohistoric Sciences
1932 – Experiment in International Living
1934 – Nordic Union for Non-Alcoholic Traffic
1936 – International Numismatic Commission
1936 – World Jewish Congress

United Kingdom

1810 – Swedenborg Society
1823 – Intercontinental Church Society
1839 – Anti-Slavery Society for the Protection of Human Rights
1864 – Early English Text Society
1865 – Salvation Army
1867 – Lambeth Conference of Bishops of Anglican Communion
1868 – Royal Commonwealth Society
1869 – International Brotherhood of Old Bastards
1875 – International Abolitionist Federation
1877 – St. John Ambulance
1881 – Pali Text Society
1882 – International Bible Reading Association
1885 – International Statistical Institute
1887 – Commonwealth Institute
1894 – World Young Women's Christian Association
1899 – International Council of Nurses
1891 – Royal Life Saving Society Commonwealth Council
1893 – Girls Brigade International

1901 – League for Exchange of Commonwealth Teachers
1901 – International Association of Seismology and Physics of the Earth's Interior
1903 – Theosophical Society in Europe
1905 – International Association of Lyceum Clubs
1905 – Baptist World Alliance
1909 – CAB International Institute of Entomology
1909 – International Cricket Council
1909 – Commonwealth Press Union
1909 – International Shipping Federation
1909 – International Federation of Ironmongers and Iron Merchants Associations
1910 – International Association of Seed Crushers
1910 – The Textile Institute
1911 – Order of the Star
1911 – Commonwealth Parliamentary Association
1912 – World's Poultry Science Association
1913 – International Congress for Tropical Medicine and Malaria
1913 – Association of Commonwealth Universities
1914 – Chartered Institute of Transport
1914 – International Bible Students Association
1914 – International Union of Housing Finance Institutions
1915 – Kiwanis International
1917 – Commonwealth War Graves Commission
1918 – Oil and Colour Chemists Association
1918 – Scout Esperanto League
1919 – Save the Children Fund
1919 – International Federation of University Women
1920 – CAB International Mycological Institute
1920 – Women's International Zionist Organization
1921 – International Society of Medical Hydrology and Climatology
1921 – British Commonwealth Ex-Services League
1921 – International Chamber of Shipping
1921 – Quaker Esperanto Society
1921 – Commonwealth Forestry Association
1922 – International Cooperative Banking Committee
1922 – Rehabilitation International

1924 – Association for Information Management
1924 – World Energy Council
1924 – International Confederation of Jewellery, Silverware, Diamonds, Pearls, and Stones
1924 – Council of Mining and Metalogical Institute
1925 – International Commission on Radiation Units and Measurements
1925 – Commonwealth Countries
1926 – International Federation of Settlements and Neighborhood Centers
1926 – International African Institute
1926 – International Fertilizer Industry Association
1926 – World Union for Progressive Judaism
1926 – International Table Tennis Federation
1927 – CAB International Institute of Biological Control
1927 – International League for the Protection of Horses
1927 – International Federation of Library Associations and Institutions
1928 – Association of International Accountants
1928 – Commonwealth Telecommunications Bureau
1929 – CABI Bureau of Animal Breeding and Genetics
1929 – CABI Bureau of Health
1929 – CABI Bureau of Horticulture and Plantation Crops
1929 – CAB International Bureau of Nutrition
1929 – CAB International Institute of Parasitology
1929 – CABI Bureau of Pastures and Field Crops
1929 – CABI Bureau of Plant Breeding and Genetics
1929 – CABI Bureau of Soils
1929 – International Council of Hides, Skins and Leather Trade Association
1929 – International Association for Properties of Water and Steam
1929 – International Association of Agricultural Economists
1931 – International Friendship League
1931 – International Gas Union
1931 – International Solid Wastes and Public Cleansing Association
1932 – International Tin Research Institute
1932 – World Goodwill
1932 – International Towing Tank Conference

1933 – International Wine and Food Society
1933 – International Tea Committee
1933 – Susila Budi Dharma
1933 – World Jewish Relief
1933 – World Petroleum Council
1934 – International Inner Wheel
1936 – World Congress of Faiths
1936 – International Glaciological Society
1937 – Society for the History of Alchemy and Chemistry
1937 – Zinc Development Association
1937 – International Cremation Federation
1938 – Moral Rearmament
1938 – CABI Dairy Science and Technology
1938 – CABI Forestry Bureau
1938 – Society for the Study of the New Testament
1939 – International Association of Margaret Morris Method
1941 – Outward Bound International
1942 – OXFAM
1943 – European Dental Society
1943 – Federation of Commodity Association
1943 – International Tracing Service
1944 – Hansard Society for Parliamentary Government
1944 – International Rubber Study Group

Yugoslavia

1930 – Alliance of Russian Solidarists

Middle East

1844 – Baha'I International Committee
1921 – Maccabi World Union
1926 – World Muslim Congress
1926 – All India Women's Conference
1944 – General Arab Women Federation

Location of Founding Not Given

1863 – Federation of Oil Seeds and Fats Association International
1894 – International Commission on Snow and Ice

1905 – International Bowling Board
1909 – Union for the International Language
1910 – International Society of Urology
1920 – World University Service
1922 – Medical Society for the Study of Venereal Diseases
1925 – Universal Love and Brotherhood Association
1929 – World Federation of Building and Woodworkers Unions
1942 – Foundation for Health and Human Rights‘

(*Source*: Union of International Associations, *2000/2001 Yearbook of International Organizations*, 37th edition, Volume 1.)

BIBLIOGRAPHY

Abbott, Kenneth W., Robert O. Keohane, Andrew Moravcsik, Anne-Marie Slaughter, and Duncan Snidal (2000). "The Concept of Legalization," *International Organization*, Vol. 54, No. 3, Summer, pp. 401–419.

Abbott, Kenneth W. and Duncan Snidal (2000). "Hard and Soft Law in International Governance," *International Organization*, Vol. 54, No. 3, Summer, pp. 421–456.

Aero, Rita (1980). *Things Chinese* (Garden City, N.Y.: Doubleday & Company, Inc.).

Aggarwal, Vinod K. (2001). "Economics: International Trade," in *Managing Global Issues, Lessons Learned*, P. J. Simmons and Chantal de Jonge Oudraat (eds.), pp. 234–280.

Alston, Philip (1994). "The UN's Human Rights Record: From San Francisco to Vienna and Beyond," *Human Rights Quarterly* 16, 375–390, reprinted in *International Law: Classic and Contemporary Readings*, Charlotte Ku and Paul F. Diehl, eds., pp. 355–368.

Anheier, Helmut, Marlies Glasius, and Mary Kaldor, eds. (2001). *Global Civil Society 2001* (New York: Oxford University Press).

Annan, Kofi (1998). "The Quiet Revolution," *Global Governance*, Vol. 4, No. 2, April–June, pp. 123–138.

Archer, Clive (1983). *International Organization* (Boston: Allen and Unwin).

Armstrong, David (1982). *The Rise of International Organisation: A Short History* (New York: St. Martin's Press).

Axford, Barrie (1995). *The Global System: Economics, Politics and Culture* (New York: St. Martin's Press).

Axworthy, Lloyd (2001). "Human Security and Global Governance: Putting People First," *Global Governance*, Volume 7, Number 1, January–March.

Bahador, Babak (1998). "Globalisation: A Conceptual Clarification," paper presented at the Third Annual Pan-European International Relations Conference, Vienna, Austria, September 16–19. Mimeo.

Baldwin, David, ed. (1993). *Neorealism and Neoliberalism: The Contemporary Debate* (New York: Columbia University Press).

Bartelson, Jens (1995). *A Genealogy of Sovereignty* (Cambridge, UK: Cambridge University Press).

Bartlett, Robert V., Priya A. Kurian, and Madhu Malik, eds. (1995). *International Organizations and Environmental Policy* (Westport, Conn.: Greenwood Press).

Bayefsky, Anne (2002). "Ending Bias in the Human Rights System," *The New York Times*, May 22, p. A27.

Baylis, John, and Steve Smith, eds. (1997). *The Globalization of World Politics* (Oxford: Oxford University Press).

Beattie, Alan (2001). "Campaigners offer integrity for influence," *Financial Times*, Tuesday, July 17, p. 8.

Bennett, A. Leroy (1995). *International Organizations: Principles and Issues* (Englewood Cliffs, N.J.: Prentice-Hall).

Bernauer, Thomas (2001). "Warfare: Nuclear, Biological, and Chemical Weapons," in *Managing Global Issues, Lessons Learned*, P.J. Simmons and Chantal de Jonge Oudraat, eds., pp. 610–659.

Best, Geoffrey (1999). "Peace Conferences and the Century of Total War: The 1899 Hague Conference and What Came After," *International Affairs*, Vol. 75, No. 3, pp. 619–634.

Bok, Sissela (1999). "Early Advocates of Lasting World Peace: Utopians or Realists?," in *Ethics & International Affairs, A Reader*, Joel H. Rosenthal, ed., pp. 124–147.

Boli, John and George Thomas (1997). "World Culture in the World Polity: A Century of International Non-Governmental Organization," *American Sociological Review*, April 1997, in *The Globalization Reader*, Frank J. Lechner and John Boli, eds., pp. 262–268.

Boserup, William and Uffe Schlichtkrull (1962). "Alternative Approaches to the Control of Competition, an Outline of European Cartel Legislation and Its Administration", in *Competition, Cartels and Their Regulation*, John Perry Miller, ed., pp. 59–113.

Brown, David L., and David Korten (1989). *Understanding Voluntary Organizations: Guidelines for Donors. Working Papers No. 258* (Washington, D.C.: Country Economics Department, the World Bank, September).

Brown, Seyom (1996). *International Relations in a Changing Global System: Toward a Theory of a World Polity*, second edition (Boulder: Westview Press).

Bull, Hedley (1995). *The Anarchical Society: A Study of Order in World Politics*, second edition (London: MacMillan Press Ltd.).

Burley, Anne-Marie (1993). "Regulating the World: Multilateralism, International Law, and the Projection of the New Deal Regulatory State," in *Multilateralism Matters*, John Gerard Ruggie, ed., pp. 125–156.

Bush, George H. W. (1990). "The U.N.: World Parliament of Peace," address to the U.N. General Assembly, New York, October 1, 1990, in *Dispatch* (U.S. Department of State), vol. 1, No. 6, October 8.

Caraley, Demetrios James, ed. (2002). *September 11, Terrorist Attacks, and U.S. Foreign Policy* (New York: The Academy of Political Science).

Carr, Edward H. (1939). *The Twenty Years' Crisis, 1919–1939: An Introduction to the Study of International Relations* (London: Macmillan).

Chege, Mike (2002). "Bridging the Digital Divide: ICT is not the panacea," *iConnect Online*, 14 November 2002 (accessed on December 30, 2002, at http://www.iconnect-online.org/base/ic_show_news?id=1966).

Claude, Inis L. Jr. (2000). "The Evolution of Concepts of Global Governance and the State in the Twentieth Century," address given at the Academic Council for the UN System Conference on July 17, Oslo, Norway. On the Internet at: http://www.yale.edu/acuns/NEW_activities/AM/AM.00.Claude.html

Cleveland, Harlan (1993). *Birth of a New World* (San Francisco: Jossey-Bass Publishers).

Cohen, Isaac (1999). "International Economic Diplomacy and International Organizations," in *Multilateral Diplomacy and the United Nations Today*, James P. Muldoon, JoAnn Fagot Aviel, Richard Reitano, and Earl Sullivan, eds., pp. 87–101.

Coicaud, Jean-Marc, and Veijo Heiskanen, eds. (2001). *The Legitimacy of International Organizations* (Tokyo: United Nations University Press).

Commission on Global Governance (1995). *Our Global Neighbourhood* (New York: Oxford University Press).

Conca, Ken (1996). "Greening the UN: Environmental Organizations and the UN System," in *NGOs, the UN, & Global Governance*, Thomas G. Weiss and Leon Gordenker, eds., pp. 103–119.

Cooper, Robert (2002). "Foreign policy, values and globalisation," *Financial Times*, January 31, p. 15.

Cox, Robert, and Harold K. Jacobson (1997). "The Framework for Inquiry," in *The Politics of Global Governance: International Organizations in an Interdependent World*, Paul F. Diehl, ed., pp. 75–90.

Cox, Robert W., with Timothy J. Sinclair (1996). *Approaches to World Order* (Cambridge: Cambridge University Press).

Cutler, A. Claire (1999). "Private Authority in International Trade Relations: The Case of Maritime Transport," in *Private Authority and International Affairs*, A. Claire Cutler, Virginia Haufler, and Tony Porter, eds., pp. 283–329.

Cutler, A. Claire, Virginia Haufler, and Tony Porter, eds. (1999). *Private Authority and International Affairs* (Albany, N.Y.: State University of New York Press).

D'Anieri, Paul (1995). "International Organizations, Environmental Cooperation, and Regime Theory," in *International Organizations and Environmental Policy*, Robert V. Bartlett, Priya A. Kurian, and Madhu Malik, eds., pp. 153–169.

Dallmayr, Fred (2002). "Lessons of September 11," *JUST Commentary*, Vol. 2, No. 6, pp. 6–9.

Dell, Sydney (1990). *The United Nations and International Business* (Durham, N.C.: Duke University Press).

Development Assistance Committee (2001). *Aid Activities in Least Developed Countries 1999—Creditor Reporting System: Aid Activities* (Paris: OECD).

De Wilde, Jaap (1991). *Saved from Oblivion: Interdependence Theory in the First Half of the 20th Century. A Study on the Causality Between War and Complex Interdependence* (Aldershot, England: Dartmouth).

Diehl, Paul F., ed. (1997). *The Politics of Global Governance: International Organizations in an Interdependent World* (Boulder: Lynne Rienner Publishers).

Dieter, Heribert (2002). "World Economy—Structure and Trends," in *Global Trends & Global Governance*, Paul Kennedy, Dirk Messner and Franz Nuscheler, eds., pp. 65–96.

Dijkzeul, Dennis, and Yves Beigbeder, eds. (2003). *Rethinking International Organizations: Pathologies and Promise* (New York: Berghahn Books).

Dijkzeul, Dennis, and Leon Gordenkor (2003). "Cures and Conclusions" in *Rethinking International Organizations: Pathologies and Promise*, Dennis Dijkzeul and Yves Beigbeder (eds.), pp. 311-336.

Donnelly, Jack (1994) "Human Rights and International Organizations: States, Sovereignty, and the International Community," in *International Organization: A Reader*, Friedrich Kratochwil and Edward D. Mansfield, eds., pp. 202–218.

Drake, William J. (2001). "Communications," in *Managing Global Issues: Lessons Learned*, P. J. Simmons and Chantal de Jonge Oudrant, eds., pp. 25–74.

Duggan, S. (1919). *The League of Nations: The Principle and the Practice* (Boston: Atlantic Monthly Press).

Economic and Social Council (ECOSOC) (1974). "The Impact of Multinational Corporations on the Development Process and on International Relations." Report of the Group of Eminent Persons to Study the Role of Multinational Corporations on Development and on International Relations, E/5500/Add. 1, Part I–24 May 1974, Part II–12 June 1974.

Elshtain, Jean Bethke (1995). *Democracy on Trial* (New York: Basic Books).

Emmerij, Louis, Richard Jolly, and Thomas G. Weiss (2001). *Ahead of the Curve? UN Ideas and Global Challenges* (Bloomington, Ind.: Indiana University Press).

Erlanger, Steven (2002). "For NATO, Little Is Sure Now but Growth," *New York Times*, May 19, p. 8.

Fafo (1999). *Command from the Saddle: Managing United Nations Peace-Building Missions, Report 266* (Oslo, Norway: Fafo Institute for Applied Social Science).

Falk, Richard A. (1999). "World Orders, Old and New," *Current History*, Vol. 98, No. 624, January, pp. 29–34.

______ (1991), "Theory, Realism, and World Security," in *World Security: Trends & Challenges at Century's End*, Michael T. Klare and Daniel C. Thomas, eds., pp. 6–24.

______ (1975). *A Study of Future Worlds* (New York: Free Press).

Fang Songhua (1998). "The Predicaments and Prospect of Traditional Chinese Philosophy in Its 20th Century," *SASS Papers*, No. 7, (Shanghai: Shanghai Academy of Social Sciences).

Fawcett, Louise, and Andrew Hurrell, eds. (1995). *Regionalism in World Politics: Regional Organization and International Order* (New York: Oxford University Press).

Feinberg, Richard E. (1988). "The Changing Relationship Between the World Bank and the International Monetary Fund," *International Organization*, Vol. 42, No. 3, Summer, reprinted in *The Politics of Global Goverance: International Organizations in an Interdependent World*, Paul F. Diehl, ed., pp. 217–232.

Feld, Werner J., Robert S. Jordan, and Leon Hurwitz (1994). *International Organizations: A Comparative Approach*, third edition (Westport, Conn.: Praeger).

Fomerand, Jacques (1996). "UN Conferences: Media Events or Genuine Diplomacy?" *Global Governance: A Review of Multilateralism and International Organizations* 2, no. 3, reprinted in *Multilateral Diplomacy and the United Nations Today*, James P. Muldoon Jr., JoAnn Fagot Aviel, Richard Reitano, and Earl Sullivan, eds., pp. 121–135.

Forman, Shepard, and Abby Stoddard (2002). "International Assistance Organizations" in *The State of Nonprofit America*, Lester M. Salamon, ed.

Gilpin, Robert G. (1986). "The Richness of the Tradition of Political Realism," in *Neorealism and Its Critics*, Robert O. Keohane, ed., pp. 301–321.

Goldstein, Judith, Miles Kahler, Robert O. Keohane, and Anne-Marie Slaughter, eds. (2000). "Legalization and World Politics," *International Organization*, Special Issue, Vol. 54, No. 3, summer.

Gordenker, Leon, and Thomas G. Weiss (1996). "Pluralizing Global Governance: Analytical Approaches and Dimensions," in *NGOs, the UN, & Global Governance*, Thomas G. Weiss and Leon Gordenker, eds., pp. 17–47.

Grieco, Joseph M., and G. John Ikenberry (2003). *State Power and World Markets* (New York: W. W. Norton and Company).

Gwin, Catherine (2001). "Development Assistance," in *Managing Global Issues, Lessons Learned*, P. J. Simmons and Chantal de Jonge Oudrant, eds., pp. 151–195.

Haas, Ernst B. (1958). *The Uniting of Europe: Political, Social, and Economic Forces, 1950–1957* (Stanford: Stanford University Press).

Haas, Peter M. (2001). "Environment: Pollution," in *Managing Global Issues: Lessons Learned*, P. J. Simmons and Chantal de Jonge Oudrant, eds., pp. 310–353.

______ (1990). *Saving the Mediterranean: The Politics of International Environmental Cooperation* (New York: Columbia University Press).

Hewson, Martin, and Timothy J. Sinclair, eds. (1999). *Approaches to Global Governance Theory* (Albany: State University of New York Press).

Hill, David Jayne (1911). *World Organization as Affected by the Nature of the Modern State* (New York: Columbia University Press).

Hobsbawn, Eric (1996). *The Age of Capital, 1848–1875* (New York: Vintage Books edition, original publication in 1975).

Hobson, J. (1916) *Towards International Government* (New York: Macmillan Co.).

Hollick, A. L., and R. N. Cooper (1997). "Global Commons: Can They be Managed?" in *The Economics of Transnational Commons*, Partha Dasgupta, Karl-Göran Mäler, and Alessandro Vercelli, eds., pp. 141–171.

Hoy, Paula (1998). *Players and Issues in International Aid* (West Hartford, Conn.: Kumarian Press).

Hume, Cameron (1994). *Ending Mozambique's War: The Role of Mediation and Good Offices* (Washington, D.C.: United States Institute of Peace).

Hummel, Hartwig (2002). "Global Pluralism? Merging IR and Comparative Politics Traditions in Developing a Theoretical Framework for Analyzing Private Actors in Global Governance," paper presented at the annual meeting of the International Studies Association, New Orleans, Louisiana, March 24–27.

Huntington, Samuel P. (1999). "The Lonely Superpower," *Foreign Affairs*, Vol. 78, No. 2, pp. 35–49.

Ikenberry, G. John (1999). "America's Liberal Hegemony," *Current History*, Vol. 98, No. 624, January, pp. 23–28.

Jackson, Robert H. (1990). *Quasi-states: Sovereignty, International Relations and the Third World* (Cambridge, U.K.: Cambridge University Press).

Jacobson, Harold K. (1979). *Networks of Interdependence: International Organizations and the Global Political System* (New York: Alfred A. Knopf).

Jacobson, Harold K., William M. Reisinger, and Todd Mathers (1986). "Entanglements in International Governmental Organizations," *American Political Science Review*, Vol. 80, No. 1, March; reprinted in *The Politics of Global Governance, International Organizations in an Interdependent World*, Paul F. Diehl, ed., pp. 57–71.

Joyner, Christopher C., ed. (1997). *The United Nations and International Law* (Cambridge: Cambridge University Press).

______ (2001). "Global Commons: The Oceans, Antarctica, the Atmosphere, and Outer Space" in *Managing Global Issues: Lessons Learned,* P. J. Simmons and Chantal de Jonge Oudrant, eds., pp. 354–391.

Junne, Gerd C. A. (2001). "International organizations in a period of globalization: New (problems of) legitimacy," in *The Legitimacy of International Organizations*, Jean-Marc Coicaud and Veijo Heiskanen, eds., pp. 189–220.

Karns, Margaret P., and Karen A. Mingst (1991). "Multilateral Institutions and International Security," in *World Security: Trends & Challenges at Century's End*, Michael T. Klare and Daniel C. Thomas, pp. 266–294.

Kaul, Inge, Isabelle Grunberg, and Marc A. Stern, eds. (1999). *Global Public Goods* (New York: Oxford University Press).

Keck, Margaret E., and Kathryn Sikkink (1998). *Activists Beyond Borders* (Ithaca, N.Y.: Cornell University Press).

Kegley, Charles W., and Gregory A. Raymond (1999). *How Nations Make Peace* (New York: Worth Publishers).

Kegley, Charles W., and Eugene R. Wittkopf (1981). *World Politics: Trend and Transformation* (New York: St. Martin's Press).

Kennedy, Paul, Dirk Messner, and Franz Nuscheler, eds. (2002). *Global Trends & Global Governance* (London: Pluto Press).

Keohane, Robert O. (1986). "Theory of World Politics: Structural Realism and Beyond," in *Neorealism and Its Critics*, Robert O. Keohane, ed., pp. 158–203.

Kettl, Donald F. (1993). *Sharing Power: Public Governance and Private Markets* (Washington, D.C.: The Brookings Institution).

Kirk, Russell (1953). *The Conservative Mind: From Burke to Santayana* (Chicago: Henry Regnery Company).

Kissinger, Henry (1994). *Diplomacy* (New York: Simon & Schuster).

Klabbers, Jan (2001). "The changing image of international organizations," *in The Legitimacy of International Organizations*, Jean-Marc Coicaud and Veijo Heiskanen, eds., pp. 221–255.

Klare, Michael T., and Daniel C. Thomas (1991). *World Security: Trends & Challenges at Century's End* (New York: St. Martin's Press).

______ (1989). *Peace and World Order Studies: A Curriculum Guide*, fifth edition (Boulder: Westview Press).

Knight, W. Andy (1999). "Engineering Space in Global Governance: the Emergence of Civil Society in Evolving 'New' Multilateralism," in *Future Multilateralism*, Michael G. Schechter, ed., pp. 255–291.

Kolakowski, Leszek (1978). *Main Currents of Marxism: Its Origins, Growth, and Dissolution*, translated by P. S. Falla, vol. 3: *The Breakdown* (Oxford: Clarendon Press) as quoted in *Will It Liberate? Questions about Liberation Theology*, Michael Novak.

Krasner, Stephen D. (1994). "Structural Causes and Regime Consequences: Regimes as Intervening Variables," in *International Organization: A Reader*, Friedrich Kratochwil and Edward D. Mansfield, eds., pp. 97–109.

Kratochwil, Friedrich, and Edward D. Mansfield, eds. (1994). *International Organization: A Reader* (New York: HarperCollins College Publishers).

Kratochwil, Friedrich, and John Gerard Ruggie (1994). "International Organization: A State of the Art on an Art of the State," *in International Organization: A Reader*, Friedrich Kratochwil and Edward D. Mansfield, eds., pp. 4–19.

Kratochwil, Friedrich (1993). "Norms Versus Numbers: Multilateralism and the Rationalist and Reflexivist Approaches to Institutions–a Unilateral Plea for Communicative Rationality," in *Multilateralism Matters*, John Gerard Ruggie, ed., pp. 443–474.

Krause, Keith, and W. Andy Knight, eds. (1995). *State, Society, and the UN System: Changing Perspectives on Multilateralism* (Tokyo: UNU Press).

Ku, Charlotte (2001). "Global Governance and the Changing Face of International Law," *ACUNS Reports & Papers, No. 2* (New Haven, Conn.: Academic Council on the United Nations System).

Ku, Charlotte, and Paul F. Diehl, eds. (1998a). *International Law: Classic and Contemporary Readings* (Boulder: Lynne Reinner Publishers).

______ (1998b). "International Law as Operating and Normative Systems: An Overview," in *International Law: Classic and Contemporary Readings*, Charlotte Ku and Paul F. Diehl, eds., pp. 3–16.

Kuehl, Warren F. (1969). *Seeking World Order: The United States and International Organization to 1920* (Nashville, Tenn.: Vanderbilt University Press).

Kurth, James (1999). "War, Peace, and the Ideologies of the Twentieth Century," *Current History*, Vol. 98, No. 624, January, pp. 3–8.

Landes, David S. (1999). *The Wealth and Poverty of Nations* (New York: W. W. Norton and Company, paperback edition).

Laurenti, Jeffrey, ed. (2002). *Combatting Terrorism: Does the U.N. Matter . . . and How* (New York: United Nations Association of the USA).

Lechner, Frank L., and John Boli, eds. (2000). *The Globalization Reader* (Malden, Mass.: Blackwell Publishers Inc.).

Lévi, Jean (1993). *The Dream of Confucius* (New York: Harcourt Brace Jovanovich).

Lindenberg, Marc, and J. Patrick Dobel (1999). "The Challenges of Globalization for Northern International Relief and Development NGOs," *NonProfit and Voluntary Sector Quarterly*, 28, 4, "Supplemental Issue: Globalization and Northern NGOs: The Challenge of Relief and Development in a Changing Context," ARNOVA, Sage Publications Inc.

Litan, Robert E. (2001). "Economics: Global Finance," in *Managing Global Issues, Lessons Learned*, P. J. Simmons and Chantal de Jonge Oudraat, eds., pp. 196–233.

Long, David. (1996). *Towards a New Liberal Internationalism: The International Theory of J. A. Hobson* (Cambridge: Cambridge University Press).

Luo Xiaowei (2000). "The Rise of the Social Development Model: Institutional Construction of International Technology Organizations, 1856–1993," *International Studies Quarterly*, Volume 44, No. 1, March, pp. 147–175.

Mahbubani, Kishore (1998). *Can Asians Think?* (Singapore: Times Editions Pte Ltd.).

"Managing in a World of Fear and Conflict," An IBLF Briefing Paper, London: The Prince of Wales International Business Leaders Forum (IBLF), October 12, 2001. Mimeo.

Martin, Lisa L. (1999). "An institutionalist view: international institutions and state strategies," in *International Order and the Future of World Politics*, T. V. Paul and John A. Hall, eds., pp. 78–98.

Mastanduno, Michael (1999). "A realist view: three images of the coming international order," in *International Order and the Future of World Politics*, T. V. Paul and John A. Hall, eds., pp. 19–40.

Mathews, Jessica T. (1997). "Power Shift," *Foreign Affairs*, Vol. 76, No. 1, January-February, pp. 50–66.

Mayotte, Judy (1999). "NGOs and Diplomacy" in *Multilateral Diplomacy and the United Nations Today*, James P. Muldoon Jr., JoAnne Fagot Aviel, Richard Reitano, and Earl Sullivan, eds., pp. 167–176.

Mendlovitz, Saul (2000). "The Prospects for Abolishing War: A Proposal for the Twenty-First Century," *Rutgers Law Review*, Vol. 52, Winter, pp. 621–631.

Messner, Dirk (2002). "World Society—Structures and Trends," in *Global Trends & Global Governance*, Paul Kennedy, Dirk Messner, and Franz Nuscheler, eds., pp. 22–64.

Mill, John Stuart (1873). *Autobiography.* Accessed full text at http://www.ccn.bris.ac.uk/het/mill/auto.

Miller, John Perry, ed. (1962). *Competition, Cartels and Their Regulation* (Amsterdam: North-Holland Publishing Co.).

Mitrany, David (1966). *A Working Peace System* (Chicago: Quadrangle).

______ (1975). *The Functional Theory of Politics* (London: St. Martin's Press).

Morgenthau, Hans J. (1948). *Politics Among Nations: The Struggle for Power and Peace* (New York: Alfred A. Knopf).

______ (1967). *Politics Among Nations*, fourth edition (New York: Alfred A. Knopf).

Muir, Ramsay (1933). *The Interdependent World and Its Problems* (Washington/London: Kennikat Press).

Muldoon, James P., JoAnn Fagot Aviel, Richard Reitano, and Earl Sullivan, eds. (1999). *Multilateral Diplomacy and the United Nations Today* (Boulder: Westview Press).

Mytelka, Lynn K., and Michel Delapierre (1999). "Strategic Partnerships, Knowledge-Based Networked Oligopolies, and the State," in *Private Authority and International Affairs*, A. Claire Cutler, Virginia Haufler, and Tony Porter, eds., pp. 129–149.

Naim, Moises (2002). "A virulent new strain of crisis," *Financial Times*, May 13, p. 13.

Nanda, Ved P. (1997). "Environment," in *The United Nations and International Law*, Christopher C. Joyner, ed., pp. 287–308.

Natsios, Andrew S. (1996). "NGOs and the UN System in Complex Humanitarian Emergencies: Conflict or Cooperation?," in *NGOs, The UN, & Global Governance*, Thomas G. Weiss and Leon Gordenker, eds., pp. 67–81.

Naughton, John (2001). "Contested Space: The Internet and Global Civil Society" in Helmut Anheier, Marlies Glasius, and Mary Kaldor, eds., *Global Civil Society 2001* (Oxford: Oxford University Press), pp. 147–168.

Nayyar, Deepak (2002). "The Existing System and the Missing Institutions" in Deepak Nayyar, ed., *Governing Globalization: Issues and Institutions* (Oxford: Clarendon Press).

"Non-governmental Organisations," *The Economist*, January 29, 2000, pp. 25–28.

Novak, Michael (1986). *Will It Liberate? Questions About Liberation Theology* (New York: Paulist Press).

Nuscheler, Franz (2002). "Global Governance, Development, and Peace," in *Global Trends & Global Governance*, Paul Kennedy, Dirk Messner, and Franz Nuscheler, eds., pp. 156–183.

Nye, Joseph S. (2002). "A whole new ball game," FT Weekend, *Financial Times*, December 28–29, pp. I & III.

Olson, Mancur (1968). *The Logic of Collective Action: Public Goods and the Theory of Groups* (New York: Schocken).

Osiander, Andreas (1998). "Rereading Early Twentieth-Centruy IR Theory: Idealism Revisited," *International Studies Quarterly*, Vol. 42, No. 3, pp. 409-432.

Oxman, Bernard H. (1997). "Law of the Sea," in *The United Nations and International Law*, Christopher C. Joyner, ed., pp. 309–335.

Paul, T. V., and John A. Hall, eds. (1999). *International Order and the Future of World Politics* (Cambridge, U.K.: Cambridge University Press).

Peel, Quentin (2001). "How militants hijacked NGO party," *Financial Times*, Friday, July 13, p. 7.

Perrault, Paul, Hunt Hobbs, and Dennis Dijkzeul (1997). "Governance: Responding to Pluralistic Societies," a conceptual paper prepared for the Institute for Services to National Agricultural Research (ISNAR). Mimeo, The Hague.

Pirages, Dennis (2002). "Globalization: States, Markets, and Global Public Goods," paper presented at the annual meeting of the International Studies Association, New Orleans, Louisiana, March 24–27.

Porter, Tony (1999). "Hegemony and the Private Governance of International Industries," in *Private Authority and International Affairs*, A. Claire Cutler, Virginia Haufler, and Tony Porter, eds., pp. 257–282.

Potter, Pitman B. (1948). *An Introduction to the Study of International Organization* (New York: Appleton-Century-Crofts).

______ (1932). "International Organization," in *Encyclopaedia of the Social Sciences*, Vol. 8, edited by R. A. Seligman, pp. 177–185. (New York: Macmillan Co.).

______ (1923). "Political Science in the International Field," *American Political Science Review*, 27, pp. 381–391.

Price, Richard (1998). "Reversing the Gun Sights: Transnational Civil Society Targets Land Mines," *International Organization*, Vol. 52, No. 3, Summer.

Puchala, Donald J. (2000). "Marking a Weberian Moment: Our Discipline Looks Ahead," *International Studies Perspectives*, Vol. 1, Issue 2, August, pp. 133–144.

Reinicke, Wolfgang H. (1998). *Global Public Policy: Governing without Government?* (Washington, D.C.: The Brookings Institution).

Reinecke, Wolfgang H., and Francis Deng with Jan Martin Witte, Thorsten Benner, et al. (2000). *Critical Choices. The U.N., Networks, and the Future of Global Governance* (Ottawa: IDRC Publishers).

Reynolds, David (2000). *One World Divisible: A Global History Since 1945* (New York: W. W. Norton and Company).

Rivlin, Benjamin, ed. (1990). *Ralph Bunche, The Man and His Times* (New York: Holmes & Meier).

Rochester, J. Martin (1993). W*aiting for the Millennium: The United Nations and the Future of World Order* (Columbia, S.C.: University of South Carolina Press).

Rosenau, James N., and Ernst-Otto Czempiel, eds. (1992). *Governance Without Government: Order and Change in World Politics* (Cambridge, U.K.: Cambridge University Press).

Rosenau, James N. (1992). "Governance, Order, and Change in World Politics," in *Governance Without Government: Order and Change in World Politics*, James N. Rosenau and Ernst-Otto Czempiel, eds., pp. 1–29.

______ (1997). *Along the Domestic-Foreign Frontier, Exploring Governance in a Turbulent World* (Cambridge, UK: Cambridge University Press).

Rosenthal, Joel H., ed. (1999). *Ethics and International Affairs, A Reader,* second edition (Washington, D.C.: Georgetown University Press).

Ruggie, John Gerard (1998). *Constructing the World Polity: Essays on International Institutionalization* (New York: Routledge).

______, ed. (1993). *Multilateralism Matters: The Theory and Praxis of an Institutional Form* (New York: Columbia University Press).

______ (2001). "global_governance.net: The Global Compact as Learning Network," *Global Governance*, Vol. 7, No. 4, October-December.

Salamon, Lester, ed. (2002). *The State of Nonprofit America* (Washington, D.C.: Brookings Institution Press).

Sandler, Todd (1999). "Intergenerational Public Goods—Strategies, Efficiency and Institutions," in *Global Public Goods, International Cooperation in the 21st Century*, Inge Kaul, Isabelle Grunberg, and Marc A. Stern, eds., pp. 20–50.

Sassen, Saskia (1996). *Losing Control? Sovereignty in an Age of Globalization* (New York: Columbia University Press).

Schechter, Michael G., ed. (1999a). *Future Multilateralism: The Political and Social Framework* (Tokyo: United Nations University Press).

______, ed. (1999b). *Innovation in Multilateralism* (Tokyo: United Nations University Press).

______ (1999c). "International Institutions: Obstacles, Agents, or Conduits of Global Structural Change?" in *Innovation in Multilateralism,* Michael G. Schechter, ed., pp. 3–28.

______ (1998). *Historical Dictionary of International Organizations* (Lanham, Md.: Scarecrow Press).

Schmidt, Brian C. (1998). "Lessons from the Past: Reassessing the Interwar Disciplinary History of International Relations," *International Studies Quarterly,* Vol. 42, No. 3, pp. 433–459.

Schmidt, Heinz (1950). *Cartels and Trusts* (International Union of Food and Drink Worker's Association).

Schulz, William F. (2001). *In Our Own Best Interest, How Defending Human Rights Benefits Us All* (Boston: Beacon Press).

Seary, Bill (1996). "The Early History, from the Congress of Vienna to the San Francisco Conference," in '*The Conscience of the World' The Influence of Non-Governmental Organisations in the U.N. System*, Peter Willetts, ed., pp. 15–30.

Simai, Mihály (1994). *The Future of Global Governance: Managing Risk and Change in the International System* (Washington, D.C.: United States Institute of Peace Press).

______ (2001). *The Age of Global Transformations: The Human Dimension* (Budapest: Akadémiai Kiadó).

Simison, W. Brian (1995). "Malthus"–biographical essay posted 10/04/95 on the Internet, www.ucmp.berkeley.edu/history/malthus.html.

Simmons, P. J., and Chantal de Jonge Oudraat, eds. (2001). *Managing Global Issues, Lessons Learned* (Washington, D.C.: Carnegie Endowment for International Peace).

Smith, Steve (1997). "New Approaches to International Theory," in *The Globalization of World Politics*, John Baylis and Steve Smith, eds., pp. 165–190.

______ (1999). "Is the truth out there? Eight questions about international order," in *International Order and the Future of World Politics*, T. V. Paul and John A. Hall, eds., pp. 99–119.

Smouts, Marie-Claude (1999). "Multilateralism from Below: A Prerequisite for Global Governance," in *Future Multilateralism*, Michael G. Schechter, ed., pp. 292–311.

Spar, Debora L. (1999). "Lost in (Cyber)space: The Private Rules of Online Commerce" in *Private Authority and International Affairs*, A. Claire Cutler, Virginia Haufler, and Tony Porter, eds., pp. 31–51.

Spear, Joanna (2001). "Warfare: Conventional Weapons" in *Managing Global Issues, Lessons Learned*, P. J. Simmons and Chantal de Jonge Oudraat, eds., pp. 564–609.

Spero, Joan Edelman (1981). *The Politics of International Economic Relations*, second edition (New York: St. Martin's Press); the first edition was published in 1977.

Stern, Alissa, and Tim Hicks (2000). *The Process of Business/Environmental Collaborations: Partnering for Sustainability* (Westport, Conn.: Quorum Books).

Sun Haichan (1993). *The Wiles of War: 36 Military Strategies from Ancient China* (Beijing: Foreign Language Press).

Sun Rongrong (1999). "The Culture of 'Emulating the Sages' and 'Honoring the Classics,'" paper presented at the faculty luncheon, Hopkins-Nanjing Center for Chinese and American Studies. Mimeo, Nanjing, China, March 18.

Szasz, Paul C. (1997). "General Law-Making Processes," in *The United Nations and International Law*, Christopher C. Joyner, ed., pp. 27–64.

Taylor, Phillip (1984). *Nonstate Actors in International Politics, From Transregional to Substate Organizations* (Boulder: Westview Press).

"The world's view of multinationals," *The Economist*, January 29, 2000, pp. 21–22.

Thompson, Kenneth W. (1994). *Fathers of International Thought: The Legacy of Political Thought* (Baton Rouge, La.: Louisiana State University Press).

______ (1992). *Traditions and Values in Politics and Diplomacy, Theory and Practice* (Baton Rouge, La.: Louisiana State University Press).

Toulmin, Stephen (1997). "Networks & the Future of Global Politics," The Center for Multiethnic and Transnational Studies, College of Letters Arts and Sciences, University of Southern California, unpublished paper accessed on the Internet.
Turner, Mark (2001). "Where NGOs step into the shoes governments cannot fill," *Financial Times*, Monday, July 16, p. 3.
United Nations (1996) *The Blue Helmets: A Review of United Nations Peace-keeping*, third edition (New York: United Nations).
United Nations (2000). *World Economic and Social Survey 2000*. E/2000/50/Rev. 1 ST/ESA/273 (New York: United Nations).
United Nations (2002). "Strengthening of the United Nations: an agenda for further change, Report of the Secretary-General," A/57/387, 9 September.
United Nations Centre on Transnational Corporations (UNCTC) (1990). "The New Code Environment," *UNCTC Current Studies*, Series A, No. 16, April.
United Nations Commission on Transnational Corporations (1980). "Transnational Banks: Operations, Strategies and Their Effects in Developing Countries," Report of the Secretariat E/C.10/67, 10 April.
United Nations Conference on Trade and Development (UNCTAD) (2000). *World Investment Report: Cross-border Mergers and Acquisitions and Development* (New York: United Nations Publications).
United Nations Development Programme (UNDP) (1997). *Reconceptualising Governance, Discussion Paper 2*. (New York: UNDP).
______ (2002). *Human Development Report 2002: Deepening Democracy in a Fragmented World* (New York: UNDP).
van Creveld, Martin (1999). *The Rise and Decline of the State* (Cambridge, U.K.: Cambridge University Press).
Van Doren, Charles (1991). *A History of Knowledge: Past, Present, and Future* (New York: Ballantine Books).
Wade, Robert Hunter (2002). "Bridging the Digital Divide: New Route to Development or New Form of Dependency?" *Global Governance*, Vol. 8, No. 4, (October-December), pp. 443–466.
Walker, Thomas C. (2000). "The Forgotten Prophet: Tom Paine's Cosmopolitanism and International Relations," *International Studies Quarterly*, Vol. 44, No. 1, March, pp. 51–72.
Wallerstein, Immanuel (1974). *The Modern World System: Capitalist Agriculture and the Origins of the European World Economy in the Sixteenth Century* (New York: Academic Press).
Waltz, Kenneth (1959). *Man, the State and War: A Theoretical Analysis* (New York: Columbia University Press).
______ (1979). *Theory of International Politics* (New York: Random House).
Webster, C. (1933). *The League of Nations in Theory and Practice* (London: Allen and Unwin).
Weiss, Thomas G., David P. Forsythe, and Roger A. Coate (1997). *The United Nations and Changing World Politics*, second edition (Boulder: Westview Press).

Weiss, Thomas G., and Leon Gordenker, eds. (1996). *NGOs, The UN, & Global Governance* (Boulder: Lynne Rienner Publishers).
Wendt, Alexander (1992). "Anarchy Is What States Make of It: A Social Construction of Power Politics," *International Organization 46*, 391–425.
Werner, Wouter G., and Jaap H. De Wilde (2001). "The Endurance of Sovereignty," *European Journal of International Relations*, Vol. 7 (3), September, pp. 283–313.
White, Lymon Cromwell (1951). *International Non-Governmental Organizations. Their Purposes, Methods and Accomplishments* (New Brunswick, N.J.: Rutgers University Press).
Wight, Martin (1992). *International Theory, The Three Traditions* (New York: Holmes & Meier).
Willetts, Peter, ed. (1996). *'The Conscience of the World' The Influence of Non-Governmental Organisations in the U.N. System* (London: Hurst & Company).
Willoughby, W. W. (1896). *An Examination of the Nature of the State* (New York: Macmillan Co.).
Witte, Jan Martin, Wolfgang Reinicke, and Thorsten Benner (2002). "Networked Governance: Developing a Research Agenda," paper presented at the annual meeting of the International Studies Association, New Orleans, Louisiana, March 24–27.
Wood, Frances (1993). *Blue Guide China* (New York: W. W. Norton).
Woolf, Leonard S. (1916). *International Government* (New York: Brentano's).
______ (1928). *The Way of Peace* (London: Ernest Benn).
Zimmern, Alfred E. (1931). *The Study of International Relations* (Oxford: Clarendon Press).
______ (1936). *The League of Nations and the Rule of Law 1918–1935*, second edition (London: MacMillan Press Ltd.).

INDEX

Afghanistan, 2
Africa, 3–4, 80, 82, 103, 139, 143, 147, 169, 226, 229, 231
African Development Bank, 140, 161, 246
Alexander the Great, 21, 22, 30
Al Qaeda, 1, 190, 229
American Political Science Association (APSA), 68
American Revolution, 47–48, 44, 52, 55, 57
Amnesty International, 146, 186
Anarchy, 38, 40, 69–70, 79
Andean Common Market (ACM), 139
Andean Development Corporation, 140
Angell, Norman, 68, 71, 72
Annan, Kofi, 191–193
Aquinas, St. Thomas, 25, 27–28, 34, 43, 64
Arbitration, 108–109
Aristotle, 15, 21–22, 25, 27, 28, 29, 30, 34, 86
Arms control, 107, 215, 227
  Chemical Weapons Convention, 227
  Convention on Conventional Weapons, 227
  Non-Proliferation Treaty, 227, 228
ASEAN Regional Forum, 159
Ashoka, 17
Asia, 17–19, 80, 82, 103, 107, 120, 130, 139, 141, 143, 169, 226, 231, 246
Asian Development Bank, 140, 161
Asian Financial Crisis, 3, 246, 249
Asian values, 17, 19, 36
Asia Pacific Economic Cooperation forum (APEC), 161, 253
Association of Southeast Asian Nations (ASEAN), 130, 138, 161, 253
Atlantic Charter, 133, 153, 154
Augustine, Saint, 15, 25–27, 28, 32, 64

Balance of power, 6, 40, 48, 78, 103, 106, 109, 111, 113, 160
Balkans, 3, 80, 108, 147, 226, 229
Bank for International Settlements (BIS), 161, 248
Basel Convention, 239, 240
Behavioralism, 83
Bentham, Jeremy, 38, 53, 58–59, 60, 70
Bernadotte, Count Folke, 223
Bodin, Jean, 31, 33, 34
Bok, Sissela, 32–33
Bosnia-Herzegovina, 3, 268
Brandt, Willy, 11
Bretton Woods Conference, 127, 134, 172
Brown, Seyom, 5–6, 236–237
Brundtland Commission, 240–241
Brundtland, Gro Harlem, 11, 240

Buddha (Siddhartha Gautama), 16. 18, 19
  teachings of, 17
Buddhism, 17, 19
  Golden Age of, 17
Bull, Hedley, 6, 34, 35, 103
Bunche, Ralph, 223–224
Burke, Edmund, 38, 50–52
Business for Social Responsibility, 182

Capitalism, 65, 81, 86, 257, 271
CARE International, 144, 145, 188, 225, 235
Caribbean Development Bank, 140
Carlsson, Ingvar, 11
Carr, E.H., 68, 72, 75–76
Cartels, 141, 169–171
  types of, 170
Casablanca Conference, 127
Catholic Relief Services, 145, 225, 235
Central American Common Market (CACM), 138, 253
Central American Bank for Economic Integration, 140
Central Europe, 3, 254
Charter of Economic Rights and of States Duties, 139
Chiang Kai-shek, 126
China, 17, 18–19, 36, 46, 56, 103, 107, 109, 125, 126, 169, 228, 230, 248
Christianity, 25, 29, 30, 115
Churchill, Winston, 126, 127, 154
Cicero, Marcus Tullius, 23–24, 34
Civilizations, 3, 113
  clash of, 1, 36
  ancient, 15–16
Civil Society, 4, 12, 118, 151, 152, 183–189, 190, 192, 193, 201, 204, 208, 209, 222, 227, 240–241, 265, 269–270, 272
  and conflict mediation, 225–226
  and humanitarian relief, 187–188, 225, 235
  role in international relations, 202, 259, 267
Cleveland, Harlan, 261–262
Cold War, 3, 4, 6, 11, 66, 67, 81, 82, 125, 129, 136, 184, 191–192, 214–215, 245, 259
Collective security, 111, 126, 128, 159–160, 162
Commission on Global Governance, 3, 11
  report of, 11–12
Commonwealth (British), 163
Commonwealth of Independent States (CIS), 159
Communism, 60, 62, 65, 66, 169
Communist revolution, 65
Community Aid Abroad, 144
Community of Sant' Egidio, 225–226
Concert of Europe, 106–107, 109, 112, 116
Confucianism, 17–19
  domination of Chinese philosophy, 18–19
Confucius, 15, 16, 17
  teachings of, 18
Congress of Vienna, 57, 104–106, 110
Conservation Foundation, 241
Conservatism, 50–52, 56, 65
Constantine, 25
Convention for Pacific Settlement of International Disputes, 108–109
Coopération internationale pour le développement et la solidarité, 144
Cosmopolitanism, 53–54
Council for Mutual Economic Assistance (CMEA), 132, 136, 137
Council of Europe, 129, 223
Cox, Robert, 212
Cross-border Mergers and Acquisitions (M&As), 175–176
Crucé, Émeric, 38, 36

Dallmayr, Fred, 1–2
Debt crisis, 3
Decolonization, 82, 130, 139, 144, 174
DeGaulle, Charles, 126
Delian League, 102
Democratic Republic of Congo, 3
Democracy, 3, 20, 22, 48, 53, 54, 65, 66, 81, 86, 222
Democratization, 3, 261, 271
De Tocqueville, Alexis, 31, 38
Development, 231–236, 238, 240, 242, 246, 255
  and basic human needs, 232–236, 243
  strategies, 235, 238, 266–267
Dickinson, Gladsworthy Lowes, 68, 71
Diehl, Paul, 268–269
Digital divide, 266–267
Diplomacy, 6, 38, 67, 111
  multilateral, 112
  Track II, 222, 226
Disarmament, 107, 226–227
  and the United Nations, 227
Drummond, Sir Eric, 112
Dumbarton Oaks Conference, 127

East Timor, 3
Eastern Europe, 3, 113, 136, 169, 246, 254
East-West conflict, 125
Economic Community of West Africa States (ECOWAS), 139, 162, 253
Economic growth, 116, 134, 140, 174, 235, 243, 244, 247, 250, 255
Economic integration, 138, 214, 248, 250, 254
Economic liberalization, 202, 247, 248, 250, 253, 254, 271
Economics, 49–50, 57, 77, 117
Economic systems, 160
  models of, 167–169
Egyptians, 15–16, 24
Elshtain, Jean Bethke, 20, 22
Empire, 15–16, 25, 27, 55
Environment, 236–243, 255,
  and development, 236, 238, 240
  protection of, 238, 240, 270
Environment and Development Action in the Third World, 241
Environmental Defense Fund, 241
Erasmus, Desiderius, 32–33, 34
Eritrea, 3
Ethiopia, 3, 46, 126
European Free Trade Association (EFTA), 138, 253
European Union (EU), 80, 137–138, 163, 186, 187, 224, 234, 253, 261, 268, 271
  Commission, 216

Fascism, 6
Food and Agricultural Organization (FAO), 136, 161, 232, 233, 234, 239
Foreign Direct Investment (FDI), 174, 207, 247
France, 46, 60, 104, 106, 109, 114, 126, 129, 168, 228, 230
French Revolution, 47–48, 51, 52, 53, 55, 56, 57, 58
Friends of the Earth, 146
Functionalism, 84, 88–89

General Agreement on Tariffs and Trade (GATT), 135–136, 162, 243, 250–253
Geneva Conventions, 119(n1)
Germany, 56, 81, 85, 108, 109, 110, 114, 126, 127, 128, 168
Global Business Council on HIV & AIDS, 182
Global commons, 193, 204
Global Compact, 207
Global economy, 3, 66, 83, 92, 134, 136, 141, 183, 202, 215, 222, 254, 256, 271

Global governance, 3, 4, 5, 11, 12, 94, 268, 269, 274
anarchic structure of, 5–6
basic domains of, 9–10
characteristics of, 7–10, 272
institutional pillars of, 9–10, 101, 270, 272
primary actors of, 9
Globalism, 2
Globalization, 1, 6, 7, 8, 12, 92, 93, 118, 182, 189, 190, 207, 208, 248, 255, 256–257, 262–265, 274
challenges of, 4, 201
management of, 255, 272
and state sovereignty, 261
Global order, 4, 6, 268, 270
Global public policy networks, 203, 208
Global Reporting Initiative (GRI), 205–206
Global system, 4, 6, 9, 11, 12, 149, 272
Gorbachev, Mikhail, 137
Governance, 4, 6, 7–8, 37, 91, 102, 149, 152, 190, 193, 205, 267, 270, 272
Gramsci, Antonio, 85–87
Great Britain, 48, 49, 50, 56, 104, 106, 109, 126, 138, 228. *See also* United Kingdom
Great Depression, 118, 133, 244
Greenpeace, 146, 241
Grotius (Hugo de Groot), 31, 38, 39, 40, 41, 44
Gulf Cooperation Council, 159, 253

Haas, Ernst, 88
Haas, Peter, 241–242
Hague Conferences, 74, 107–109, 112, 118, 226
Hanseatic League, 53, 102
Hegel, Wilhelm Friedrich, 38, 60–61, 65, 86
Hegemonic stability, 90
Hinduism, 17
HIV/AIDS epidemic, 4
Hobbes, Thomas, 25, 38, 39–40, 43–44, 90
Hobsbawn, Eric, 65, 114–115
Holy Roman Empire, 27, 34, 37, 103
Humanitarian emergencies, 3, 147, 229, 230
Humanitarian intervention, 41, 229, 230, 263
Human rights, 54, 118, 147, 192, 193, 202–203, 215, 233, 243, 262, 263, 270, 271, 272
Covenants, 220
NGOs, 146, 220
standards, 219–221
United Nations Commission of, 220
UN Convention on the Elimination of Discrimination Against Women (CEDAW), 221
UN Convention on the Rights of the Child, 221
Universal Declaration of Human Rights, 207, 219, 220, 233
Human Rights Watch, 146, 186, 228
Human security, 215, 230–231, 243, 263, 270
concept of, 230
Hume, David, 38, 48–49

Idealists, 28, 63, 67, 70, 71, 72, 76, 79, 83, 88
Ikenberry, G. John, 151, 264–265
India, 17, 81, 103, 228
Industrialization, 113–114, 140
and the environment, 236
Industrial Revolution, 37, 57, 72, 116, 141
effect of, 113, 114–115
and international standardization, 114–115
spread of, 113

Information and Communication Technology (ICT), 206–207, 266–267
Institutions, 7–9, 90. *See also* International institutions
Integration, 88, 253. *See also* Economic integration
Inter-American Development Bank, 140, 161
Interdependence, 3, 57, 71–72, 254, 265–266
Intergovernmental Conference of Experts on a Scientific Basis for a Rational Use and Conservation of the Resources of the Biosphere, 237
International administration, 123–124
International Atomic Energy Agency (IAEA), 136, 212, 239
International Bank for Reconstruction and Development, 127, 134–135. *See also* World Bank
International business, 141, 151, 172–174, 175, 188, 222, 241
  alliances, 174, 177–178
  structure, 172–174
  trade and industry associations, 178, 181, 241
International Campaign to Ban Landmines (ICBL), 189
International Chamber of Commerce, 119, 121, 183
International Civil Aviation Organization (ICAO), 136, 161, 216
International Committee of the Red Cross (ICRC), 119, 146, 185, 225, 227–228
International community, 1, 6, 82, 110, 120, 140, 144, 191, 215, 220, 231
International Council of Marine Industry Associations (ICOMIA), 181–182
International Council of Scientific Unions, 120
International Court of Justice (ICJ), 109, 121
International Criminal Court (ICC), 221, 270, 272
International economic order, 82, 134, 139, 141, 161, 162, 172, 182, 234, 255. *See also* New World Order; Global order
International economic system, 118, 125, 136, 139–140, 160, 162, 174, 244, 245, 246
International Federation of Business & Professional Women, 119
International finance, 214, 244–250
International Financial Institutions (IFIs), 245, 246–247
International Governmental Organizations (IGOs), 108, 116, 117, 120, 124, 130–131, 132, 139, 140, 143, 152, 174, 183, 186, 190, 222, 232, 259, 267
  decision-making, 163–164
  and international conflicts, 223
  and international law, 154–155, 215, 218–219
  and international regulatory system, 117, 161, 215, 216
  key structural features of, 121, 155, 157–166
  secretariats of, 165–166
  and security, 130–132
  special representatives and envoys, 223–234
International institutions, 3, 9, 92, 123–124, 152, 191, 241, 243, 264, 268, 272
  building of, 211
  dimensions of, 211, 215, 216, 217
Internationalism, 1, 49, 74, 76

International Labor Organization (ILO), 121, 123, 136, 161, 207, 212, 216, 233
International law, 6, 31, 35, 40, 41, 42, 68, 73–74, 76, 107, 113, 154, 155, 215, 271
  and the environment, 238–241
  and human rights, 219–222
  and international governmental organizations, 218
  norms, 216, 219
  scope of, 218
International Meteorological Organization, 115, 116
International Monetary Fund (IMF), 127, 134–135, 139, 161, 163, 172, 212, 243, 244–246, 250, 273
International Nongovernmental Organizations (INGOs), 119, 120, 124–125, 143–148, 183, 235
  and international development, 144
  See also Nongovernmental Organizations (NGOs)
International organizations, 3, 9, 10, 12, 45, 46, 73, 80, 91, 94, 116, 117, 119, 126, 137–138, 259, 268–269, 272, 274
  classification systems for, 99–102, 120(n2), 121
  and the Cold War, 160, 214–215
  decision-making in, 163–164, 213
  essential characteristics of, 100–101
  evolution of, 102–149
  and foreign aid, 234–235
  functions of, 11, 123, 153, 211, 212, 268
  mandates, 132
  operational activities, 212–215
  private, 118–119, 141, 143, 169, 182, 269
  roles of, 101, 213–214, 242–243, 268, 272
  secretariats of, 165–166, 213, 216
  structure of, 121–125, 152, 158
  tasks of, 117, 211–212
International order, 3, 4, 6–7, 9, 46, 54, 66, 68, 80, 92, 103, 105, 111, 120, 125, 189, 243, 259, 262
  American view of, 151, 153
  after World War II, 130, 132, 151–153, 260
  three sectors of, 152
  See also Global order; International economic order
International Planned Parenthood Federation, 144
International politics, 1–2, 67, 68, 71, 73, 76, 77, 92, 160, 164, 191, 202, 240
International Publishers Association, 119
International relations, 6, 15, 31, 38, 46, 48, 49, 54, 66, 67, 68, 70, 71, 76, 77, 81, 82, 83, 89, 92, 93–94, 95, 120, 148, 202, 262
International Rescue Committee, 225
International society, 6, 10, 31, 35, 39, 41, 42, 44, 47, 64, 67, 70, 77, 211, 222, 255
International system, 9, 51, 71, 72, 75, 91, 102, 103, 105, 114, 120, 122, 143, 149, 152, 154, 155, 190, 203, 208–209, 215, 222, 259, 260, 262, 267, 269–270
  legalization of, 215–218
  rules and standards, 216–222
International Telecommunications Union (ITU), 117, 136, 161, 205, 212
International Telegraph Union, 115, 116, 117
International theory, 38–39, 40, 47, 70, 76, 77, 80, 93, 95
International thought, 15, 50, 54, 55, 66, 76, 84

International trade, 49–50, 58, 114, 134–136, 141, 214, 243, 244, 248, 250–254. *See also* Trade
International Union for Conservation of Nature and Natural Resources-World Conservation Union (IUCN), 146, 241
Internet, 202, 203–205, 266
Internet Corporation for Assigned Names and Numbers (ICANN), 205, 206
Interorganizational networks, 207–208
Inter-Parliamentary Union, 118, 170–171
Intra-state conflict, 3, 223, 261
Islam, 17, 25, 28–30, 115
Islamists, 1

Jacobins, 47–48, 51, 52, 134–136
Jacobson, Harold, 84, 85, 88, 89, 99, 100, 134
Japan, 56, 80, 81, 90, 107, 113, 126, 127, 128, 168, 173, 233, 271
Jefferson, Thomas, 38, 44, 47–48, 203
Judaism, 24–25, 29
Juristic theory, 68–70, 73

Kant, Immanuel, 38, 52–53, 54–55, 70
Kegley, Charles, 82, 83–84, 103–104, 126
Knight, W. Andy, 265
Knowledge-based networked oligopolies, 174, 177, 179–181
  characteristics of, 177–178
Koran, 29
Kosovo, 3, 202
Krasner, Stephen, 89
Kratochwil, Friedrich, 88, 90, 91, 158
Kuehl, Warren, 45–46, 53–54

Landes, David, 113
Latin American Free Trade Association (LAFTA), 138, 253
Laski, Harold, 68, 73
League of Arab States (LAS), 158, 159, 223
League of Nations, 67, 69, 75, 88, 108, 109, 121, 126
  Assembly and Council, 112, 121
  Covenant of, 75, 111–112, 119(n1)
  voting in, 112
  secretariat of, 112–113, 121
Least developed countries, 3, 192, 234
Legal Positivism, 74
Less developed countries, 139, 140
Liberal institutionalism, 84
Liberalism, 49, 56, 65, 66, 81, 84, 115
Liberia, 3
Locke, John, 38, 39, 43–44, 47, 48, 50

Machiavelli, 25, 31, 33, 34, 38, 39, 40
Malthus, Thomas, 58, 113
Mansfield, Edward, 90–91
Marcuse, Herbert, 85–87
Markets, 4, 8, 9, 142, 152, 166–167, 172, 173, 174, 175, 177, 183, 190–191, 209, 244, 248–249, 253, 264, 270, 272
Mathews, Jessica, 4, 259–260
Marshall Plan, 136, 245
Marx, Karl, 38, 60, 61–62, 65, 86
Marxism, 62, 66, 84, 85–87
Marxist-Leninist theories, 84–85
Médecins Sans Frontières (MSF), 147, 187, 188, 225
Mencius, 18
Mercado Común del Cono Sur (MERCOSUR), 139, 162, 165, 253, 256
Middle East, 80, 120, 147, 226, 229
Mill, John Stuart, 38, 58, 59–60, 70
Millennium Development Goals (MDG), 201
Military alliances, 129–130
Mitrany, David, 68, 88
Modernity, 65, 94

Montesquieu, 48
Montreal Protocol, 238, 239
Morgenthau, Hans, 67, 76, 77–78
Moscow Conference, 127
Mozambique, 225–226
Muir, Ramsay, 68, 71–72
Muhammed, the Prophet, 28–29
Multilateralism, 3, 84, 212, 260
Multilateral treaties, 108, 155, 156, 157, 219
Multinational corporations, 81, 141, 142, 171, 172–174
  and environmental protection, 241–242
  and the UN Conference on Environment and Development, 241
  See also International business; Transnational corporations

Napoleonic wars, 55, 66, 101–105
Nationalism, 54, 55, 60, 61, 62
Nation-state, 2, 5, 9, 32, 37, 42, 52, 55, 56, 61, 62, 66, 73, 78–79, 102, 110, 113, 130, 190
Natural law, 27–28, 34, 40, 41, 42, 44
Neo-Scholastics, 34, 42
New Deal, 153
New International Economic Order (NIEO), 139
Newly Industrialized Countries (NICs), 141
New Partnership for African Development (NEPAD), 207
New social question, 255–258
New World Order, 1, 3, 67, 84, 125, 152, 260, 271, 272
Nongovernmental Organizations (NGOs), 4, 12, 101, 145, 151, 183, 192, 202, 222
  activism, 146
  defining characteristics of, 184–185
  and development, 144, 145, 146, 185
  and disarmament, 226, 227–228
  and the environment, 146–147, 237–238, 240–241
  forums, 147–148, 238, 241
  and IGOs, 146–147, 148
  operational, 187–188
  and principled issue networks, 221
  relations with business, 6, 187–188, 207
  relations with governments, 6, 186–187
  special types, 184–185
Non-state actors, 4, 6, 11, 73, 151, 173, 183, 189, 190, 202, 209, 211, 213, 224, 259, 271
Norms, 2, 5, 89, 90, 139, 152, 204, 216, 217
North American Free Trade Agreement (NAFTA), 139, 162, 253, 256
North Atlantic Treaty Organization (NATO), 80, 129, 130, 132, 158, 224, 229, 261, 268, 273
North-South conflict, 82, 139–141, 242
Nuclear weapon states, 228

Official Development Assistance (ODA), 174, 233
Olson, Mancur, 89
Organization for the Prohibition of Chemical Weapons, 227
Organization for Security and Cooperation in Europe (OSCE), 158, 186, 224
Organization of African Unity (OAU), 100, 130, 159, 160, 223
Organization of American States (OAS), 129, 130, 158, 160, 223
Organization of Economic Cooperation and Development

(OECD), 130, 132, 136, 161, 174, 233, 234
Development Assistance Committee (DAC), 233, 234
Organization of the Islamic Conference (OIC), 163
Organization of Petroleum Exporting Countries (OPEC), 90, 162
Ottoman Empire, 103, 109, 110
Oxfam, 145, 185, 187, 225, 235

Paine, Thomas, 54–55, 203
Peace of Westphalia, 4, 45, 103
Peace plans, 45–46, 53–55
Penn, William, 38, 46
Permanent Court of Arbitration, 108, 121
Persian Gulf War, 1, 11
Plato, 19–21, 25, 30, 32
Pluralism, 73
Political economy, 50, 58–60, 82, 114
Political philosophy, 15, 24, 31, 76, 77
Political theory, 15, 31, 32, 49
Political thought, 25, 30, 36, 41, 45, 49, 60, 76
traditions of, 38–39
Western, 20, 22, 23, 36, 55, 56
Positive law, 42, 44, 52, 74
Post-Cold War, 95, 148, 192, 229, 259, 260, 261–262
Postmodernism, 93–94
Potsdam Conference, 128
Potter, Pitman Benjamin, 68, 123–124
Power, 4, 7, 8, 22, 32, 39, 43, 45, 67, 75, 76, 77–78, 90, 149, 153, 158, 226, 259, 260, 262, 265, 272
Prince of Wales International Business Leaders Forum, 182
Private sector, 151, 152, 166–167, 169, 172, 182, 188, 190, 192, 201, 203, 206, 231, 236, 242, 246, 248, 257, 269
Public goods, 89, 208, 209, 262–264
theory of, 84, 89
Public international unions, 73, 117, 121, 136, 189
Public private partnerships, 203, 206, 208
Puchala, Donald, 83, 92, 93–94, 95
Pufendorf, Samuel, 38, 39, 40

Quebec Conference, 127

Rainforest Action Network, 146, 147
Rationalists, 38, 39, 40, 43, 62
Realists, 28, 38, 39–40, 48, 62, 63, 67, 71, 75–76, 79, 83, 90
assumptions of, 78–79
Reformation, the, 31
Reflectivism, 93
Refugees, 4, 218
Regimes, 21, 205, 272
theory of, 84, 89–91
Regional organizations, 129–130, 136–139, 160, 260
Religion, 24
and politics, 24–30, 36
Renaissance, 30–35
Revolution, 47, 48, 86
Revolutionists, 38, 39, 47–48, 52, 62
Rhine Commission, 106, 116
Ricardo, David, 38, 58
Rochester, J. Martin, 9
Roman Empire, 22, 24, 25, 26, 27, 28, 30, 43
Roman law, 23, 48
Roman Republic, 23, 24, 30
Roosevelt, Franklin D., 126, 127, 154, 155
Rousseau, Jean-Jacques, 25, 38, 47–48, 50, 52, 53, 64
Rosenau, James, 6,8, 10
Rotary International, 121
Ruggie, John Gerard, 90, 91, 94, 207–208

Russia, 27, 65, 80, 84, 104, 106, 107, 187, 228
Rwanda, 3, 268

San Francisco Conference, 128
Save the Children, 121, 145, 146, 188, 225
Schechter, Michael, 105–106, 117, 128, 260–261
Schools of thought, 15, 79, 93
 classical, 15–24
 rationalist, 40–46, 62
 realist, 39–40, 62–77
 revolutionist, 47, 62
Security, 3, 16, 20, 24, 32, 40, 63, 79, 82, 85, 106, 108, 130, 132, 134, 158, 215, 222, 228–230, 262
 See also Human security
Sierra Leone, 3
Simai, Mihály, 167–168, 169, 174, 233, 253–254
Smith, Adam, 38, 49–50, 57, 58, 167
Sociability, 44
Social contract, 40, 42, 68
Social constructivism, 93, 94
Socialism, 56, 65, 66
Socrates, 16, 19–20
Somalia, 3, 145, 268
South Africa, 226
South Asian Association for Regional Cooperation (SAARC), 162, 253
South East Asian Treaty Organization (SEATO), 129
Sovereign state, 38, 40, 46, 102, 191, 262
Sovereignty, 4, 5, 31, 40, 45, 48, 68–70, 78, 88, 116, 130, 191, 214, 253
Soviet Union, 3, 4, 81, 82, 85, 90, 125, 127, 128, 136, 137, 141, 147, 169, 228, 259. *See also* Union of Socialist Soviet Republics (USSR)
Spain, 56, 104
Specialized agencies, 124, 129, 136, 161, 216, 238–239, 255
Special Representative of the Secretary-General (SRSG), 224–225
Spero, Joan Edelman, 82, 172–173, 244–245
Stalin, Joseph, 85, 86, 126
States, 5, 8, 26, 27, 79, 117, 134, 152, 190–191, 211, 230–231, 246, 259
 and cooperation, 78, 90, 116
 and welfare, 78, 132, 154, 232
Stockholm Conference. *See* United Nations Conference on the Human Environment
Stockholm International Peace Research Institute (SIPRI), 222
Supranational, 6, 31, 88, 137, 214, 253
Sustainable development, 3, 206, 222, 242–243, 263, 270, 271

Taliban, 2
Technology, 88, 125, 136, 137, 179, 182, 189, 254
 and globalization, 182, 256, 264–266
Tehran Conference, 127
Terrorism, 1–2, 229–231, 262, 271, 272
 and international organizations, 2, 229
 international organizations response to, 229–230
 September 11 attacks on United States, 1, 229, 271
Theocracy, 27
Third World, 133, 140, 144, 184
Thompson, Kenneth, 20, 21, 22, 26, 27, 28, 32, 39, 41, 43–44, 47, 48–49, 50, 60, 61, 62, 67, 76, 77
Trade, 35–36, 114, 138, 161, 242, 254, 264. *See also* International trade
Transnational corporations, 101, 141, 142, 148, 174–178, 188, 189, 191, 202, 254, 259, 269

and human development, 235–236
and NGO activism, 236
Transnationalism, 1, 84
Transnationality Index, 175–177
Treaty of Utrecht (1713), 103
Treaty of Versailles, 109–111

Union douanière et économique de l'Afrique centrale (UDEAC), 138
Union of International Associations (UIA), 99, 120(n2), 121, 140
Union of Socialist Soviet Republics (USSR), 85, 110, 127, 129, 137, 187. *See also* Soviet Union
United Kingdom, 64, 114, 129, 115. *See also* Great Britain
United Nations, 80, 85, 100, 126, 127, 147, 186, 260, 268
Charter of, 128–129, 159, 164, 165, 192, 219, 220, 232
and collective security, 130
Commission on Sustainable Development, 148, 261
Conferences, 147–148, 202, 237–238
Development Decades, 233
Economic and Social Council, 148, 193, 218, 237
General Assembly, 108, 139, 159, 193, 218, 219, 222, 260
and international peace and security, 160, 192, 193
and international terrorism, 229–230
Membership, 80, 129, 231, 232
Peacekeeping operations, 129, 218, 223, 224–225, 229, 268
and reform, 191–193
Secretariat, 123, 129, 193, 223
Secretary-General, 165, 191, 193, 224
Security Council, 3, 127, 130, 159–160, 164, 222, 230, 260, 268
Military Staff Committee, 129
Structure, 129
United Nations Children's Fund (UNICEF), 186, 233, 236, 255
United Nations Conference on Environment and Development (UNCED), 147, 240–242, 243
process of, 240–241
United Nations Conference on Financing for Development, 207
United Nations Conference on the Human Environment, 146, 237–238
United Nations Conference on Trade and Development (UNCTAD), 140, 175–177, 255
United Nations Convention on the Law of the Sea, 240
United Nations Development Program (UNDP), 140, 186, 206, 233, 235, 255
United Nations Educational, Scientific and Cultural Organization (UNESCO), 136, 212, 233, 234, 239
Man and the Biosphere Program, 237
United Nations Environment Program (UNEP), 205, 206, 217, 238–240
and environmental law, 238–240
Governing Council, 239
United Nations Industrial Development Organization, 140
United Nations Millennium Declaration, 193, 194–201
United States, 48, 53, 54, 55, 56, 64, 68, 76, 82, 107, 114, 125, 127, 129, 136, 138, 141, 142, 154, 160, 171, 173, 184, 187, 228, 229, 233, 244–246
and hegemony, 90, 260–261, 270–271
and post-war world order, 151

sole superpower, 66, 260
unilateralism, 261
Universal Postal Union (UPU), 115, 116, 117, 136, 161
Utilitarianism, 58–59
Uruguay Round, 250, 252

Values, 6, 8, 15–16, 20, 222
Western, 3
Van Creveld, Martin, 34, 55, 132–134, 137–139
Van Doren, Charles, 16, 17, 21, 23, 24, 25, 28, 29, 30, 35–36, 44–45, 52–53, 55–56, 57, 62

Waltz, Kenneth, 70, 78
War, 1, 5, 26, 32, 33, 44, 70, 103
on terrorism, 2
Warsaw Treaty Organization (Warsaw Pact), 80, 129, 132, 137, 160
Washington Consensus, 247, 273
Weapons of mass destruction, 227, 230
West African Development Bank, 140, 161
Western Europe, 27, 30, 37, 39, 81, 88, 113, 125, 142, 168, 173
Wight, Martin, 31–32, 34, 38–39, 40, 42, 44, 47, 52, 62–64, 79
Willoughby, Westel Woodbury, 68, 69
Wilson, Woodrow, 63, 68, 75, 112
Wittkopf, Eugene, 82, 83–84
Women's International League for Peace and Freedom, 118, 121
Woolf, Leonard, 68, 71, 72
World Bank, 139, 163, 172, 206, 217, 218, 234, 243, 246–247, 255, 273
World Business Council for Sustainable Development, 182, 241
World Commission on Environment and Development, 240
World Confederation of Labor, 119
World Economic Forum, 182
World economy, 141, 182, 248, 253
World Health Organization, 100, 136, 161, 206, 212, 217, 232, 233, 234, 236, 239
World Intellectual Property Organization, 136, 205, 216
World Meteorological Organization, 136, 161, 239
World polity, 5
World Trade Organization (WTO), 161, 162, 205, 211, 217, 250–253, 255
World Vision, 187, 188, 235
World War I, 57, 65, 68, 71, 75, 109, 141, 143
World War II, 66, 67, 75, 76, 81, 82, 90, 118, 125, 132, 141, 142, 143
World Wide Fund for Nature (WWF), 146
Wright, Quincy, 68, 73

Yalta Conference, 127

Zimmern, Alfred, 68, 72–73